The End of Cheap Labour?

T0345025

International Labour Studies

Edited by Klaus Dörre and Stephan Lessenich

Volume 9

*Florian Butollo* is assistant professor at the Department for Labour, Industrial and Economic Sociology at the University of Jena.

Florian Butollo

# The End of Cheap Labour?

Industrial Transformation and "Social Upgrading"
in China

Campus Verlag
Frankfurt/New York

This study was supported by a PhD grant of Rosa-Luxemburg-Foundation Germany which also gave financial support for the printing of this book.

Bibliographic Information published by the Deutsche Nationalbibliothek.
The Deutsche Nationalbibliothek lists this publication in the Deutsche Nationalbibliografie; detailed bibliographic data are available in the Internet at http://dnb.d-nb.de
ISBN 978-3-593-50177-2

All rights reserved. No part of this book may be reproduced or transmitted in any form or by any means, electronic or mechanical, including photocopying, recording, or by any information storage and retrieval system, without permission in writing from the publishers.
Copyright © 2014 Campus Verlag GmbH, Frankfurt-on-Main
Cover design: Campus Verlag GmbH, Frankfurt-on-Main
Printed on acid free paper.
Printed in the United States of America

This book is also available as an E-Book.

For further information:
www.campus.de
www.press.uchicago.edu

# Contents

# Acknowledgements

My interest in the outcomes of industrial transformation in China was raised during my work at the German NGO "World Economy, Ecology and Development (WEED)" between 2006 and 2009. I was responsible for a project entitled "PC Global", the aim of which was to raise awareness about labour rights violations in the globally organised computer industry. During this project, and especially after the global economic crisis of 2008/09, the rapid dynamics of change in the Chinese industry caught my attention. I eventually took the decision to entirely dedicate myself to researching these changes and their impacts on workers on a scientific level. I owe special thanks to Sarah Bormann, who created the project PC Global, for introducing me to the issue of working conditions in global supply chains and for an inspiring and productive collaboration during those years.

For the implementation of this project, the guidance of my supervisor Dr. Boy Lüthje was decisive. He helped me to develop my ideas and to structure them within a meaningful research framework. Above all, I benefited from the profound results of his own work on industrial transformation in China, his broad network of contacts in the Pearl River Delta (PRD) and his intuition for field work. I realised on the very first day of my field studies how relevant his guidance turned out to be. I had selected the knitwear cluster of Dalang as a research object, but had no idea where to begin. So he suggested to just travel there together and have a look at what was happening there. When we visited the local knitwear market, I was invited to the upcoming knitwear fair, where in turn I was able to establish the contacts for the subsequent case studies. From then on I knew how to proceed.

Of no less importance was the help of the organisers of the thriving "International Center for Joint Labor Research" at Sun Yat-sen University in Guangzhou which was founded in 2010 as a cooperation between Sun Yat-sen University, the UCLA Berkeley and the University of Frankfurt. The researchers at the labour centre have conducted groundbreaking research on the transformation of labour relations in the PRD and particularly on the 2010 strikes at the Honda Nanhai factory. Moreover, the centre provides an unparalleled intellectual environment by organising regular talks by Chinese and international labour experts. I consider myself lucky for being able to participate in these discussions right from the start. I am particularly grateful to Prof. He Gaochao, Ellen Friedman, Liang Guowei and Tian Miao at the labour centre for their constant support in coping with any issues related to my stay in the PRD and my research. Their intellectual capacities and broad contact networks are amazing and proved to be indispensable for the success of my studies. I also want to thank Prof. Qiu Haixiong and his assistant Dr. Li Gan from the Research Center for Social Development at Sun Yat-sen University who introduced me to the LED industry in the PRD and thus provided valuable initial aid for my field research.

Of elementary importance were the admirable efforts of my main translators in 2010 and 2011, Zhang Ye and Qin Yu. They not only managed to translate the precise meanings of my detailed conversations on often complicated issues, but also supported my research in various other ways including backup research tasks and help with practical issues. They also helped me to reflect upon the experiences we made together in numerous Chinese factories. Furthermore, I want to thank Nellie Chu and the late Brigitte Tiedge, who both possess deep knowledge about garment production, for joining me on some factory visits and providing important thoughts and good company. I came to know Brigitte as a constant source of encouragement and good humor. She will be dearly missed.

Many more people provided encouragement and practical support during my field research trips in China, especially Prof. Huang Qiaoyan, Prof. Li Longyi, Dr. Eli Friedman, Oscar Siu, Peter Sack, Diana Beaumont, An Wei, Ji Mu as well as Liao Huan Biao, Jun Fang and their colleagues at Qichuang Social Work Center. I also owe special thanks to employees in local government institutions and industry associations for their commitment, their willingness to share their contacts with me, and their readiness in helping me to approach companies. In particular, I am grateful for the help of Chen Yi Chun (Dalang), Luo Li Ying (Humen), Shen Hai Yang and He Li Ting (Xiqiao), Wang Hao and Li Zhi Ji (Guangdong LED Association), and Zhou Yi (Guangdong Solid State Lighting Alliance). Furthermore, Chen Weiguang and Wu Lei from the Guangzhou Federation of Trade Unions provided access to some companies covered in my empirical investigation. Of course, I am also deeply grateful for the honesty and patience of my interview partners in 63 conversations. Their helpfulness and readiness to respond to even seemingly odd questions went far beyond my expectations and enabled me to process a profound set of data.

Dr. Tobias ten Brink, who is a distinguished China expert and has been a friend for many years, provided valuable comments on drafts of this work. Another good friend, Jan-Peter Herrmann, did a fantastic job in proofreading the whole text which decisively contributed to turning it into comprehensible English. I also thank Prof. Klaus Dörre and Dr. Stefan Schmalz for valuable support, academic inspiration, and ongoing cooperation. Furthermore, I want to express my gratitude for the generous support of the Rosa-Luxemburg-Foundation in Berlin which supported my work during three years with a PhD grant, covered travel expenses, and provided extra funding for my field research expenses.

Last but not least, I owe gratitude for support to my family and friends who always encouraged my work, helped me to cope with the involved difficulties and provided plenty of love and companionship, especially my parents Andrea and Willi, my brothers and sisters Simon, Vera, Asisa, Leo and Manuel, my grandmother Leopoldine Kerciku and my aunt Miriam Porta. Most of all, I am deeply grateful to my wife, partner and intimate friend, Maria Alexandrino Butollo, with whom I share my passion for China. She not only kept showing me that there exists a colourful and pleasant life beyond work, but also provided valuable assistance for completing it backed by her profound academic experience.

# 1 Introduction: A leap beyond the global factory model?

During the last decade, Chinese leaders have not been reluctant to point out and criticise the weaknesses of the country's economic development model. Most outspoken about this was China's former premier Wen Jiabao. In 2007, he coined an expression by now known as the "four uns" among China observers when he said that the economy was "unstable, unbalanced, uncoordinated, and unsustainable" (cf. Roach 2009: 229–233). He repeated this critique in almost the same words at a speech at the National Congress in 2012 to underline the urgency of reforms (The Guardian 05.03.2013). In the 12th Five Year Plan, adopted in 2011, the country's structural problems are summed up as follows:

"[I]t is important to have a clear sight of the imbalanced, incompatible and non-sustainable elements within China's development, which mainly turn out to be a tightened constraint between economic growth on one hand and resources and environment on the other, an imbalance between investment and consumption, a relatively large income disparity, uncompetitive technological innovation ability, unreasonable industrial structure, vulnerable agricultural basis, a gap between rural and urban development [...] a significant increase in social conflicts and a still considerable number of institutional obstacles that restrain scientific development" (FYP 2011).

From a European perspective in the year of 2014, such a gloomy assessment appears odd. After all, China's economy has acted as a locomotive of the world economy since the recent crisis whereas the European economy, and with it the project of European economic and political integration, is stuck in grave difficulties that seem endemic.

But China indeed faces mounting contradictions in its recent development model. Unlike it is the case with Europe, these are not the result of sluggish economic growth, but of the very economic success that lets China appear infallible in the eyes of many in the West. The "global factory model" (Ernst 2007), according to which China assumed the role of an assembly platform for consumer goods that were exported to advanced industrial regions, has reached its limits. The economic crisis of 2008/09 graphically demonstrated the risks of an overtly export-oriented growth pattern, and it underlined that high growth rates in the future will barely be sustained through exports of mass consumer goods to Europe and the US alone. And while stagnant growth in the West is putting a strain on China's export performance, domestic consumption up until now has barely generated sufficient demand to act as an alternative source of economic growth. After all, China's success of the last three decades has deepened social inequality which is reflected in a steadily shrinking share of wage incomes as a proportion of GDP and the parallel rise of the GINI co-efficient that measures social inequality (Zhu and Kotz 2011; Guo and N'Diaye 2009). Ecological damages contribute to a rather bleak perspective. They not only compromise the quality of life for hundreds of millions that breathe polluted air, drink contaminated water, and harvest from intoxicated soils, but also turn into an economic risk because of expensive measures that need to be undertaken in order to maintain basic conditions for investment and trade. In short, China is facing a turning point: Chinese political leaders and most international commentators share the view that either there is a reorientation towards a more sustainable and just economic growth pattern based on domestic demand or China's apparently limitless growth engine will lose steam (Eurasia Group 2011; Lardy 2011; World Bank 2012; FYP 2011). The notion that slower growth somehow could turn out to be a desirable alternative is deceptive in the case of China. For if the sources of the country's economic growth run dry, China's historic societal transformation could also get stuck. The result in all likelihood would be growing unemployment, a resurgence of poverty and an escalation of social and political conflict with uncertain outcome. The Chinese leadership therefore is performing the balancing act of achieving the transformation towards a more sustainable growth pattern while avoiding a substantial slowdown of economic growth that could undermine political and social stability.

In response to the contradictions of the current economic growth pattern, the Chinese central government is pursuing the dual target of economic rebalancing and a transformation of China's industrial base. The strategy of rebalancing, a guiding theme in the Eleventh and the Twelfth Five Year Plan, aims at increasing the share of domestic demand in overall economic growth. There are several dimensions to this objective including a rise in the share of wage incomes, the construction of social security systems, and a regional rebalancing between the relatively affluent coastal regions and the poorer regions of the interior. These projects are being pursued with great fervour, though so far with limited effect in terms of a change in the overall composition of growth.

The second strategy, industrial upgrading, aims at developing innovative capabilities of domestic enterprises in order to enable their emancipation from a subordinate role of low-tech assemblers in global production networks (GPN). By enriching the enterprises' functions, as is the assumption behind this strategy, Chinese entrepreneurs could siphon off higher revenues from advanced manufacturing as well as from design and marketing activities. It is widely agreed that this is the only perspective of escaping the trap of a profit squeeze in manufacturing industries triggered by sluggish export performance, rising prices for the most important factors of production, and the continuous appreciation of the Renminbi (RMB) that is undermining the competitiveness of Chinese exporters of low-end goods (Yu and Zhang 2009; World Bank 2012; HKTDC 2011a). In fact, the desire to overcome low-end production and to reach a higher level of economic development has shaped Chinese industrial policy not only in recent years, but effectively since the beginnings of the reform era in 1978 (Naughton 2007, 349–351). But in the course of mounting economic problems of low-end assemblers and the temporary breakdown of many export-oriented companies with low technological capabilities, such efforts are undertaken with a new urgency. No one expressed this more clearly than the former secretary of Guangdong's Communist Party, Wang Yang, who stressed that the economic crisis of 2008/09 was an opportunity for change and said at the height of the virtual breakdown of much of Guangdong's export industry that is was "time to open the bird cages for new birds to settle down", implying that the economic crisis was an opportunity for a sweeping replacement of low-end industries by more advanced successors (cf. Businessweek 15.06.2009).

This study addresses the interrelatedness of both issues, the challenge of rebalancing on the one hand, and the goal of industrial upgrading on the other hand. A transformation of industries that leads them beyond production models based on cheap labour is a precondition for eventually raising the level of domestic consumption and thereby bringing about economic rebalancing. But industrial transformation in itself does not necessarily imply more just patterns of labour relations or income redistribution. In fact, as a growing body of empirical studies in the field of economic sociology has analysed in great detail (Barrientos et al 2010; Bernhardt and Milberg 2011; Bernhardt 2013; Lüthje et al 2013a), much of the literature on industrial upgrading in developing countries proved to be too naïve in assuming such a direct relationship between industrial transformation and what has come to be known as "social upgrading" of wages and working conditions.

Hence, the principal aim of this study is to analyse recent transformations of industries in China with special regard to the question as to how far the chosen strategies for industrial upgrading lead to improvements for workers in terms of wage levels and working conditions. It approaches this issue by means of case studies from factories in the Pearl River Delta (PRD), China's main hub for export production and at the same time the site of an unmatched conglomeration of those enterprises that were labelled as "old birds" in Wang Yang's metaphor. The case studies investigate two industries in this region. The first is the LED lighting sector, a rapidly transforming industry which belongs to the so-called Strategic Emerging Industries (SEI) that are particularly supported by the Chinese authorities. The second is the textile and garment industry, which has a centuries-old history in China and constituted one of the pillars of the country's recent period of rapid industrialisation from the early 1980s on. By choosing two industrial sectors with remarkably different characteristics, the investigation highlights the diversity of industrial upgrading strategies and their effects. A comparison of differences and parallels of industrial transformation in these industries provides ample insights for a discussion of general development tendencies in the region.

The Pearl River Delta was chosen as the site for the empirical investigation not only because it is presumably the largest industrial area in the world with a particularly long history of low value-added manufacturing for overseas markets, but also because it has emerged as a laboratory for economic and political reform. Nowhere else in China has the economic crisis been felt as intimately, the scale of labour conflict been as high, and the reform programmes of the government been as ambitious as in this region. It is therefore assumed that an in-depth study of economic and social relations in the PRD will offer particularly valuable insights about the future of Chinese industrial and social development.

## 1.1 Rebalancing, industrial upgrading, and social upgrading in academic literature

By viewing economic rebalancing, industrial upgrading, and social upgrading as combined issues, this investigation pursues an innovative approach and links debates from different disciplines that have barely been put into dialogue so far. In particular, this study covers new ground by (1) identifying the issue of "social upgrading" as a key issue for economic rebalancing, (2) developing an operable concept for the analysis of social upgrading which can be used for empirical case studies on an enterprise and industry level and (3) delivering rich case studies of two relevant Chinese industrial sectors the upgrading dynamics and labour relations of which have scarcely been investigated to this day.

Ad 1)   Social upgrading as key issue for economic rebalancing

In the disciplines of Economy, Economic Sociology and Political Science there is a lively ongoing debate about the contradictions of China's current growth model and the prospects for its transformation (Zhu and Kotz 2011; Akyüz 2011; Lardy 2011; Breslin 2011; McNally 2013). Academic studies are thereby complemented by analyses from business observers and researchers in international institutions (Eurasia Group 2011; Credit Suisse 2012; World Bank 2012; Ahuja et al 2012). In China, the issue of rebalancing has been the subject of extensive debate and commentary around the release of the 12th Five Year Plan the central theme of which is the transformation of China's economic growth model (cf. Y.Yu 2009 and 2012; CCCWS 2009; FYP 2011). All of these accounts acknowledge that the sustainability of the Chinese growth model depends on the ability to shift its growth composition from a high share of exports and investment towards household consumption. To a certain extent, they also agree that a rise in wage incomes is a precondition to achieve this task. Yet, none of these accounts discusses the impact of industrial transformation on wage incomes in detail. On the basis of macroeconomic reasoning, there often exists an underlying assumption that industrial transformation is taking place and that this will contribute to a rise in incomes, but there is no attempt to investigate this correlation empirically by looking at changes in remuneration at the enterprise level. While the mentioned macroeconomic analyses are indispensable for monitoring China's economic imbalances, quantifying recent changes and identifying problems of political reform, the omission of the question how economic change affects labour relations is a serious shortcoming. After all, a rise of wages as a share in national income decisively depends on the question whether the distribution of income within Chinese enterprises takes on more just forms than has been the case in export-oriented manufacturing industries during the last decades.

Ad 2) Tools for assessing the relationship between industrial upgrading and social upgrading

The neglect of the issue of labour relations is also characteristic for most studies on industrial upgrading in China. Various accounts by Chinese authors and institutions paint an increasingly detailed picture of recent transformations, but usually do not address the impact on labour in their analyses (cf. M.Yu 2011; Qiu 2012; Yu and Zhang 2009; HKTDC 2011a; Schiller 2013). At the same time, there are some studies that deal with the relationship between China's economic growth model and the rise of income inequality in recent years (cf. H.Yu 2009 for the case of Guangdong), yet here again they do not address the character of production models and labour relations on an industry basis. Comprehensive empirical studies that combine an analysis of recent economic changes with the analysis of labour relations are the exception (cf. Lüthje et al 2013b).

These shortcomings mirror the narrow focus on technological changes, which is inherent in theories about industrial upgrading in the discipline of economics (cf. Porter 1985). In the field of economic sociology, the issue of social upgrading, defined in a broad way as "improvements in the rights and entitlements" as well as the "quality of employment" of workers (Barrientos et al 2010, 7), has recently received considerable attention. A broad international network of researchers collaborating under the umbrella of a project entitled "Capturing the Gains" (CTG) is dedicated to investigate how economic[1] and social upgrading "relate, and what strategies can help to combine them" (CTG Website). This project corrects a blind spot

---

1 The term "economic upgrading" is preferred in the framework of Barrientos et al because it is conceived to provide a broader focus than the term "industrial upgrading": "in recent years GPNs [Global Production Networks, F.B.] have widened beyond manufacturing to include sectors such as agro-food, and services like call centres, tourism, and business-process outsourcing, where the term 'industrial upgrading' is less appropriate. A more generic concept used here is that of economic upgrading which applies across sectors" (Barrientos et al 2010, 6). "Economic upgrading" is defined analogously to "industrial upgrading" as "the process by which economic actors – firms and workers – move from low-value to relatively high-value activities in global production networks" (ibid).

of previous research on industrial upgrading in global value chains which "often implicitly assumed that economic upgrading in GPNs will automatically translate into social upgrading through better wages and working conditions" (Barrientos et al 2010, 7). Under the CTG framework a rich body of literature has already been published, a part of which also addresses the relationship between economic upgrading and social upgrading in China. The available analyses on China, however, are based on a "parsimonious approach" of social upgrading which is methodologically limited to a cross-country comparison of employment and wage figures in different sectors (Bernhardt and Milberg 2011; Bernhardt 2013). While these developments in academic discussion are a suitable point of departure for this investigation, empirical studies need to go beyond the analysis of macroeconomic data and must develop a more precise conceptual framework if they are to produce meaningful insights about recent changes within Chinese enterprises and their consequences, as will be discussed in more detail in the chapters 4 and 5. The critical task in this respect is to analyse concrete upgrading strategies that are implemented by enterprises and to assess their impacts on skill requirements, employment patterns and wages. So far, such instruments are missing in analytical frameworks which is why empirical studies either reproduce a bias towards technological changes without thoroughly assessing their impacts on the workforce (cf. Brandt and Thun 2011; Sturgeon and Marakami 2011) or remain limited to swift judgements on the basis of aggregate wage and employment figures which do provide some insights about general development tendencies, but fall short of explaining their profoundness and root causes (cf. Bernhardt and Milberg 2011; Bernhardt 2013; Lee and Gereffi 2013). What is needed therefore is an approach that combines the merits of research on global production networks, which discusses the preconditions for industrial upgrading on enterprise level, on the one hand, and concrete tools developed by industrial sociologists, by which the impact of industrial change on the workforce can be assessed, on the other hand. This study develops such a framework which is used in the analysis of the case studies drawing on important groundwork from, and close dialogue with, a team of researchers at the Institute for Social Research in Frankfurt. Their empirical studies of the "regimes of production" in Chinese key industrial sectors (Lüthje et al 2013b) inspired the development of a set of indicators for the assessment of social upgrading which is introduced in chapter 5.

Ad 3)  The analysis of industrial and social upgrading in the LED lighting and textile and garment industries

Thorough analyses of the shape and development of Chinese industries remain scarce, be it in the academic world or beyond. Despite the outstanding performance of Chinese manufacturing sectors in recent years, there is often surprisingly little known about their history, their basic structure, the division of labour between companies, and their dominant models of production. To the author's knowledge, this also largely is valid for the literature by Chinese authors. Often the only available general analyses about Chinese industries are provided by business analysts, sold at high prices and sometimes of doubtful quality (cf. BMI 2009; IBISWorld 2011). Beyond that, anyone who wants to find out more about Chinese industries needs to painstakingly collect information from Chinese and international business media, Chinese industry associations and government sources. When it comes to the question of labour relations, labour scholars and NGOs have published extensively about the conditions in typical mass manufacturing industries geared to export such as the IT and the textile and garment industries. Such analyses and the related advocacy work deserve credit for having raised the awareness on frequent labour rights violations in the supply chain of transnational corporations (TNCs) (A.Chan 2001; C.Chan 2010; Egger et al 2013). Especially the studies on working conditions in the IT industry, most recently on the giant electronics contract manufacturer Foxconn, have shown that low wages and bad working conditions are pervasive in this supposedly modern and advanced high-tech industry (Pun 2005; WEED 2008; Pun et al 2012). They thereby demonstrate that there is no linear relationship between industrial and social upgrading, though without explicating this conclusion at a theoretical level. Notwithstanding their merits, most labour scholars also fail to relate their comprehensive analyses about conditions in Chinese enterprises to an assessment about the wider dynamics in global and regional production networks. The debate often focuses on cases of labour rights violations whereas the impact of the profound industrial transformations on labour relations is insufficiently assessed (cf. H.Yu 2011 for an exception). As labour research and labour activism constitute the background of the author's interest in China, the ambition here is to contribute some insights to close the gap between labour studies and structural analyses of economic change in China.

In concrete terms, both of the industrial sectors under consideration have barely been the object of comprehensive analyses that combine an assessment about recent industry dynamics with the monitoring of labour relations. Recent global developments in the textile and garment industry have received extensive coverage (Fernandez-Stark et al 2011; Lopez-Acevedo and Robertson 2012; Frederick and Gereffi 2011), but so far there are few comprehensive analyses of production networks and labour relations in the Chinese industry with the exception of the already mentioned study by Lüthje et al (2013b, 251–314) and an overview provided by the Hong Kong-based NGO Globalization Monitor (GM 2010). The study presented here adds to this knowledge by delivering additional insights about recent dynamics in China, providing more profound findings about the textile segment and contributing a rich set of case studies about industrial and social upgrading at the level of industrial clusters which constitute an important structural characteristic in this sector. Thereby, the case studies also highlight the relationship between government policies and industrial upgrading on an enterprise basis, which is often neglected in analyses on inter-firm networks (cf. Bair 2005 for a critique).

The dynamic developments in the global LED industry are covered in a broad range of studies from business analysts which constitute an important source for this investigation (JPMorgan 2010; HSBC 2011; McKinsey 2011a and 2012a). Some detailed analyses of the Chinese industry do exist, but are barely accessible because they are sold by commercial market research institutes at prohibitive prices. Some preliminary studies about the industry have also been published by Chinese scholars (Li and Qiu 2010). This study combines a groundbreaking analysis of the Chinese LED industry with the first thorough investigation of industrial upgrading strategies and working conditions based on case studies of enterprises in Guangdong.

## 1.2 Structure of the presentation and research methods

The general point of departure for this investigation is the assumption of a correlation between China's outward-oriented mode of development and its current macroeconomic imbalances. Because China's economy is strongly shaped by export-oriented industrial sectors that grew based on the comparative advantage of a large pool of cheap labour, there has been a widening gap between the strength of China's productive capacities and the volume of domestic consumption, a disequilibrium which is threatening the sustainability of economic development. Industrial upgrading is seen as a potential way to escape from this contradiction because it could generate higher value added, require more sophisticated skills from employees, and eventually lead to higher incomes for broad sections of the workforce. Yet, global economic relations as well as the economic and institutional structures that grew on the basis of the established Chinese growth model condition the outcome of industrial upgrading, in particular with regard to its social effects on the workforce.

By framing the research question in this manner, the systemic conditions for changes on the enterprise level are highlighted, which is insufficiently the case in many analyses of global production networks which focus on firm interrelationships while largely ignoring institutional factors (cf. Bair 2005; Selwyn 2011 for a critique). As will be shown, this consideration of institutional conditions is of particular relevance when discussing the feasibility of social upgrading.

Because of the assumption of a close relationship between macroeconomic and institutional factors and the outcomes of industrial transformation, the empirical investigation on industrial upgrading in the Pearl River Delta is framed by a comprehensive analysis of the character and genesis of China's recent growth model, the origins of its present contradictions and recent initiatives for reform. Accordingly, the main body of this investigation is divided into three parts, in each of which different research methods are applied.

Part I:    Theoretical interpretation of the Chinese growth model and the conditions for its transformation

The aim of the first part of this study is an interpretation of the Chinese economic development model on the basis of existing theories about economic growth models, and an assessment of recent tendencies for its transformation. The method applied to this end is the analysis of three bodies of literature: (1) theoretical works about economic growth models from the fields of international political economy and economic sociology, (2) analyses of the genesis of the Chinese economic model with a special focus on the interaction of global world market integration on the one side and the domestic forms of economic development on the other, and (3) an assessment of the internal contradictions of the Chinese growth model and the recent government-led attempts towards its transformation.

Following insights formulated in recent theoretical appraisals of the Chinese political economy (ten Brink 2013; McNally 2006, 2012 and 2013), China's economic model is interpreted as a peculiar form of capitalism which justifies the application of political concepts from theoretical discussions in the West—in particular the application of institutionalist concepts from "regulation theory"—to the Chinese case. At the same time, the analysis of the genesis of the Chinese growth model and its imminent transformation strives to come to terms with the peculiarities of China's political and economic conditions as identified by international and Chinese authors.

The result of the comprehensive literature review is a deeper understanding of the relationship between China's outward-oriented mode of development and the proliferation of "exportist", "extensive" regimes of accumulation that rely on a steady quantitative expansion of production volumes while simultaneously suppressing workers' wages. It therefore becomes comprehensible that the issue of economic rebalancing critically depends on the ability to transform China's industrial structure towards more inclusive forms of development in which economic growth is combined with rising incomes for workers. A closer look at the current government-led attempts for overcoming the contradictions of the Chinese growth model reveals substantial efforts and progress in this direction, but also identifies persistent challenges rooted in those structures to which China's past mode of development has given rise.

## Part II: Development of a research framework for industrial and social upgrading in Chinese industries

The second part of the investigation develops a theoretical understanding of the conditions for industrial upgrading at the enterprise level and the relationship of industrial upgrading and social upgrading. Based on the discussion of the theoretical literature on this issue and under consideration of the insights about the general macroeconomic and institutional conditions in China as analysed in part I, detailed research hypotheses and a set of indicators for the empirical analysis of the case studies are developed.

The method of investigation in part II is a discussion of the existing literature about industrial upgrading in global production networks, in particular the so-called global value chain (GVC) school, and a review of recent discussions about the relationship between industrial upgrading and social upgrading. As mentioned before, these discussions constitute an important theoretical progress because they acknowledge that there is no automatic relationship between industrial upgrading and an improvement of social conditions for the workforce. Yet, they are also seen as deficient because they fail to sufficiently acknowledge how internal segmentations of the workforce between and within companies limit the profoundness of social upgrading. Furthermore, they do not provide a satisfying framework for the assessment of social upgrading in empirical case studies. Hence, an appropriate set of indicators is developed with reference to insights from industrial sociology and analyses that acknowledge the specifics of Chinese industrial relations.

The result of part II is a comprehensive framework for the sector analyses of industrial and social upgrading in Chinese industries that integrates institutional factors and economic relationships on the global, national and regional level.

Part III: Empirical analysis of industrial upgrading and social upgrading in the LED lighting and the textile and garment industries

The framework developed in part II is applied in part III for the analysis of industrial upgrading and social upgrading in selected enterprises in the Pearl River Delta. The analysis proceeds in each chapter by first investigating recent changes in global production networks within both industrial sectors under consideration. Secondly, the structure and recent developments within the respective Chinese industries are analysed. Finally, the data from enterprise case studies in the Pearl River Delta is presented.

The method of analysis is a thorough review of academic literature and business sources about the structure of both industrial sectors on the one hand, and a comprehensive field study based on 64 semi-structured interviews on the other hand. The data on industrial upgrading in Chinese enterprises was collected during two field research trips to the Pearl River Delta in the autumn of 2010 and 2011, respectively. The data covers developments in 13 enterprises that were selected because of their pronounced efforts for industrial upgrading. The rationale of the research therefore aims at the identification of industrial upgrading strategies in a "vanguard" of progressive enterprises, since it is assumed that the effects of industrial upgrading can be observed in the clearest possible manner in advanced firms. The interview data was processed and interpreted according to the method of "qualitative content analysis" (Gläser and Laudel 2010). The precise research method for the empirical case studies and its underlying assumptions are explicated in detail in chapter 5.

## 1.3 Main results and their interpretation

The results of the empirical investigation are summarised and interpreted with view to the main research question in the concluding section (chapter 8). All in all, the results show pronounced efforts towards industrial upgrading in both sectors under investigation. Although the results are not representative of all enterprises in the Pearl River Delta, they do reflect a more profound trend of industrial transformation throughout the region. Significantly, this is valid not only in the newly emerging and dynamic LED lighting industry, but also for the "traditional" textile and garment industry. While production models in the latter continue to be highly labour-intensive, they are combined with higher value-added functions of design and marketing while parts of the manufacturing process are being automated.

In terms of social upgrading, the assumption of higher value-added functions in both industries requires enhanced R&D capacities and marketing functions which are performed by highly skilled and better-paid employees. In this sense, there is a positive correlation between industrial upgrading and social upgrading. Chinese enterprises in particular acquire functions which previously had been performed by enterprises outside of China when Chinese companies used to be largely limited to basic manufacturing tasks. Thus, this study provides ample evidence of the fact that Chinese companies are now "climbing up the value chain" and thereby create a higher demand for highly skilled and better-paid employees. However, this tendency is complemented by a strong trend towards a renewed internal task segmentation within single enterprises, which leaves basic manufacturing tasks to be performed by low-skilled and badly paid migrant workers who in most of the investigated enterprises constituted the large majority of the workforce.

The results of the empirical investigation therefore demonstrate in detail a failure of social upgrading for manufacturing workers in the Pearl River Delta. Industrial upgrading does not lead to qualitative improvements in terms of skills and training, remuneration systems and working conditions. Wage rises do occur in the surveyed industries, but they do not go beyond a general tendency of rising wages induced by macroeconomic factors such as a regional labour shortage, and therefore cannot be interpreted as resulting from industrial upgrading. What is more, the case studies demonstrate how modern production techniques are being combined with employment systems that continue to rely on large quantities of low-skilled migrant labour and that such production models are relatively stable despite pressures of rising costs and competition from low cost producers abroad. Frequently voiced expectations about an "end of cheap labour" in China (cf. Braun 2010, Li et al 2012, Das and N'Diaye 2013a) therefore overstate the case. Even if a secular trend for rising minimum wages and the introduction of social security schemes is undeniable, there is a simultaneous preservation of the basic characteristics of the cheap labour regime, at least in the IT industry and the textile and garment industry of the Pearl River Delta—sectors that do upgrade, but leave most migrant workers behind.

Relating the results of the empirical investigation to the conclusions drawn in part I about China's present efforts to rebalance the economic growth model, it can be assumed that industrial upgrading combined with the general tendency of rising wages for manufacturing workers does have a positive effect on income growth and hence on economic rebalancing. However, the potential for a qualitative transformation of the overall growth model is not fully realised because strong segmentations of workforces within Chinese enterprises persist. This is not a matter of sheer backwardness of enterprises since such divisions are being reproduced even when companies overhaul their production systems and introduce new production technologies. For these reasons, the integration of migrant workers into urban consumption patterns remains shallow—which harvests powerful social contradictions that often erupt in industrial conflicts. Notwithstanding steady quantitative changes, the basic contradiction of the Chinese growth model, characterised by the build-up of huge productive resources on the one hand and an endemic structural underconsumption on the other hand, remains unresolved. The failure of social upgrading in Chinese industries therefore constitutes an obstacle for a profound transformation of the Chinese economy towards a more sustainable development path.

# Part I:
## China's growth model and the conditions for its transformation

# 2 Origins and character of the Chinese economic growth model

This chapter provides a theoretical interpretation of China's peculiar economic growth model which has persistently generated extraordinarily high growth rates but also brought about economic imbalances that necessitate its transformation. The analysis identifies China's export-led form of world market integration as the main reason for these imbalances. Large industrial agglomerations were built up in coastal regions on the basis of China's competitive advantage of cheap resources and a suppression of income growth for a large share of workers in manufacturing industries whose wages did not keep track with growth in industrial output and productivity. Since this model of development increasingly is plagued by internal contradictions, the issue of "social upgrading", an industrial transformation that entails social benefits for workers, is identified as one key issue in China's quest for economic rebalancing.

The analysis of China's growth model is conducted on the basis of theories about distinct phases and types of capitalist growth which were developed within the framework of regulation theory. Its main concepts will be introduced in section 2.1 and then complemented in section 2.2 by considerations about how a global integration of national (or regional) economic systems into the world economy under the circumstances of a globalisation and disintegration of production shapes their economic structure. The resulting theoretical framework is then applied to the case of China's recent economic history in section 2.3. Drawing on recent literature from the field of international political economy, China is identified as a peculiar form of capitalism which legitimises the application of theoretical concepts from social science that had been developed to analyse modes of capitalist growth. Acknowledging recent insights from international and Chinese research about the specifics of the Chinese political economy, the analysis reveals how the combination of market-driven, outward-oriented accumulation and China's peculiar institutional forms have resulted in a heterogeneous mix of industry structures and labour relations. Yet, a common denominator of industrial relations in different industries is the weak representation of workers and the dysfunctional regulation of labour relations which is seen as the prime reason for the divergence between the growth of GDP and household incomes in recent years. This analysis serves as a theoretical background for the interpretation of recent government attempts to meet the combined challenge of a reform of China's development model and industrial upgrading.

## 2.1 Extensive and intensive regimes of accumulation: The regulationist legacy

A suitable point of reference for the theoretical interpretation of capitalist growth models can be found in regulation theory. Authors from this theoretical tradition distinguish between different phases of capitalist growth with regard to their predominant patterns of accumulation and discuss the evolution of institutions and labour relations from this vantage point. As China's institutional settings continue to evolve in the context of an economic structure that is heavily shaped by its peculiar form of world market integration, regulation theory offers an adequate perspective for the analysis of China's societal transformation.[2] In particular, this approach offers a perspective for the discussion of the interrelationship between forms of accumulation and the respective patterns of industrial relations. For these reasons it constitutes the most adequate framework for the present study whose aim is to disentangle the relationship between macro-economic reform, industrial change and labour relations.[3] However, regulation theory was developed with an eye on advanced economies and with a framework centred on national modes

---

2 Of course, the interpretation of China as a form of capitalism is a controversial matter. The reasoning behind this assumption will be explicated below (cf. section 3.1) when the case of China is analysed by using the theoretical terms developed in this section.

3 Regulation theory is in particular preferred to approaches of the Varieties of Capitalism paradigm because the latter categorise capitalist societies primarily according their institutional settings (Hall and Soskice 2001; Streeck 2010). An interpretation of China's (constantly evolving) political economy along these lines is a legitimate and theoretically stimulating task (cf. ten Brink 2013), but less suited for this investigation because of its more specific focus on the relationship between forms of accumulation, regimes of production within different industries and the corresponding forms of labour relations.

of development. Its theoretical elements therefore must be adapted to the specific situation of latecomer economies that are integrated into the world economy based on their roles in globally disintegrated production networks.

The fundamental theoretical contribution of regulation theory is the identification of different phases of capitalist growth, so-called "modes of development", using the concepts of "regimes of accumulation" (RoA) and "modes of regulation" (MoR) (Aglietta 2000, 66–67).[4] According to a definition by Alain Lipietz a RoA is:

"the fairly long-term stabilization of the allocation of social production between consumption and accumulation. This implies a certain correspondence between the transformation of the conditions of production and the transformation of the conditions of the reproduction of wage-labour, between certain of the modalities in which capitalism is articulated with other modes of production within a national economic and social formation, and between the social and economic formation under consideration and its 'outside world'" (1987, 14).[5]

If a relatively stable development of a RoA is to succeed it needs to be complemented by "norms, habits, laws and regulating networks", the so-called "mode of regulation", that assure that the behaviour of agents conforms to its basic logic of reproduction (ibid, 14–15). A MoR for instance defines the forms of monetary exchange, the forms of economic competition and the competences and institutional forms of the state.

Based on this conceptual framework, further differentiations have been introduced to characterise specific patterns of growth in historic periods. Discussing the economic development in the US, Aglietta develops the distinction between predominantly "extensive" and "intensive" regimes of accumulation (2000, 71–72; cf. Becker 2002, 67–70): an extensive RoA describes a scenario of successive industrialisation of formerly non-capitalist societies in which workers are drawn into the processes of industrial produc-

---

4 The following paragraphs contain a simplified summary of the most proliferated, the so-called "Parisian School" of the regulation approach. Yet, Jessop and Sum distinguish between seven different theoretical schools associated with regulation theory (2006, 13-57; cf. also Becker 2002).

5 Since this definition takes the relationship between national regimes of accumulation and the 'outside world' into account, it can be seen as a modification to prior regulationist concepts which selected the nation state as primary unit of analysis. Thereby Lipietz offers a theoretical venue to discuss the interaction between an intensification of global trade and the internationalisation of production, on the one hand, and the development of national regimes of accumulation, on the other hand.

tion, but in which they barely become consumers of industrially produced goods: "the traditional way of life may persist or be destroyed, but it is not radically recomposed by the logic of utilitarian functionalism", i.e. shaped by mass consumption of standardised goods from industrial production (ibid, 71). The dominant logic of such a configuration is one of quantitative expansion. Revenues are increased by hiring ever more workers, expanding working time to the physical maximum and producing an ever higher quantity of products based on increasing volumes of raw materials. Due to this inherent expansionist mode of development, extensive regimes of accumulation tend to run into contradictions since consumption does not keep track with the expansion of productive resources. A temporary solution for this contradiction may be the quest for exterior markets which is why extensive RoAs tend to be "extraverted" (cf. Lipietz 1987, 29–46; Becker 2002, 67–73).

An intensive RoA is different from, and in Aglietta's conception a succession of, the extensive growth pattern. In intensive RoAs, "a new mode of life for the wage-earning class" is established that incorporates workers entirely into the circles of capitalist commodity consumption (Aglietta 2000, 71–72). Traditional life-styles are eliminated and subsistence-based production patterns are marginalised or disappear. Accordingly, workers' consumption comes to constitute an important source of demand. Intensive RoA are facilitated, on the one hand, through jumps in productivity based on technological progress and new patterns of work organisation (historically: the Taylorist and then Fordist revolutions brought about by advanced forms of the division of labour), and, on the other hand, through a rise of workers incomes that matches the growth of productivity (Lipietz 1987, 35–37). A virtuous circle of "introverted" production may arise when expanding domestic markets, based on rising incomes of workers, continuously spurn economic growth which in turn creates a leeway for wage gains by workers. (Aglietta, 67–171; Lipietz 1987, 29–46).

Reality rarely neatly fits these categories which will subsequently be interpreted as ideal types (cf. Becker 2002, 67). The following qualifications have been made by the adherents of regulation theory themselves, as well as by their critics. First, the character of a RoA is seldom clear-cut, as elements of an extensive and an intensive logic of accumulation may coexist. A mainly quantitative mode of growth, for instance, may also involve constant progress in productivity and a steady increase in workers' consumption and therefore not be "purely" extensive. Aglietta writes of the history of the US that "the two regimes of accumulation [extensive and intensive, F.B.] were combined together, and yet the process of capital accumulation assumed a different pattern according to whether one or the other dominated" (2000, 71). For this reason, Aglietta and other regulationist authors refer to "predominantly" extensive or intensive RoA. The analysis of national economic structures can also further be differentiated according to regional RoAs below or across the level of nation states or RoAs in different industrial sectors. As will be further elaborated in the next section, the notion of a relative heterogeneity of regimes of accumulation is of great importance to grasp modes of capitalist development in the context of globally disintegrated production in which technologically sophisticated norms of production are spread to less developed regions and thus create a highly heterogeneous economic structure in the target regions of investment.[6]

The second qualification concerns the historic evolution of RoAs. Regulation theory assumes a succession from extensive to intensive forms of accumulation. This assumption seems fairly sensible according to the framework established so far. Once it is accepted that predominantly extensive RoAs based on continuous quantitative expansion of production and a simultaneous suppression of workers consumption do exist, contradictions are endemic due to the quantitative boundaries of resources (natural resources, raw materials, labour, land) and market volumes. At a certain point, a progress towards a more balanced regime of accumulation which rests on an even development of productivity and workers consumption must supersede the extensive RoA if further stable social and economic development is to be realised. Increases in productivity may then create a leeway for a growth in workers' wages and consumption, which could unleash a pattern of growth based on the demand from the very workers who produce these goods. Adherents of regulation theory identify the period from the late 1930s until the late 1960s as such a constellation. It was baptised "Fordism", with reference to the combination of mass production and constant growth of wages at the Ford motors company, which for the first time allowed workers to purchase the products of their own labour, a pattern which shaped economic history in the US and in advanced European economies after the Second World War. But in the view of Aglietta and his followers, the advent of such a

---

6 Yet, the institutional embeddedness of economies levels the heterogeneity to a certain extent since it provides a set of legal regulations and norms concerning employment, wages, and social systems, i.e. a mode of regulation, that shape the patterns of consumption and therefore the overall character of an RoA.

constellation is far from automatic. On the contrary, it is emphasised that the emergence of Fordism was the product of a prolonged series of social struggles and state intervention galvanized in Roosevelt's New Deal (Aglietta 2000, 130–135). The product was a new mode of regulation, a set of norms and laws governing production and distribution which allowed for a substantial rise in workers consumption. However, there is no reason to assume that such a trajectory would be the model case for all other processes of capitalist transformations. As Lipietz writes,

"It is pointless to attempt to fit all social formations into the framework of a regime of accumulation adapted to a model situation (such as Fordism). It is not simply that they do not necessarily all conform to that regime of accumulation; it may be that they conform to no stabilized regime of accumulation. In other words, they may simply be in a state of crisis" (1987, 15).

Such a relativistic understanding of the key concepts of regulation theory is vital if the framework of extensive/intensive RoA is not to regress into another form of mechanistic modernisation theory according to which the contradictions of extensive RoAs are overcome through an inherent process of systemic evolution. Concrete analysis of societal formations is needed to determine the factors supporting and inhibiting a transformation of extensive RoA with their inherent contradictions. As will be further elaborated below, this insight is of high relevance when it comes to the issue of a rebalancing of the Chinese growth model, characterised by a large proportion of industries operating on an extensive mode of growth. Rebalancing is a contested process in which adherents of thorough economic reform are challenged by interest groups associated with the old growth model.

A third qualification of the concept of extensive/intensive accumulation pertains to the overall validity of the historical interpretation inherent in regulation theory. In fact, there has been considerable debate about whether both its periodization and its theoretical conclusions are valid. Critics have pointed out that Aglietta's interpretation of US history is flawed because rather than being a model case for extensive accumulation in the 19 century, growth depended to a large scale on leaps of productivity and workers' consumption (Brenner and Glick 1991, Walker 1995). Consequently, the validity of the overall theoretical juxtaposition of crisis-ridden extensive RoAs and more stable intensive RoAs is questioned (Brenner and Glick 1991). This has important implications for the interpretation of 20th century economic history. Aglietta, representative of many other regulationists, sees a higher share of workers' consumption based on rises in productivity through Taylorist production as the root cause for a more stable development of capitalism which was complemented by a more coherent pattern of investment and by effective demand facilitated through monopolistic regulation (2000, 151–161). But there exist various competing explanations of the Golden Age of post-war capitalism that see mass consumerism rather as an effect than as the primary cause of stability (cf. Callinicos 1991; Brenner and Glick 1991). A closer assessment of such debates lies beyond the scope of this study. Yet, the controversy about the preconditions under which "virtuous growth cycles" of intensive accumulation may arise is relevant in so far, as they highlight the conditioning influences of the global economic context on the evolution of capitalist regimes of accumulation on a national scale.

Keeping such caveats in mind, the distinction between extensive and intensive RoAs is useful for the analysis of the modifications of the Chinese growth pattern. As will be elaborated in section 2.3, the formation of an export-led growth model entailed the development of a peculiar kind of a predominantly extensive RoA, especially in those industrial sectors that are oriented towards overseas markets. In fact, the structures of Chinese industries that have grown on the basis of labour-intensive export production in a sense fit the concept of an extensive RoA even better than the "model case" of the USA, because they are based on a type of semi-proletarianised labour that is largely excluded from urban patterns of consumption.[7] Since this growth model gives rise to macroeconomic imbalances, an advancement toward what has been described as an intensive RoA, i.e. one based on workers' consumption and increases in productivity, or, in the terminology of the reform discourse, rising domestic demand and higher value-added produc-

---

7 Brenner and Glick critically note that Aglietta's notion of workers that are subsumed to capitalist production while they are still dependent on subsistence production in early US capitalism is erroneous: "[T]he very fact of proletarianization would seem to imply a process by which the direct producers have been, or are being, separated from the means of subsistence […] [I]f workers have been made subject to the authority of capital in the labour process, it would, under normal conditions, seem difficult for them just in practical terms to secure their means of consumption from agricultural households and plots in rural communities" (1991, 61). Yet, exactly this paradox of a working class partially dependent on subsistence production has been a reality in the case of migrant labour in China. Migrant workers generally have kept use rights on land in their places of origin while they went to the city to earn additional income through wage labour. Their families often have earned a basic income on basis of subsistence production, but benefitted from the remittances of their family members in the cities (cf. Lee 2007, 204–216).

tion through industrial upgrading, is widely conceived to be necessary. The feasibility of such a transformation to a great extent rests on a transformation of labour relations, in particular on whether some tens of millions of migrant workers toiling in export industries will come to be resident city dwellers with incomes that can support their families and thereby generate rising domestic demand for industrially produced goods. Aglietta's question, whether industrial transformation entails "a new mode of life for the wage-earning class", therefore lies at the heart of China's rebalancing conundrum which justifies a framing of the research subject about the social impact of industrial transformation in regulationist terms.

The caveats outlined above, however, advise us to use these terms cautiously and with certain scepticism towards the wider historical interpretations associated with them. Neither is the advent of an intensive RoA automatic, nor does it automatically generate self-sustained and stable growth. In concrete terms, China's attempts to mimicry Fordism may be compromised by the ongoing weak economic performance in advanced industrial regions, regular excesses of investment and bursts of speculative bubbles, as well as the corresponding intense competition on international markets. These circumstances are very different from those in the period after the Second World War indeed, and it will be argued that they put a strain on China's ambitious strategies for reform.

For these reasons, the concept of extensive/intensive RoA is used in a purely analytical sense in the course of this examination. It serves to highlight the relationship between specific forms of accumulation in Chinese industries, their corresponding forms of wage labour, and the emerging patterns of consumption. A reference to the historic experience of Fordism as a tentative blueprint is relevant only in so far as it generates stimulating questions concerning China's prospects for a more balanced growth model: To what extent can an intensive RoA, similar to the one in the US after the Second World War[8], emerge under the highly different context of globalisa-

8 A similar question about the analogy between developments in the US history and in contemporary China is raised in a recent report by Credit Suisse: "What has happened in China over the last 30 years—i.e., massive pace of industrialisation, significant improvement in people's livelihood, but surging income inequality and related social problems—is quite similar to what was experienced in the US during the "Gilded Age" in the late 19th century. The "Gilded Age" was followed by the "Progressive Era" in the early 20th century, in which government involvement in regulating business and redistribution of income increased significantly [...]. Will China follow the same path?" (2012, 7).

tion? And in particular: to what extent do global norms of production, established in disintegrated global production networks that are shaped by intense competition, undermine the introduction of more just patterns of work and employment (cf. Lüthje et al 2013a, 17–31)? These questions will serve as a background for both the analysis of the current attempts to transform the Chinese growth model as well as the relationship between industrial upgrading and its effects on the workforce.

## 2.2 Uneven and combined development and its impact on forms of accumulation in latecomer economies

The discussion about different modes of capitalist growth up until now has not acknowledged international economic and political interpenetrations of national formations. Yet, the proliferation of global production networks in which different functions of production are allocated in different regions requires putting the analysis of national or regional RoAs in a transnational perspective. Especially when it comes to analysing patterns of economic growth and social development in developing economies, the analysis must overcome the methodological nationalism that is inherent, for instance, in classic modernisation theories that assumed a linear evolution of economies along quite uniform stages (cf. Rostow 1960), or in some neoclassical interpretations of economic development that see the abstract principles of competition as harmonising factors generating a convergence between national economies (cf. critically: ten Brink 2008, 81–82). Rather, economic relations in latecomer economies are shaped by an already existing economic structure on the global scale that involves certain technological standards, an existing level of capital accumulation, for example in the form of transnational corporations (TNCs), and an established economic and political world order. Hierarchies in the global political and economic system can inhibit development in weaker economies which may have limited resources to compete against more powerful economic actors. Yet, they can also be a source of technology transfer and thereby stimulate the development of modern industrial sectors.

The notion of uneven and combined development can help to integrate the contradictory tendencies of uneven power relations on the one hand, and catch-up growth of the other (cf. Dunn and Radice 2006; Ashman 2009;

Callinicos 2009, 88–93). According to this perspective, a hierarchical global order, created by non-determinable competitive interactions and not by an all-encompassing steering subject, is open for change because hierarchies are not static, but must be reproduced. As the underlying economic development is dynamic, opportunities for latecomers to jump in and to upgrade their operations can open up, for example when new technologies are conquered that lead to a creation or reconfiguration of industrial sectors. Most importantly, their development does not start from scratch, but on the basis of already existing technologies that can be imitated, adapted, or simply taken over. Capitalist development in latecomer economies therefore is not a simple repetition of previous growth patterns, but a combination of traditional and advanced forms of production. An analysis of national growth models needs to take this coexistence of influences into account.

A rich body of research in the field of economic sociology focuses on the changing forms of an international division of labour, the interpenetration of economic relations in global production networks and the effects of industrialisation on developing countries (cf. Lüthje et al 2013a: 7–27; Bair 2009; Gereffi 2005 for an overview). One early theoretical interpretation of the experience of export-led industrialisation and its impact on countries in the global South can be found in descriptions of a "New International Division of Labour" (NIDL) (Fröbel et al 1980). They reflected that underdeveloped economies did not remain confined to a role of raw material export. Rather, certain regions were chosen by TNCs as sites for Foreign Direct Investment (FDI) in labour-intensive industries. Economic activities, however, remained highly dependent on decisions in the advanced economies. Technologies remained under firm control of multinational corporations which also siphoned off the bulk of profits. It was basically denied that industrialisation in the newly industrialised countries (NIC) would lead to more than a mere allocation of basic assembly steps which persisted only on condition of the exploitation of cheap labour. Theories of a NIDL therefore emphasised the ongoing dependence of industrialisation in the periphery. Third World industrialisation in this view largely remained another form of "development of underdevelopment" (cf. Lüthje et al 2013a, 13–17).

From a regulationist perspective, Alain Lipietz (1987, 75–81) challenged this notion of a static bifurcation of the world between economies of the centre and the periphery. He introduced a distinction between "primitive Taylorisation" and "peripheral Fordism" that implied the possibility for developing economies to advance. The expression "primitive Taylorisation" referred to those forms of world market production that dominated the early division of labour in GPNs. Production was "labour-intensive in the strictest sense" whereas technologic development, as well as more sophisticated tools and processes that require skilled workforces, remained controlled by enterprises in advanced economies. There was a Taylorist division of labour on the shop floor, but no automatic machinery. In fact, capital intensity often was lower than in domestic industries (built e.g. during phases of import substitution industrialisation). Production therefore relied on an army of low-skilled, often female, migrant workers recruited from rural areas of the hinterland of the industrialising zones. In these extensive RoA, revenues heavily relied on the extraction of absolute surplus value by prolonging the working day and depressing wages. Lipietz coined the term "bloody Taylorisation" to characterise the extreme forms of exploitation that could be found in these forms of world market production.

Yet, not all patterns of Third World industrialisation conformed to this picture. For Lipietz, "peripheral Fordism" is distinct from primitive Taylorisation. It is characterised by the existence of autonomous local capital, the presence of a sizeable middle class, and significant elements of a skilled working class (Lipietz 1987, 78). Peripheral Fordism remains a form of export-led industrialisation with links to the world market, but "[i]ts markets represent a specific combination of consumption by the local middle classes, with workers in the Fordist sectors having limited access to consumer durables, and exports of cheap manufactures to the centre" (ibid, 79). Peripheral Fordism involves mechanisation of industrial processes, but remains peripheral since most functions of skilled manufacturing and engineering remain located in the advanced economies. Rather than evolving from primitive Taylorisation, peripheral Fordism is often based on previous capital accumulation that created domestic industries (e.g. in the heavy industry on which ISI strategies especially had focused) and urban middle classes.

Lipietz' model of peripheral Fordism was taken up in a modified form by Bob Jessop and Ngai-Ling Sum (2006). They criticise Lipietz' terminology for remaining too narrowly attached to Fordism as a model case, but they share his notion that industrialisation in export-oriented developing countries shape a peculiar form of economic development which they call "exportist regimes of accumulation" with explicit reference to the East Asian newly industrialised countries (EANIC). By applying this term, they wish to capture an "interiorization of world market dynamics" and "the interconnection between an external demand-driven virtuous cycle and the overall flexibilization of production and distribution across time and space", which they see insufficiently covered by Lipietz' conceptual framework. Exportist RoA rely on various forms of regulation which are based on the state's effort to allocate FDI or foster domestically owned export industries and to organise technological catch-up. Under neoliberalism, a new paradigm of a "Schumpeterian state" has become prevalent which especially aims at raising competitiveness and technological capabilities. With regard to the labour process, there is a task fragmentation among many globally dispersed production sites with a prevalence of a Taylorist work organisation in exportist RoAs (ibid, 163–171).

The interpretations of Lipietz or Jessop and Sum both focus on the combination of export production with production models based on low-waged labour. Both approaches at the same time describe how the allocation of export-led industries leads to an internal variegation of growth models. In fact, various sector-specific patterns of accumulation with respective differences regarding their capital intensity, patterns of work and their market orientation can be identified. Lipietz refers to the case of South Korea in the early 1980s, in which patterns of accumulation in export industries, mostly in the textile and garment sector, could be classified as "bloody Taylorization", whereas other domestic industries and even internationalised industries like the automotive sector showed different forms associated with peripheral Fordism (1987, 79–81).

This distinction offers a suitable vantage point for a theoretical assessment of the heterogeneous forms of accumulation in different industries of latecomer economies. However, the outlined concepts offer only a vague idea of how transnational norms of production and regional systems of regulation combine to give rise to distinct patterns of accumulation in different industrial sectors. They remain limited to a description of some paradigmatic forms without assessing more closely their genesis and conditions for transformation.

One solution to this problem is offered by the theoretical model of norms of technology, production and productivity, as outlined by Esser et al (1997, 15–27), and its application to forms of accumulation in disintegrated production networks (cf. Lüthje et al 2013a). The concept builds on Aglietta's term of "norms of exchange and production", by which he understands relatively stable standards that define the dominant production methods and price levels for certain product categories. Norms of production and exchange, which can, but do not need to, consist of codified standards, are determined through competitive processes mainly within single industrial sectors. They are in constant transformation due to innovations in products and production technologies that also affect the boundaries of the respective sectors. They reflect the outcome of struggles between economic actors and the relations between capital and labour that co-determine specific forms of production (cf. Aglietta 2000, 288–297). Esser at al specify this abstract concept in Aglietta's work as a sector-specific consensus of the involved actors about the boundaries of spheres of interest between single enterprises concerning forms of market regulation, price setting, licence and patent rights, and techniques of production (1997, 23).

In Aglietta's conception, norms of production and exchange are formed through competitive processes under the condition of a monopolistic regulation within the *national* sphere. Under Fordism, they implied a vertically integrated form of enterprises and provisions with view to the organisational form of production, i.e. a Taylorist division of labour (ibid, 22). Yet, under the conditions of a *global* dispersion of production, such norms become fragile and take on different, more diffuse forms.

According to Esser et al (1997, 24–27), norms of technology in certain industries assume an important role for the formation of sector-specific transnational norms of production and exchange. Technological development in this understanding is just as much a competitive struggle between social actors. The dominant norms of technology prefigure certain aspects of the norms of production and exchange, and therefore for the distribution of profits between firms and industry segments. Hence, the capacity to influence norms of technology assumes a high importance in sectors such as the IT industry, in which dependencies between companies do not mainly rest on direct hierarchic control, but on the acquisition of dominant positions within production networks that are subject to rapid reconfigurations which constitute the hegemony or marginalisation of certain production models and also redefine enterprise relations and sector boundaries (cf. Lüthje 2001, 48–49).

As norms of production and exchange can take on a transnational character, often in the form of codified standards negotiated under the participation of industry associations, national states, and international institutions, the relation between such transnational standards and localised forms of production becomes a crucial problem for companies engaged in global production networks. Strategies for global supply chain management address the necessity of global lead firms to enforce norms of production and productivity, i.e. the methods of work organisation and control in supplier factories. Such strategies also take advantage of different conditions with regard to labour supply and regulation in various regions, thereby allowing for variations concerning the organisation of production according to the respective regulative frameworks in sourcing regions (cf. Sauer and Döhl 1994; Lüthje 2001, 38–43).

The introduced concepts about norms of technology, production, and productivity offer a non-reductionist framework for the analysis of accumulation patterns in emerging economies. As norms for production and exchange are thought to be primarily sector-specific, the interpenetration of industry-specific supply chain relations and their combination with domestic economic structures gives rise to heterogeneous structures of production (or "regimes of production", cf. section 2.3.3) with different ownership forms, production models, and labour relations. This framework therefore is suited better to acknowledge the variety of intermediate and hybrid forms of production than early interpretations of industrialisation in developing countries like, for instance, Lipietz' rough distinction between primitive Taylorisation and peripheral Fordism.

## 2.3 The rise of China from a global perspective

The outlined theoretical notions about phases of capitalist development, their combined and heterogeneous forms in latecomer economies, and the necessarily diverse landscape of forms of accumulation resulting from them are now applied to the case of China based on insights about the Chinese political economy generated by Chinese and international authors. An overall synthesis or of this vast literature will not be attempted here (cf. Naughton 2007; Cai 2010; Heilmann 2004 for comprehensive overviews). Instead, the following paragraphs focus on China's specific form of world market integration and its implication for the emergence of peculiar regimes of production. The overall objective is a description of China's growth pattern and the specific position of Guangdong Province within this pattern. The resulting picture reveals the contradictions of the present growth model and the economic and institutional conditions for its reform through the combined task of rebalancing and industrial upgrading. The analysis of China's political economy and its transformation thereby provides the background for the examination of concrete upgrading trajectories that will be conducted in the empirical chapters.

The analysis reveals a thoroughly heterogeneous industrial landscape resulting from the superimposition of various layers of private investment on top of the (reformed) state-controlled economic units. The result are diverse and hybrid ownership forms and production systems. Rather than a coherent RoA, there is a combination of extensive and intensive RoA distributed across different industrial sectors and regions. The political heterogeneity engendered by dispersed "local development states" as well as by a lack of regulation of the conditions of wage labour support the diversity of production models and labour relations in Chinese industries. The Pearl River Delta, the site of the empirical investigation of this study, is a special case of economic development with a massive concentration of labour-intensive industries with "extensive" accumulation patterns, yet often in combination with ultra-modern production techniques imported from abroad. Here, the contradictions of the present mode of development are experienced in the sharpest manner, which results in a rapid upgrading dynamic.

## 2.3.1 China as a form of capitalism

The peculiar form of the Chinese political and economic system is continuing to puzzle observers that aim to classify it according to established categories of political theory. After all, the economic reforms after 1978 led to a flourishing of private investment and market relations which defy its categorisation as a clear-cut version of "socialism". Yet, market opening did not lead to the erosion of the formally socialist structures of the state which continue to be controlled by the Chinese Communist Party (CCP). The state also continues to play a particularly strong economic role through its control of state-owned economic assets, comprehensive macro-economic planning, and economic interventions by deploying diverse instruments at the central and the local level (ten Brink 2013, 243–252).

The following analysis is based on studies from the field of international political economy that interpret the Chinese case as a specific form of capitalism, albeit one with unique institutional characteristics (McNally and Chu 2006; McNally 2012; ten Brink 2013; Yeung 2004).[9] These works defy

---

9 The Chinese leadership's own definition of China's political and economic system is characterised by alterations and ambiguities, epitomised in the formula of the "socialist market economy" used since the 1980s, which reflects the factual mix of private economic

the expectation, as inherent in most works of transformation theory that take the development of CEE countries as a blueprint (cf. ten Brink 2013, 35–36; Heilmann 2004, 33–34), that the market reforms would trigger a process of profound political transition leading to an erosion of the party state and its associated institutions. Rather than assuming an ongoing transition towards a "complete" market economy in the form of a retreat of the state from economic functions, these authors insist on analysing the Chinese political and economic system as a novel kind of formation in its own right. Change is seen as ubiquitous in China's dynamic capitalism. This also leads to an "embryonic bifurcation of the secular realm", i.e. a relative independence of private capital, a codification of the legal system, and the strengthening of private property rights. Yet, the resulting relations remain "heavily tilted in favour of state interests or interests closely aligned with the state" (McNally 2006, 28; 34). In particular, interests between private actors and the state at various points merge and intermingle and give rise to unique institutional settings to which the forms of political rule then adapt. The assumption of a brusque antagonism between state and private capital, on which many theories of market transformation rest, therefore does not fit the case of China. According to McNally, "[o]ne of the most misunderstood aspects of capitalist development in popular concepts is that it is a purely "private" economic system. Quite to the contrary, the expansion of capital-owning classes serves to expand and reconstitute state power, since capital demands more effective state power. In essence, capitalist development leads to a process of mutual

---

relations and state planning, but remains evasive in an identification of the relationship between state and market. Academic debates reflect such ambiguities. As ten Brink (2013, 37–43) observes, some authors echo the views of the Chinese leadership that the market reforms constitute a stage of transition towards socialism (Itoh 2003) or aim to define China as some sort of non-capitalist market society (Arrighi 2007). With a focus on processes of market competition and largely ineffective and incomplete labour regulation, others view the Chinese economy as a specific form of "neoliberalism" or capitalist restoration, yet, for the most part, without making efforts to interpret in a detailed way how market relations intermingle with China's particular institutional setting (Harvey 2005, 120–151, Hart-Landsberg and Burkett 2005). Most authors avoid a closer theoretical description by calling China as a "post-socialist" (Heilmann 2004, 191–193), or, simply, a largely unspecified hybrid and transforming society (Meyer 2011). The advantage of the above-mentioned analyses of ten Brink, McNally and Yeung is that they depart from theoretical definitions of the term "capitalism" which they then confront with an examination of the societal peculiarities of the Chinese political economy. This analytical precision goes beyond a declamatory use of the term capitalism for the case of China which has become common in recent years (e.g. Huang 2008; Coase and Wang 2012).

empowerment whereby both the realm of the "economy" and that of the "state" expand. The structural power of capital can keep in check the vagaries of state power and reshape state action" (ibid, 50; cf. also McNally 2013).

The Chinese system is categorised as a form of capitalism because it is held that the drive to capital accumulation is the main imperative of economic activity (ten Brink 2013, 169; 311–312; McNally 2006, 20–25). Ten Brink uses the expression "variegated state-permeated capitalism" as a term for describing the Chinese political economy (2013, 312). He demonstrates that state institutions do not only allow for the flourishing of capitalist accumulation, but often also act as its agents through their command over state-owned enterprises (SOEs), their involvement in joint ventures with foreign companies, various levers of industrial policy to channel investment and by capital-state alliances on the local level. McNally describes the decentralised character of China's economic development which has given local economic actors space for experimentation and evolvement, and which has led to the emergence of "many separate and distinct local political economies" (2006, 48). He draws parallels to historic cases of capitalist development which also have engendered sustained industrialisation, urbanisation, infrastructure development, and social stratifications, but emphasises that the developing institutional forms have distinct characteristics (ibid, 35–36). In particular, China's private sector development is based on typical East Asian forms of "network capitalism" similar to those of predecessors of private sector-driven industrialisation like Korea and Taiwan. Unlike in these cases, however, there exists a close interaction between private business networks and local "developmental states" that "build close relations with the emerging private sector" (ibid, 40). Conscious initiatives of local state apparatuses to support local economic development by attracting private investment, raising competitiveness, and fostering industrial clusters forge a comprehensive alignment of private and public interests.

2.3.2 Integration into Global Production Networks as key factor of China's rise

Since the beginnings of the reform policies, Chinas GDP has grown more than 38-fold from USD 189.4 billion in 1980 to USD 7.3 trillion in 2011 at an average annual growth rate of 10.0 percent, according to World Bank statistics. This extraordinary fast pace of growth needs to be understood in the context of China's integration into global and regional production networks. As McNally argues, "China's development is taking place in the era of global capitalism. This is structuring the choice sets open to Chinese policy makers and business leaders, in turn generating novel responses to the challenges of late development and globalization" (2006, 36; cf. also Gereffi 2009, 48). China's private sector development was first triggered by structural reforms that unleashed domestic private or collective economic units, most importantly the so-called Township and Village Enterprises (TVEs). In 1980, the government set up the first Special Economic Zones in coastal area. In the subsequent decade, there was an increase of investment by overseas Chinese, although originally at comparably low volumes. Only in the 1990s, there was a strong influx of FDI, and economic growth was increasingly driven by the performance of export industries in the coastal provinces (Schmalz 2013). As a consequence, China's economy developed a tight outward orientation with exports constituting a volume of almost 35 percent of GDP shortly before the financial crisis (Credit Suisse 2012, 21–22). This outward orientation of the Chinese economy was supported by the following exogenous factors:

- *A disintegration of production and the proliferation of global production networks:* More or less simultaneously to the onset of China's market reform policies, the global dispersion of industries accelerated. Whereas, in the early phase, FDI was dominated by vertically integrated transnational corporations, fragmented production chains soon became the dominant pattern, especially in the production of mass consumer goods such as garments or electronics. This supported the allocation of export-oriented manufacturing industries in low-wage regions, particularly in Asia (Gereffi 2005, 2009; Herrigel and Zeitlin 2010).
- *A restructuring of production networks within Asia:* From the early 1980s on, the first generation of EANICs were becoming less attractive as a site for labour-intensive assembly due to rising production costs. Hence, companies from these countries began to outsource assembly functions to less developed sites which had a large pool of cheap labour and other advantageous factors of production at their disposal. From the late 1990s on, China therefore more and more assumed the role of an assembly hub in Asian production networks. (Hart-Landsberg and Burkett 2006; Gaulier et al 2007).
- *Overinvestment in the advanced industrial countries:* In the 1990s and 2000s, investment in industrial assets slowed down in Japan, Europe

and the US. The result was idle excess capital which was available for other channels of investment. While much of it spurned the speculative frenzies of the last two decades that triggered the "dotcom" and the "subprime" crises, FDI in emerging economies constituted another outlet (Hung 2009a; ten Brink 2013, 187–191).

In the course of the reform period, the private sector assumed a leading role in economic development. It developed on top of the existing state-controlled industry, which was thoroughly transformed, partly privatised, but not given up. The previously existing industrial structure presented favourable conditions for the growth of privately invested enterprises (PIEs) through stocks of capital, infrastructure, technologies, human capital, and markets (McNally 2006, 24).

Export-led growth was first propelled by overseas Chinese investors in the surrounding Asian countries which used their cultural and kinship ties to the Chinese mainland to set up export-oriented companies in the coastal regions. Overseas Chinese investors from Hong Kong and Taiwan also received preferential treatment from mainland authorities in order to attract their investments. From the 1990s on, after the growth of export-oriented industries had already developed a strong dynamic, overseas Chinese investment was complemented by a strong influx of FDI from advanced industrial countries which consolidated economic growth (Hart-Landsberg and Burkett 2006, 4–17; McNally 2006, 45–49; ten Brink 2013, 187–191).

The Chinese government initially pursued a strategic course that supported private investment while at the same time keeping it in check and only gradually easing restrictions for free investment and trade. Under the framework of a "dualist trade regime", FDI was originally only permitted in Special Economic Zones where it was granted privileged conditions. At the same time, domestic markets remained protected through high tariffs and other barriers. The result was strong foreign investment in processing industries that heavily relied on imports of components from abroad and were solely directed at overseas markets (Naughton 2007, 377–388). The export trade regime did not differ much from counterparts in East Asia except for its size. After successful experiments in a few coastal cities, "China created a gigantic export processing zone throughout the entire coastal region" (ibid, 387). After China's accession to the WTO, most limitations for private investors were lifted. In particular, foreign invested enterprises (FIEs) gained relatively unrestricted market access, although the authorities maintained means to regulate and influence markets, e.g. through industrial policies, public procurement, tariffs and credits (Schmalz 2013). The huge Chinese market subsequently all the more attracted foreign investors who gained increasing market shares vis-à-vis Chinese competitors (Brandt and Thun 2010, 1–2).

*Table 2.1: Domestic value-added share in manufacturing exports by sector, 2007*

| Product category | Foreign value added | Domestic value added | Share of processing | Share of FIE |
|---|---|---|---|---|
| Electronic components | 67.7 | 32.3 | 83.1 | 89.8 |
| Electronic computers | 66.2 | 33.9 | 97.9 | 93.3 |
| Household electrical appliances | 48.2 | 51.8 | 65.1 | 61.7 |
| Motor vehicles | 24.7 | 75.3 | 23.7 | 42.0 |
| Furniture | 23.8 | 76.2 | 34.2 | 56.0 |
| Wearing garments | 21.0 | 79.0 | 29.7 | 36.9 |

Source: Koopmann et al 2008.

This manner of integration into GPNs shaped the character of industrialisation in the coastal provinces. A specific form of "triangular trade" developed through which intermediate goods were imported mainly from other Asian countries, then assembled in China, and finally exported (Gaulier et al 2007, 2, 14). Economic development through the allocation of foreign enterprises was a historically new choice that existed due to the proliferation of globalised production in the 1990s. In fact, the strong role of FDI in China's recent growth dynamics distinguishes it from its predecessors in Taiwan, Korea and Hong Kong (McNally 2006, 48, 58). As a result, China's economic development, especially in the coastal provinces, is characterised by a very strong dependence on foreign enterprises. This is most evident in high-tech industries. As table 2.1 shows, FIEs were responsible for 93.3 percent of computer exports in 2007, for instance. The table also reveals that more sophisticated export products are generally characterised by a particularly high import content (denominated as "foreign value added" in the table) indicating that higher value-added production steps are mostly performed outside China.

*Figure 3.1: Share of wages in China's GDP, 1992–2009*

percent of GDP

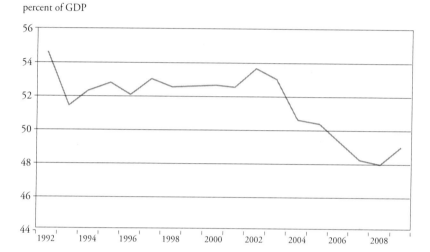

Source: Lardy and Borst 2013.

The result is what has been termed a "shallow integration" of China into GPNs (Steinfeld 2004). China's growth has been fuelled by a flourishing development of processing industries in industrial sectors geared to export production, but the performed functions have remained mostly limited to basic manufacturing tasks with, at least in its early stages, limited effects on the technological capabilities of domestic firms:

"Precisely because China specialized in the least technologically demanding stages of production, these linkages initially had few implications for technological development. Even when China was exporting finished goods that embodied high-technology components—such as laptop computers—the actual spillovers into indigenous technological capabilities were minimal. The global production networks involved in these high-tech commodities were largely closed, and Chinese domestic producers did not participate much, if at all" (Naughton 2007, 368).

Since the late 1990s, processing trade, a production model that denotes the pure assembly of products, has constituted about half of China's total exports (Li and Song 2011, 72), a share which only recently has fallen to a level of 39 percent in 2013 (HKTDC 2014). China thereby harvested its competitive advantage of abundant labour. The export-led growth pattern based on foreign investment in coastal provinces therefore is closely related to those conditions that by now shape the public perception of Chinese world market production in the West: the employment of low-skilled workers who toil under tough conditions for meagre wages (A.Chan 2001; Hart-Landsberg and Burkett 2005; Li and Song 2011, 77–79).

Such exportist regimes of accumulation have played a decisive role in China's economic ascension during the last three decades and continue to do so today. It is important, however, not to reduce China's industry to low value-added assembly models, as some accounts tend to do (cf. Steinfeld 2004; cf. Brandt and Thun 2010 for a critique).

First of all, cheap labour was not the only pull factor for FDI, and China is not only a site for export production. Its development path differs from its predecessors in the first generation of EANICs in so far as that it combines an open policy with regard to FDI with a huge domestic market. Much of FDI therefore has been motivated by a quest to access the Chinese market. This accounts for a large share of recent FDI after China's accession to the WTO and the corresponding relaxation of restrictive import rules. Yet, foreign investors in certain industrial sectors, most importantly the automotive industry, managed to participate in gains from domestic market sales in an even earlier period by entering joint ventures with Chinese SOEs in which access to technology effectively was traded for market access. Today, foreign firms openly compete with Chinese enterprises on the domestic market. This is creating spillover effects to domestic suppliers and opportunities for firms to upgrade (Brandt and Thun 2010).

Second, the model of a "triangular trade" primarily fits the patterns in the high-tech industry which predominantly relies on the supply of sophisticated components from abroad. Yet, many other sectors, such as the garment or the automotive industry, today operate on the basis of lower import content (cf. table 2.1). In these sectors, production is not limited to assembly. Export production (and production for the domestic market) therefore has spurred the development of domestic companies or the allocation of sophisticated foreign suppliers with differentiated functions along the production chain.

Third, despite the mentioned "closed" character of production networks, export-led industrialisation entails an ongoing dynamic of industrial learning and upgrading across Chinese industries (Arvantis et al 2006; Gereffi 2009). Whereas foreign investors continue to take advantage of cheap costs in China for labour-intensive manufacturing, there are also cases in which they actually require enhanced functions from their suppliers. This conforms to a general trend across many industries after the global economic crisis, in the wake of which lead firms consolidated their supply chains and thus tended to rely even more on full-package or turn-key suppliers with comprehensive capabilities (Gereffi 2014). Furthermore, there are strong tendencies for an allocation of higher value-added activities in China which now even include R&D functions of FIEs, thus fostering various forms of knowledge diffusion (Herrigel et al 2013; Ernst 2008; Schüller 2008, 55–74).

As a result, export-oriented activities in China are not confined to low value-added assembly functions any more. This is not only traceable in a shift of the export composition towards more capital-intensive and high-tech products (cf. Gereffi 2009), but also in a rise of the domestic content of export products, i.e. a diversification of functions performed by Chinese companies. According to one calculation, the share of domestic content of all export goods increased from 51.3 percent in 2002 to 59.7 percent in 2007, indicating industrial upgrading and a deeper integration into GPNs (Koopmann et al 2008, 24; cf. also Jiang and Milberg 2012). A new calculation by UNCTAD even estimates the share of domestic value added in Chinese exports to be at 70 percent—which is no less than the ones in most industrial countries and even more than the respective values of Germany and France (UNCTAD 2013, 129).[10]

Whereas basic export processing continues to constitute a large share of industrial production in coastal provinces, the quoted figures suggest that industrial upgrading has been a continuous accompaniment of industrial

---

10 Of course, these figures of the average share of domestic value added are no perfect measure for industrial upgrading as such. A country with a high share of agricultural exports, for instance, would also achieve a high share of domestic value added—which certainly would not indicate industrial upgrading. However, these figures do indicate that China has moved beyond the stage of merely being an assembly platform for export production with a shallow world market integration. Yet, more detailed analyses of individual sectors are necessary to grasp the respective forms and impacts of backward integration and regional sourcing.

development in China for a long time. In recent years, this has become particular evident through the ascendance of strong Chinese-owned technology enterprises that develop sophisticated R&D capabilities and pursue marketing strategies that also target foreign markets in advanced industrial countries. Prominent examples of this tendency are the IT companies Lenovo, Huawei and ZTE, as well as a number of Chinese sportswear brands that have gained large market shares in recent years (cf. Schüller et al 2010; Ernst and Naughton 2008).

### 2.3.3  Labour relations in China's heterogeneous industrial landscape

Starting with investments from overseas Chinese, foreign investment poured into China in consecutive (and overlapping) phases the latest of which is marked by FDI from multinational companies. Consequently, several layers of investment of different origin and in different sectors were placed on top of the existing state-controlled industrial structure (Arvantis et al 2003). This is reflected today in divergent enterprise ownership forms and hybrids like joint ventures between foreign enterprises and state controlled assets. This patchwork is distributed unevenly across different sectors. Furthermore, China's recent dynamic development is reflected in a peculiar uneven geographic structure. There is a pronounced gap in the output of coastal provinces, the locomotives of economic growth since the reform era, and that of interior regions. The proportion of six coastal provinces plus in the City of Shanghai in national income has been continuously rising since the turn of the century until it reached a value of 44 percent in 2008 (up from about 37 percent in 1980). These provinces also accounted for around three quarters of China's exports in 2009 (DB Research 2010, 3–4). The Pearl River Delta, the site of the first SEZ in Shenzhen and the destination of particularly dense investment from Hong Kong and other overseas Chinese investors most distinctively exemplifies the exportist pattern of growth based on labour-intensive assembly industries and a large migrant workforce from interior provinces (cf. section 3.3).

Political decentralisation exacerbated the economic disequilibrium. As already mentioned, the Chinese economy in effect consists of local developmental states acting in relative independence and in competition among each other, with their own strategies of attracting investment and distinct priorities of economic development.

Taking this diversity within the Chinese industrial structure into account, one can speak of "patchwork of political economies" (McNally 2006, 49) or "varieties of capitalism in one country", in which there is a "co-existence of industrial sectors of various levels of development, distributed over various regions ruled by competing local governments, and socially separated along the divide between the urban and rural population" (Lüthje 2014, 6).

This economic heterogeneity has resulted in a multiplicity of patterns regarding the organisation of production and the related patterns of work and employment in different industrial sectors. As discussed in the previous section, labour relations are shaped by the respective norms of production and productivity, which can be assumed to be formed on sector basis and under the influence of global technology leaders, on the one hand, and by the specific local institutional setting on the other hand. In order to analyse labour relations on the level of certain industries it is necessary to ask how production models that are mainly based on the application of imported or adapted production technologies as well as Western or Asian management concepts are combined with the peculiar institutional context in China. In particular, it is necessary to acknowledge the following characteristics that shape Chinese labour relations:

*(1) An imbalance of power between capital and labour on the enterprise level*
As singled out by Chinese and international researchers, market transformation has so far not resulted in effective mechanisms to regulate labour relations (Taylor et al 2003; Traub-März 2011). Government initiatives in recent years have created a legal framework for individual labour rights, most importantly through the introduction of the Labour Contract Law in 2008, and the introduction of tripartite mechanisms for labour regulation. However, there is an absence of regulations concerning collective labour rights, which results in a lack of collective bargaining mechanisms to define wages, working hours and working conditions. The resulting constellation has been described as "tripartism with four parties" or "quatropartism" (Chang et al, 2008; Chen 2010): Since the state-controlled trade union ACFTU does not play any effective role in negotiations over conditions at the enterprise level, the official tripartite structures are ineffective and hollow. Workers have therefore frequently resorted to spontaneous protests in which they appealed mostly to government institutions, either by handing in petitions and appealing for litigation of conflicts, or by outbursts of protests during which they often blocked public spaces (Shen 2007). Increasingly, workers have

also opted for strike actions, as was the case in a widely reported series of strikes centred in the automotive industry in the summer of 2010 (Butollo and ten Brink 2012; Chan and Hui 2012). The ACFTU usually has been bypassed in such forms of protest and it also lacks the legal authority to stage strikes as there exists no official right to strike in China. Yet, the growing level of conflict has spurned some experiments with trade union reform and certain forms of collective negotiations, especially in Guangdong Province, which has been the epicentre of recent labour unrest. These experiments face their own contradictions, however, and are far from setting the standard for labour relations all over China (Butollo and ten Brink 2012).

*(2) A segregation of labour markets and legal discrimination of migrant workers*

Market opening and the development of exportist patterns of accumulation in the coastal provinces have led to major changes in Chinese employment patterns. On the one hand, the coupling of stable incomes, employment guarantees and enterprise-based social security schemes of the "iron rice bowl" system were gradually dissolved in the course of SOE privatisations (Lee 2007, 69–153). On the other hand, the rise of export-led production in coastal areas has resulted in the migration of some 200 million workers from rural areas to urban regions. This pattern of migration was based on temporary employment in the cities during the last three decades. Typically, rural workers accepted dire conditions and low pay in factories producing for the world market as a supplement to a meagre living standard of their households: "Tilling the land and toiling in factories complement and require each other. For many migrant workers, agriculture provides a floor of subsistence and city jobs allow for material improvement of their families and better life opportunities for the next generation. For others in impoverished households and villages, *dagong* (taking odd-jobs in the city, F.B.) is not an option but a necessity" (ibid, 205). The segmentation of industrial workers into one group that is permanently resident and another group that temporarily migrates to the cities is cemented by the *hukou* regulations, a remnant of the Mao period. These regulations tie rights to social services and education to the place of household registration (Watson 2009, 94–105; Lee and Friedman 2010, 516). Although there have been signs of change in recent years, with regard to both the pattern of migration as well as the legal framework of the *hukou*, employment relations in Chinese industries are characterised by the ongoing segmentation of

workforces which is reflected in diverging wage levels and working conditions: "The rural-urban divide in the Chinese working class is increasingly
an integral part of complex regimes of production. These combine several
layers of urban and non-urban workers in different segments of production
and labor markets." (Lüthje et al 2013b, 336).

Matching Lipietz' description of varieties of accumulation patterns in
Korean industrial sectors in the 1980s, the heterogeneity of industrial settings resulting from China's peculiar form of world market integration has
produced various patterns of accumulation on a sector basis. The most systematic profile of the Chinese industrial landscape in this respect is provided
by extensive empirical investigations in five Chinese core industries (auto-
motives, electronics, textile and garments, steel, chemicals) by Lüthje et al.
Based on this data, various "regimes of production" (RoP) in Chinese core
industries are identified in reference to the respective combination of industry-specific forms of the organisation of production and the institutional
forms of regulation specific to Chinese capitalism (cf. 2013b 18–24). On the
basis of their field studies, Lüthje et al identify five types of RoP that differ
with regard to their regimes of work, employment and labour control:

- *State bureaucratic:* predominant in (restructured) SOEs, e.g. in the steel or
  petrochemical sectors; employment of medium-skilled or highly skilled
  workers with local *hukou* under relatively stable employment conditions;
  typically a high share of performance-based, flexible wage components;
  co-management by the official state unions; collective contracts (given
  that they exist) usually do not contain regulations that pertain to wages,
  working-hours, or other workplace-related conditions.
- *Corporate bureaucratic:* typical for transnational corporations (TNCs) or
  joint ventures, e.g. in the automotive industry; management and work
  systems shaped by TNCs; stable employment of resident workers with
  local *hukou* who often are paid the highest wages in the respective regions; relatively high base wages; regulated working hours and long-
  term career patterns; presence of trade unions which play some role in
  co-management of factories, but weak contract-based regulation of wages
  and working conditions
- *Corporate high performance:* typical for US or Western electronics companies, but also to be found e.g. in the chemicals industry and in newer
  Chinese TNCs; similar to "corporate bureaucratic" production regimes,
  but with stronger performance-based management systems in terms of

workforce selection, work organisation, career patterns, and wage determination; base wages often do not constitute more than half of the total wage; high employment flexibility; weak trade union representation and a rising number of non-regulated workplace conflicts.

- *Flexible mass production*: an extreme form of performance-based management systems; predominant in electronics mass manufacturers, especially contract manufacturers[11]; the distinguishing feature is a combination of modern manufacturing technologies and organisation with large-scale exploitation of low-paid rural migrant workers; strong segmentation and flexibilisation of employment; typically, accommodation in factory-owned dormitories; excessive overtime hours; very high wage differentials between technicians and managers on the one hand, and line-workers whose base wages usually amount roughly to the local minimum wage on the other hand; usually no trade union presence.

- *Low wage classic*: common in export-oriented light industries and in lower-tier suppliers in the automotive and electronics industry; low technological standards of production and patterns of control based on authoritarian paternalism; employment of rural migrant workers; low-wages often paid according to piece rate schemes (that may undermine legal minimum wages); excessive overtime hours.

This brief overview underlines the divergent trajectories of labour relations in Chinese industries. Notwithstanding the differences between the identified RoP, Lüthje et al (ibid, 334–336) observe the following common problems found across industries that reinforce the social divisions at the point of production:

- Low base wages and high amounts of variable pay which creates permanent incentives for extensive overtime work
- Strong wage hierarchies including status discrimination against migrant workers, women and temporary workers that undermine principles of "equal pay for equal work"

---

11 Electronics contract manufacturers are companies that are specialised on the manufacturing of consumer electronics products for such "fabless" brandname companies that gradually outsourced most of their production capacities during the 1980s and 1990s and instead focused on functions of product development and marketing (cf. Lüthje et al 2013a, 33-68).

- A lack of seniority-based workplace regulations, job classifications and job-security provisions
- A high degree of employment flexibility and low job security

These common features may be seen as one decisive structural reason for the divergence of high productivity growth and sluggish increases of wage incomes which has been characteristic in recent decades. According to one estimate, labour unit costs—a measure for wage costs per unit of production—declined by 40 percent between 1995 and 2004 (HKTDC 2011b). Although a shortage of labour has reversed this trend since the middle of the last decade especially in coastal provinces (cf. section 3.1.2), insufficient codified labour standards and a lack of workers representation continue to inhibit more comprehensive wage increases. The very heterogeneity of China's industrial structure complicates the setting of collective standards due to the outlined divergent forms of accumulation within and across industries.

The result of this, as Lüthje concludes, is an imbalanced regime of accumulation based on underconsumption:

"[A]n accumulation model based on simultaneous growth of capital intensity, productivity and wages—once the virtuous circle of Fordism in industrialized countries—does not have much of a base in China's new capitalism, neither at the macroeconomic nor at industry levels […]. [M]odernization of production and the related increases in capital intensity and productivity appear disconnected from the development of wages and employment conditions" (2014, 22).

According to this view, the task of rebalancing the economy towards a higher share of domestic consumption should not be limited to building social security systems and increasing minimum wages, but must also address the inbuilt asymmetries in China's RoP. The fundamental question in this respect is whether the current period of restructuring of Chinese industries also leads to different patterns of work. This challenge is most virulent in the extensive regimes of accumulation in the coastal provinces which emerged on the basis of extraordinarily high growth rates of exports, low value-added assembly activities and a suppression of wages for a workforce which predominantly consisted of migrant workers who only temporarily resided in the cities and who, until shortly, therefore were barely included into urban consumption patterns.

## 2.4 Summary

In this chapter, the theoretical distinction between extensive and intensive regimes of accumulation was taken as a starting point to discuss the inter-relatedness between China's integration into the world economy and the corresponding growth patterns and RoP in different industries. Due to un-even and combined development on a global scale, the industrial structure of China is markedly heterogeneous and can be interpreted as a combination of extensive and intensive regimes of accumulation. Relations in "low wage classic" RoP most closely match the ideal type of extensive RoA because they rely on labour-intensive production models under the exploitation of low-skilled and meagrely paid migrant workers who remain excluded from urban consumption patterns in the sense that their wage levels remain be-neath what is necessary to support a permanent existence in urban zones of the coastal areas. Conditions in the "flexible mass production" RoP do only partially match the definition of extensive RoA in regulation theory since they rely on the widespread application of modern production technology. Yet, relations in enterprises of this type combine modern technology with "extensive" patterns of employment characterised by an often very large mi-grant workforce that may not suffer from equally harsh conditions that exist in small scale sweatshops, but usually also is affected by low wages, excessive working hours, insecure flexible employment and authoritarian forms of workplace control. In other industrial segments, such as in certain segments of the electronics, chemical or automotive industries, Chinese companies are developing strong technological capabilities supported by intense efforts of the Chinese authorities to raise the technological standards of local in-dustries. The competitive strength of such companies is drawn from knowl-edge-intensive and capital-intensive functions, not merely from a large pool of cheap labour. Labour relations in these segments tend to be more stable and based on the employment of resident workers.

Due to the persisting lack of a regulation of industrial relations, all of these RoP are characterised by a power asymmetry between capital and la-bour which is the root cause for a disarticulation of productivity and wage growth. These structural inequalities, which are inbuilt in RoP in Chinese industries, are one reason for the virulent contradictions of the Chinese eco-nomic model which has become increasingly dependent on investment and exports, whereas the proportion of domestic consumption as driver growth has decreased steadily.

# 3 Industrial upgrading and the rebalancing conundrum: Contested trajectories of reform

The analysis in chapter 2 describes China as a heterogeneous regime of accumulation in which the export industry has played a pivotal role for economic development during the last three decades. This next chapter deals with the present contradictions of the Chinese growth model and attempts by the Chinese government to overcome them. The aim is to outline the context for industrial upgrading initiatives on an industry basis and their strategic importance to government efforts towards rebalancing the economy. The discussion therefore underlines the relevance of the research question about the relationship between industrial and social upgrading and outlines its political and economic context which conditions the outcomes of industrial transformation.

## 3.1 Mounting contradictions of the Chinese growth model

As of early 2014, the Chinese authorities, representatives of international institutions, business analysts, and academic observers almost unequivocally share the conviction that the Chinese economy needs to be thoroughly readjusted to avoid a severe slowdown of growth due to mounting internal contradictions (c.f. for instance: Eurasia Group 2011; FYP 2011; World Bank 2012; Credit Suisse 2012; Breslin 2011; Lardy and Borst 2013; McNally et al 2013). While such intentions already had been voiced before the global economic crisis of 2008/09, this experience led to a reinforcement of reform efforts. After all, the crisis had vividly demonstrated the perils of excessive export dependency. A drop in foreign demand had led to a virtual breakdown of industrial production in the coastal provinces in late 2008 and early 2009. The result was a contraction of Chinese exports by 10.4 percent in 2009. Only a huge increase of capital investment by 19.8 percent, mainly a result of high infrastructure investment under the umbrella of a massive government stimulus programme, outweighed this slump in foreign trade and led to an overall positive growth performance of 9.1 percent in 2009 (Akyüz 2011, 12).

There are certain variations in how commentators perceive the structural contradictions plaguing the Chinese economy and there are significantly different accentuations when it comes to estimating the severity of these problems and the capacity of the Chinese leadership to overcome them (cf. section 3.5.1). Yet, most accounts depart from a description of the same problems which are outlined subsequently.

### 3.1.1 Excessive dependency on exports and investment coupled with a low level of domestic consumption

China's household consumption as a share of GDP decreased pronouncedly from a value of over 50 percent in the late 1980s to a low of 35.8 percent on average in the years 2006–09 (Credit Suisse 2012, 12). During the same period, GDP growth came to depended more and more on investment and, until the global economic crisis, on exports. This disproportion escalated in the period before the economic crisis in 2008/09, as exports grew twice as fast as GDP (25.5 percent on average between 2002 and 2005) while consumption growth rates lagged behind (cf. table 3.1).

*Table 3.1: GDP growth and its components in China (percent)*

|      | GDP  | Consumption | Investment | Exports | Imports |
|------|------|-------------|------------|---------|---------|
| 2002 | 9.1  | 7.4  | 13.2 | 29.4  | 27.4 |
| 2003 | 10.0 | 6.6  | 17.2 | 26.8  | 24.9 |
| 2004 | 10.1 | 7.1  | 13.4 | 28.4  | 22.7 |
| 2005 | 10.4 | 7.3  | 9.0  | 24.3  | 11.4 |
| 2006 | 11.6 | 8.4  | 11.1 | 23.8  | 15.9 |
| 2007 | 14.2 | 10.8 | 14.2 | 20.0  | 14.2 |
| 2008 | 9.6  | 8.5  | 11.0 | 8.6   | 5.1  |
| 2009 | 9.1  | 8.5  | 19.8 | –10.4 | 4.3  |

Source: Akyüz 2011.

The resulting growth pattern is hardly sustainable because investments in productive capacities and infrastructure need to be accompanied by rising household consumption if a steadily growing volume of products is to be absorbed. Is this not the case, overinvestment eventually results in economic instability and slower growth. High growth rates of exports during the last two decades mitigated this basic contradiction because they absorbed a large share of manufactured goods. Yet, the crisis of 2008/09 indicated that such high growth rates can barely be sustained in the face of a sluggish and structurally limited growth of foreign demand. The extraordinary high export growth rates in the 1990s and 2000s reflected China's ascendancy as manufacturing hub at the cost of other regions in Asia and elsewhere (Hart-Landsberg and Burkett 2006). It is highly unlikely that such a high pace of growth—at an annual rate of 18.5 percent during the period between the late 1990s and the onset of the crisis in 2008—can be sustained in the future as average economic growth in China's main export markets is projected to constitute not more than 2–3 percent per year (Guo and N'Diaye 2009; Zhu and Kotz 2012, 24).

The main reasons for the observed macroeconomic economic imbalances can be summarised as (1) the suppression of household incomes, particular of wages and rural incomes (cf. figure 3.1), (2) a high saving rate of private consumers who tend to make provisions for old-age pensions and healthcare in the face of missing or non-functional social security systems, (3) a consistently high level of private investment directed either at export production or at conquering a share of the expanding domestic market[12], and (4) high levels of government spending, especially in the field of infrastructure construction (cf. Guo and N'Diaye 2010; Lardy 2011, 43–65; Pettis 2013, 69–99).

---

12 Although the growth rates of household consumption lagged behind those of GDP growth, consumer markets are expanding much faster than those in advanced industrial economies and absorbing a growing chunk of global markets, a tendency which is projected to continue in the future (cf. McKinsey 2012d). Symbolically, China overtook the US as the largest market for automobiles in 2009 (China Daily 11.01.2010).

*Figure 3.1: Share of wages in China's GDP, 1992–2009*

percent of GDP

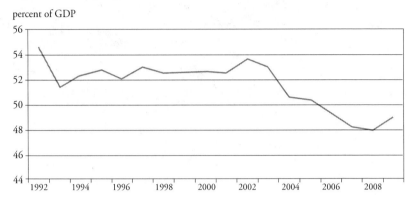

Source: Lardy and Borst 2013.

While observers agree on the need for rebalancing the economy, they perceive the graveness of China's economic difficulties differently. Some commentators doubt an excessive export dependency of the Chinese economy because the contribution of net exports (i.e. the margin of exports over imports) to GDP growth peaked at a level of around 20 percent between 2005 and 2007 and has declined ever since (cf. figure 3.2).

*Figure 3.2: Composition of China's GDP growth (standard accounting method)*

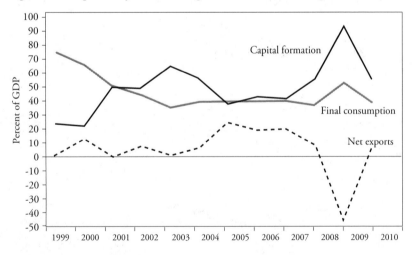

Source: Eurasia Group 2011.

A steady reduction of exports therefore would not compromise growth as much as it is sometimes claimed (cf. He and Zhang 2010, Anderson 2007). Yet, some economists (Zhu and Kotz 2011; Akyüz 2011; Liu et al 2009, 307–309) argue plausibly on the basis of alternative calculations that the factual growth contribution of the export sectors has been much higher, as the figures for net export suggest.[13] Akyüz claims that about one third of GDP growth in the years before the economic crisis was based on exports and that this figure rises to up to 50 percent if indirect effects of export growth, mainly through higher consumption of workers employed in export industries and additional investment in export sectors, are included. Thus, he sees China as particularly vulnerable to external economic shocks which lead to a slump in foreign demand as was shown during the economic crisis of 2008/09 (ibid, 3). Of course, this all the more pertains to the coastal regions where most of China's export production is concentrated (Huang and Chen 2009).

### 3.1.2 Diminishing competitiveness of low value-added industries

Dynamic growth during the last decades has led to a scarcity and related price increases of those factors of production the abundance of which originally constituted much of the attractiveness of China as a site for investment in manufacturing. This is most obvious with regard to labour. The coastal regions have been plagued by shortages of migrant labour since the mid-2000s. A combination of demographic factors, growing employment opportunities in the interior provinces, and a reluctance of the younger generation of migrant workers to accept harsh labour conditions is responsible for this development (Das and N'Diaye 2013b; Zhao and Huang 2010).

---

13 These accounts doubt that the category "net exports" is suitable for measuring the actual impact of the export economy to GDP growth. After all, "net exports" are calculated by subtracting all imports from the total export demand, although a high share of them is used for domestic consumption and investment. In other words, because there is a structurally high level of imports to China which is not related to export processing, foreign trade would have a thoroughly negative impact on growth were it not for the persistent growth of exports. A better measure for assessing the factual impact of exports on GDP growth is what Akyüz calls "value added exports", i.e. the difference between all exports and the import content of these exports. The growth contribution of this variable is much higher than the formal calculation of net exports (cf. Akyüz 2011, 3-6; Zhu and Kotz 2011, 10–12).

*Table 3.2: Minimum wages in selected cities of the PRD, 2006–2013 (RMB)*

|  | 2006 | 2010 | 2011 | 2013 |
|---|---|---|---|---|
| Shenzhen | 810 | 1,100 | 1,500 | 1,600 |
| Guangzhou | 780 | 1,030 | 1,300 | 1,550 |
| Zhuhai, Foshan, Dongguan, Jiangment | 690 | 920 | 1,100 | 1,310 |

Source: China Briefing 23.03.2010 and 10.06.2010; HKTDC 2013a.

As a result, the bargaining power of migrant workers, which had been low in the 1990s and early 2000s because of an oversupply of labour, has increased in recent years resulting in higher wage demands, a rise in workplace conflicts, and individual bargaining by which workers leave dissatisfying jobs in favour of better paid ones. In order to counteract labour shortages, and in line with the general government target of raising domestic consumption, local governments across the country and especially in coastal regions have repeatedly raised minimum wages substantially (cf. table 3.2). Recently, average wage rises in the manufacturing industry have even outpaced average productivity growth, thereby reversing the trend of declining unit labour costs which had been prevalent between the mid-1990s and mid-2000s (cf. figure 3.3, cf. also Li et al 2012).

*Figure 3.3: Annual growth rate of unit labour costs in the manufacturing industry*

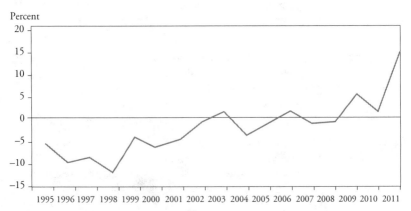

Source: HKTDC 2012b.

In recent years, enterprises also had to cope with the introduction of obligatory social security payments, rising cost for basic inputs like electricity and a strong volatility in commodity markets. The garment industry, for instance, suffered from rising cotton prices in 2010 which squeezed profits in the recovery period after the financial crisis (Interview data (=ID) 27.10.2010). The competitiveness of exporting enterprises is furthermore negatively affected by the continuous appreciation of the RMB the value of which increased by 23 percent against the US Dollar between 2005 and late 2011 (HKTDC 2011b).[14]

Such pressures particularly affect labour-intensive processing industries which operate on low margins and whose competitiveness in the past rested on access to cheap inputs. Hence, such factories were plagued with economic difficulties even before the economic crisis. In Guangdong, there were reports about an unusually high number of more than 7,000 factory closures even in the first nine months before the effects of the global crisis led to a slump in foreign demand. This tendency came to a head in the last quarter of 2008 when an estimated number of 50,000 factories closed their gates, according to the Guangdong government (figures quoted in K. Chan 2010, 665).

### 3.1.3 Escalating social inequality and a rising tide of workplace conflicts

In the absence of effective forms of labour regulation, escalating inequality has resulted in a rising tide of conflict in recent years. Although only a vague indicator, the number of "mass incidents"—up until now the most reliable statistical indicator for social conflicts available[15]—more than doubled from 40,000 in 2000 to 87,000 in 2005, and then allegedly rose to over 127,000

---

14 Yet, it should be remembered that many exporting enterprises, especially in the PRD, engage in processing operations based on a high proportion of imports that become cheaper through RMB appreciation.

15 There are no official strike statistics in China. The statistics about "mass incidents" lists a broad range of unrest including protests against land reforms and the like. Frequent reports about workplace conflicts and a skyrocketing figure of litigation and arbitration cases, however, support the assumption that labour conflicts are one main reason for the rising number of "mass incidents". One account estimates that of 90,000 mass incidents in 2009 about one third consisted of labour conflicts (CLB 2011, 10–11).

in 2008, according to an unofficial source (CLB 2009, 8).[16] Whereas protests of migrant workers in the 1990s and 2000s had mostly been defensive in nature, migrant workers now end to demand higher wages. This trend was most pronounced in a series of strikes centred in Guangdong's automotive sector in 2010 (Butollo and ten Brink 2012, CLB 2012). The rising tide of labour strife in China is reminiscent of Lipietz's description of the inner contradictions of primitive Taylorisation: "The model is redolent of the nineteenth century, and it will not be long before the working classes begin to react in nineteenth-century fashion. As the model exhausts the locally available labour force and has to bring in more and more immigrant labour from the countryside or from neighbouring countries, the social question is further complicated by an urban question and a racial question" (1987, 78), except for the fact that the discrimination of migrant workers is not based on racial differences, but social distinction.

### 3.1.4 Ecological constraints to growth

Massive capital accumulation under an extensive growth model has led to staggering dimensions of ecological destruction. This adds to severe pollution caused by the construction of the heavy industry during the Mao period and already existing long-term damages resulting from a large population in a country with limited natural resources.[17] The effects of high-speed industrialisation and the development of mass consumerism have brought pollution to a thoroughly unsustainable level, which makes an environmental U-turn one of the most serious challenges China is confronted with. Land, air and water are affected by high degrees of pollution which not only threaten the reproduction of natural resources, but also affect public health severely. A report which was published by the World Bank in cooperation with the Chinese government in 2007 estimates that about 750,000 people die prematurely each year, mainly due to air pollution in large cities.[18] While this

---

16 The latest official figure for mass incidents was released in 2005. The 2008 figure was quoted by a Hong Kong-based magazine with reference to an anonymous senior CPP source (quoted in CLB 2009, 8).

17 The latter is seen as the prime reason, for instance, that China had been stripped of forests already a hundred years ago (cf. Naughton 2007, 487).

18 Astonishingly, this and other key results of the report were not released as part of the official presentation out of fear that they would "cause social unrest", as one adviser to the

shocking figure should be sufficient to demonstrate the urgency of an ecological turnaround, this also becomes a necessity out of economic reasons.
The report estimates that the damages caused by air and water pollution in
2003 amounted to a value of up to 5.78 percent of GDP, depending on the
method of calculation (World Bank 2007, xvii). The extent of the imminent
challenges to China's political leadership especially becomes clear with view
to the task of the development of further urbanisation and mass consumerism. The World Bank predicts that "[o]ver the coming two decades, the
increase in the urban population will be the equivalent of more than one
Tokyo or Buenos Aires each year as the share of urban residents in the total
population climbs from about one half to near two-thirds in 2030 (World
Bank 2012, 8). Widespread ecological destruction is inevitable if this drive
towards urbanisation is based on consumption patterns similar to those pioneered in advanced industrial countries. China therefore rapidly needs to
come up with new solutions how to combine its modernisation path with
sustainable production technologies and lifestyles. Mass consumerism, unequivocally seen as the only solution for rebalancing China's growth pattern, thereby could further undermine ecological sustainability. The fact that
China overtook the US as the largest market for automobiles in 2009 is a
worrying signal in this context.

## 3.2 Government initiatives for rebalancing and industrial upgrading

The growing awareness of the structural difficulties of the Chinese growth
model has provoked a series of interconnected reform measures at the central
and the local level that aim at rebalancing the economy in terms of relieving
it from excessive dependency on exports and investment, and strengthening
the role of the domestic market as driver for growth. This is connected to an
overarching strategy of industrial upgrading which is supposed to overcome
China's specialisation on labour-intensive assembly functions. The discussions about the need for rebalancing the economy date back to the middle
of the past decade and already shaped the 11th Five Year Plan which was
implemented in 2006. Yet, the experience of the economic crisis in 2008/09

study told the Financial Times (FT 02.07.2007).

additionally underlined the urgency of economic transformation and reinforced the government's commitment to reform.

The immediate reaction to the crisis by the central government, however, was primarily concerned with maintaining stability. It aimed at a support of financially stricken companies and a huge stimulus programme of RMB 4 trillion which was financed from central, provincial and private sources (Schüller and Schüler-Zhou 2009). These measures were remarkably successful in preventing a further economic downturn and in achieving a growth rate of 9.1 percent in 2009, contrary to the global trend. To this end, the government accepted a temporary deviation from its overall rebalancing targets. It granted tax rebates to export processing companies (which only shortly before had been restricted for the sake of rebalancing). In Guangdong, some prescriptions of the labour law were also temporarily suspended and increases of the minimum wage were postponed to 2010 nationwide. By lowering interest rates, the government ensured cheap monetary supply in order to spurn investment. Above all, the economy was lifted out of ashes by the stimulus package primarily aimed at the construction of infrastructure. The government thereby was effectively substituting the growth contribution of foreign demand through government-led investment which aggravated the problem of excess investment in China's GDP composition (de Haan 2010; Naughton 2009; Schüller and Schüler-Zhou 2009).

Yet, subsequent government programmes have reinforced the efforts to change the Chinese growth model. The rebalancing efforts of the government are galvanised in the 12th Five Year Plan (FYP) which was approved by the National People's Congress in March 2011. Its general orientation is not much different from the 11th FYP of the years 2006 to 2011 that had equally aimed at raising domestic consumption, lowering export dependency, and upgrading the industrial structure. The 12th FYP is mainly an "extension and acceleration of the themes of the 11th FYP", yet with an even more pronounced focus on domestic consumption and ecological transition (Casey and Kolesky 2011, 3–4). These goals are epitomised in the slogans "high quality growth" and "inclusive growth" which both refer to a pattern in which GDP growth goes hand in hand with an increase in household consumption (KPMG 2011, 1). The rebalancing course is characterised by a mix of macro-economic measures, political reforms, and measures for industrial upgrading. It consists of a bundle of reform measures the most important of which are introduced in the following paragraphs.

### 3.2.1 Construction of social security systems

A necessary precondition for raising domestic consumption is a diminution of the share of income that consumers are saving instead of spending. The private savings rate doubled between the early 1990s from about 15 to 30 percent in 2009 (Roach 2011, 4). This reflects the absence of effective social security systems which forces consumers to stock money for healthcare, pensions, or as a provision in case of unemployment. In the Mao period, workers were included into social security systems through their association to factory collectives. In the course of SOE privatisations, this system was dismantled and only in recent years supplemented by rudimentary tax-financed systems (de Haan 2010, 76–84). After hesitant and unsuccessful attempts to introduce such systems during the 1990s, the construction of social security systems gained momentum in the context of the strategy of building a more equitable "harmonious society" during the Hu/Wen administration (2003–13). Since then, the government has primarily tried to increase the coverage of pension, medical care, unemployment, maternity, and work-injury funds. In the framework of the 12th FYP the government also committed itself to construct 36 million new housing units, reacting to social tensions due to the lack of affordable accommodation in metropolitan areas as well as to the prospected intensification of urbanisation (Casey and Kolesky 2011, 4). In 2011, a general regulation of social insurance was issued by the central government. According to this scheme, amounts of contributions of employers to the system may be set by city governments which can also set different rates for FIEs, SOEs and private Chinese companies. The obligatory contributions from employers vary considerably between regions. In Beijing, they constituted 44.3 percent of gross wages in 2010, in Guangzhou 33.5 percent and in Dongguan 25 percent (cf. GTAI 2011; AustCham 11.07.2011).

The speed at which the coverage of social security is being extended is breath taking. In August 2012, for instance, 622 million people, or 55 percent of the adult population, were covered in the national pension scheme, 240 million more than two years before, mainly through the expansion of the pension scheme to include rural inhabitants (The Economist 11.08.2012). Efforts to construct a meaningful health insurance system led to a surge in coverage, as well. In 2011, 95 percent of the population were included in the scheme, up from 43 percent in 2006 (McKinsey 2012b, 3).

The flipside of this success is that, up until now, social security systems are lacking substance because of insufficient funding. The staggering amount of RMB 2.4 trillion which was managed by the national social security fund in 2009 translates into a lifetime pension payment of just USD 470 for an average Chinese worker (Roach 2011, 5). As China will struggle with the consequences of a profound demographic change which will prospectively raise the number of people above 60 years from currently 181 million to 390 million in 2035 (The Economist, 11.08.2012), it is very uncertain whether the financial assets of the system will suffice, and it is also doubtful whether it will contribute to a meaningful rise in living standards, at all. Stephen Roach, an observer who otherwise is outspokenly optimistic about the capacity of the Chinese leadership to rebalance, comments:

"I would have preferred a much stronger signal from the 12th Five-Year Plan on the funding side of the safety net equation. With its outsize surplus of domestic saving, China certainly has the wherewithal to move aggressively in expanding the benefits of its still embryonic social safety net. For reasons that are not altogether clear, China has been unwilling to take such a step in recent years" (Roach 2011, 5).

Similarly, healthcare insurance coverage is still shallow as there are high co-payments by patients for treatments and the most expensive drugs are not being reimbursed. The government is now focusing on improving the quality of provisions to patients. But as with the pension insurance, demographic change is projected to put additional strains on the system which requires large amounts of extra funding (McKinsey 2012b, 6–7).

Despite the colossal advances in the extension of social security systems, expenses still only constituted 5.7 percent of GDP in 2011, or "less than half the level that is typical for countries at similar levels of development" (Lardy and Borst 2013, 7). Additional services will certainly contribute to a higher private spending power, but up until now consumers remain reliant on their own savings in order to provide for medical treatment and their old-age provisions.

### 3.2.2 A reform of income distribution

The renewed publication of the GINI coefficient by the Chinese government in January 2013 for the first time since 2005 showed disappointing results with regard to the attempts to overcome income inequality. The value of 0.474 was slightly down from its peak of 0.491 in 2008, but still is significantly higher than in the middle of the last decade. The publication lead to calls for urgent reform and an acceleration of a projected income distribution reform (Reuters 18.01.2013). While the official calculation of the GINI coefficient already expresses a stark income inequality, alternative calculations suggest an even higher rate of up to 0.61, which would imply that China is one of the most unequal countries in the world (cf. Lardy and Borst 2013, 7).

Yet, China's income distribution reform, a set of changes in the tax system and regulations to redistribute wealth, is still waiting to be implemented. The reform had first been announced in 2004, but has frequently been postponed ever after. Recently, the implementation was once more adjourned after the government could not reach a consensus over the draft proposed by the National Development and Reform Commission (Bloomberg 17.12.2012). Such delays not only reflect the difficult procedure of implementing a reform in a broad range of policy fields that cut across boundaries of ministries and areas of competence, but also power struggles between winners and losers of such measures.

Even so, the 12th FYP sets targets for income increases which would considerably exceed the projected GDP growth rate for the same period if implemented (Casey and Kolesky 2011, 4). In particular, the government targets an annual rise of the minimum wage by at least 13 percent until 2015. Between 2006 and 2010, average minimum wages in China had already increased by 12.5 percent per year (Reuters 08.02.2012). Wage incomes are also expected to rise as an indirect effect of accelerated urbanisation, a key project of the 12 FYP. According to one observer:

"With migration shifting between 15 and 20 million citizens a year from impoverished wages in the rural countryside to urban areas where they are making more than three times as much, this transition imparts an enormous windfall to Chinese wage income generation. Moreover, with rural-urban migration expected to total another 310 million over the next 20 years, this trend should provide an enduring tailwind to sustained growth in Chinese labor income" (Roach 2011, 4).

While such swift assessments suggest a sea-change with regard to the share of domestic consumption, it remains to be seen how far demographic and structural changes actually translate into higher wage incomes that substantially surpass the levels of productivity growth and therefore serve to realign China's growth pattern.[19] Strong increases in minimum wages and a rise in

---

19 Even more so because this automatic correlation between urbanisation and rising household consumption may well be doubted. A study about the income effects of urbanisa-

annual average incomes in urban areas from RMB 11,759 to RMB 19,109 between 2006 and 2010 (HKTDC 2011b) only marginally reversed the overall trends of rising income inequality and of a falling share of wage incomes as a proportion of GDP.[20] Important questions in this respect concern the distribution of urban incomes and the mechanisms by which a general rise of minimum wages can actually translate into substantially higher wage incomes for broad sections of the working population.

### 3.2.3 Regulation of labour relations

Due to a rising tide of uncontrolled labour conflicts since the beginning of the millennium, the reform strategy of the Hu/Wen administration has especially focused on a harmonisation of labour relations. This included the implementation of the Labour Contract Law (LCL) in 2008 which strengthened workers' rights in terms of stable employment under contractually fixed conditions and confirmed the position of the ACFTU in negotiating the terms of employment (Lan and Pickles 2011).[21] These legal changes were linked to attempts to revitalise the ACFTU which up to then had not gained a foothold in private enterprises and was struggling to find a new role after its role as co-management in SOEs became more and more obsolete. After a campaign to increase its membership, the ACFTU registered 229 million members, up from a figure of 87 million members in 1999. Among the newly signed-up members were some 70 million migrant workers who,

---

tion comes to the conclusion that urbanisation in fact has had positive income effects for migrant workers, but that there were also strong motivations for precautionary savings among this group. Among resident inhabitants with rural or urban *hukou* there were "very little positive effects on income growth" (Huang 2010). What is more, the belief that urbanisation results in higher incomes for workers rests on the assumption that there is sufficient employment growth in urban regions. However, due to the difficulties of labour-intensive industries referred to above, this does not seem to be the case automatically.

20 Yet, growth composition started shifting towards domestic consumption in the years 2011 and 2012 (cf. discussion in 3.5.1).

21 The most important provisions of the LCL are: (1) employers need to consult employee representatives (i.e. the ACFTU) when revising work rules, (2) employers need to provide written work contracts, (3) probationary periods are limited according to the total duration of employment, (4) premature termination of employment requires severance payments (ibid).

up until 2003, had not been allowed to join the organisation (Traub-Merz 2011, 15). Following a high-profile campaign, the ACFTU claimed to have founded factory branches in 483 large foreign enterprises of the "Fortune 500" list (ibid, 16). Yet, these impressive figures do not reflect a substantial increase of organisational strength of the workers. Most new union branches were founded in a top-down manner in cooperation with factory managers who very often also hold leadership positions within them (ibid, 18; CLNT 2008).[22] Since factory union branches therefore barely represent the interests of rank and file workers, the mechanisms for tripartite consultations continue to be hollow. Most importantly, most implemented collective contracts do not contain detailed stipulations concerning working conditions. They usually are limited to formal framework agreements and do not set wage levels, working hours, or other vital aspects of industrial relations around which labour conflicts continue to erupt in great number and frequency (Lüthje et al 2013b, 334–337).

It is in the context of such conflicts that reform initiatives can gain in substance. Most evident is the case of a series of strikes that was centred in Guangdong's automotive industry in 2010. After a local trade union branch at the Honda factory where the strikes first broke out was confronted with public criticism because of its management friendly behaviour during the strike, the trade union leadership in the neighbouring city of Guangzhou outspokenly supported the workers in pushing through substantial wage increases. The provincial government subsequently drafted regulations for collective negotiations which would give workers a bigger say in the co-determination of wages in negotiations with the management. Due to strong resistance from local and foreign business groups, the draft for the regulations eventually was watered down to a general proposition that does not contain formal prescriptions about the mechanisms of wage negotiations. Yet, some local branches of the ACFTU in this region are experimenting with forms of democratic worker representation and collective negotiations over wages and have achieved some significant results (Butollo and ten Brink 2012; Lüthje 2011). Despite such experiments, which remain relatively isolated on

---

22 According to a study about the background of factory branch union presidents in 1811 enterprises, "40.6 per cent hold positions of middle-level managers. 17.9 per cent of union presidents serve concurrently as the director or deputy director of CPC committees. Another 13.3 per cent are retired factory heads or managers" [and] only 4.2 per cent [...] were ordinary employees before being elected" (quoted in Traub-Merz 2011, 19).

a national scale, the lack of mechanisms to determine collective wage levels remains a serious shortcoming and makes the government's efforts to raise wage incomes somewhat frail. After all, employers can evade their obligations to raise minimum wages, e.g. by cutting other wage components. Precisely this act by the Honda management had triggered the strikes at the factory in Foshan which then constituted the trigger for the wider strike wave of 2010.

### 3.2.4 Ongoing efforts for regional rebalancing

The tight integration of China's coastal regions into GPN has resulted in massive regional imbalances. Since the turn of the century, the government has shown increased efforts to develop the interior provinces and to link them to the dynamic growth centres in the East. The latest out of a series of programmes is the National Territory Development Plan which was issued by the State Council in 2011. The plan contains a tiered development strategy to raise the performance of regions of different economic strength. In particular, it identifies 18 key development zones, most of which are located in the interior provinces. It also designates the leading industrial zones of the PRD, the YRD and the Bohai region as zones for an optimisation of development (Li&Fung 2011). State authorities support the allocation of industries to interior provinces through preferential policies with regard to land, credit, taxes and subsidies. Furthermore, a large share of government spending in the framework of the post-crisis stimulus plan was dedicated to massive infrastructure investments which link interior regions closer to the coastal areas.

As a result of policy efforts for the allocation of industries to the interior, and of increased cost pressures in the traditional growth centres in coastal areas, a new geographical division of labour is gradually emerging. This is particularly evident in the electronics industry. The high growth figures for sales of electronic companies in these regions, among other things, reflect major investments by multinational companies such as the Taiwanese contract manufacturer Foxconn that has invested in large-scale production facilities in several cities in the interior since 2009 (cf. Pun and Chan 2012, 388–392).

The strategy of regional rebalancing has been quite successful in creating enclaves of modern development in formerly little developed regions. This trend has accelerated in 2012 when growth rates in many interior provinces surpassed 12 percent while they stayed below or slightly above 8 percent in the traditional coastal growth hubs of Guangdong, Zhejiang and Shanghai (The Economist 03.04.2012). Such tendencies, which are reinforced by the weak performance of export industries in coastal areas in recent years, will prospectively alter the regional composition of China's economic development significantly. Yet, skyrocketing growth figures in metropolitan areas in the interior provinces do not necessarily suffice to achieve comprehensive regional rebalancing. After ten years of implementing such policies, the figure for the share of Western regions[23] in China's total GDP only increased from 17.1 percent in 2000 to 18.7 percent in 2010 (H.Yu 2012).

## 3.2.5  Industrial upgrading

The issue of rebalancing the Chinese economic growth model is not identical with, but closely linked to the issue of industrial upgrading. The exportist regimes of production in the Pearl River Delta are historically associated with labour-intensive low-value-added export production. The quest for overcoming this extensive mode of growth is intertwined with the strategic aim of creating capital-intensive and knowledge-intensive industries which potentially could allow for more inclusive growth patterns because they would not rely exclusively on rising quantities of cheap production factors. However, the strategy of upgrading the economy through technological catch-up is not new. In fact, it has shaped Chinese industrial policy for many years:

"[I]ndustrial policy has increasingly been subsumed into technology policy. […] [P]romotion of high-technology industry is arguably the central economic development policy of the Chinese government today. Technology development is the unifying thread that links together many aspects of economic policy in the Hu Jintao-Wen Jiabao administration" (Naughton 2007, 365–366).

With view to successful policies in neighbouring states, especially in Japan, the government applied several strategies to raise innovative capabilities of firms and to shift the industrial structure towards high-tech development. Important milestones of this policy were (1) the harmonisation and coordination of industries to facilitate synergetic effects and foster national flagship

---

23 The Western Development Strategy launched in 1999 includes twelve provincial administrative regions including Inner Mongolia, Guangxi, Chongqing, Sichuan, Guizhou, Yunnan, Tibet, Shaanxi, Gansu, Qinghai, Ningxia, and Xinjiang (cf. Lu and Deng 2011).

enterprises, (2) agreements with foreign investors in which market access was traded for technology transfer, (3) long-term projects for science development partially carried out by large state funded research centres, and (4) the creation of high-tech development zones and particular support programmes for designated high-tech industries. The authorities thereby used the instruments of taxation, subsidisation and legal regulation to promote their development goals. State-controlled banks also played an important role in the implementation of high-tech development programmes because they allowed for preferential access to credit according to the government's development goals (Naughton 2007, 349–374; Schüller 2008, 43–53; Liu et al 2007).

In recent years these efforts have been reinforced and linked to the goal of economic rebalancing. The result is a set of policies that explicitly aims at changing the industrial structure to reach beyond labour-intensive manufacturing activities and to acquire technological leadership in selected industries that are deemed to be of strategic importance. As a response to the economic crisis in 2008/09, the State Council issued plans for a revitalisation of ten industrial sectors in an attempt to eliminate overcapacities and modernise products and processes (cf. Tong and Zhang 2009, 17–18). The 12th FYP furthermore contains a comprehensive programme to support industries of particular strategic importance. The seven fields of development identified by the plan, the so-called strategic emerging industries (SEI), concern (1) energy-saving and environment protection, (2) new-generation information technology, (3) biotechnology, (4) high-end equipment manufacturing, (5) new energy, (6) new materials, and (7) new-energy cars. These industries, or rather: fields of technological development that cut across sector boundaries, are expected to constitute the backbone of the Chinese economy in the future. The 12th FYP sets the target of raising the combined share of the SEIs from currently 3 percent of GDP to 8 percent in 2015 and 15 percent in 2020 (Roach 2011, 5). By supporting them through subsidies, preferred financing, and tax breaks, China hopes to leapfrog development and acquire technological leadership (Casey and Kolesky 2011, 9). One account estimates the sum that prospectively will be spent by national, provincial and local authorities to this end at a dizzying RMB 14 trillion (APCO 2011, 6). The SEI were selected with a particular focus on energy efficiency and ecologically sustainable technologies. The strategy for acquiring technological leadership in SEI is therefore connected to the goals of the 12th FYP of reducing energy consumption per unit of GDP by 16 percent and $CO_2$ emissions per unit of

GDP by 17 percent (KPMG 2011, 3). Apart from the concerted initiatives to support SEI, the 12th FYP also sets targets for increasing the pace of indigenous innovation, in particular by raising the expenditure on research and development to 2.2 percent of GDP and elevating the number of patents to 3.3 per 10,000 inhabitants (KPMG 2011).

Industrial transformation is a crossover target which is implemented by means of various instruments on a central, provincial and local level. In particular, the goal of attracting advanced manufacturing is pursued through preferential treatment of FDI in these fields (while reversing some of the benefits that had been granted to processing industries during the 1990s and 2000s), easy access to credits for high-tech enterprises, changes in taxation and subsidies (Reuters 23.07.2012). While the central government formulates general policy objectives, provides subsidies, and creates national research institutions, industrial upgrading to a large degree depends on the actions of provincial and local-level governments that try to modify the regional industrial structure.

## 3.3 Industrial transformation in the PRD

The Pearl River Delta has been the economic powerhouse of China's recent economic ascent. More than any other region in China it represents the model of an exportist, extensive regime of accumulation, and more than anywhere else the contradictions of this mode of growth have become obvious in this region. The huge industrial agglomeration in an area of only about 40,000 square kilometres—i.e. about the size of Switzerland—contributed 9.2 percent to China's GDP and 26.7 percent to China's export volume in 2011 (HKTDC 2013b). The region gained prominence as a site for labour-intensive production since the early 1980s and subsequently was the destination of several waves of FDI. While investment was initially concentrated on light industries, mainly in the form of cross-border relocations by Hong Kong entrepreneurs, the 1990s saw a strong influx of FDI in a broader range of industries including heavy industry, high-tech electronic equipment, and chemicals. Following a major wave of restructuring in GPNs in the wake of the so-called dotcom crisis of 2000/01, the region subsequently emerged as one of the most important sites for electronics assembly (Lüthje et al 2013a, 118–129) and recently attracted large investments from automotive companies (HKTDC 2013b). In recent years, the provincial government of Guangdong particularly supported the allocation of heavy industries and promoted the relocation of some labour-intensive light industries. The ratio of light industries in relation to heavy industries therefore decreased significantly from 1.39:1 in 1995 to 0.61:1 in 2011 (ibid). Still, the agglomeration of processing enterprises that produce consumer goods for export is extraordinarily high. This is reflected in a very high rate of exports which stood at around 85 percent of GDP in 2008 (Yu and Zhang 2009, 4). The region truly is the workshop of the world for some products. Its share of worldwide production for some articles of the toy industry, for instance, surpasses 60 percent (HKTDC 2013b). Industrial investment is strongly shaped by foreign enterprises. In 2011, 61 percent of Guangdong's export value (the bulk of which is manufactured in the PRD) was produced by foreign enterprises. The PRD accounted for 17 percent of China's FDI stock in the same year (ibid).

After years of extensive growth, the region has experienced shortages of land, labour and energy since about the middle of the last decade (OECD 2010, 18–20, 77–138; HKTDC 2011a).[24] It has also been the epicentre of a rising tide of protest from migrant workers during the same period. Faced with these difficulties, the provincial government, until recently under the leadership of the pronounced reformer Wang Yang, is particularly eager to restructure local industries. The reform of the PRD is also an objective pursued by the national government, which is spelled out in the Plan for the Reform and Development of the Pearl River Delta (2008–2020) by the National Reform and Development Commission (NRDC 2008). In this plan, the PRD is seen as a pilot area for industrial upgrading. The region thereby resumes its role as a reform laboratory which it had already played in the early 1980s when the first Special Economic Zone was set up in the city of Shenzhen.

The provincial development plan especially supports the allocation of heavy and high value-added industries on the one hand, and the development of the service sector on the other hand. This is coupled with a strategy of discouraging further investment of labour-intensive and energy-intensive low-end enterprises which are encouraged to relocate to specially set up industrial parks in less developed zones within Guangdong Province (GPRD-

---

24 The Guangdong's Labour and Social Security Office estimated as early as 2006 that there was a shortage of 2.5 million workers in Guangdong (HKTDC 2007).

BC 2010; 28–43, NRDC 2008). The Guangdong government furthermore is supporting innovative capabilities of local companies and has established various high-tech development zones with the support of the central government. The city of Dongguan, in which export-oriented processing industries abound, has been designated as one of two national pilot cities for industrial upgrading along with the city of Suzhou in Jiangsu Province. Apart from the allocation of high-end manufacturing and the allocation of advanced research facilities, the upgrading policy in Dongguan particularly aims at transformation of the local processing industries which are supposed to acquire R&D and marketing capabilities and help boost sales on the domestic market (HKTDC 2010a; DG Government 2010).

The devastating effects of the economic crisis on companies across the PRD provided the background for an intensification of upgrading efforts framed by a series of polemic interventions by CCP leader Wang Yang. He argued that Guangdong should be grateful for the financial crisis because it had been instrumental to reach a consensus about the need to transform its development model (Businessweek 15.06.2009). In a particularly controversial statement he argued at the height of the crisis that it was "time to open the bird cages for new birds to settle down", implying a sweeping replacement of labour-intensive industries by advanced manufacturing (ibid).[25] Yet, in other statements the party leadership advocates a transformation, rather than a replacement, of traditional industries. This view is expressed by Wang's metaphor that "there are no sunset industries, only sunset technologies" which expresses that there is a chance of transformation towards higher value-added activities in any industrial sector (Nanfang Ribao, 26.08.2010b).

Although the political discourse about industrial upgrading in Guangdong usually is centred on technological issues, it has recently been complemented by a notion of comprehensive social change. Echoing the national orientation, the provincial government argues for a more inclusive mode of growth under the catchphrase "happy Guangdong". The official government

---

25 The birdcage metaphor is a conscious allusion to a historic debate by which Wang Yang put additional weight behind his intervention. The metaphor originally stems from Chen Yun, one of the most influential political leaders in China during the Mao period and the time after. He argued during the period of reforms in the early 1980s, that the free market should be contained by a central plan like a bird in a cage. Neither should the bird be set free, nor choked by the cage. When Wang now speaks about the necessity to exchange the birds, he conveys the message that the change of the course of economic development should be fundamental (Schmalz 2013, 329).

line advocates a priority of human happiness over GDP growth and thus expressed some willingness to slow down growth for the sake of industrial transformation and a mediation of social contradictions (cf. Gore 2012).

## 3.4 Structural constraints for rebalancing

The overview of government efforts on a national and regional level that tackle the combined task of rebalancing and industrial upgrading bears witness to a rapid transformation of China's economic and social situation. Whatever the precise outcomes of this process, it is safe to assume that change is ubiquitous. Government sources and international observers agree that China faces a fateful turning point. Either the prospected transformation succeeds or the country will be plagued by the internal contradictions of the present development model. Though China's accomplishments during the last decades are impressive, its political leaders emphasise that the present path is "unsustainable", and the World Bank discusses whether China may become caught in a "middle income trap", i.e. that its economy will lose steam once a certain standard of wealth is accomplished (World Bank 2012, 3–14).

A discussion of China's reform prospects must go beyond a mere observation of government planning and acknowledge the structural constraints that affect social actors in China, including the political leadership. This is related to the discussion in chapter 2 about the peculiar relationship between global linkages and the internal development of the Chinese development model. As Joachim Hirsch writes, national systems of accumulation and regulation are embedded in the world market and international exchange relations and thus shaped by this peculiar form of world market integration (2005, 101f). China's challenge to transform its economic growth model is therefore subject to (1) the overall competitive situation and ongoing processes of restructuring in global production networks in different industrial sectors which condition the opportunities for industrial upgrading and prefigure norms of technology and production, and (2) the balance of forces within China, which reflect the past models of growth and world market integration, and which condition the scope of macroeconomic reform as well as the direction for innovation and industrial transformation. A strategy for transforming China's economy therefore has to tackle the specific constellation of interests that has grown during the past three and a half decades of world market integration, i.e. it has to face those social forces that are linked to the exportist, extensive growth model and seek to preserve it. Taking this mutual dependency between the global economy and the national development path into account, a strategy of changing the Chinese growth pattern is then confronted with the following dilemmas:

*(1) The pressure to sustain high growth rates*
Since the Chinese economy is excessively dependent on investment and exports, the easiest way of rebalancing would be to cut down on both which would amount to slowing down the economy as a whole. The government made a step towards this direction by deliberately lowering the goal for annual GDP growth to 7.5 percent in the 12th FYP for the sake of rebalancing, which symbolically remained slightly below the value of 8 percent which up to then had been regarded to be the minimum figure to create sufficient employment. However, especially the fast pace of urbanisation induces high pressures to maintain high growth rates since about nine million people enter formal labour markets per year and need to find employment, which could turn out to be difficult in case growth slows down (cf. Schucher 2009, 122f). Consequently, the prospect of renewed economic slowdown in 2012 provoked worried responses. In general, the Chinese central government is performing a delicate balancing act of pursuing far-reaching macroeconomic reforms while at the same time preventing any impediments to growth, which in turn could result in a rising tide of social conflict. The commitment to sustained high growth works as a buffer against a radical structural transformation because growth is still highly dependent on the competitiveness of China's labour-intensive industries. As Barry Naughton wrote in 2007, "The root of China's comparative advantage is still in labor-intensive manufacturing, where the highly elastic supply of cheap semi-skilled labor will continue to work to China's benefit for at least a decade" (2007, 398). While the share of processing enterprises that operate mainly on the basis of this comparative advantage has dropped recently (cf. section 3.5.2), they continue to generate a substantial share of GDP growth. China's leadership, as well as local cadres, whose internal evaluation still largely rests on their ability to generate economic growth, therefore may sacrifice targets of macroeconomic reform in case the economic situation worsens. Under such circumstances the po-

litical balance of forces may also tilt towards more conservative solutions (Schucher 2011).

## (2) The entanglement of local governments with private capital

As outlined in section 3.1, the rise of the Chinese variety of capitalism depended on close linkages between businesses groups and local governments. Due to these symbioses, conflicts between the overall objective of macroeconomic reform and the interests of local governments may arise since the latter are not only closely linked to local capital, but also depend financially on its continued flourishing to a large degree (ibid). Reformers in the central government therefore may encounter limitations to their capacity to govern and direct socio-economic development vis-à-vis local governments and private actors (ten Brink 2013, 268–278).

## (3) Resistance from entrepreneurs

Although there is strong evidence for a lack of sustainability of the low-end exportist growth model, efforts for a reform need to tackle those forces that are historically attached to it. The most vivid example for the ongoing political influence of these groups in recent years was a coordinated action by business associations to stop government regulations for collective wage negotiations in Guangdong in 2010 (Butollo and ten Brink 2012). While entrepreneurs from Hong Kong associated with low-end export industries in this region played a prominent role in staging opposition in this case, a reluctance to improve the conditions for workers is not limited to industries with "low-wage classic" regimes of production. As there are also highly competitive pressures in the fields of advanced manufacturing and even in the so-called strategic emerging industries, employers may seek ways to combine modern manufacturing methods with established patterns of cheap and largely unregulated employment. In Neo-Taylorist regimes of production in the field of IT manufacturing, for instance, high technology is combined with cheap migrant labour. If industrial upgrading remains as narrow as in these cases and does not translate into significant improvements for all employees, the basic contradiction of China's extensive growth model will rather be maintained than overcome (cf. Lüthje 2014).

## (4) Competition in the field of technology development

As outlined above, Chinese industries have benefited from technology transfer in recent years and the allocation of functionally diversified industrial clusters in China creates favourable conditions for ongoing technological learning in the future (Ernst 2008, Herrigel and Zeitlin 2010). Yet at the same time, Chinese companies still face an uphill battle because foreign companies control most of the intellectual property, have better R&D capabilities, and are thus in a strong position to define the norms of technology and production that shape economic development. What is more, the challenges tend to increase as Chinese companies come to compete directly with powerful peers in advanced industrial countries. Chinese companies will be less able to benefit from a mere transfer of existing technologies as they approach the "technological frontier" of new product development (World Bank 2012, 183). Development strategies based on the opportunities of catch-up growth therefore need to be gradually replaced by an emphasis on stronger capacities for indigenous innovation. The status quo in this respect is not sufficient: "Although the research infrastructure and number of researchers has expanded manifold, quality, experience, and the institutions that undergird innovation, remain weak" (ibid, 181–183).

The last two aspects highlight that the issues of economic rebalancing and industrial upgrading are closely connected. Industrial upgrading is a precondition for escaping those contradictions which have become endemic in export-oriented extensive RoAs in recent years. Because of competitive pressures and a limited volume of foreign demand, industrial upgrading needs to be part and parcel of a broader transformation towards a domestically-led pattern of economic development. It is therefore of critical importance for the future of economic development in China whether the patterns of employment and work in modernised industries entail different forms than those which have produced escalating social inequality in the past.

## 3.5 Rebalancing and industrial upgrading: Half full or half empty glass[26]?

The rebalancing efforts of the Chinese economy have received extensive coverage from international observers. After all, they not only concern the

---

26 I owe this formulation to Nicholas Lardy (2011).

sustainability of the Chinese economy, but that of the whole world economy. Until the economic crisis, international economic relations were in particular shaped by a symbiosis between American debt-financed consumption and Chinese foreign trade surpluses, a constellation also baptised "Chimerica" by commentators (Ferguson and Schularick 2009). The USA as a consumer of last resort absorbed exports from China, while Chinese accumulated currency reserves that were, among other things, invested in US government securities, kept interest rates in the US low and credits cheap. This relationship was deemed unsustainable and the global economic crisis in fact violently disrupted it. From the perspective of China, it means that a period of strong and steady export growth has probably come to an end. From the perspective of the world economy, the question arises whether China's considerable contribution to sustaining economic growth will continue and whether China comes to create strong demand for imported goods from abroad based on expanding the spending capacity of its population (Hung 2009b; Silver and Zhang 2009).

In the last years there have been extensive debates about the extent to which recent changes are pointing towards a qualitative transformation of the Chinese growth model. The closing section of this chapter provides an overview of this debate and a rough general discussion of the state of industrial transformation.

### 3.5.1 Successful transformation or ongoing imbalances?

Most international commentators meanwhile give a rather optimistic assessment of China's capacity to rebalance its growth path. The report "China 2030" by the World Bank mentions potential headwinds in China's development but estimates that China will be able to maintain an average growth rate of 6.6 percent between 2012 and 2030, equivalent to an incremental output 15 times the size of Korea's GDP, and eventually emerge as the world's largest economy by 2030. By then it will also have "pulled abreast" with advanced industrial economies with regard to technologies and innovative capabilities (World Bank 2012, 3, 16, 163). In a more short-term perspective, a report by Credit Suisse expects that the share of private consumption as a percentage of GDP will rise from currently about 35 percent to between 39 and 42 percent in 2015, while exports will decrease from currently 26 percent to little above 20 percent in the same year. The economy is expected to achieve this readjustment while maintaining a slightly lower but still high growth rate of 8–9 percent (Credit Suisse 2012). Such optimistic forecasts about the feasibility of rebalancing and simultaneously maintaining growth seem to be vindicated by recent developments. In 2011 and 2012, domestic consumption for the first time in a decade surpassed investment as the main driver of growth.

*Figure 3.4: Components of China's GDP growth 2000–2012*

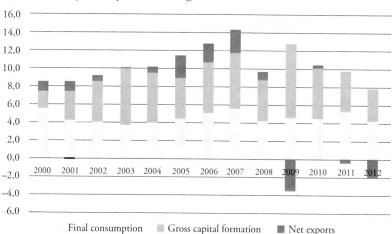

Final consumption  Gross capital formation  Net exports

Source: China Statistical Yearbook 2013.

At the same time, the volume of imports was higher than that of exports in this period, thus leading to a negative growth contribution of net exports according to the formal accounting method (World Bank 2014, 2).[27] The change in the growth composition was interpreted as a critical shift and the beginning of a comprehensive phase of rebalancing which is likely to continue, according to this view (Wong 2013, cf. figure 3.4).

Other accounts are more sceptical about the political and economic scope for reform. In contrast to the cited mid-range growth forecasts, they stress ongoing contradictions and the so far limited success of a thorough turnaround in China's growth pattern. In particular, they are wary of taking

---

27 It should be kept in mind, however, that this focus on the balance of trade entails a distorted view on the real growth contribution of exports which can be calculated by subtraction of processing imports from net exports (cf. footnote 11).

the proclamations of government plans literally. After all, economic rebalancing has dominated the political agenda in Beijing for nearly a decade without showing major progress. The 11th FYP did centrally tackle the problem of rebalancing but largely failed to achieve any progress in this direction (Casey and Koleski 2011, 3; Schucher 2011). As Barry Naughton argues, state intervention after the global economic crisis has even aggravated imbalances because the growth of domestic consumption could not keep track with the high levels of investment triggered by the stimulus programme (Naughton 2009). The fact that domestic consumption in 2011 and 2012 played a larger role in the overall growth composition does not necessarily contradict this view. It mainly reflects a particularly weak performance of foreign demand due to the crisis in Europe. What is more, economic recovery in the latter half of 2012 rested on high growth rates of investment, especially in the field of real estate. It was triggered by another RMB 1 trillion stimulus programme of the government to counter the "longest slowdown in growth since the global financial crisis" in the first half of the year (Reuters 20.01.2013).

Ongoing failure to rebalance can create high risks for economic stability, as some observers argue. According to this view, the deceleration of export growth and the disappointing performance of domestic demand further tilt the Chinese growth model towards investment which creates dangerous tendencies of over-accumulation and speculative bubbles (Hung 2009a; ten Brink 2013; 215–238; Zhu and Kotz 2012).[28] These tendencies are all the more worrying since there exists an excessive level of local government debt and additional, non-state-controlled financial supply by a shadow banking system which quadrupled in size between 2008 and 2012 (Washington Post 02.10.12; FT 26.02.2012). For these reasons, the debate among economists in recent years revolved around the question whether or not there will be a "hard landing" for the Chinese economy, i.e. a sustained economic crisis with more damaging consequences than the averted crash of 2008/09 (cf. FT 19.08.2012; China Daily 28.07.2012). Such an implosion has not

---

28 Stephen Roach takes a decisively different position on the issue by arguing that high investment in real estate rather were necessary to sustain the "greatest urbanisation story the world has ever seen". Empty ghost towns therefore could soon turn out to be "tomorrow's thriving metropolitan areas", rather than being testimony to hazardous real estate speculation (Project Syndicate 29.08.2012). While this argument indeed puts the frequent accounts about "China's ghost towns" (cf. BBC News 13.08.2012) into perspective, it seems doubtful whether the investment spree that has been triggered by cheap credits as a whole will actually serve development purposes in a reasonable way.

taken place so far, but intensifications of GDP growth in recent years have repeatedly created speculative bubbles, especially in the field of real estate investment. The government consciously tries to keep overinvestment in check, while it is again tempted to widen investment when the economy cools down. This tightrope walk became obvious in 2012 and 2013 when growth slowed down because of weak foreign demand. The government first pursued a course of tight monetary policy and consciously restrained from granting another strong fiscal stimulus like in 2009. Yet, as economic perspectives did not brighten up towards the end of the year, a concern with stability replaced long-term strategic considerations as the government issued another huge investment package (though smaller in volume than in 2009). A failure to generate high growth based on consumption alone therefore led to a new turn towards large-scale investment. One consequence is a resurgence of a worrying real estate price bubble (Reuters 09.03.2013) and an escalating amount of loans from the shadow banking system which was recently identified as a "source of systemic financial risk over the next few years" by the chairman of the bank of China (quoted in Businessweek 21.03.2013).

All in all, it appears reasonable to assume that there is some progress in terms of economic rebalancing, but that this so far does not suffice to generate stable growth. This is emphasised in some studies which consider macroeconomic rebalancing as feasible, but identify insufficient wage distribution and other obstacles for a more pronounced change (cf. Eurasia Group 2011; Lardy and Borst 2013). One recent account states that:

"Overall, things are moving in the right direction on most fronts, but at a glacial pace. The slow rate of reform is at odds with the urgent rhetoric that policymakers use when describing the necessity of economic rebalancing" (China Economic Watch 2013).

The decisive question in this respect seems to be whether rebalancing at a "glacial pace" will be sufficient to control the mentioned systemic risks and to generate stable growth. Quantities definitely matter in this respect. If rebalancing proceeds only slowly, China may become riddled with contradictions (overinvestment, internal conflicts, political inertia) that impede a further advancement of macroeconomic reform.

It would be foolish to attempt a definite forecast about future developments which depend on a variety of factors that are hard to foresee. Suffice it to say that due to its characteristic global entanglement, much of China's prospect to rebalance will again depend on global economic developments. A revival of strong demand from the advanced industrial economies would create more scope for tackling internal contradictions because exports would contribute to sustaining economic growth rates at a high level. Ongoing stagnation in these regions, on the contrary, may translate into domestic difficulties and possibly lead the governments at central and local levels to prefer stability over a determined implementation of reforms. It may also lead to enhanced international competition and protectionist measures that undermine technology transfer.

### 3.5.2 Beyond cheap labour? A preliminary assessment of industrial upgrading

As the discussion in section 2.3.2 has shown, there is no doubt about the question whether a transformation of industries is actually taking place. In a way, the whole reform period can be interpreted as a successful case of industrial upgrading, since companies have continuously adapted technologies, raised their productive capabilities and adapted product technologies through imitation as well as through their own efforts to innovate. The rise of Chinese enterprises in sophisticated fields of technology, epitomised in the rise of Chinese high-tech enterprises like Huawei or Lenovo, is only the tip of the iceberg of a much more fundamental dynamic of permanent change. Against this background, a general assessment of recent transformations must first and foremost look at the speed and possible contradictions of this movement, rather than merely account for its existence.

Across various sectors there are favourable conditions for industrial upgrading and some companies or regions have made impressive progress as the following examples illustrate. The clustering of high-end manufacturing in regions such as Beijing's Zhongguancun Science Park or around the City of Shenzhen, for instance, favour an allocation of R&D functions and associated services which in turn fosters the development of local enterprises in this field. In the mobile handset industry, for example, the depth of vertical integration of the Shenzhen region gives this region an increasingly privileged status for high-tech investors which nowhere in the world can find a comparable supply chain density and a similar integration of design and manufacturing (ID 17.11.2011). What is more, the expanding domestic market creates tremendous opportunities for local manufacturers since they can offer products that are well adjusted to the spending power and preferences of Chinese customers. Their ties to these markets render them more competitive in relation to foreign producers targeting the same markets. Competition on the domestic market (and on export markets with a similar cost structure) thereby fosters industrial upgrading by Chinese enterprises (Brandt and Thun 2011; cf. Cattaneo et al 2010). Success stories such as those in the mobile handset industry are not limited to the field of high-tech development. There is also an impressive dynamic of technological upgrading in traditional industries like the garment sector. Chinese companies in this industry have outcompeted peers in other traditional sourcing destinations like Mexico in recent years precisely because they advanced from simple assembly operations towards full-package supply functions that include supply chain management and co-design (Frederick and Gereffi 2011; cf. chapter 7). The allocation of diverse functions to China is also supported by the emergence of industrial clusters, sometimes referred to as "supply chain cities", which consist of a myriad of SMEs that provide various steps of the supply chain in a complementary fashion (cf. Barbieri et al 2012; Zeng 2011; Gereffi 2009).

One indicator for the rapid upgrading dynamics in China is the changing composition of exports. Since the early 1990s, the share of high-tech manufacture has increased rapidly, whereas the share of low-tech manufacture has been continuously decreasing (cf. figure 3.5). As argued above (cf. section 2.3.2), the rise of high-tech exports does not necessarily imply the allocation of higher value-added functions to China, since much of the high-tech export volume consists of products which are assembled in China but possess a particularly high import content. Yet, recent studies show that the global integration of the Chinese industries is becoming deeper, i.e. that producers across industries have continuously increased the share of components sourced locally and widened the functions performed by them (Koopmann et al 2008, Jiang and Milberg 2012).[29]

---

[29] The World Bank further enumerates the following achievements that demonstrate ongoing progress in China's quest for industrial upgrading and innovation: The amount of full-time R&D personnel has tripled in recent years; Chinese authors account for 8.5 percent of global scientific publications with leading contributions in natural science and maths; the number of patents rose from 5,386 in 1995 to 76,379 in 2006 (although most are registered by foreign corporations); the number of science and technology-based firms rose from 5,386 in 1995 to about 150,000 in 2006; companies based in China are master-

*Figure 3.5: Composition of China's exports to the US market 1987–2006*

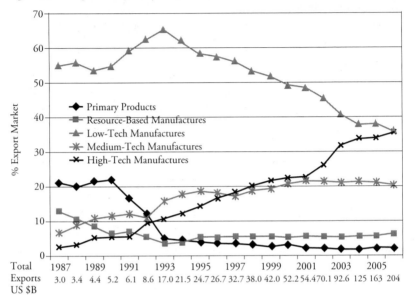

| Total | 1987 | 1989 | 1991 | 1993 | 1995 | 1997 | 1999 | 2001 | 2003 | 2005 |
| Exports | 3.0 3.4 | 4.4 5.2 | 6.1 8.6 | 17.0 21.5 | 24.7 26.7 | 32.7 38.0 | 42.0 52.2 | 54.4 70.1 | 92.6 125 | 163 204 |
| US $B | | | | | | | | | | |

Source: Gereffi 2009.

But although the rise in the proportion of high-tech exports displayed in fig-ure 3.5 is impressive, a mere look at the composition of total exports masks the ongoing relevance of low-tech exports in quantitative terms. After all, the decrease of low-tech manufacture as a *proportion* of exports to the US by some 30 percent between 1993 and 2006 occurred during a phase of rapid expansion of the total export *volume* to the US from USD 17 billion in 1993 to USD 204 billion in 2006. The quantitative development of low-tech manufacture which still constituted about 35 percent in 2006 is therefore contrary to the impression derived from figure 3.5: exports of low-tech arti-cles to the US increased more than six-fold during this period. This under-lines that high-end manufacturing, up until now, has not replaced industries

ing latest technologies in the fields of auto assembly and components, PVCs, biopharma-ceutics, nanotechnology, stem cell therapeutics, high density power batteries, high speed trains, telecommunication equipment and wind turbines, among other things; several lead firms like Huawei, the solar power producer Suntech and Dalian Machine Tool Group are approaching the technological frontier in their industries (World Bank 2012, 177–179).

operating on low technological capabilities and extensive usage of labour and other resources. Rather, they have developed on top of a broad layer of low-tech assembly operations.

A different consideration which does not ask about the technological content of products, but about the type of operations performed by Chinese companies (which can be basic also in high-tech manufacturing when they are limited to simple assembly tasks), shows similar results. As figure 3.6 shows, products from processing operations constituted more than half of all exports from China between 1995 and 2006. Again, this high share was maintained while the volume of exports was rising exponentially during this period which means that the volume of processing exports (left column) has expanded at almost as fast a pace during the last decade. As is the case with low-tech exports, the share of processing exports recently dropped to a lower value, i.e. a proportion of 39 percent in 2013 (HKTDC 2014). But even so, the absolute volume of processing trade is still on the rise, even if it is complemented by products with a higher domestic value added content. Far from becoming marginalised, China's competitive strength therefore continues to depend strongly on processing operations, notwithstanding the adverse pressures of rising costs that by and large make it more difficult to sustain production models that are limited to assembly operations. What is more, a relocation of processing operations towards provinces with lower production costs constitutes one possible outlet for low-end manufacturers to react to adverse pressures in the coastal provinces while still maintaining their facilities in China.

*Figure 3.6: Share and absolute values of processing exports 1981–2006[i]*

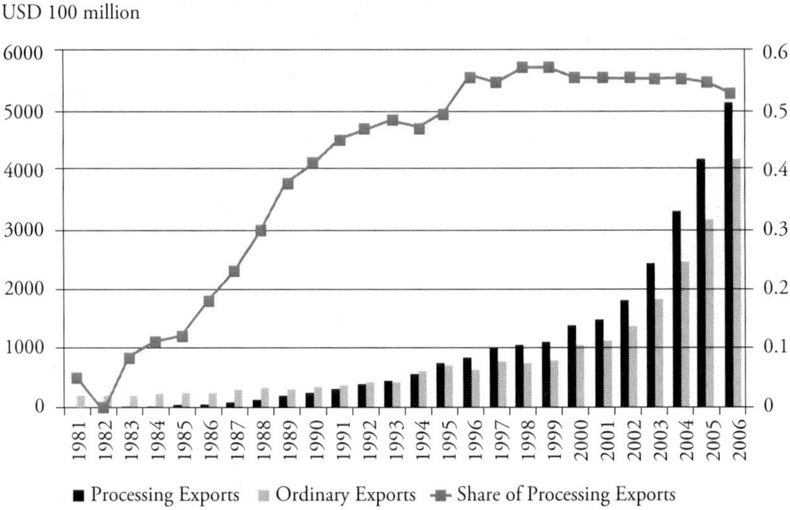

USD 100 million

- Processing Exports   ■ Ordinary Exports   ■- Share of Processing Exports

i   The left-scale refers to the absolute values of exports displayed by the columns, the
    right-hand scale refers to the proportion of processing exports as a share of total ex-
    ports.

Source: M.Yu 2011.

Even in the Pearl River Delta, where the contradictions of the extensive
growth model have provoked a series of factory closures and relocations
in recent years, processing industries seem to be more persistent, as many
political proclamations and media reports imply. This is shown by a comprehensive empirical investigation conducted by researchers at Guangzhou's Sun Yat-sen University with the collaboration of local government
officials (Qiu et al 2012). On the one hand, this survey of industrial upgrading in some 2,000 enterprises of the region showed a heavy emphasis
on measures to improve quality and raise independent R&D capabilities.
On the other hand, a majority of companies that operate according to an
assembly production model reported no obvious change in their growth
performance (55.7 percent) or even slow (22.9) or fast (4.0) growth. These
figures are lower than the corresponding responses by more sophisticated
ODM (45.2/31.7/12.7) and OBM (40.2/35.0/17.3) producers, but suggest
that assembly-type production models can still be sustained even under the
condition of an increasingly disadvantageous cost structure. Surprisingly,

the company responses documented in this investigation also revealed a relatively low inclination towards a relocation of operations to other provinces or other countries (ibid). The persistence of low-end manufacturing is also reflected in recent newspaper reports about industrial upgrading in Dongguan, the designated pilot area for industrial upgrading in which a transformation of processing enterprises towards more sophisticated functions ranks high on the government agenda (Nanfang Ribao 15.01.2012; Chinaview 08.03.2013). These sources reveal considerable progress in industrial transformation, but also show the discontent of local leaders in the face of ongoing difficulties to reach the set targets.[30]

As is the case with the discussion about the feasibility of economic rebalancing, these considerations do not allow for making bold forecasts about the further trajectory of the Chinese industrial structure, especially since conditions differ markedly between different industrial sectors and regions. However, these preliminary considerations underline the markedly heterogeneous development of the Chinese economy which is characterised by leaps in high-tech development and rapid industrial upgrading on the one hand and a persistence of low-tech and low value-added production models on the other hand. This persisting heterogeneity all the more presents a challenge for the combined efforts for macroeconomic rebalancing and industrial upgrading.

---

30 Efforts were in particular hampered by the difficult global economic situation in 2012 which resulted in a relatively low growth performance of 6.1 percent in Dongguan. This was even lower than the target of 7.0 percent GDP growth, which was deliberately set to a lower value by the city government with view to the difficult task of industrial transformation. Despite these obstacles, more than 4,000 processing enterprises have been transformed and 670 research and development institutions inaugurated. The government has also forced 670 businesses to suspend operations because of pollution concerns and rejected administrative approval for another 2,500 enterprises (Chinaview 08.03.2013).

Part II:
A research framework for industrial and
social upgrading in Chinese industries

# 4. Industrial and social upgrading: Definition and theoretical concepts

Up to this point, the theoretical discussion has dealt with an interpretation of the peculiar Chinese growth model in a global context, the resulting internal contradictions, and the government strategies for reform. The analysis revealed that the future stability of the Chinese economy depends on the combined challenge of economic rebalancing towards domestic consumption of wage earners on one side, and industrial upgrading towards higher value-added activities on the other. Starting from this macroeconomic understanding, the following paragraphs narrow down the perspective on industrial change in order to reach a closer definition of industrial upgrading, its different forms, its preconditions, and the relation between industrial and social upgrading. This serves as a basis for the development of a research framework for the empirical analysis.

## 4.1 Industrial upgrading in disintegrated production networks

In the course of the last three decades or so, the discourse on economic development of latecomer economies has been nearly completely submerged into the question of how these economies can integrate into global production networks through an export-led growth strategy. As Jennifer Bair observes, "even critics of the market-radical versions of the prevailing orthodoxy [...] appear to take as self-evident the proposition that the goal for developing countries is increased competitiveness in world markets" (2005, 153). In the associated developing concepts, the idea of "industrial upgrading" takes centre stage, which is broadly defined as "the process by which economic actors—nations, firms, and workers—move from low-value to relatively high-value activities in global production networks" (Gereffi 2005, 171). The strategy of industrial upgrading reacts on and takes advantage of fundamental transformations in the global economy since the 1970s, which have been described as a "disintegration" of Fordist, vertically integrated manufacturing (Herrigel and Zeitlin 2010, 1093–1100; Feenstra 1998). Tendencies for disintegration, by no means all-encompassing and without contradictions, were a reaction to the volatile, unpredictable, and rapidly changing character of the competitive environment to which smaller, more specialised producers in many sectors could adapt better. The financialisation of corporate governance, i.e. the determination of enterprise decisions by short-term profit expectations of financial investors, contributed to this trend. Financial investors tended to focus on highly profitable segments of production and thereby induced pressures on integrated manufacturers to slice up their portfolios and strip them from less profitable activities which were then outsourced (cf. for the IT sector: Lüthje et al 2013, 33–45). The disintegration and globalisation of production were intertwined processes:

"Soon after disintegrated production emerged in the advanced industrial economies, it began to globalize. The process began in the 1970s with lighter, simpler, labor-intensive products like garments, footwear, and some electronics, but by the late 1990s had engulfed a wider range of industries, including heavier, more technologically complex, capital-intensive sectors, such as motor vehicles; aerospace; industrial, construction, and agricultural machinery; electrical equipment; steel; and pharmaceuticals [...]. Globalization both intensified and modified the process of disintegration in production" (Herrigel and Zeitlin 2010, 1106).

In the course of these developments, a "shallow" integration of the world economy, such as the one prior to the First World War, when a high level of international trade remained limited to the exchange of final goods produced on a national level, was replaced by a "deep" integration that involved the production of goods on an international scale reflected in an intensification of trade in intermediate goods (Gereffi 2005, 163). The pressures to reduce costs by tapping cheaper pools of labour were a major driving force for the relocation of manufacturing. The result was a form of "systemic rationalisation" by which regional differences in productivity, flexibility and cost were utilised to raise returns, and which thereby also created new lines of segmentation between regions and workers along the production chain (Sauer and Döhl 1994, 202). From the beginning, however, access to large consumer markets, especially in the case of countries with large populations such as China, constituted a parallel motive for setting up production abroad. Both motives subsequently shaped the structures of GPN driven by flagship enterprises in the advanced industrial countries (Herrigel and

Zeitlin 2010, 1107–1109). Contrary to the expectations of early theories of a new international division of labour as outlined in section 2.2, outsourcing of economic activities from developed economies did not remain limited to labour-intensive functions. The relocation of basic assembly functions merely constituted an early stage in a more comprehensive fragmentation of the production process which meanwhile also includes high-end manufacturing and R&D functions. (Gereffi 2005, 163).

The dispersion of production networks around the globe, or at least to some regions that offered beneficial conditions to engage successfully in production of export goods, inspired new lines of research that took transnational inter-firm linkages, not national economies, as their point of departure for the analysis of economic relations. Various conceptions of "commodity chains" or "value chains" tried to assess how production was sliced up into different functions and how they were distributed across locations (cf. Hopkins and Wallerstein 1977; Kogut 1984; Porter 1985). The Global Value Chain (GVC) concept, by now the most proliferated approach for the analysis of global production chains[31], explicitly integrates issues of development policy to GPN analysis. It evolved from early attempts of authors associated with World Systems Theory to trace the different inputs of a final product from the raw material extraction to its sale to end users. The aim behind this was to uncover the structural conditions for the reproduction of inequality and global hierarchies (Bair 2005, 154–158). In the aftermath of the experience of the EANICs, and facilitated by a general ideological shift towards market-based export-oriented strategies of development, the debate about value chains took a new turn, now emphasising opportunities rather than obstacles to economic progress. This switch of perspectives was criticised for losing sight of the systemic reasons for the reproduction of persistent inequality in the world economy. Some authors also argued that

---

31 The diversity of research approaches is reflected in the deviation in terms used to characterise the phenomenon under investigation. Apart from "global value chains", there also exist the terms "supply chains", "global commodity chains", "international" or "global production networks" and (in French) "filières" for the same phenomenon, each with a specific emphasis reflecting the theoretical perspective on it (cf. Gereffi 2005, 168; Bair 2009). Despite efforts to put these approaches in dialogue and harmonise them (cf. Bair 2005, 153-159; Bair 2009; Sturgeon 2009), there still are significant differences in theoretical perspectives. Subsequently, the term "GVC" is used when referring to the particular *theoretical framework* developed by Gereffi and others whereas the term "GPN" (because it is less associated with one particular research tradition) is used when the author refers to the *subject matter* of transnational supply chains.

there was a tendency among GVC researchers to equate industrial upgrading on firm-level with economic development of whole regions instead of asking more precisely about the winners and losers in such processes (Bair 2005, 171; Selwyn 2011, cf. section 5.6 below). At the same time, it is widely acknowledged that the analytical focus on inter-firm relations inherent in various forms of research on GPNs has stimulated productive questions about the organisation, coordination and power relations in such networks and thereby has contributed to their better understanding. In particular, there has been a productive relationship between theoretical concepts and empirical case studies which helped to modify and further elaborate the basic categories of research on GPNs.

## 4.2 Governance, global hierarchies, and entry barriers

According to the GVC and related concepts, lead firms which for historical reasons are located in advanced industrial countries assume a coordinating and controlling function in global production networks. Such firms source products from globally dispersed suppliers, but mostly do not own them directly. Hence, questions of control over the production chain assume vital importance for lead firms. The forms of supplier relations strongly depend on the solutions developed by lead firms to maximise profits and ensure control over the dispersed production process. GVC theory frames these as issues of "governance" (cf. Gereffi et al 2005; Humphrey and Schmitz 2001).

Drawing on analyses of value chains in the production of typical mass consumer goods such as garments and toys in which outsourcing to developing countries was particularly widespread, Gary Gereffi (1994) analysed the role of "big buyers" in advanced industrial countries that assume a dominating position in supply chains. He called such production networks "buyer driven commodity chains" (BDCC) and contrasted them to "producer driven commodity chains" (PDCC) in which enterprises exerted control on the basis of their vertically integrated manufacturing facilities. Gereffi showed how firms in BDCC retreated from manufacturing or gave it up altogether and rather focused on functions of design and marketing which offered higher returns than "commodified" manufacturing, i.e. manufacturing of standardised, technologically mature goods. This drew on the Schumpeterian view that "intangible assets" of R&D, supply chain management, and marketing put companies in a position to siphon off most profits in GVCs (cf. Kaplinsky 2000, 122–129). The dominant position of global buyers therefore rested on their ability to control, not to directly own, production. At the bottom end of the value chain, firm roles remained limited to functions of commodified manufacturing in which entry barriers for new competitors, and thus profit margins, were low—this in turn put these companies under high cost pressures to which they reacted by keeping the levels of exploitation of their workforces high (Gereffi et al 2001, 8).

While this hierarchical relationship assured the dominance of lead firms in advanced economies, it also provided opportunities to upgrade for companies in developing countries through technological learning which occurs, among other, because companies have to meet elevated standards for world market production, most of which surpass quality requirements on domestic markets. Lead firms thereby have acted as "primary sources of material inputs, technology transfer, and knowledge" in successful cases of upgrading (Humphrey and Schmitz 2001, 7–8). What is more, subsequent analyses showed that a retreat of lead firms from manufacturing in some sectors could also create space for a "vertical integration from below" through which "full-package suppliers" or "contract manufacturers" acquire more comprehensive functions including some forms of co-design and own responsibility for supply chain management and logistics (Lüthje et al 2013, 33–68; Gereffi and Frederick 2010, 176–182). GVC theory therefore holds that the inclusion into GPNs may act as a source of technology transfer and industrial upgrading, notwithstanding their persistent inequalities.

The theoretical identification of BDCC raised important questions about the direction that sourcing strategies of lead firms would take and about their capacities to control value chains to their advantage. However, the BDCC/PDCC distinction proved to be too simplistic to adequately depict the great variety of supply chain relations across industries, since some industries and developments did not fit this picture altogether (cf. Bair 2009, 19–28; Sturgeon 2009, 114–117). The most evident example for this is the IT industry, in which production on the one hand is highly fragmented into producers which supply specific "modules" like hard disk drives, chipsets, or displays, but in which, on the other hand, manufacturers of core components, not only "big buyers", exert significant control over supply chains by defining system architectures and standards. Hence, this production model was baptised

"Wintel" model in the literature with reference to the companies Microsoft ("Windows") and Intel who control the standards of technology development and production in most of the supply chain of personal computers (cf. Lüthje et al 2013, 33–68). The BDCC/PDCC approach also tends to neglect internal variations between production models within certain sectors. For example, there were also countervailing tendencies to the overall tendency of manufacturing outsourcing in the garment industry, which contradicted the assumption of a retreat of buyers from manufacturing. Most notably, the economic success of the Spanish garment producer Inditex (the owner of the labels Zara and Bershka), who initially exclusively relied on their own production capacities, contradicted the expectation of a retreat of lead firms from manufacturing. Similarly, the Korean electronics companies Samsung and LG stuck to a production model which relied on in-house production contrary to the trends of outsourcing that were pursued by most American competitors.

Recent analyses therefore rather stress the heterogeneity of supply chain relations on a continuum between direct hierarchic control (in vertically integrated companies) and indirect "arm's length" relations mediated through the market (cf. Gereffi et al 2005; Humphrey and Schmitz 2002). Suppliers do not necessarily remain in a "captive", subordinate position in the supply chain. They may assume positions of strategic importance to lead firms, especially in cases of so-called "relational" or "turn-key" suppliers that provide important technologies and subsystems and therefore can assume a more powerful and co-determining role in supply chains (cf. figure 4.1).[32]

As a general hypothesis about the forms of supplier relationships, Gereffi et al assume that there is a tendency of lead firms to customise and standardise requirements for products and components in order to reduce transaction costs. These are thought to be lower in market or modular supplier

---

32 In GVC theory, a tight relationship between lead firms and suppliers is seen to reflect a high level of power asymmetry, whereas arm's length market-based relations are understood to be more equal (cf. figure 4.1). There is reason to contest this view, however. Relational suppliers, for instance, may increase their power position in GPN because they deliver solutions adapted to the needs of buyers and developed within a dialogical relationship. Recent successes in upgrading in China's mechanical engineering and automotive industries have been analysed to be the result of "mutual learning" dynamics based on close interactions between lead firms and suppliers (Herrigel et al 2013). Market relations may guarantee the independence of suppliers. Yet, this tells little about their power position which could be very low in case they supply standardised components without any further customer-controlled specifications.

relationships (2005, 97). However, as Gary Herrigel and Jonathan Zeitlin have shown, such efforts for modularisation are continuously undermined, among other, by technological changes and competing production models which may turn out to be more efficient (2010, 1109–1116). They argue that GVC literature exaggerates the proliferation of modular supply chain models (and therefore inherent hierarchies in spatial configurations). Especially in the automobile and construction equipment industries and in the field of mechanical engineering, production models rather rely on "integral product architectures" in which "technical sub-systems interpenetrate and cannot be easily standardized" (ibid, 1115). As a result, production models that are based on interactions and cooperative development between suppliers on a relatively equal status turn out to be most successful.

*Figure 4.1: Five types of governance in global value chains*

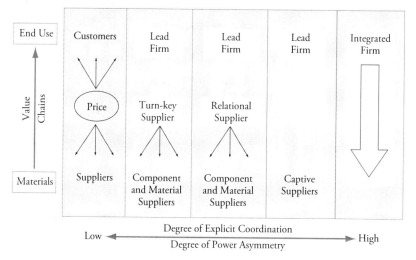

Source: Gereffi et al 2005.

Such disagreements also reflect sector-specific differences in supply chain relationships. The cited interpretations of the varieties in production models and supplier relations therefore underline that the perspectives for industrial upgrading decisively depend on the relationships between suppliers and lead firms which need to be investigated on a sector-specific basis, acknowledging the distinctiveness of the respective products and the competition between different production models.

In all such relationships, supply chain management through the definition and control of standards for products and processes becomes the vital task for lead firms. They rely on their successful implementation in order to coordinate supply chains, ensure control, and arrange production models in a way that provides them with high shares of profits. The distribution of functions and profits across the supply chain decisively depends on the content of such standards. According to Humphrey and Schmitz (2001), parameters for product definition and production processes, as well as for the timing and quantity of production, are set by lead firms (or in some cases by external agents such as government institutions) to ensure product quality and specifications. Product standards may be defined more or less narrowly depending on the supply chain relation and the capabilities of the respective suppliers.

As discussed in chapter 2, the same issue is addressed in a similar way in regulation theory on the basis of a more comprehensive framework that recognises the embeddedness of economic agents in a wider social environment. This perspective emphasises the competitive processes between economic agents and social classes in the course of which specific norms of technology, production and productivity are established. Norms of production and productivity in particular are set on a sector-specific basis (and in fact also constitute sector boundaries). Yet, within sectors, there is endemic competition among actors that experiment with distinctive production models which also entail different ways of combining technologies and forms of labour control. This competition is enhanced by the fast pace of technological development, especially in the various branches of the IT industry, as well as by the regulatory fragmentation on the world market which can lead to the evolution of regionally specific production models (Esser et al 1997).[33] This understanding challenges the claim by Gereffi et al that inter-firm relationships based on market interactions are equivalent to a lower degree of power asymmetry. Norms of production are informal or institutionalised reflections of power relations in which lead firms tend to maintain the upper hand. They therefore transcend the concrete forms of interaction between buyers and suppliers because they tend to define underlying conventions regarding innovation, product design, and production processes.

---

33 One example for the latter is the competition between OEM and ODM contract manufacturing models in the IT industry (cf. Lüthje et al 2013a, 45–51).

## 4.3 Innovation offshoring and the quest for emerging market access: A destabilisation of spatial hierarchy?

The theoretical interpretations of governance, that is to say, power relations, within global production networks have certain implications with regard to the interpretation of spatial hierarchies between advanced and developing economies. As outlined in section 2.2, the first waves of outsourcing by TNCs demanded limited capabilities from suppliers which were either directly owned by lead firms or remained in a "captive" relationship in which all specifications and functions of supply chain management remained under the control of lead firms. Entry barriers to such kinds of arrangements were low, given state authorities provided access and the necessary infrastructure to set up production (Kaplinsky 2000, 122–123).[34] Suppliers neither needed much technological know-how, nor a skilled workforce; hence the proliferation of so-called "cut, make and trim" (CMT) arrangements in the garment industry and similar basic assembly production models in other light industries in various developing countries. As reflected in theories about a new international division of labour, lead firms in advanced economies maintained tight control over all sophisticated functions and siphoned off the bulk of profits. Their power to determine the conditions of supply contracts vis-à-vis suppliers led to the well-documented cases of extreme exploitation in Third World "sweatshops" as depicted in Lipietz' description of "bloody Taylorisation".

As analysed in the chapters 2 and 3, such arrangements are not a thing of the past and remain particularly widespread in light industries in China's Pearl River Delta. In the course of the historical evolution and diversification of supply chain relations outlined in the previous paragraphs, however, suppliers in some emerging economies were able to develop more comprehensive skills. Most notably, this accounts for IT companies in Taiwan and Korea in which developmental states took advantage of technological ruptures in order to boost their domestic industries. Entry barriers to the core

---

34 While this is true for the great majority of outsourcing arrangements in labour-intensive industries during this period, FDI that targeted the domestic market had different implications right from the start. One striking example is the engagement of foreign automotive companies in joint ventures with Chinese SOEs like the one of Volkswagen in 1984. In joint venture factories the workforce consisted of local workers with urban *hukou* who earned relatively high wages in contrast to migrant workers in export processing factories (cf. section 2.3.3).

high value-added functions of the supply chain exerted by countries in the US, Europe and Japan remained high, but EANICs companies nevertheless managed to gain a foothold in these industry segments by either developing technologically sophisticated core suppliers and mass manufacturers (Taiwan) or own brand name companies that challenged the hegemony of Western lead firms (Korea) (cf. Pohlmann 2002; Amsden 2001). As mentioned before, these upgrading successes in some cases were also supported by lead firms which shifted their sourcing strategies to more advanced "full-package suppliers". This was often complemented by renewed waves of outsourcing of more basic functions to second-tier and third-tier suppliers which in many cases involved a further geographic relocation to regions that offered cheaper conditions for basic assembly tasks (cf. Gereffi 2005, 171–173). This vertical differentiation of production networks in Asia is part of the explanation for the so-called "flying geese" model according to which development in Asia is headed by the strongest regional economy Japan which elevates the technological and economic levels of a cascade of successive economies (cf. Akamatsu 1962).

The geographical repercussions effected by sourcing strategies of lead firms in a hunt for the most cost-effective production models are intertwined with other impacts that stem from the second investment rationale of gaining access to the increasingly important consumer markets in large emerging economies (Herrigel and Zeitlin 2010, 1116–1127).[35] In their analysis of the automotive sector and other industries that require advanced engineering capacities, Herrigel and Zeitlin highlight how lead firms that aim to acquire market shares in emerging economies may not uphold a stringent division of labour between "intangible" functions located in high-wage regions and basic assembly tasks in low-wage regions. The need to adapt to specific market properties rather leads them to allocate R&D functions to the vicinity of their assembly operations in emerging markets and to act upon their suppliers to follow suit. The result is the creation of modern manufacturing complexes in emerging economies that do not, or only marginally, lag behind traditional core operations in their places of origin. There are strong spillover

---

35 The GVC literature from its onset devoted its attention to export relationships of developing countries and therefore tended to neglect the importance of the domestic market in target countries for FDI in its framework. After the financial crisis, however, the issue of a shift of end-markets to the South and its effects on GPNs has gained renewed attention (cf. Cattaneo et al 2010).

effects to regional economies because of needs for an integration of product development and manufacturing as well as constantly changing supplier relationships in industrial districts. Herrigel and Zeitlin interpret this as a "destabilization of spatial hierarchy" which in their view is "radically redefining the division of labor between high and low-wage regions" (ibid, 1118).

These observations are related to a more general tendency of innovation offshoring (Ernst 2011a; Naughton 2007). This trend on the one hand results from the fact that a modularisation of tasks has also become common in the field of R&D. Countries like China are an attractive location for innovation offshoring because of its vast, relatively well trained and cheap labour pool in the field of engineering.[36] In this sense, "the same trends that led firms to slice up and relocate the manufacturing value chain are now increasingly coming to bear on the services embedded in the high-technology value chain, including research and development" (Naughton 2007, 370). On the other hand, innovation offshoring follows the need for geographical proximity between suppliers. In many cases this is a reaction to the limits of modularity of value chains. In the field of computer chip production, for instance, a "decoupling of design and fabrication became impractical [...]. This required a re-coupling of design and fabrication, giving rise to much closer interaction between chip designers, design service providers, mask makers, foundries, EDA tool providers and IP providers" (Ernst 2007, 447).[37]

All of these tendencies do not amount to a sudden rupture in the established hierarchies in GPNs. But they undermine their rigidity and create opportunities (1) for the allocation of knowledge intensive functions performed by foreign invested companies to emerging economies and (2) for the rise of domestic enterprises that gain from technology transfer. The observation that global hierarchies are not static, but in constant transformation, is reminiscent of Lipietz' proposition that the international division

---

36 The Chinese government is investing massively in the expansion of higher education. Between 1997 and 2008 the number of colleges doubled and the number of students quintupled. Between the early 1990s and 2006, the number of doctorate awards rose tenfold to a similar number than in the US (quoted in Ernst 2011, 5). Additionally, there is a significant, government-supported "reverse brain drain" of highly educated Chinese citizens who graduated at foreign universities and now receive attractive job offers in China (Businessweek, 19.11.2009).

37 Electronic Design Automation (EDA) tools are programmes used to support chip design processes. Internet service providers (IP or ISP) are companies that serve as intermediate knots to connect end users with the internet.

of labour is not a "deliberately created order: It is a random configuration resulting from the myriad strategies adopted by different companies and states" (1987, 99; cf. ten Brink 2008, 83–85). Despite lasting technological backwardness, China is in a favourable position to take advantage of the opportunities that arise from such spatial reconfigurations. Its potential to attract or develop higher-skilled functions in GPNs particularly stems from (1) clustering effects through a concentration of diverse production steps in certain regions that is virtually unmatched by global competitors; (2) its related attractiveness as a location for innovation offshoring; and (3) the dynamic growth of consumer markets in China (which until recently has been lagging behind productivity growth, but nevertheless expanded rapidly in quantitative terms).

Whereas these factors contribute to a destabilisation of spatial hierarchy, it is also important to be aware of the limitations and contradictions of this geographic reconfiguration. First, tendencies for an outsourcing of more sophisticated functions to developing countries is not only creating opportunities to upgrade, but also cutting off those regions which cannot keep track with higher requirements on the side of lead firms. For instance, it is questionable whether the garment industry can maintain its role as "pillars of export-oriented industrialisation" for developing countries that it had assumed during the last thirty years in which the progression of suppliers in some countries towards higher value-added functions at the same time was accompanied by the rise of a new generation of low-wage regions (cf. Frederick and Gereffi 2011, 68; Gereffi 2005, 171–173). While this tendency still can be observed, for instance, in the rising importance of Cambodia and Bangladesh as sourcing destinations, lead firms reacted to the crisis of 2008/09 by a consolidation of supply chains which resulted in pronounced "downgrading" of some regions. The ascent of strong full-package suppliers furthermore raises entry barriers for suppliers in other regions that strive to engage in more comprehensive supply functions (cf. chapter 7). While some regions therefore increasingly are being cut off or marginalised in global supply chain arrangements, industrial upgrading becomes "precarious" in others. This is particularly evident in the IT sector, where the reconfiguration of sourcing arrangements results in frequent geographic shifts that raises competitive pressures and undermines stable regional development (cf. Lüthje et al 2013a, 224–225 for the case of contract manufacturing in the IT sector). Second, an allocation of R&D to emerging economies and knowledge spillover is not equivalent to a flattening of global hierarchies.

Notwithstanding, for instance, the rise of flagship companies like Huawei and Lenovo in China, most domestic companies still lack the innovative capabilities of their peers in advanced economies and so do the private-public innovation systems in which they are embedded (Schüller 2008; World Bank 2012, 179–183). For the time being, technological development remains mainly a matter of catching up for Chinese firms even though the conditions for doing so have improved markedly. Yet, the game defining standards regarding norms of technology and production are still mainly set by stronger peers in the developed nations.

## 4.4 State intervention, innovative capabilities, and the domestic market

The GVC framework deliberately focuses on inter-firm relations whereas the regulatory institutions are taken as an "exogenous variable" (Gereffi 2005, 170).[38] While this perspective has contributed to the understanding of globalisation "in situ" (Bair 2005, 159) by highlighting the importance of transnational enterprise relations and overcoming the methodical nationalism inherent in many institutionalist theories, it is limited in understanding the acquisition of innovative capabilities in emerging economies. In fact, the ability of companies in these countries to take advantage of technology transfer decisively depends on the regulatory context under which they operate, including industrial and tax policies, market regulations, the education system and infrastructure spending (Ernst 2007). Precisely the most shining examples of industrial upgrading in the case of Taiwan and Korea furthermore benefited from a peculiar world political constellation and the interventions of a developmental state (cf. Amsden 2001; Pohlmann 2002). Hence the calls from some researchers to stronger integrate the institutional

---

38 Timothy Sturgeon stresses that institutions do play a role for GVC development and therefore should be acknowledged in order to take the entire complexity of supply chain relations into account. However, he interprets GVC theory as a "bottom-up, research driven method that accounts for the governance characteristics that tend to arise in global value chains *absent other factor and influences*" (2009, 27. Emphasis by author). In other words, GVCs would develop according to certain mechanisms unless public institutions would not interfere. Institutions are not seen as constitutive for GPNs, but as a factor external to them.

setting into GPN analysis (Bair 2005; Hess and Yeung 2006, 1199–1200). In the case of China, such a "political" view on firm-level upgrading is of particular importance given the ambitious programmes for technological catch-up by the central government and the important role of "developmental states" on the local level. In order to situate research on firm-level upgrading in a broader context, Dieter Ernst furthermore argues for a broader understanding of "innovative capabilities" that also acknowledges the mutual relationships between firms:

> "[F]or firm-level upgrading to succeed, upgrading must take place simultaneously at the level of 'industry linkages'. To broaden the pool of firms that are fit for sustained firm-level upgrading, strong support industries are required, so are dense linkages with universities and research institutes. The challenge is to enable firm-level and industry-level upgrading to interact in a mutually reinforcing way, so that both types of upgrading will give rise to a 'virtuous circle'" (Ernst 2007, 443).

This view echoes the results of research on industrial clusters that highlighted the merits of mutual firm linkages for competitiveness. In fact, as Herrigel and Zeitlin (2010, 1,100–1,106) argue, the "industrial district/local production system" model is a second form of disintegration of production which runs parallel and interacts with the logic of geographical dispersion of vertically disintegrated inter-firm networks. Consequently, the analysis of firm-level upgrading should acknowledge the role of global and national regulations and policy frameworks, but also the importance of local political economies and industry clusters for knowledge diffusion and complementary vertical specialisation. As results from a broad line of research reveal, the emergence of industry clusters was of critical importance for the advance of Chinese industries and continues to be a vital structure for upgrading policies and technological learning (Zeng 2010; Barbieri et al 2012).

The spatial environment constitutes an important condition for firm-level upgrading in yet another way. Expanding domestic markets in emerging economies can present a beneficial context for the development of local firms. Due to their privileged access, their better knowledge of consumer behaviour, and a strong demand for goods that may not correspond to most advanced product standards, but are available at a cheaper price, domestic companies can harvest consumer markets in their places of origin and thereby develop own branding and marketing strategies (Brandt and Thun 2010). In these "middle markets" between top-notch and low-end product quality standards, which are often growing at an extraordinarily fast pace, domestic producers can successfully offer products which are well adapted to domestic tastes and needs at lower prices. Competition with foreign companies on the home market, in turn, drives innovation and industrial upgrading, especially in terms of "good enough" product designs and inventions in "manufacturability", i.e. developing efficient ways of advancing from prototyping to the manufacturing of high volumes (ibid; Nahm and Steinfeld 2013). Success on the home market can also support the growth of exports to other emerging economies with similar demand structures, which constitute a rising share of global demand (Cattaneo et al 2010).

A good example for the success of "good enough" products on the domestic market is the mobile phone industry. There was skyrocketing growth of previously unknown Chinese mobile phone producers like ZTE, Coolpad and Oppo, which are able to offer smartphones at prices substantially cheaper than foreign competitors. In some cases, these are fabless enterprises that source functionally elaborate chipsets, so-called turnkey solutions, from chip design companies, which partially relieves them of the burden of sustaining independent developing capabilities because much of the functional design of end products is already incorporated in the chips (Pawlicki 2010; Brandt and Thun 2011). Another example for industrial upgrading through a concentration on the domestic market is the meteoric rise of Chinese fashion brands discussed in chapter 7.

Like on the global scale, markets in emerging economies are no purely economic phenomenon, but politically structured. Even under the condition of the WTO principle of "non-discrimination" with regard to market access, governments can set certain rules through foreign investment and trade regimes that protect and support local producers (cf. ten Brink 2013, 240–249). A strong example of a game-changing political intervention into the Chinese market was the development of an independent domestic telecommunication standard, a high-profile government project which lead to the adoption of the standard in 2009 at the world's largest telecommunication provider China Mobile. The standard helps domestic companies to lower their dependency from foreign technologies and to reduce licence fees for the application of foreign telecommunication standards (cf. Brandt and Thun 2011, 169–170). In this case, indigenous norms of technology were implemented, which puts Chinese flagship companies in a position to reduce their dependency on foreign product technologies. The result is an enhanced space for independent innovation on which Chinese companies potentially can flourish.

## 4.5 Types of firm level upgrading

Based on the above considerations about the structures of value chains and the conditions for industrial upgrading, the following paragraphs aim to further distinguish between various forms of upgrading strategies on the level of single enterprises. Although industrial upgrading has become a catch phrase in policy documents in China and around the world, the concrete meaning of the term beyond some general notion of technological development often remains obscure.[39]

Starting from the already mentioned general definition about a move of economic actors "from low-value to relatively high-value activities in global production networks" (Gereffi 2005, 171), an account of industrial upgrading strategies must acknowledge the multiplicity of possible forms. This is unduly omitted when Gary Gereffi narrows down his broad definition of industrial upgrading by asserting that "we can think about upgrading in a concrete way as linked to a series of economic roles associated with production and export activities, such as assembly, original equipment manufacturing (OEM), original brand name manufacturing (OBM), and original design manufacturing (ODM)" (ibid). Certainly, such full-scale changes in production models are one important strand of industrial upgrading, but not necessarily all upgrading strategies involve such changes.[40] Especially in the IT industry, patterns of incremental innovation are widespread in which companies enhance their vertical specialisation in the field of key components, often without adhering to major changes in their production model (cf. Ernst 2009, 7–12).

A more precise discussion of the variety of upgrading trajectories is offered by a typology by Humphrey and Schmitz (2002, 6). They distinguish between three main upgrading types:

- Process upgrading through a re-organisation of the production system or the introduction of superior production technology
- Product upgrading through a move towards more sophisticated products

---

39 A case in point are the slightly contradictory statements of Wang Yang in which he, on the one hand, equates industrial upgrading with a replacement of traditional industries by high-tech enterprises, and, on the other hand, emphasises that enterprises in traditional industries have equal opportunities to upgrade (cf. section 3.3).

40 This suggested sequence (first brand building, then ODM supply functions) is quite dubious and most likely an unintended factual error in the quoted passage.

– Functional upgrading through the acquisition of new functions which increase the overall skill content of activities

Additionally, they also refer to the variant of "inter-sectoral upgrading" which occurs when firms use prior experience in one sector or sub-sector to enter production in another field. Some authors amended this meanwhile widely used model by adding further categories. Frederick and Gereffi, for instance, also identify "integration into the supply chain" through backward linkages in the supply chain, and "channel upgrading" through a market diversification that reaches out to new consumer groups in their framework for the analysis of the garment industry in China and Mexico (2011, 73).

While these typologies offer a useful point of departure for the distinction of concrete strategies, it is important to note that different upgrading approaches are not mutually exclusive. Functional upgrading towards brand building, for instance, necessarily rests on product upgrading and often involves some forms of process upgrading. Similarly, Sturgeon and Kawakami argue in a recent article on the electronics industry in Guadalajara, Mexico, that product upgrading "required firms to upgrade processes to accommodate rapid changeover and to add new functions" (2011, 136). An analysis of concrete upgrading approaches on cluster or company level must therefore take into account that strategies necessarily overlap. The types of upgrading identified in the literature therefore are instrumental in identifying a specific *mix* of strategies in concrete cases.

## 4.6 Economic and social upgrading

The GVC framework and most other theoretical models of global production networks face a paradox: they were developed to trace the economic linkages between developing countries and advanced economies in order to identify possibilities for development, but they rarely actually assess the concrete effects of firm-level upgrading on social development in general and on workers in the investigated industries in particular. Rather, "[i]t is often implicitly assumed that economic upgrading in GPNs will automatically translate into social upgrading through better wages and working conditions" (Barrientos et al 2010, 7; cf. Bair 2005, 171). Beyond these implicit notions, however, there exists a gap of knowledge about the relation between industrial (or economic[41]) upgrading and "social upgrading". According to Staritz et al:

> "[t]he upgrading debate has largely focused on economic upgrading and has not specifically taken into account social upgrading understood as improved working conditions, higher-skilled and better paid jobs. Economic and social dimensions of upgrading are often intertwined, but one does not necessarily lead to the other. In fact, we understand relatively little about the conditions under which they occur together" (2011, 4).

This blind spot also has to do with the barriers between academic disciplines. While economic sociologists primarily have focused on tracking the technological and organisational patterns of industrial change without sufficiently addressing their implications for labour relations, few labour scholars and NGOs have systematically dealt with the impacts of industrial transformation on labour relations (Barrientos et al 2010, 4–5).

Recent case studies have highlighted the problems of assuming a linear relationship between industrial upgrading and what became to be known as "social upgrading", mostly defined in relation to the "decent work" agenda of the International Labour Organisation (ILO).[42] In particular, the results of these studies as well as theoretical discussions have shown that:

– Successful upgrading at firm-level does not necessarily ensure a more powerful position of such enterprises and the ability to gain a higher share of profits since they often still remain in a subordinate position in relation to lead firms (cf. Bair 2005, 166).

– Upgrading of some firms may furthermore lead to a marginalisation of smaller and less capable competitors and therefore entail processes of exclusion of workers and communities from social benefits (ibid).

– Upgrading may not provide benefits for workers, or may even contradict their interests, for example, when a company raises its competitiveness through increased exploitation of the workforce (Selwyn 2013).

41 As stated before, the term "economic upgrading" is used in the literature to broaden the perspective to include forms of upgrading that do not affect industrial sectors, but, say, the service sector (cf. Barrientos et al 2010, 6). As this research focuses on manufacturing industries, however, the author will maintain the term "industrial upgrading".

42 The "decent work agenda" defines four strategic objectives of "creating jobs", "guaranteeing rights at work", "extending social protection", and "promoting social dialogue" with "gender equality" as a crossover objective, cf. http://www.ilo.org/global/about-the-ilo/decent-work-agenda/lang--en/index.htm, accessed 19.04.2013.

– Benefits from industrial upgrading may be distributed in a highly unequal manner within enterprises due to an internal polarisation between
of highly skilled and low-skilled work (Lüthje et al 2013a).

Since 2010, a major research project entitled "Capturing the Gains" (CTG),
under partnership of the ILO, is devoted to correcting this blind spot of
previous GVC research with regard to social upgrading by exploring on an
empirical basis under which circumstances economic upgrading translates
into improvements of working conditions.[43] A corresponding framework by
Barrientos et al (2010, 7–10) traces the potential gains for workers according
to a progression of industries from small-scale household work (associated
with very early stages of export-led industrialisation) towards technology-intensive or knowledge-intensive work (associated with the IT and service
sectors). They also point to the "competing pressures" in global production
networks that on the one hand provide incentives for a "high road" of transformation based on a more stable, skilled, and formalised workforce and, on
the other hand, induce cost constraints that can lead to a "low road" which
may depress labour standards. In effect, they argue, industrial transformation
leads to mixed results, e.g. by a bifurcation between regular, skilled work
and, for instance, lower-skilled contract work (Barrientos et al 2010, 15).

   This approach provides a useful point of departure for an empirical analysis of industrial upgrading processes. Yet, the concept of "social upgrading",
up until now, has been insufficiently elaborated to inform concrete research
projects. In cross-country analyses, for instance, Pickles and Godfrey apply a "parsimonious" approach to social upgrading which takes quantitative
data on wages and employment in different sectors as indicators for social
upgrading (2012; cf. Bernhardt 2013). While such studies provide a useful
overview of recent economic and social progress in different countries, they
are ill-equipped to actually explore the relationship between both. China,
for instance, is identified as an example for "clear-cut upgrading", in which
economic upgrading is accompanied by social upgrading, in reference to
observed average wage rises by 88 percent between 2004 and 2009 as well
as gains in employment (Pickles and Godfrey 2012, 4). Yet, rising wages
in China driven by a labour shortage, labour conflicts, and government efforts to stimulate domestic consumption are among the main *motivating*

---

43 Cf. the project description at http://www.capturingthegains.org/about/, accessed
   19.04.2013.

forces for companies to engage in industrial upgrading, as the discussion in section 3.1.2 showed.[44] It would be highly misleading to interpret them as a consequence of upgrading strategies that succeed in elevating income levels and working conditions of employees as the term "clear-cut upgrading"—intentionally or unintentionally—implies. The case studies presented in the following chapters rather demonstrate that industrial transformation in Chinese industries often implies process upgrading through investment in machines, due to which the workforce in the respective companies is substantially reduced. In the case of China, these negative employment effects of industrial upgrading, however, are compensated for by an ongoing fast growth dynamic of the economy which balances such losses in employment. Negative effects on employment caused by industrial upgrading therefore become invisible in aggregate figures.

Another problem of current accounts of social upgrading is the lack of differentiation and method with regard to the question how skills are distributed across and within enterprises. This is particularly evident in a typology offered by Barrientos et al (2010, 7–10; cf. figure 4.2) which offers a breakdown of the type of work in different industrial sectors. This stylised model, which is not based on actual data, but on qualitative descriptions of skill requirements in the concerned sectors, provides a general idea of how the labour process in different industries is composed of tasks of varying skill levels. But first, the illustration is somewhat obscure since, for example, the share of labour-intensive work in IT hardware production is lower than that in the automotive sector, although the latter is a very capital-intensive industry and IT manufacturing often implies large amounts of low-skilled manufacturing work, as numerous studies on the sector have highlighted (cf. Smith et al 2006; Lüthje et al 2013a). Secondly, and more importantly, even if one accepts the assertion that the share of high-skilled functions in IT manufacturing amounts to almost half of the total workforce, it remains unclear as to how the different functions are distributed across enterprises and regions. Thus figure 4.2 gives the impression that the allocation of IT hardware manufacturing would by itself strongly augment the demand for knowledge-intensive and other high-skilled functions, whereas there would be less need for labour-intensive tasks. However, modularised production networks in the IT industry are a prime example of outsourcing of

---

44 The category "employment growth" as an indicator for "social upgrading" is therefore particularly misleading in the case of China.

labour-intensive manufacturing to developing countries with the resulting effect of a polarisation of highly skilled and low-skilled functions across the globe. Employment schemes at electronics contract manufacturers in emerging economies do imply some highly skilled functions of product development, but their manufacturing workforce is strongly dominated by low-skilled and meagrely paid workers on the level of product assembly (Lüthje et al 2013a). The suggested typology therefore neglects the very insights about the global dispersion and fragmentation of functions that constitute the core of GVC research.

*Figure 4.2: Typology of workforce composition across different sectors in GPN*

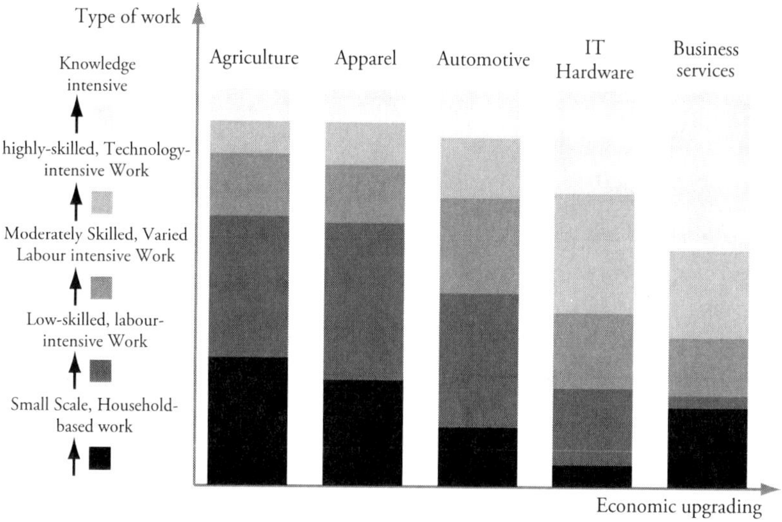

Source: Barrientos et al 2010.

# 4.7 Conclusions for the research strategy

On the basis of the discussion of the conditions for industrial upgrading in global production networks and the shortcomings of contemporary research frameworks to assess the relationship between industrial upgrading and social upgrading on regional and/or company level, a number of conclusions regarding a general research framework for the analysis of the social implications of industrial upgrading in Chinese industries can be drawn. This serves as a foundation for the research method and for the research hypotheses which are explicated in chapter 5.

1. Given the multiplicity of governance forms in different industries, as well as the sector-specific norms of technology, production, and productivity, questions about industrial upgrading in a regional context and the corresponding forms of work must be based on sector analyses.

2. The core elements of such analyses are the assessment of global industry linkages and the involved hierarchies based on the unequal control of technology and allocation of high value-added functions. As these spatial arrangements are not static, but subject to sourcing decisions by lead firms and shifts in the competitiveness of firms and regions, the analysis in particular needs to track recent changes in the structure and "governance" of production networks which condition the upgrading space for firms in certain regions.

3. Acknowledging the outlined weakness of GVC research to integrate the forms of labour into analysis, the analysis of GPNs explicitly should not only aim to determine the opportunities for industrial upgrading of enterprises in developing countries, but depart from a comprehensive perspective of how different forms of work under different socio-economic conditions are interconnected and modified by forms of "systemic rationalisation" characteristic of post-Fordist production in disintegrated production networks (cf. Sauer and Döhl 1994; Lüthje et al 2013a). The question of regional industrial upgrading, of how labour-intensive functions in developing countries can be supplemented by higher value-added functions in advanced manufacturing and the service sector, is therefore complemented by a view on renewed segmentations and outsourcing arrangements which may lead to an ongoing fragmentation of tasks between high-skilled and low-skilled functions and the corresponding polarisation of employment patterns.

4. The opportunities for industrial upgrading at the level of individual enterprises are heavily influenced by the regional environment in which they operate. Based on the outlined broad understanding of "innovative capabilities", the sector-specific analyses of Chinese industries therefore need to acknowledge the role of industrial policies, inter-firm linkages on a national, regional and cluster level, and the specific context of (rapidly expanding) domestic consumer markets that grant additional

space for the proliferation of functionally diversified Chinese enterprises. As for the global scale, the analysis of Chinese industrial sectors aims to generate a profile of the distribution of functions across enterprises which influence the character of labour on the level of individual enterprises. In particular, the analysis needs to disentangle whether the evolving norms of production in Chinese industries imply a strong segmentation of tasks between enterprises as it is the case in modular supply chain relations (which would hint at a separation of highly skilled and low-skilled work) or whether they are based on production models that rely on a stronger interpenetration of functions either within vertically integrated enterprises or in regional production systems that involve a high amount of collaboration and feedback between different production steps.

5. With regard to the effects of industrial upgrading on workers *within* enterprises, it is necessary to study if or how the respective enterprise's functions involve higher skills that require either formal training or profound working experience since it can be assumed that conditions for workers in such functions are better than in unskilled functions (cf. Barrientos et al 2010, 7–10). It is furthermore critical to assess how these functions are distributed across the workforce. One decisive question in this respect is whether the evolving norms of productivity in Chinese enterprises are built on a strong segmentation of skills or a rather comprehensive skill upgrading of the whole workforce which may be a result of a strong need to involve manufacturing workers in processes of product improvement and quality control, for instance.

6. While it seems plausible to assume a correlation between a skill upgrading of the workforce and social upgrading, there is no automatic linkage between both. It is assumed that the feasibility of social upgrading also strongly depends on labour laws and regulations, the structure of labour markets, and the agency of workers and their organisations which may establish certain standards regarding wages, working hours, and general working conditions. With regard to the Chinese case, the segmentation of the workforce into rural migrant workers and regular, resident workers, the latter of whom usually work under better conditions, plays an important role in this context. The analysis of the patterns of work at the enterprise level needs to ask to what extent a strong segmentation between relatively privileged workers with a local residential status and largely unskilled migrant workers persists, and to what degree these work

patterns are modified, e.g. by more extensive training, permanent employment, and higher remuneration of migrant workers.

7. In order to answer these questions, the general notion of "social upgrading" as found in the literature needs to be broken down into a more specific definition and corresponding indicators, a task which is undertaken in the following chapter.

# 5 Object of research, hypotheses, and methods for the empirical investigation

The aim of the empirical investigation of industrial transformation in China is to identify specific industrial upgrading strategies at the level of single enterprises and to find out whether they affect employment patterns, wage structures, and working conditions in a way that benefits the employees, i.e. whether they entail "social upgrading". As discussed in the previous chapters, the wider implication of this question is whether the present forms of industrial upgrading are instrumental to overcome those "extensive" employment patterns that have been the hallmark of export-oriented light industries on which much of China's recent economic ascent has rested. Social upgrading is therefore seen as a fundamental contribution, if not precondition, for a rebalancing of the Chinese economy from excessive dependence on exports and investment towards domestic consumption.

## 5.1 Object of research

Given the pronounced heterogeneity of the Chinese industrial landscape and the necessarily sector-specific nature of supply chain relations and upgrading patterns, the empirical analysis is undertaken with a regional and sector-specific focus.

The *Pearl River Delta* in Guangdong province was chosen as the site for investigation for several reasons. First, it constituted the pioneering region of China's export-led industrialisation after the onset of the reform policies in the late 1970s. As outlined in section 3.3, economic growth historically rested on a strong influx of FDI, first from overseas Chinese investors and subsequently from multinational companies. The predominant form of investment was one of export-oriented assembly operations which until today shape the region's industrial structure. As a result, the PRD is a paradigmatic case of an exportist, predominantly extensive regime of accumulation which rests on the widespread exploitation of migrant labour from Guangdong's and China's interior regions. The contradictions of this growth model have become particularly evident in recent years in the form of escalating social inequality, a proliferation of labour conflicts and a crisis of low-end export-oriented industries due to a deceleration of foreign demand and rising costs for land, labour, and raw materials. Secondly, because of the provincial government's acknowledgement of inherent contradictions in the prevailing growth model, the region has become a laboratory for reform in recent years with strong initiatives for industrial upgrading, a harmonisation of labour relations and other reforms summarised under calls for "inclusive growth" and a "happy Guangdong" (cf. Gore 2012). The transformation towards knowledge-intensive manufacturing and the service sector assumes a high priority in the policy of the provincial government, and the reform of the PRD is also strongly supported by the central government. Since the attempts to leap beyond the old growth model are particularly pronounced in the PRD, the region constitutes the ideal ground for the investigation of the relationship between industrial and social upgrading. The rationale of the case studies therefore does not aim at representativeness—regarding industrial change in China, typical upgrading patterns in all enterprises, etc.—but at the clearest possible expression of the phenomenon. Third, the case of the PRD was also chosen because of its quantitative relevance. The possibility of a shift towards a development model based on intensive accumulation not least depends on the feasibility of reform in the PRD, given that the region contributed 9.2 percent to China's GDP and 26.7 percent to China's export volume in 2011 (HKTDC 2013b).

The sector analyses cover the LED lighting industry on the one hand, and the textile and garment industry on the other hand. This choice was made deliberately in order to contrast diverging upgrading trajectories in industries with a markedly different history and structure. The case studies therefore offer rich material for a comparison of upgrading strategies and their effects on the workforce.

The *textile and garment industry*, with a history that dates back for centuries, constitutes one of the pioneering industries responsible for the quick pace of industrialisation of the early reform period. Although its relative share in total industrial output has declined during the last decade, the industry has still grown at a fast pace—a fact that is largely ignored in most debates about industrial change in China. Its combined output doubled during the years 2005 and 2009, backed by a surge of foreign demand for Chinese products (China Customs Statistics 2011). The PRD emerged as a destination for export processing arrangements of garment suppliers in the 1980s after much of Hong Kong's manufacturing capacity was relocated. Today, Guangdong Province belongs to the largest production sites of the garment industry in China and also accommodates a large textile manufacturing base which provides competitive advantages since garment companies can build on strong backward linkages to textile enterprises in the region.

The *LED lighting industry* is of much more recent date in comparison. As a new source of lighting based on semiconductor technology, it has evolved as a mass manufacturing industry during the past decade as a subsector of the IT industry. It has recently received very strong support from the central and provincial governments as one of the "strategic emerging industries" (Digitimes, 01.07.2011). The 12th FYP sets ambitious targets for strengthening the innovative capabilities of domestic enterprises in the LED industry. The industry has its strongest production base in Guangdong province. About 70 percent of Chinese and 50 percent of global output of LED packages[45] were manufactured in Guangdong in 2012 (Nanfang Ribao 07.04.2014).

The comparison of industrial upgrading in these industries is particularly interesting because they paradigmatically represent the "traditional" and the "strategic emerging industries" in reform programmes, or, according to Wang Yang's metaphor, the "old" and the "new birds" in the PRD's bird cages.

Notwithstanding the marked differences between the textile and garment and the LED industries, there exists a certain common ground with respect to the widespread employment of low-skilled migrant labour.[46] A comparison of the evolving employment patterns, wage structures, and working con-

---

45 LED packages are ready-made light sources which can be built into applications, cf. section 6.1.3.

46 According to Lüthje et al (2013a, 345–347), "low-wage classic" RoP prevail in the textile and garment industry, although there also exist "state-bureaucratic" and "flexible mass production" RoP. Due to a strong segmentation, relations in the IT industry are more diverse although "corporate high performance" may be seen as the dominant RoP. However, most of the manufacturing segments of the IT industry are shaped by "flexible mass production" RoP. This study is the first systematic investigation of RoP in the LED industry. Due to its relatedness to the field of IT manufacturing, employment patterns based on migrant labour can be expected. One crucial question in relation to the issue of social upgrading is how these are combined with other production steps similar to those in "corporate high performance" or "corporate bureaucratic" RoP in the IT industry.

ditions therefore promises to generate meaningful results in terms of parallels and differences in social upgrading.

## 5.2 Hypotheses

Based on the theoretical considerations concerning the position of Chinese industries in GPNs and the corresponding regimes of production within them (cf. chapter 2), on the insights about conditions and forms of industrial upgrading (cf. Chapter 4), and on preliminary considerations about the sectors in question stated above, the empirical investigation is guided by the following hypotheses about the relationship between industrial and social upgrading:

1.  There are overall favourable conditions for a vertical upgrading of Chinese industries in GPN

From a broad perspective on the respective sectors as a whole, industrial upgrading primarily depends on a vertical extension of performed functions due to which a vertical specialisation on low value-added manufacturing can be overcome (also dubbed "vertical upgrading" in literature (cf. Jiang and Milberg 2012)). Whereas vertical upgrading to a large degree depends on shifts in the sourcing strategies of lead firms in global production networks which may or may not demand more sophisticated capabilities from their suppliers, China's ambitious industrial policy, the effects of industrial clustering, and a large domestic market constitute beneficial factors for an allocation of higher value-added functions on an industry level. In particular, it can be expected that companies in domestically-oriented industry segments are in a good position to develop independent R&D and marketing functions.

2.  Functional upgrading supports skill upgrading of the workforce

By adding enterprise functions in the fields of R&D, advanced manufacturing and marketing, the involved companies also need to raise their level of capital investment and hire skilled employees, thereby overcoming "extensive" forms of employment that solely rest on China's (diminishing) comparative advantage of cheap production factors, above all labour. It can therefore be expected that functional upgrading on a company level supports skill upgrading of the workforce.

3. The profoundness of social upgrading depends on the forms of segmentation of the workforce as well as on political factors, in particular:

*3.1    The manner in which highly skilled functions and basic manufacturing tasks are distributed between enterprises*

As on the global scale, the critical issue concerning the distribution of skills along the production chain is whether knowledge-intensive functions are concentrated in technology-intensive enterprises while manufacturing is outsourced to captive or modular manufacturers with low technological capabilities (i.e. a hierarchic polarisation of functions between enterprises), or whether there are integrated or coordinated supply chain relations in which knowledge-intensive functions are spread more or less evenly across companies. It can be expected that social upgrading remains limited to a small number of lead firms or strategic suppliers in the first scenario, whereas it can affect workers across the supply chain in the latter.

*3.2    The forms of task segmentation within enterprises*

It can be assumed that functional upgrading toward higher value-added activities on a company level raises the skill requirements for the workforce which by and large may entail benefits in terms of wages and working conditions. But to what extent individual workers are affected by these requirements decisively depends on the forms of internal task segmentation. If a rigid segmentation between high-skilled functions and basic manufacturing tasks within enterprises prevails, social upgrading is limited to small segments of the workforce. If cooperative forms of work prevail in which tasks of planning, coordination and execution are combined, it can be expected that social upgrading effects are distributed more widely since companies need to invest in a comprehensively skilled workforce and develop an interest in creating stable and socially sustainable employment relations for workers.

### 3.3 The regulation of labour relations and the agency of workers

Whereas it can be expected that the demand for higher-skilled employees in general has positive effects in terms of social upgrading since companies need to attract and keep talent, the substance and the distribution of such benefits also depends on the effectiveness of the regulation of labour relations and the ability of workers to pursue their interests on an enterprise and an industry basis. If these conditions are not or only partially met, norms of productivity may prevail in which requirements for flexibility and cost-effectiveness are met by relying on renewed segmentations of the workforce into highly skilled and low-skilled employees as well as on disadvantageous remuneration systems, work schedules, and working conditions.

4. Social upgrading is undermined by new segmentations into low-skilled and highly skilled work

As cost-driven competition continues to play an important role in both industries in question, and labour regulations and labour relations in China continue to be incomplete or dysfunctional, it can be expected that industrial upgrading strategies in both industries will rely on new segmentations of highly skilled and low-skilled tasks that undermine social upgrading.

## 5.3 Research method

In line with the conclusions about a general research strategy laid out in section 4.7, the sector-specific analysis proceeds in three steps:

1. The examination of the structure of global production networks and recent changes therein. Special attention is thereby devoted to the existing forms of hierarchies based on the imposition of norms of technology and production by lead firms and the distribution of knowledge and labour-intensive functions across the value chain.

2. An analysis of the present position of the Chinese industry in sector-specific production networks, the respective allocation of functions and their main orientations for industrial upgrading. The latter in particular acknowledges government attempts to support the modernisation of local industries and the context of an expanding domestic market for industry development.
3. Empirical case studies from a sample of companies in the Pearl River Delta which aim to identify the companies' particular blends of upgrading strategies and their respective effects on the workforce.

### 5.3.1 Research method for the structural analysis (steps 1 and 2)

The structural analysis of sector-specific GPN and the respective state of the Chinese industry were executed by means of an extensive review of secondary literature and an observation of current developments in the sectors through business journals or sector-specific online news services. The textile and garment sector has been one of the pioneering industries of globalised production. In fact, much of contemporary theoretical knowledge, especially within the GVC framework, was developed with explicit reference to the garment industry (cf. Gereffi 1994; Gereffi and Memedovic 2003). Due to this background, current developments in the global textile and garment industry are particularly well-documented in academic literature (Frederick and Gereffi 2011; Frederick and Staritz 2012; Fernandez-Stark et al 2011). Yet, the same cannot be said about the state of the Chinese industry, which is surprising since it emerged as the World's largest production base in the 1990s and has expanded at a particularly fast pace over the last decade. The analysis here relies on some publicly available business reports, research publications from NGOs, and some data from Chinese government and industry sources.

As a rapidly expanding environmental technology, the LED industry has received much attention from analysts (McKinsey 2011a and 2012a; HSBC 2011; JPMorgan 2010), whereas so far, little academic literature exists in the field of economic sociology about the structure of GPN in this sector (but cf. Gereffi et al 2011; Li and Qiu 2010). The publicly available material from private research institutes provides a detailed picture of the eventful recent development of the sector and its further growth prospects.

As China comes to play an increasing role in the sector, some of the analyses also cover the state of the Chinese industry. For more detailed information about developments in China, and in the PRD in particular, a series of interviews with representatives from local business associations proved to be indispensable. They also provided some insightful documents about the development of the Chinese industry which up until now have not been published in English language.

### 5.3.2 Research method for the empirical case studies (step 3)

The case studies in the PRD's industries were conducted during two field research periods between October and December of 2010 and 2011, respectively. The selection of the cases followed the rationale of finding companies which were engaged proactively in a transformation of their operations in order to identify meaningful examples for industrial upgrading. This rested on the assumption that the effects of the respective upgrading strategies on the workforce could be most clearly observed by focussing on a "vanguard" of advanced enterprises. At the same time, the cases should reflect developments in a variety of companies of different size and function in order to provide a relatively comprehensive picture.

Desk research and initiatory expert interviews soon revealed that a different strategy had to be applied for the two sectors under consideration. In the textile and garment industry, a strong segmentation of the industry in clusters on the basis of townships is characteristic. The case studies therefore focused on localities with large concentrations of companies from different subsectors: the textile industry in Xiqiao, Foshan, the woollen knitwear industry in Dalang, Dongguan, and the general fashion industry in Humen, Dongguan. Each of these clusters represents a micro-environment for peculiar upgrading strategies specific to the respective subsectors. Local township governments in each case strongly support the development of their industries. The case studies based on interviews with government representatives of the middle and upper level as well as on company visits that included management interviews therefore also shed light on the role of government-led upgrading policies for the respective company strategies.

Industrial clusters and linkages between local governments and enterprises are also of great importance for the development of the LED industry which is predominately concentrated in the City of Shenzhen and has strong bases in the Cities of Guangzhou, Huizhou and Foshan, the latter of which is a traditional production base of the conventional lighting industry. However, industrial clusters in these places are not as densely concentrated as in the textile and garment industry and not organised on the basis of specialised towns that mainly focus on the manufacture of one particular product. Therefore, the cases were not selected on a geographical basis, but following a distinct vertical segmentation between so-called upstream, midstream and downstream functions which are typically executed by different enterprises.[47] The target of the investigation was to cover companies of all these fields in order to assess the corresponding vertical segmentation of workers between companies.

*Figure 5.1: Location of the surveyed industry clusters and companies in the PRD*

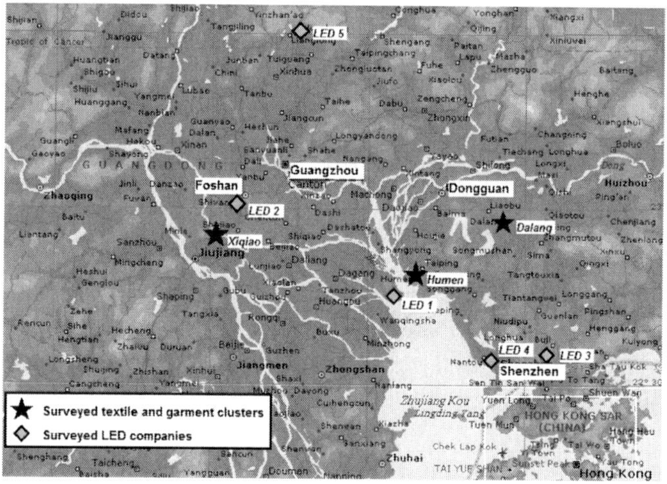

Source: ChinaToday.com, adapted by author.

Access to the companies was gained through various channels. After selecting the textile and garment industry clusters by means of desk research, local industry fairs proved to be an adequate way to approach entrepreneurs and government contacts. Foreign investment bureaus of the respective clusters were another valuable source of contacts and information, and helped to establish contacts to companies. In the LED industry, the main channels of

---

47 The definitions for the different industry segments are introduced in section 6.1.3.

access were local industry associations at a provincial and city level which provided rich information about the often confusing local industry structures and established contacts to companies on my behalf. While the research sample therefore partly depended on arbitrary contacts and the willingness of contact persons to establish further contacts, the author deliberately followed a strategy of balancing the selection, e.g. by choosing companies of a similar size in each cluster of the textile and garment industry or by trying to cover all vertical LED industry segments. In many cases, representatives of government institutions and industry associations courteously and with great success established those contacts the author had asked for. This manner of case selection, which took advantage of the willingness of conversation partners to demonstrate their successes in industrial transformation, involves a certain bias towards showcase examples which should be reflected upon. Yet, as the research strategy aimed at the identification of companies with a strong upgrading impetus, this bias could not only be accepted, but turned out to be useful to the overall research objective.[48] Besides, as especially the case studies of the LED industry demonstrate, the investigated companies do not conform to a rosy picture of straightforward success. Many companies were struggling with economic difficulties during the research period and two even went out of business in 2012.

The presented data stems from semi-structured interviews with government officials (7 interviews at 3 institutions), representatives of industry associations (8 interviews at 6 associations), company managers (31 interviews at 16 companies), and other experts (18 interviews). Data from interviews in 2010 was updated by subsequent interviews in 2011 except in two cases where this turned out to be impossible because of a lack of access. Supplementary information about the visited companies was gathered through online sources, government contacts and additional interactions with company contacts via telephone or e-mail. All in all, the empirical study is based on 64 in-depth interviews and 20 supplementary communications (cf. list of interviews pp. 393–397). They were either conducted in English language or by means of consecutive translation between English and Mandarin Chinese. All names of companies and interview partners are anonymised throughout this study.

---

48 Of course, this judgement about the "usefulness" of the mentioned bias for the *case selection* does not mean that it is unproblematic with regard to the *content* of the provided information. See the discussion in section 5.3.2.2 below.

*5.3.2.1  Questions and indicators*

The interviews with company representatives generally consisted of three parts: (1) a general introduction to the company, its products, its production model, and its position in the industry supply chain; (2) questions referring to the company's upgrading strategy, the implemented measures, and possible plans for relocation; and (3) questions about the organisation of the production process, the composition of the workforce, the distribution of wages and skills, and general working conditions (cf. figure 5.2).

*Figure 5.2: Catalogue of questions for interviews with company representatives*

---

1. **General information on company and production model**
   – Information about products, markets, production model, position in production network
   – Assessment of the general economic situation

2. **Industrial upgrading strategy**
   – Pursued upgrading strategies as perceived by interviewee
   – Concrete measures to implement these upgrading strategies
   – Access of company to technology, R&D
   – Role of government support for industrial upgrading
   – Obstacles and challenges to the company's development
   – Geographical position and possible intention of relocation

3. **Production process and social upgrading**
   – Overview of production steps and involved tasks for workers
   – Breakdown of the workforce (functions, social composition)
   – Skill distribution, training times, required work experience
   – Wage distribution and wage systems
   – General working conditions: overtime hours (OT), occupational safety and health (OSH), working and living environment

---

Initial research soon revealed peculiarities in the upgrading strategies within each sector which led to slight adaptations of the questionnaire. For example, the issue of codified intellectual property in the form of national or international patents plays an important role for LED companies, whereas product innovation in the fashion industry does not mainly depend on patents but on the employment of in-house fashion designers and external design input through agencies and the like. Hence, it seemed appropriate to include questions about the possession and the access to patents in questionnaires at LED companies whereas fashion companies were scrutinised more closely with regard to their design staff and consultants. Apart from such amendments, however, the questionnaires were deliberately kept the same in order to highlight derivations between the cases in both industries.

In order to systematically assess the respective developments regarding industrial and social upgrading, the following criteria and indicators were used:

### a) Industrial upgrading

Given that the discourse on industrial upgrading (*chanye shengji*) in Guangdong is ubiquitous, most representatives tended to advertise the transformations that are being implemented in their enterprises. As the definition of industrial upgrading is also somewhat ambiguous in the daily use of the term, the above mentioned typology by Humphrey and Schmitz (2002, 6; cf. table 5.1) was used in order to sort out the specific mix of upgrading strategies in a certain enterprise. Instead of introducing additional upgrading types, the framework was limited to the three main categories identified by Humphrey and Schmitz because they are unambiguous and most proliferated, which does not account for other upgrading types suggested in literature.[49] Yet, questions about industrial upgrading strategies were deliberately asked in an open way in order to record the genuine perception of my interview partners who in some cases also named initiatives that did not conform to the suggested upgrading typology. As argued in section 4.5, upgrading types are not mutually exclusive, but instead often complementary. Furthermore, upgrading strategies that fit the same category can imply diverging approaches. In the case of functional upgrading, for instance, companies can, among

---

49 The category of "inter-sectoral upgrading" (by which companies use knowledge that they have obtained in one sector to enter other more sophisticated industries (cf. Humphrey and Schmitz 2002, 6)), is a special case that is not as proliferated as the other upgrading types, which are considered to be elementary. It was learned from interview partners that inter-sectoral upgrading does frequently occur in the PRD, but this was not the case in the surveyed companies. Some forms of product, process, and functional upgrading, on the contrary, were present in virtually all the investigated cases. The categories of "channel upgrading" and "integration in supply chain" (through building backward linkages) as used by Frederick and Gereffi (2011, 73) are both of high relevance, e.g. for newly founded garment brands that need to develop their sales channels. Yet, these are considered as special cases of functional upgrading here.

other things, either aim at a *vertical integration* of functions within the same enterprise, or at a form of *vertical specialisation* by which a company gives up its former core business in order to focus on higher value-added activities.

The information from management interviews was complemented and scrutinised by impressions from shop floor visits during which particular aspects of a company's upgrading strategy could be observed while interviewees supplied additional information. In order to create an objective measure for evaluating the upgrading strategy at a surveyed company, a specific set of indicators was chosen for each upgrading type. These differ slightly between sectors, for instance in the case of product upgrading for which lighting efficiency is one important indicator in the LED sector, whereas style and unit price are the appropriate measurement in the garment industry (cf. table 5.1).

*Table 5.1: Upgrading types, possible articulations and indicators*

| Upgrading type | Possible articulation | Indicators |
|---|---|---|
| Product upgrading | Better product quality and/or functionality | Unit price, style, functions, efficiency, etc. |
| Process upgrading | New production equipment, modifications in organisation of production | Number, price and type of machines; management systems, systems of quality control |
| Functional upgrading | Addition of functions to core operation (vertical integration); replacement of certain functions by higher value-added functions (vertical specialisation) | Production model (OAM, OEM, ODM, OBM), number and type of production steps, allocation of R&D and marketing |

Source: Own compilation adapted from Humphrey and Schmitz 2002.

## b) Social upgrading

As argued in section 4.6, up until now there is no satisfying concept to measure "social upgrading". An important task for the empirical investigation of social upgrading on a company basis therefore is the selection of meaningful indicators which acknowledge the regional specificity of labour relations and, furthermore, can trace the interrelatedness between concrete measures for industrial upgrading on a company basis and the social conditions of the workforce.

An assessment of "social upgrading" in the Pearl River Delta solely by means of aggregate figures about wage levels would convey a partial and distorted picture about whether such changes actually result from industrial upgrading initiatives of individual companies. As outlined in chapter 3, the peculiar context of a general tendency of rising wages and a shortage of manufacturing workers is an exogenous regional phenomenon rooted in demographic changes and the unwillingness of migrant workers to accept wage levels and working conditions as they were common in the 1990s and 2000s. It can be assumed that these factors drive wage increases quite independently of the upgrading efforts of an individual enterprise. Similarly, as argued in section 4.6, aggregate data on employment growth in a certain region tells little about the concrete impacts of industrial upgrading as employment losses through automation can be compensated for by employment gains in other companies resulting from general economic growth. Above all, increases in employment generally are a questionable indicator for social upgrading in the context of the PRD. Given the predominance of highly labour-intensive manufacturing industries that absorb more workers than are currently available, social improvements are above all related to the *quality* of employment. This concerns basic issues of wages and working conditions, but also the issue of whether there emerge more stable forms of employment which entail equal conditions for resident and migrant workers.

In order to develop a more meaningful set of indicators that matches the peculiar case of the PRD, it is useful to resort to the more comprehensive understanding of social upgrading which can, for instance, be derived from the ILO decent work framework and consists of the four pillars "creating jobs", "guaranteeing rights at work", "extending social protection", "promoting social dialogue" with the additional crossover target of "gender equality".[50] Based on these general fields, Barrientos et al further provide a distinction of "measurable standards" and "enabling rights":

"Measurable standards are those aspects of worker well-being that are more easily observed and quantifiable. This includes aspects such as category of employment (regular or irregular), wage level, social protection and working hours. It can also

---

50 Cf. the definition at <http://www.ilo.org/global/about-the-ilo/decent-work-agenda/lang--en/index.htm>, accessed 19.04.2013.

include data related to gender and unionisation, such as the percentage of women supervisors or the percentage of union members in the workforce. However, measurable standards are often the outcome of complex bargaining processes, framed by the enabling rights of workers. These are less easily quantified aspects, such as freedom of association and the right to collective bargaining, non-discrimination, voice and empowerment. Lack of access to enabling rights undermines the ability of workers (or specific groups of workers such as women or migrants) to negotiate improvements in their working conditions which can enhance their well-being" (2010, 7).

This holistic understanding of social upgrading provides a suitable point of departure for the identification of indicators for social upgrading. However, these still need to be adapted to the peculiarities of labour relations in China, and the Pearl River Delta in particular, which in the latter case are shaped by predominantly extensive forms of accumulation under the widespread discriminatory employment of migrant workers. In order to identify a benchmark in relation to which changes through industrial upgrading can be detected, the general issues deducted from the ILO decent work framework are therefore complemented by issues that are specific to the region under investigation. These have been identified by a number of analyses of labour relations in China and Guangdong (A.Chan 2001; CLB 2012, 3–15; Lee 2007, 204–231; Shen 2007), and were recently highlighted in a cross sector investigation by Lüthje et al (2013b, 366–368):

- *Wage systems* that are built on low base-wages and high amounts of variable pay resulting in unstable remuneration and constant incentives for excessive overtime work
- *Strong wage hierarchies* along with status discrimination against migrant workers, women and temporary workers which undermine principles of "equal pay for equal work"
- *A lack of seniority-based workplace regulations, job classifications and job-security provisions* which reflects the prevalence of individualised schemes of performance evaluation, arbitrary distribution of jobs and tasks, and a general high flexibility of employment
- *A high degree of employment flexibility and low job security* which has been only partially limited by provisions of the Labour Contract Law of 2008

These deficiencies could be observed across various regimes of production in Chinese industries. However, they are particularly virulent in "low wage classic" and "flexible mass production" RoP which respectively dominate the textile and garment as well as the IT manufacturing industries of the region (ibid, 315–319).

Based on these considerations, the following criteria and indicators were chosen for the empirical study of social upgrading in enterprises in the PRD:

*(1) Employment schemes*
This concerns the social composition of the workforce, especially with regard to its segmentation into migrant workers and resident workers with a local household registration (*hukou*). A strong segmentation, if accompanied by an equally strong polarisation in wage and skill levels, suggests a continuation of status discrimination and schemes of employment associated with extensive regimes of accumulation. A related criterion concerns the stability of the workforce measured by an overall turnover rate, the duration of employment (measurable by information about the average period workers stay with one company and observable through the age of workers), and the existence and application of seniority type of payments.

*(2) Skills, training times and required working experience*
These criteria aim to trace whether changes in the production process result in a task distribution which requires a higher share of skilled employees. The analysis consequently aims to uncover which processes require highly skilled workers and how skill levels are distributed across the whole workforce. The skill level can be either measured in formal training times provided by companies themselves or in requirements for working experience and/or formal training formulated by the respective company when hiring new workers. Previous studies have observed a relative correlation between skill and social upgrading. As Barrientos et al note, "case study evidence suggests that a shift from lower to higher skilled types of work may directly lead to social upgrading, but this is not automatically the case. The challenge, therefore, is how to pursue strategies that will enhance labour standards for all workers in all types of work" (2010, 17).

*(3) Wages and wage systems*
This includes the absolute wage levels, the amount of performance-based wages as a share of the total wage and the general wage differentials within a company. The absolute wage sums are measured against each other in order to identify which groups of workers earn above average wages compared to their peers at other factories. Another critical question concerns

the nature of applied wage systems and their effects on the total wage. Thereby it is acknowledged that a change in the wage system can have contradictory effects on workers. The replacement of a piece wage system by an hourly wage system, for instance, which in theory could assure a more stable income for workers and reduce their dependency on overtime hours (cf. Chan and Siu 2010), can also have negative effects on skilled workers who may earn less on an hourly wage scheme than they would make on piece rate where they can benefit from their working experience (Lüthje et al 2013b, 268–269). Accordingly, the plain data on wages, wage systems, and wage differentials in each factory had to be assessed on the basis of a qualitative interpretation of the impact of recent changes on different sections of the workforce.

### (4) Overtime hours and general working conditions

The amount of overtime hours is rated with reference to the propositions of the Labour Contract Law which sets the maximum amount of overtime hours to 36 hours per month on top of a regular 40-hour work week. As these standards are rarely met in the concerned sectors, this indicator rather reveals the severity of the labour law violations in the respective companies. Other indicators pertaining to working conditions are occupational safety and health (OSH) standards, the physical and mental strain of different tasks, the conditions on the factory shop floor (i.e. tidiness, air-conditioning, etc.), and the living environments of the workforce. Apart from entertainment offers and social programmes, the latter especially concerns the question of the quality of factory dormitories, which represents the norm for accommodation of migrant workers in the region, and whether workers need to pay for accommodation and food. The prevalence of dormitory housing indicates the continuation of temporary employment systems of migrant workers since there are generally no conditions to accommodate families in dormitories.

*Table 5.2: Overview of indicators for the measurement of "social upgrading"
in PRD factories*

| Category | Criteria | Indicator | Sources |
|---|---|---|---|
| Employment structure | | | |
| | Social composition | Share of migrant workers, existence of status discrimination | Interview data, observation |
| | Gender composition | Share of female workers, existence of gender discrimination | Interview data, observation |
| | Workforce stability | Age of workers, average time of employment | Interview data, observation |
| Workers skills | | | |
| | Skill levels | Training times and/or required work experience | Interview data |
| | Task distribution | Distribution of highly skilled tasks across workforce | Interview data, observation |
| Wages | | | |
| | Absolute wage levels | Total wage for different groups of workers | Interview data |
| | Wage differentials | Difference between highest-paid and lowest-paid functions | Interview data |
| | Wage systems | Mode of wage calculation, hare of flexible wage components, stability of wage payments | Interview data |
| Working conditions | | | |
| | Working hours | Amount of OT in normal and peak production times | Interview data |
| | OSH | Protective gear, health risks through materials and equipment, physical and mental strain of work | Observation, interview data |
| | Shop floor conditions | Cleanliness, noise, smell, air-conditioning | Observation |
| | Working and living environment | Existence of and conditions in dormitories, entertainment facilities | Interview data |

Source: Own compilation.

These indicators combine quantitative measures for some criteria with a qualitative description of the labour process and the general working conditions. Social upgrading occurs when positive changes in a number of the listed indicators can be detected which point towards relevant overall changes in relation to the core problems in the PRD's employment systems discussed above. As some of them, such as the composition of the workforce, the task distribution and wage differentiations, are loosely related, it can be expected that they occur together. Yet, diverging results are equally possible, for example, when a reduction of overtime hours leads to income losses. Most importantly, social upgrading does not necessarily affect the entire workforce, but may remain limited to a share of scarce professionals, for instance, while not affecting the bulk of the manufacturing workforce.

For the purpose of applicability, the listed indicators remain limited to "measurable standards" and do not account for "enabling rights" of the workforce. Whereas questions about this issue were also included in interview questionnaires, the presence of a factory trade union branch is an imperfect indicator for the capacity of workers to pursue their interests because such branches mostly are dysfunctional in representing workers. A closer assessment of the state of "enabling rights" and the subjective condition of workers to enforce positive changes in wages and employment conditions would be desirable because this could help to overcome a top-down perspective on social change. The theoretical approach inherent in GVC theory was rightly criticised for such a bias because ultimately social improvements were seen as a result from management-induced decisions, not of the capacity of workers to enforce better wages and working conditions (cf. Selwyn 2013). Yet, the assessment of the balance of forces between management and workers on a factory level lies beyond the methodological possibilities of this study. After all, it can hardly be expected that details about labour conflicts and internal bargaining processes would be disclosed by the management.

### 5.3.2.2 Reliability of the data

As mentioned, the interviewees at company visits generally were managers of the middle or upper segments. As they mostly constituted the only source of information on the conditions within a single company, the potential for a triangulation of the provided information was generally limited.[51] It is

---

51 Empirical investigations by labour scholars about labour relations in this region are often

therefore important to reflect upon the accuracy of the obtained data and their limitations.

With regard to the efforts for industrial upgrading, interview partners mostly referred to concrete measures (the acquisition of machines, the introduction of new product lines, the addition of certain functions) the implementation of which could be verified during shop floor visits and through additional desk research. What is more, ambiguities could often be eliminated through more concrete information during a second interview or *ex post* conversations via telephone or e-mail. Company updates during the second round of visits in 2011 furthermore revealed which planned initiatives had actually been executed and to what results this had led. The author therefore holds that the data on the industrial upgrading strategies at the surveyed companies is accurate. In case ambiguities remained, they are highlighted in the presentation of the material.

The reliability of data on social upgrading is less clear, given the controversial and sensitive nature of the subject. Whereas it seemed unproblematic for the author's conversation partners to boast about their company's technological progress, it often appeared less natural to them to reveal details about working conditions to a stranger. Nevertheless, almost all interview partners revealed information on skill requirements, working conditions and wages in a quite detailed way. Often, however, they show a characteristic vagueness, for example by giving gross lump-sums about wage payments. This must not necessarily be judged as evasiveness, since it also can reflect a lack of awareness of the respective interviewees who either reported about issues that were beyond their own responsibility or who could themselves not see through the complex individualised remuneration schemes that make it difficult to quote concrete aggregate wage figures.

Although the obtained data thus could not be ultimately verified, it can be argued that it conveys a roughly accurate impression of the *tendencies* in the respective factories. Significantly, many interview partners disclosed

---

based exclusively on workers interviews which are viewed as a more reliable source of information than assessments by the management. Yet, this method was not applicable within the present study due to a lack of access and resources. Moreover, an exclusive reliance on workers interviews was not an option since this would have provided only partial insights about the pursued upgrading strategies and the subjective views of the management behind it, which constitutes an important aspect of the research question. The author therefore needed to rely on management information about the indicated criteria which was then subjected to a critical interpretation.

information which does not let their company appear in a positive light, for instance, when they gave figures for working hours which surpassed the legal maximum by far or when they admitted that wages were lower than at other companies in the same area. In rare cases, in which interview partners obviously expressed exaggerated claims with regard to wages or training periods, subsequent conversations provided a more accurate picture. In some instances, information could be confirmed by triangulation through a second interview partner or, in one case, through a short conversation with workers. Finally, some indicators for social upgrading, such as the age of the workforce or the strain of work, not only depend on management information, but are observable at company visits. The presented data therefore meaningfully and to the author's best knowledge reflects the state of industrial and social upgrading in the surveyed companies. Yet, it would be desirable to complement this information by studies derived from other sources of information, above all by interviews with workers in the respective industry segments.

### 5.3.2.3 *Method of data evaluation*

The processing of the obtained information was done based on the method of qualitative content analysis (cf. Gläser and Laudel 2010). The method consists of the following three steps:

1. Extraction of data from interview transcripts according to a grid of aspects determined with reference to the research question.
2. Editing the data by sorting it according to matching themes, summarising identical information and eliminating factual mistakes.
3. Evaluating the data by identifying causal relationships and comparing mechanisms in different cases.

The method offers a documented way of data presentation which reduces arbitrariness of interpretation by insisting on data evaluation according to explicated research parameters and a strict evaluation procedure. It also allows for the reconstruction of the final interpretation from the original data. In both sector studies, the task of qualitative content analysis consisted in a summarisation of information obtained at single-company level to a systematic presentation of aggregate data without neglecting important differences between the cases.

# Part III:
# Empirical analyses of industrial upgrading and social upgrading

# 6 The "LED revolution"—Disruption of production networks in the lighting industry and the rise of China

The application of LED lighting technologies on a mass scale amounts to a change so fundamental in nature that it was called a "revolution" and described as "the biggest change in the global lighting industry since the invention of the light bulb" by industry analysts (HSBC 2011; JPMorgan 2010, 3). The LED industry has experienced high growth rates in the recent past as LED light sources have become the standard technology in screen backlighting, e.g. for mobile phones, computer monitors and LCD TV sets. Yet, forecasts project even steeper growth in the immediate future since LED products are becoming increasingly competitive on consumer markets.[52] This transition is supported by regulations for a phase-out for conventional "incandescent" lighting by governments in the USA, Europe, Japan, and China. The rise of LED lighting implies a technological rupture in the lighting industry that will thoroughly transform conventional production methods as well as the international division of labour in GPNs. As such, it presents opportunities for industrial upgrading of Chinese industries as well as for a further regional shift of the lighting industry towards Asia. This chapter will first outline the main structural characteristics and development trends in the global LED industry (6.1). It will then analyse the structure of the Chinese LED sector and discuss the general conditions for an upgrading of Chinese enterprises (6.2). This serves as an introduction for the in-depth analysis of upgrading strategies and their impact on the forms of work, based on empirical data from field studies in 2010 and 2011 (6.3).

---

52 Currently the three main segments of the lighting industry are general lighting, automotive lighting and backlighting. The field of general lighting consists of the sub-categories residential, office, shop, hospitality, industrial, outdoor and architectural lighting. In 2011, the general lighting segment constituted around three quarters of the total lighting market. (McKinsey 2012a, 15; 23-26)

## 6.1 LED lighting—successor of conventional lighting technologies

LED lighting works according to a completely different principle than incandescent lighting. In the latter case, light bulbs disseminate light by igniting a wire under vacuum conditions in the process of which up to 90 percent of energy is transformed into heat and lost. This principle has been unchanged since the invention of the light bulb at the beginning of the 19th century and its subsequent refinement by Thomas Edison in the 1870s. LED light, on the contrary, is a semiconductor technology. It is composed of photons that are disseminated when electrons change their atomic energy level after they have been led from one semiconductor compound to another when attached to electric circuits. After use, the compounds take on their original shape which gives LEDs a theoretically eternal lifespan. This principle of "electroluminescence" was discovered at the beginning of the 20th century and commercialised in the late 1960s in the US. Typical early uses were electronic digits in watches or electronic devices.

*Figure 6.1: Life-cycle primary energy consumption of light sources (MJ per 20 million lumen hours)*

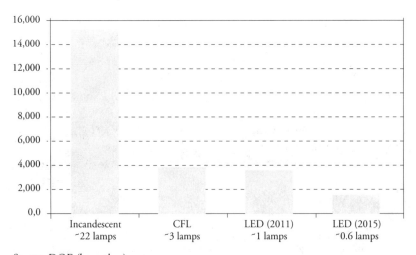

Source: DOE (by author).

LED lighting is highly energy efficient because much less energy is lost to creating heat. State-of-the-art LEDs in 2011 required about 75 percent less energy than incandescent light sources and slightly less than alternative energy-saving "Compact Fluorescent Lamps, CFL" (cf. figure 6.1). Yet, even higher savings are projected for the future because of further optimisation of lighting efficiency.[53]

There are several other advantages of LED lighting. For instance, the colour of light can be conditioned by the selection of the applied semiconductor materials which determine the wave length of lighting rays and LEDs of different colours can be blended to cover the entire colour range. This supports a great versatility in the technology's application. Furthermore, LED light sources are much more durable with an average life span that is 40-50 times longer than that of conventional bulbs and 5–8 times longer than the one of CFL light sources (HSBC 2011, 14; JPMorgan 2010, 21). Life cycle analyses also highlighted other comparative advantages of LED lighting with regard to its impact on the consumption of resources and the contamination of soil, water and air (DOE 2012a). In all categories, LED lighting also performs better than state-of-the-art energy-saving lighting based on CFL or halogen lighting, which is why these are considered to be transitional technologies that will be replaced by LED lighting in the future. Given that lighting in general currently accounts for 19 percent of global energy consumption and thereby is responsible for about 6 percent of $CO_2$ emissions, LED lighting is also considered to be a major technological contribution to climate protection against the background of rising demand for light sources due to population growth, economic development, and urbanisation (HSBC 2011, 3; McKinsey 2011a, 14–17; The Climate Group 2012). Such technological leaps in energy efficiency are a precondition to meet political goals like the one set in China's 12th Five Year Plan which aims at a 15 percent reduction of energy consumption per unit of GDP until 2016 (cf. Roach 2011, 5).

Because of the LED technology's energy-saving benefits, and due to the fact that LED prices are continuously dropping, the change towards more energy-efficient lighting may come at a low cost. The US Department of Energy expects an overall saving of energy costs of USD 120 billion until 2030

---

53 Theoretically, LEDs can reach a lighting efficiency of more than 250 lumen per Watt (lm/W). According to a projection of the US Department of Energy, LED packages will reach a maximum lighting efficacy of 164 lm/W in 2013 and of 235 lm/W in 2020. Conventional light bulbs have a lighting efficiency of 10 – 19 lm/W (DOE 2012b; McKinsey 2011a, 43).

due to LED application (calculated in 2010 energy prices; cf. NSR 2010, 7). The prospect of such savings not only raises the attractiveness of LED products for private consumers, but also facilitates government programmes such as the Chinese "Energy Management Contract (EMC)" scheme, by which current public investment in LED lighting devices is financed by future energy savings. Governments around the world have supported the growth of the LED industry by investment and stimulus programmes, as well as through regulations like the roadmap for a phase-out for incandescent light bulbs to be completed in 2012 in Europe, in 2014 in the US and in 2016 in China (McKinsey 2012a, 11; HSBC 2011, 26). The emergence of a new standard lighting technology is bound to thoroughly transform the production networks of the lighting industry.

6.1.1 The global LED market: growth perspectives and main markets

Driven by the rise of LED applications in the consumer electronics market and the expected boom in relation to the replacement of incandescent lighting, McKinsey&Company forecasts very high annual growth rates of above 30 percent for the global LED industry in the period between 2011 and 2016 (cf. figure 6.2). Most industry analysts share the tendency of this projection, although there remain considerable uncertainties due to several factors including the speed by which conventional lighting technologies are replaced, the annual gains in lighting efficiency of LED light sources and the price erosion of LED packages.[54]

---

54 The latter led the market research firm "Strategies Unlimited" to drastically revise its projection of a compound annual growth rate (CAGR) by 20 percent between 2011 and 2016 which it had released in 2012 (cf. LEDs Magazine March 2012). Its most recent projection released in February 2013 now only expects a CAGR of 1.8 percent until 2017 for the LED lighting industry (McKinsey: 33 percent until 2016) with a CAGR of 7 percent in the general lighting segment (McKinsey: 45 percent until 2016) (cf. Wright 2013, 35–40). The main reason for this pessimistic forecast is a slump in LED prices which is claimed to have fallen below the level of 2 USD per kilolumen which originally was projected to be the case in 2015 only.
While this forecast highlights the various uncertainties concerning future market development, it stands in contradiction the projections of other analysts. McKinsey&Company recently published a forecast in which the drop in LED prices is interpreted in the opposite way: lower LED prices thus are seen to be beneficial for a faster penetration of LED technologies on consumer markets. Taking into account that prices have dropped faster than expected due to oversupply on the market, McKinsey now projects a market volume of

*Figure 6.2: Growth projection for the global LED industry*[i]

**LED value-based market share**
Percent

**LED lighting market**
EUR billions

i General lighting and automotive lighting refer to the whole product value chain including fixtures and electric controls whereas backlighting only refers to light sources (since they are not built into luminaires but attached directly to a variety of electronics products, cf. section 6.1.3).

Source: McKinsey 2012a.

EUR 37 billion in 2016, EUR 3 billion lower than in its 2011 forecast (McKinsey 2012a, 21; 2011, 21). However, this only marginally affects McKinsey's general growth forecast for the LED industry which still stands at a CAGR of 33 percent with a CAGR of 45 percent in the general lighting segment (cf. figure 6.2). This calculation already takes into account the recent volatility in the market (cf. section 6.1.2). The figures published by JPMorgan (2010), HSBC (2011) and Digitimes (18.03.2013) roughly correspond to the expectations about the future market volume by McKinsey.

Arthur Jaunich, one of the authors of the 2012 McKinsey report, admits that there are considerable uncertainties about the development of LED prices and the penetration rate of LEDs on the general lighting market because of the recent volatility of the market, but expressed doubts about the forecast of Strategies Unlimited (ID 09.04.2013). It lies beyond the scope of this study to provide a detailed assessment of the validity of the contrary forecasts. However, the assumption of Strategies Unlimited that LED revenues in the general lighting segment will only increase by 7 percent per year does not seem plausible given that the penetration rate in this segment is still very low and that revenues in this field more than doubled in 2012, according to Strategies Unlimited's own assessment (cf. Wright 2013, 36). The expectation of a sudden slowdown of growth also does not do justice to the growth performance in 2012, a year which generally is considered to have been a very difficult one for the industry. The LED market in 2012 grew by almost 10 percent from USD 12.5 billion to USD 13.7 billion, according to Strategies Unlimited (ibid, 35).

Growth will be mainly driven by fast penetration of LED lighting in the general lighting segment, i.e. residential, office, shop, hospitality, industrial and outdoor lighting applications (cf. McKinsey 2012a, 42). Yet, the growth performance in the field of backlighting, which used to be an important driver of the industry in recent years, is expected to be negative.

Backed on the fast proliferation of LED lighting which is expected to constitute 63 percent of the total lighting market by 2020, the general lighting industry is expected to grow at an above average rate of around five percent per year until 2016 (McKinsey 2012a, 14–15). However, analysts agree that growth, both in the LED subsector and in the general lighting industry, will considerably flatten out after this period (cf. McKinsey 2012a, 14–15; HSBC 2011, 4; JPMorgan 2010, 3). One reason for this is that demand for LEDs will decrease once high penetration rates are achieved in most application fields. Breakthroughs in the lighting efficiency of LEDs furthermore will aggravate the tendency of slower growth in the light source market in the future because fewer high-power LEDs, sold at ever lower piece costs, will be needed to create the same lighting effects. This process currently is already depressing growth performance in the backlighting segment since product architectures of TV sets, computer and mobile phone backlights tend to rely on fewer LEDs.[55] Another reason for slower growth projections of the lighting industry after the transition towards LEDs has advanced is that due to their exceptional longevity, there is no need to exchange LED light sources as often as it is the case with incandescent light sources. Therefore, the market for replacement lamps, which in 2011 accounted for around 90 percent of total light source revenues, will dry up in the future (HSBC 2011, 32).

---

55 A growing market share in this segment will also be gained by Organic LED (OLED) applications. Displays lit by OLED technologies have a higher picture resolution and can be integrated directly into the display (instead of being installed behind the display as "backlight"). Due to higher product prices, OLEDs currently are mainly used in high-end consumer electronics products, but expected to expand to cheaper applications in the future. OLED is a competing technology to conventional backlighting. OLED technologies are pioneered mainly by companies that are also active in the inorganic LED business. Its main vendors currently are Samsung, LG and Sony (McKinsey 2011a, 21; 2012a,17).

## 6.1.2 An interim low on the market: Overinvestment and volatility

Despite generally dazzling growth perspectives for the future, the industry was plagued by a relatively weak economic performance in the years 2011–2013 that aggravated competition, depressed prices and drove many companies out of business. The main reasons for this unexpected situation were large overcapacities and the global repercussions of the European debt crisis (McKinsey 2012a, 9–10, 17). The boom in LED backlighting of the past years, a generally favourable business outlook and government stimulus programmes have led to exceptionally high investment rates in recent years. Hundreds of new manufacturers have entered the market, including small scale start-ups on the one hand and multinationals in the consumer electronics industry—most notably the Korean electronics giants Samsung and LG—on the other. Particularly large investments in LED capacities in China that were backed by strong government support contributed to the installation of capacities that exceed worldwide demand (McKinsey 2012a, 17). According to the US Department of Energy, there was a growth in worldwide LED capacities by 200 percent between 2009 and 2011 whereas global demand only grew by 90 percent during the same period (Dorsheimer 2012).

The recent volatility in the LED market is best reflected in the sales figures for MOCVD reactors, the equipment that is needed to produce epitaxial LED wafers, the key component of any LED lighting device. Overinvestment led to extremely high bookings in 2009 and 2010, followed by a slump in 2011 and 2012. The volumes of bookings are expected to flatten out in the coming years, which indicates that future LED production will rely to a significant extent on the equipment that was bought in the "hot" years of investment in 2009 and 2010 (Dorsheimer 2012).

The depressing effects of overinvestment were aggravated by factors related to the European debt crisis and its global repercussions. The lighting industry was affected by an overall slowdown in GDP growth because of lower construction activity, slower sales of consumer electronics products like flat panel TVs and the faster proliferation of low cost LEDs with further depressing effects on prices (McKinsey 2012a, 9–10, 17).[56]

---

56 Especially the luminaire (i.e. complete lighting systems including light sources and fixtures) market is sensitive to the performance of the construction industry since a large share of these is directly built into new buildings.

The result of the slowdown of growth since 2011 was a drop in LED prices at a faster pace than predicted (ibid, 17–18).[57] This had contradictory consequences. On the one hand, lower LED prices enhanced the competitiveness of LED products on the general lighting market—a precondition for the proliferation in the technology. According to McKinsey&Company, the infliction point for the proliferation of certain technologies like, for instance, retrofit LED light bulbs that can be used in conventional lighting fixtures is expected at an earlier date due to "aggressive price erosion" (ibid, 16–19). Yet on the other hand, after 2011 the industry was stuck between a rock and a hard place: on one side there was a contracting backlight market and on the other a general lighting market that was not yet kicking off. Growth rates of the LED industry in 2011 and 2012, which stood at about 10 percent in both years (HSBC 2011, 28, Wright 2013, 35), therefore remained substantially below expectations which led industry analysts to revise their forecasts.[58]

In this situation, the decline of prices for LED light sources aggravated the problems for LED companies. As one commentator explains with reference to the LED chip industry:

"[T]he biggest challenges facing chip manufacturers is that chip prices are dropping at a rate significantly faster than sales volume growth. Although the LED market performance [is] better in 2012 than in 2011, the rapidly dropping prices [are] causing revenue[s] to either stay flat or to increase in minor level" (LEDinside 15.11.2012).

Despite the difficult economic situation in the industry in recent years, the situation was interpreted as an interim low which did not affect the overall favourable growth perspectives for LED revenues and the gen-

---

57 Prices of LED chips in 2011 dropped by between 35 and 45 percent and those of LED packages by 30–35 percent (Bhandakar 2012). The expectation for a regular annual price decrease due to productivity and lighting efficiency gains was 20–30 percent (HSBC 2011, 30)

58 As a reaction to the depressing effects of overinvestment on growth in 2011 and 2012 McKinsey&Company published an update of its 2011 report only one year later which "puts additional emphasis on the increasing volatility of the macroeconomic environment and the accelerated price erosion of LED components" (McKinsey 2012a, 4). The report contains a slightly lower growth projection for the general lighting industry (a CAGR of 5 percent instead of 6 percent in 2011–2016) and the LED lighting industry (CAGR of 33 percent instead of 34 percent 2011–2016). Yet, these revised forecast does not alter the expectation of a very fast expansion of global LED markets (cf. McKinsey 2011a, 21; 2012a, 21).

eral proliferation of LED technologies (cf. McKinsey 2012a, 7–8). The pronounced overcapacities in the field of LED chips were expected to be reduced until late 2014 or early 2015 and a further proliferation of LED lighting in various product categories which will provide opportunities for high growth was expected for the coming years (Bhandakar 2012, McKinsey 2012a, 23–26).

But although the general growth projections remained positive, many individual LED companies were struggling to maintain positive growth figures in a market that has become more competitive. A senior analyst even stated at a major industry event that there had been "a bloodbath in the last few years in the LED industry" (quoted Wright 2013). The potential benefits for venturing on the path of LED technology remain huge, but revenues are slimmer than expected and the gains harder to be harvested. Overinvestment is therefore expected to drive further commoditisation of the industry towards a mass manufacturing business with slimmer returns on investment.

### 6.1.3 Transformation of light source manufacturing towards a subsector of the electronics industry

The replacement of conventional lighting technologies, including most energy saving halogen or fluorescent lighting techniques currently used, also results in the establishment of a new supply chain alongside the conventional one. Established lighting companies like Philips or Osram (formerly owned by Siemens, but spun-off in July 2013) do play a prominent, and pioneering, role in the emerging LED subsector due to their large resources and profound know-how in microelectronics and optics which can be applied for LED lighting applications. Unlike the third major light source manufacturer of the present, General Electric (GE)[59], these companies also invested early in the development of independent LED technologies. However, most of their present production sites used for light source production will prospectively be dismantled (or converted) in the future as this technology—and prospectively also most currently offered

---

[59] GE has also placed investments in the LED industry in the past, most recently through the acquisition of a US-based LED fixtures producer (LEDsMagazine 27.11.12). However, the corporation's LED business lags behind that of the industry leaders significantly.

energy saving alternatives[60]—becomes increasingly obsolete. Other than these technologies, LED production requires specialised factories that employ techniques of wafer processing and chip packaging similar to those of the consumer electronics industry. Because of this technological rupture, ample opportunities for new entrants to the lighting industry, companies that are specialised in the new production technologies of the LED value chain, have arisen and continue to do so.

The general lighting supply chain today consists of the production of light sources (like conventional light bulbs), ballasts and drivers (that usually convert the voltage of the power supply to one suited to the light sources), fixtures (for desk lamps, down lights, street lamps and others—not including the light source) and control gears (switches, dimmers, etc.). All these components are assembled to luminaires that are ready to use for end consumers (cf. figure 6.3).

---

60 McKinsey&Company regard "green traditional" light sources (i.e. those non-LED light sources that consume a share of not more than 20 percent of incandescent lighting's energy consumption) as a "bridge technology before full penetration of LED lighting. Hence, its market share is expected to dwindle from over 50 percent in 2011 to little more than 25 percent in 2020. As the light source market will grow significantly during this period, the contraction is not as pronounced in absolute numbers. The market volume is expected to shrink from EUR 39 billion in 2011 to EUR 27 billion in 2020 (2012a, 21–22).

*Figure 6.3: Components of the lighting supply chain*

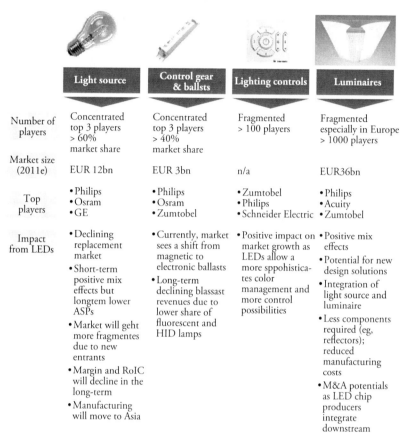

| | Light source | Control gear & ballsts | Lighting controls | Luminaires |
|---|---|---|---|---|
| Number of players | Concentrated top 3 players > 60% market share | Concentrated top 3 players > 40% market share | Fragmented > 100 players | Fragmented especially in Europe > 1000 players |
| Market size (2011e) | EUR 12bn | EUR 3bn | n/a | EUR36bn |
| Top players | • Philips<br>• Osram<br>• GE | • Philips<br>• Osram<br>• Zumtobel | • Zumtobel<br>• Philips<br>• Schneider Electric | • Philips<br>• Acuity<br>• Zumtobel |
| Impact from LEDs | • Declining replacement market<br>• Short-term positive mix effects but longtem lower ASPs<br>• Market will geht more fragmentes due to new entrants<br>• Margin and RoIC will decline in the long-term<br>• Manufacturing will move to Asia | • Currently, market sees a shift from magnetic to electronic ballasts<br>• Long-term declining blassast revenues due to lower share of fluorescent and HID lamps | • Positive impact on market growth as LEDs allow a more sppohisticates color management and more control possibilities | • Positive mix effects<br>• Potential for new design solutions<br>• Integration of light source and luminaire<br>• Less components required (eg, reflectors); reduced manufacturing costs<br>• M&A potentials as LED chip producers integrate downstream |

Source: HSBC 2011.

At first glance, the basic structure of this supply chain will not be altered by the proliferation of LED lighting. After all, change in the lighting industry is rooted merely in a different light source technology. But this technological transformation of the key component will also affect all other stages of the supply chain. The emergence of LED lighting demands new technological solutions and creates new opportunities in each business segment. For instance, LED technology will not only be applied in forms of "retrofit" light sources that fit conventional fixtures (as is the case with LED light bulbs designed to replace incandescent light bulbs), but will also create a whole new range of applications and luminaire types because of the great versatility and small size of LED light sources.

The changes do not only affect the design of every single component within each market segment, but also will lead to changes in product architectures. For instance, the importance of electronic controls and drivers prospectively will rise, but such components, unlike in the conventional lighting value chain, are now often directly integrated into LED modules (either by integrating IC chips into packaged LEDs or through integrated solutions on wafer-level, cf. HSBC 2011, 32; Mc Kinsey 2011, 45f). Such changes demonstrate that LED technology is bound to thoroughly change norms of technology and production throughout the industry, including the hierarchies that reigned the traditional industry. The emerging norms in the LED sector reflect the struggles of LED companies for market domination. The outcome of these struggles conditions the growth prospects for certain market players against others and largely determines the scope of a successful upgrading of companies that challenge the positions of market leaders.

*Figure 6.4: Vertical segmentation of the LED value chain*

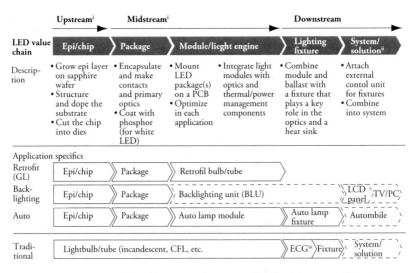

i   Vertical categories as commonly used by Chinese industry experts. Other analyses categorise LED packaging as part of upstream production, cf. McKinsey 2012a:, 51.
ii  More sophisticated external control systems that can be attached to the basic control functions of fixtures.
iii ECG = "electronic control gear".

Source: McKinsey 2012a, adapted by author.

With regard to the current supply chain structure of the LED industry, most industry analysts and practitioners distinguish between *upstream, midstream* and *downstream* production, a terminology which runs parallel to the categorisation according to product types (cf. figure 6.4). Confusingly, there is a different understanding of the respective categories by international analysts as compared to experts in China (cf. McKinsey 2012a, 51; Li and Qiu 2010). Though less rigid in its definition, I will stick to the terminology used by Chinese practitioners in the course of this analysis because the empirical data relates to these. According to the Chinese understanding, the LED industry is subdivided into the following segments:

– *Upstream* production refers to the manufacturing of LED chips from LED wafers. These wafers (also called "epitaxial wafers" with reference to the chemical coating process involved) are produced in a similar way as regular semiconductor wafers, but under application of different chemical substances, mostly gallium, an element from the "poor metal" category. Wafers are coated by various layers of semiconductor material employing so-called MOCVD (metalorganic chemical vapour deposition) reactors[61] and then cut into chips (also called "dies"). The processes of wafer production and dicing of chips is called front-end production. In LED back-end production, the chips are provided with primary optical conditioning and heat control. When wired, the final product already has the capacity to disseminate light, even though it usually cannot yet be integrated into electronic devices or luminaires.
– The finalisation of the LED light source is done in LED *midstream* production which mainly consists of the process of encapsulation, also referred to as packaging. Encapsulation factories attach a substrate (mainly for thermal management), wire the chips, and provide further optical conditioning, among other by attaching a lens. Often, midstream facilities also produce LED modules which are integrated multi-chip units with a multiple lighting output. LED midstream factories mostly supply to LED application, or *downstream,* producers. In general, midstream

---

61 The coating of LED wafers, the process of "epitaxy", i.e. the attachment of crystalline layers to a substrate, is a high-precision process that affords sophisticated and expensive machinery as well as highly skilled personnel. The bulk of MOCVD reactors is produced by two companies only, Aixtron from Germany and Veeco from the US. There has been a high volatility of demand resulting in serious bottlenecks and, currently, large overcapacities, which reflects the uneven growth rhythms in the LED industry as a whole.

production delivers ready-made light sources that can be immediately integrated into luminaires or built into other electronic devices.

–  *Downstream* production refers to the manufacturing process of LED applications, mainly in the form of luminaires in the field of general lighting or backlighting modules in the consumer electronics segment.[62] In the former, LED downstream factories combine fixtures of various shapes with the packaged LEDs and, in most cases, with a ballast. They also develop specific product designs, e.g. by creating blueprints for a beneficial placing of packaged LEDs to achieve certain lighting effects of luminaires. Apart from selling individual devices like desk lamps, down lights, street lamps, flash lights, etc., downstream companies can also offer complete lighting installations that include various light sources and external light controls. The construction industry is an important driver for the luminaire market because of its high demand for new installations. In the case of LED backlight production, downstream producers do not produce luminaires, but attach LED packages directly on PCBs which are then sold as components to electronics companies, e.g. flat TV panel manufacturers.

As will be elaborated in the next section, the theoretical distinction of industry segments does not necessarily correspond to an actual segmentation of enterprises in the supply chain. Modularised production models in which the different functions of the production chain are performed by different enterprises are widespread in the industry, but some of the largest companies, such as Philips, Osram, Samsung and LG, are vertically integrated enterprises that combine all of the production steps from upstream to downstream production within the same enterprise. Technological innovation also fosters the development of processes that cut across the established divisions, e.g. between upstream and midstream production (cf. section 6.1.4.4).

In typical LED applications, LED packages (i.e. the actual lighting units) in 2012 constituted between 30 percent and 60 percent of manufacturing costs. These shares vary according to different product types. It is

---

62 One special case in the general lighting field is the production of retrofit LED bulbs that can replace standard incandescent light bulbs. These are produced by downstream producers, but the product is not a luminaire because it does not contain a fixture. LED light bulbs are one important channel for the establishment of LED lighting products on mass consumer markets. However, they prospectively will constitute a transitional technology until the purchase of specific LED luminaires becomes more common.

highest in LED retrofit light bulbs and significantly lower in outdoor lamps which require more voluminous mechanical installations and thermal management (DOE 2012c, 24–25). In the manufacturing of LED light source, the packaging process constitutes the most cost-intensive component as figure 6.5 demonstrates based on the example of a typical 60 Watt LED retrofit light bulb.

*Figure 6.5: Relative manufacturing costs of a 60 Watt LED retrofit light bulb*

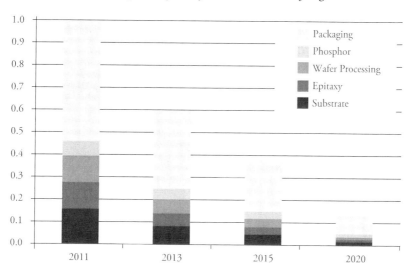

Source: DOE 2012c, adapted by author.

This figure also demonstrates that total costs of LED products will prospectively diminish until an average LED application in 2015 will only cost one fifth in comparison to its price in 2010. The greatest reduction will be achieved in the production of packaged LEDs. Manufacturing in these segments (but also in final assembly) therefore largely is turning into a cost cutting game in which manufacturers strive to raise yields. The quest for competitive advantages through higher lighting efficiency of LED packages encounters limitations, as one industry expert explains:

"Improvements in device efficacy [lighting efficiency of LED wafers, F.B.] have been driving big improvements in lumens per dollar, but that's getting close to the theoretical maximum—there's no room to double it again, but costs still need to come down much more than that. So that means it's now all about manufacturing efficiency" (Bryan Bolt, Cascade Microtech's director of technology development and systems, quoted in SEMI 05.11.2012).

Higher manufacturing efficiency in the field of LED packages can be achieved through a variety of measures including "higher quality and lower cost raw materials, improved epitaxial growth equipment and processes, optimized wafer processing equipment, and more flexible packaging methods and equipment" (DOE 2012c, 34). One important dimension to all these efforts is the automation of processes which can be achieved by adapting methods from the more mature subsectors of the electronics industry:

"Since this new lighting technology is based on semiconductor technology and manufacturing processes, the final luminaire products may be able to take advantage of automation technologies developed for the manufacturing and assembly of consumer electronics products. Automation could reduce the labor cost for the full luminaire and for the sub-components of the luminaire" (ibid, 34).

Current developments in the LED industry are therefore characterised by an increase in capital intensity, particularly in the upper segments of the industry chain as well as a tendency towards automation. But high pressure for cutting production costs is a general phenomenon across the industry that also affects companies in the downstream segments. As the case studies presented in section 6.3 demonstrate, these companies often have fewer possibilities for improving yields through automation. It therefore can be assumed that cost-driven competition negatively affects workers in labour-intensive production systems, e.g. in the field of LED application production.

### 6.1.4 Disruptions of the supply chain of the lighting industry

The rise of LED technology implies a major transformation of the production process in the lighting industry. It "will put increasing stress on the mature lighting value chain and existing business models", as it is put in one recent industry report (HSBC 2011, 4). These changes affect an industry that—at least in the field of incandescent lighting—was considered to be mature, with a slow pace of technological development. The light source market currently is highly concentrated with three companies—Philips, Osram and General Electric—controlling 60–70 percent of market volumes (JP Morgan 2010, 14). The advent of LED now leads to several changes with regard to production networks and business models which will be discussed subsequently.

*6.1.4.1 Increased competition and entry of new players*

LED production affords sophisticated knowledge in the field of semiconductor technologies, especially since there is a permanent race for higher lighting efficiency and production yields coupled with short product cycles. The traditional lighting giants Philips and Osram first emerged as major players in the LED industry because these companies had invested early in technology development and had sufficient funds to do so. They hold a large share of intellectual property rights for LED technology. For example, Philips claims to hold 70 percent of all patents on LED applications and Osram possesses the most important patents on high-energy white LEDs that are used in many advanced applications in general lighting (NSR 2010, 13). However, new specialised LED companies have gained substantial market shares especially in the lucrative field of LED chip production. The most successful newcomers in the LED sector were the current market leader Nichia as well as Toyoda-Gosei from Japan and the US-based company Cree. Together with Philips and Osram, these companies until recently dominated the upstream market. Market control of these companies is based on a delicate system of cross-licensing between LED upstream producers which each hold patents for different key technologies (e.g. Nichia for blue light through GaN LEDs, Osram for specific coatings that transform blue into white lights, etc., NSR 2010, 13). Regardless of these assets of the market leaders, opportunities for new market entrants regularly open up because international product standards are still not fixed and technology norms are fluid (JP Morgan 2010, 5). The most prominent recent example for success of LED "latecomers" is the heavy investment of Korean consumer electronics companies—mainly Samsung and LG. These companies venture on the advantage of controlling large market shares in LCD TV sales and other LED powered applications in the field of consumer electronics, which allows for a tight integration of applications and custom-made LED chips. Samsung gained access to LED technology by licensing agreements with the biggest five enterprises in LED upstream production (McKinsey 2011a, 22). In 2012 it used aggressive pricing strategies, enabled by the company's huge financial assets, to launch the first LED retrofit light bulb sold at a fairly competitive price in relation to conventional lighting products (LEDinside 15.12.2011). Other market entrants operate with fewer resources and focus on technological excellence in a specific product category. Taiwanese companies like the LED chip producer Epistar have taken advantage of the profound knowledge of the region's semiconductor producers to gain market shares. In China, there is also a myriad of SMEs that profited from the massive political support of the government for the industry. In particular, there is a growing number of LED chip producers as a result of high subsidies under the framework of the 12th FYP which lists self-sufficiency in the field of chip production as one of the primary aims of sector development (cf. section 6.2.4).

*Table 6.1: Top ten LED manufacturers 2010–12*

| Position in 2012 (2010) | Company | Country of origin | Industry segment | Revenues in million USD 2012 (E) | 2011 | 2010 |
|---|---|---|---|---|---|---|
| 1 (1) | Nichia | Japan | Midstream | 3,208 | 2,605 | 2,246 |
| 2 (2) | Samsung LED | Korea | Up/mid-stream | 1,262 | 1,148 | 1,140 |
| 3 (4) | Cree | US | Up/mid/downstream | 1,138 | 988 | 818 |
| 4 (5) | LG Innotek | Korea | Up/mid-stream | 828 | 818 | 738 |
| 5 (3) | Osram Opto | Germany | Up/mid/downstream | 808 | 780 | 822 |
| 6 (6) | Seoul Semicond. | Korea | Up/mid-stream | 795 | 678 | 726 |
| 7 (n.s.) | Lite-On optoelectronics | Taiwan | Mid/downstream | 655 | 536 | 514 |
| 8 (10) | Everlight Electronics | Taiwan | Midstream | 630 | 633 | 553 |
| 9 (n.s.) | Epistar | Taiwan | Upstream | 621 | 601 | 626 |
| 10 (9) | Toyoda-Gosei | Japan | Upstream | 600 | 395 | 438 |

Source: CS 2012, Research in China 2011.

Due to these developments, the LED industry, and the lighting industry in general, is becoming much more fragmented and there is continuous reshuffling. For instance, the LED division of Philips, one of the market leaders in the general lighting industry, for the first time in years was not among the ten largest LED sellers in 2012. Yet, there are also strong tendencies for a renewed concentration of units. The ten largest LED producers controlled 68 percent of sales in 2011 and among these the biggest three companies stood out in particular (cf. table 6.1). However, capital concentration is frequently undermined by technological ruptures that create opportunities for companies venturing on new technological paths as for instance the performance of Taiwanese upstream and downstream producers proves (ibid). By and large, market success in this fast-moving industry primarily depend on IP rights, R&D capacities, the ability to ramp up production capacities quickly in order to introduce new models, and continuous productivity gains in manufacturing (McKinsey 2011b; HSBC 2011, 33).

### 6.1.4.2 LED manufacturers target the general lighting market

Initially, the LED industry took off by supplying backlight modules for consumer electronics devices on a mass scale. But growth in this segment is flattening out while the industry is about to enter its so-called "third growth cycle" in the field of general lighting.[63] The general lighting market is huge, and the LED penetration rate is expected to skyrocket during the next five years. Consequently, the general lighting market is expected to dominate sales of packaged LEDs in the future (cf. Yole 2012; McKinsey 2012a, 8, 21). Most established manufacturers now react to this tendency by reorienting their business focus from backlighting towards the general lighting market. As one analysis points out,

"[m]ost upstream companies are now aiming to capture the general lighting opportunity as LED upstream business in general lighting is expected to be significant. […] [O]nce the LED package market in LCD TV backlighting stagnates, epi/chip/package production capacity will shift to general lighting" (McKinsey 2011a, 22).[64]

---

63 The first growth cycle was launched by LEDs for small display backlighting, and the second by LEDs for large display backlighting (Yole 2010). As noted above, the expression "general lighting" refers to the categories of residential, office, shop, hospitality, industrial and outdoor lighting.

64 In this case, the category "upstream" refers to both producers of chips and packaged LEDs. See the clarification about differing terminologies in section 6.1.3. The term "epi" refers to the production of epitaxial wafers.

Correspondingly, there is a large number of new entrants to the lighting application market. These are either manufacturers from the conventional lighting industry that settle for LED products, or companies that are new to the lighting industry.

Technologically, the focus on the LED general lighting segment requires the development of high-power LEDs with improved lighting properties as well as advanced techniques for heat control and optics. Companies that are specialised in LED backlighting face multiple challenges in the transition toward general lighting. Upstream and midstream companies in turn, need to provide products with higher lighting efficiency and/or high-power modules consisting of various chips. Companies across the value chain also need to either accumulate a new customer base of downstream luminaire companies and to engage in some technological cooperation with them[65], or to enter luminaire production themselves. If a company chooses the latter path, this mostly implies a transformation of the production model from OEM or ODM towards own brand manufacturing which allows producers to sell their lighting products directly to end consumers. This necessitates functional upgrading not only in the field of marketing, but also with regard to a broader manufacturing profile: OBM production of light sources and fixtures requires additional knowledge of optics and materials, access to and knowledge about consumer markets as well as independent design capabilities for fixtures and lamps.

### 6.1.4.3 A shift from light source towards luminaire production

Against the background of the shift from backlighting towards general lighting, the LED industry is currently experiencing a growing importance of luminaire (i.e. downstream) production in relation to light source production (upstream and midstream). These processes are interconnected, since they both reflect the growing importance of the general lighting market. Yet, they are not identical. While the growing weight of general lighting in relation to backlighting amounts to a lateral movement of companies towards another segment of applications, the growing importance of luminaire manufactur-

---

65 Due to a lack of standardisation, relations between suppliers and their customers often cannot be confined to arms-length market relations, but must involve a degree of cooperation in order to adapt supply products to the specifications of LED light sources or vice versa (cf. McKinsey 2012a, 32–33).

ing in comparison to light source manufacturing concerns a vertical relationship: the downstream segment is gaining in importance quantitatively in relation to upstream and midstream production.

This vertical shift is rooted in the longevity of LEDs. As mentioned before, the replacement market for light sources will shrink considerably with the introduction of long-lasting LEDs and thus will encounter limits once the change from conventional lighting to LED technologies advances. Relevant industry analysts agree upon the forecast that the market for LED products consequently will focus more and more on the direct sale of complete luminaires instead of light sources (HSBC 2011, 32–33; JPMorgan 2010, 15). This has a severe impact on the production models of the industry. As one analysis spells out:

"This industry shift from the light source replacement business towards new lighting fixture installation is set to transform the industry supply chain going forward. The current lightbulb-centric supply chain—where a few global light source manufacturers supply their products to local markets—is at least temporarily losing its hold, with manufacturing sites becoming more fragmented. […] [T]his structural shift in the supply chain has radical implications for all industry players and will require the development of entirely new business strategies" (McKinsey 2011a, 38–39).

Due to these changing rules of the game, industry observers expect a reconfiguration of the current pattern of value distribution in the LED industry. While currently LED chip production is considered to be the most lucrative field of LED production (because of its high share of value added and extra-profits through royalties gained by holding patents in key technologies), industry experts expect a high level of commoditisation and standardisation in the upstream industry which may depress margins in the long term. In the meantime, luminaire production, currently an industry with comparatively low returns, is expected to gain in attractiveness and achieve higher value added by producing more comprehensive and diverse lighting solutions that integrate digital mechanisms for lighting control (Yole 2012; HSBC 2011, 6).

These shifts of power relations within the industry are reflected in quarrels about product standards which still have only been rudimentary developed with view to the main properties of light sources and fixtures. The outcome also affects questions of value distribution between light source and fixtures producers.[66] There is a high level of activity to define LED product standards

---

66 As one account explains, "[t]he degree of standardization will likely vary depending on the

in international consortia. On an international level, this is organised under the framework of the Zhaga consortium in which currently 281 companies from all major manufacturing regions participate.[67] These efforts are complemented by organisations on the national level like the US Department of Energy and the Chinese Ministry of Industry and Information Technology (MIIT) (cf. Chen 2012).

Within the Zhaga consortium, development of standards focuses on specifications for LED light engines.[68] Standardised light engines would facilitate coordination between light source and luminaire producers. Currently, the industry depends on "vertical play and collaboration between light source and luminaire players" in order to adjust products to each other (McKinsey 2012a, 33). Standardised light engines would make manufacturers more independent from each other just as is the case in the conventional light bulb system in which fixtures match standardised light source sockets, thus making cooperation between upstream and downstream companies unnecessary. The definition of standards for LED light engines therefore could drive down transaction costs for manufacturers and facilitate mass production:

"Standardization [...] allows light engine manufacturers to scale their production lines, increase volume output, and focus research on defined sets of parameters. Standardization therefore gives access to economies of scale and is likely to transform the lion's share of the light engine business into a commodity industry—similar to most other electronics component industries" (McKinsey 2012a, 33).

---

application. One model is that light engines are standardized products, where fixture designs are adjusted to the commonly available LED light engines, and end users can replace LED light engines themselves. The alternative is that light engines will be individually customized to fit lighting fixture designs provided by the fixture manufacturers. In this scenario, the light engine business would be similar to today's consumer electronics business: light engine makers would need to align to fixture manufacturers' design activities" (McKinsey 2011a, 23). The way in which standards are defined therefore decides about where higher value added design functions will be allocated in the supply chain.

67 See the list of participants at http://www.zhagastandard.org/about-us/our-members/. According to the Zhaga website, "[t]he word Zhaga has no intended meaning. It is a waterfall in Sichuan" (Zhaga Website).

68 "Zhaga uses the term 'LED light engine' to describe the combination of one electronic control gear (ECG) and one or more LED modules [...]. An LED module is a unit supplied as a light source. In addition to one or more LEDs it may contain further components, e.g. optical, mechanical, electrical, and electronic components, but excluding the control gear" (Zhaga Website).

However, the development of standards faces several obstacles. This not only has to do with the fast pace of technological development which oftentimes outpaces the development of standards (ID 10.12.2010), but also with the competition between different production models. According to McKinsey&Company, "finding a common denominator that satisfies every player is a challenge" (2012a, 33). Nevertheless, there is some progress in standardisation. Meanwhile, seven "books" of standards for different LED applications such as certain down light or streetlight engines have been compiled which cover "interface specifications concerning the physical dimensions, as well as the photometric, electrical and thermal behavior, of LED light engines" (Zhaga Website). Products with Zhaga certificates are already available on commercial markets.

But given the great versatility of LED technologies it is likely that large segments of the market will remain poorly standardised. What is more, market competition can also lead challengers to offer innovative product designs that cut across existing standards. There is also the possibility of a regional diversification of standards. Recently, the development of standards has also led to conflicts between producers in different regions. It is estimated that higher technical standards for LED applications set by the EU, the US, Chile and Uganda will cost exporters in Guangdong more than RMB 4 billion, because costs for manufacturers will rise by more than 20 percent if they are to meet these requirements (China Daily 10.07.2012).

For these reasons it is rather unlikely, that there will be agreement on rigid standards for light sources like they emerged in the incandescent supply chain. McKinsey&Company expects a divided industry landscape in this respect: "A scale-driven mass market light engine business—especially for low- to medium-end market light engines—will require full standardization. However, high-end light engines will allow for customization in terms of design, features, and performance" (2012a, 33).

### 6.1.4.4 Vertical integration of light source and luminaire production

LED companies across the value chain are responding to the ongoing shifts in industry development in different ways. One major strategy in reaction to the growing importance of the luminaire market is a trend towards vertical integration of light source and luminaire production:

"[A]s value is moving to the top of the value chain (module and luminaire levels), several players that were originally involved only at LED device levels [i.e. LED chips and packages, F.B.] will develop strategies of vertical integration in order to capture more value. But accessing distribution channels represents a big challenge for those players who develop new approaches to sell their lighting products (e-commerce, new distributors, …). The rise of LED lighting will therefore depend on the right merger of the emerging LED industry with the traditional lighting industry" (Yole 2012).

In the conventional lighting value chain based on incandescent lighting and its recent energy saving successors that are designed according to the same product architectures, the light source and luminaire markets are mostly supplied by different companies. Although the vertically integrated giants GE, Philips and Osram also offer luminaires for end consumers, they do not control this market in the same way they control the light source market. A huge share of luminaires is rather sold by specialised companies such as the Austrian company Zumtobel or the US-based manufacturer Acuity. High entry barriers to regional markets that exist because of differing technological specifications as well as the need for close interaction between application designers (which also can include companies of the construction industry) and luminaire manufacturers contribute to the high fragmentation of the luminaire market on a global scale (JPMorgan 2010, 15; McKinsey 2011a, 23). For the time being, local markets are mostly served by enterprises from the respective regions—although these may outsource important parts of production to other parts of the world, above all China. This has resulted in the emergence of a relatively segmented world market with diverse properties. In the USA there is an oligopolistic market virtually controlled by four companies, whereas over 1,000 luminaire companies exist in Europe, and a similar diverse situation is true for Asia (NSR 2010, 14; HSBC 2011, 6).

The growing importance of the luminaire market relative to the light source market now creates incentives for LED producers to move downstream which will create increased competition in this field. HSBC expects "further downstream integration by non-integrated LED chip producers to increase their value added, combined with a likely increase in M&A activity" (2011, 33). Similarly, there is a trend of "well-capitalised players from the electronics industry such as Samsung Electronics or LG Electronics" moving from LED chip and module production towards the field of general lighting applications by which these companies can gain from "existing distribution channels and in-house production know-how from the LED TV business" (ibid, 4f). While there is a clear tendency of upstream producers moving downwards, the opposite phenomenon also exists. Luminaire companies that still suffer from low margins because they do not produce the core components of their products may engage in "backward integration" by entering encapsulation or LED chip production (ibid, 4). One example for this trend is the investment in upstream production by PACKAGESTAR, a large Chinese midstream company covered in the empirical investigation (cf. section 6.3).

On a practical level, companies can realise strategies for vertical integration in various ways. As illustrated by the case studies below, one possibility that is pursued by a great number of Chinese midstream manufacturers is to expand existing OEM production divisions with supplementary production lines for the production of LED luminaires. For instance, many Chinese LED midstream companies added street lights to their product portfolio, after the government launched a large investment programme for such products in 2010. Mergers and acquisitions between specialised upstream companies and luminaire producers constitute a second option for vertical integration. Recent examples of this trend include the acquisition of the downstream producers Siteco and Traxon by Osram and of Ruud lighting by Cree, both of which occurred in 2011.[69] China is seeing a trend for deeper "cross strait cooperation" with Taiwanese companies which was symbolised by the announcement of a merger between China's largest LED chip manufacturer San'an and Taiwan's second largest LED chip producer Formosa Epitaxy in November 2012 (LED inside 09.01.2013).

Lighting companies that are already vertically integrated, like Philips-Lumileds and Osram Opto, are well-equipped to benefit from advantages through vertical integration. In particular, they can combine the strengths of their upstream segments with their sales channels from the conventional lighting industry. Yet, this only partially accounts for the vertically integrated Korean multinationals Samsung and LG, which so far have barely been active in the field of general lighting. They face similar challenges like upstream and midstream lighting companies entering the downstream segment of the lighting industry and first of all need to acquire resources and knowledge in this field. However, Samsung and LG are in a favourable position to gain

---

69 The latter is only the youngest of a series of acquisitions by Cree. The company used to be an exclusive producer of LED chips and then gradually "climbed the value chain" in order to sell lighting components to end consumers (cf. Gereffi et al 2011, 7–8).

market shares due to their large capital resources and professional sales channels for other electronics products.

One particular option for vertical integration arises out of new product architectures resulting from technological breakthroughs. These allow companies to cut across the established production segments by merging some of their respective functions. A prominent and increasingly implemented example is the technique of "wafer-level packaging", a fusion of upstream and midstream production, in which LEDs are packaged while still being attached to the wafer substrate (see the example of CHIPSTAR in section 6.3). Another example are chip-on-board (COB) architectures in which chips are directly mounted on PCBs instead of being packaged individually. This technique simplifies design and manufacturing and can help to enrich COB modules with multiple functions, e.g. for lighting control. Such modules, produced by midstream packaging companies, do not make the task of LED downstream companies obsolete, but can simplify the final step of luminaire production because some functions can already be integrated in the modules (McKinsey 2011a, 59). Such innovative production techniques can be interpreted as a technological path of integration of upstream, midstream and downstream manufacturing. They can help producers to obtain a higher share of value added and often enable a streamlining of production which results in higher yields. If such practices become hegemonic they could alter the balance of forces in the industry decisively. Manufacturers of the midstream segment, for instance, could counter the loss of weight of light source production vis-à-vis luminaire manufacturers by integrating as many properties as possible into their products.

Variants of vertical integration clearly are one major trend in business strategies of companies across the value chain. But they are not the only option. Under the condition of a rapidly developing market with multiple applications, some of which are only in the process of being created, high revenues can also be gained by a narrow specialisation in one specific segment. This is exemplified by ARCHIAPP, a specialised company for entertainment and architectural lighting (cf. section 6.3). This company has experienced consistent growth by providing high-end production in a specialised, but rapidly growing market segment, without any ambitions to enter the highly competitive fields of upstream or midstream production.

*6.1.4.5 The countertendency of vertical disintegration: LED manufacturing as an EMS business*

The recent aspirations for vertical integration are rooted in the following structural conditions of the LED industry:

– High potential returns in the fast moving LED chip industry coupled with rapidly expanding demand
– Growing relevance of the luminaire market in comparison to the light source market, the latter of which will lose in quantitative weight in the long term
– Relatively low entry barriers in the luminaire market because of the highly fragmented, little standardised and quickly growing market, which leaves ample space for newcomers
– A certain need for cooperation between light source and luminaire manufacturers due to the lack of standardisation and benefits of customised products

Whereas vertical integration currently is the dominant trend by which LED companies react to these circumstances, this will prospectively be coupled with the opposite tendency soon. It is expected that major LED light source producers of the present may reduce their efforts in the upstream and midstream industry as processes and technologies become more mature. For instance, it is widely believed that the largest lighting company of the present will exit light source manufacturing altogether. One analysis concludes: "We believe that Philips has no desire to enter a scale-driven low return battle with Asian competitors in manufacturing after the experiences it has had over the past 20 years in other businesses" (JP Morgan 2010, 6).[70]

The reason for the projected bifurcation of the industry is an approximation of LED light source manufacturing to production norms that are typical for the wider electronics industry. HSBC expects the LED upstream industry to develop towards a "pure commodity business [...] dominated by Asian players and foundry-type business models" (2011: 33; cf. also McK-

---

70 This forecast is made despite the fact that Philips and Osram are currently expanding their capacities in the field of LED chip and module production (cf. LEDinside 07.11.12). Nevertheless, analysts also speculate about the exit of Osram from LED production in the long term (cf. JP Morgan 2010, 1).

insey 2012a: 33).[71] Similarly, the development of LED module assembly is expected to "become an EMS business" (JP Morgan: 1).[72] The quest for lowering LED prices, which is a precondition for the future proliferation of the technology, fosters the adoption of production models that are known from the more mature segments of the electronics industry. In fact, McKinsey recommends an adoption of such models including higher levels of automation, large-scale factories and lean production techniques in order to resolve the problem of the sales prices of LEDs, which are perceived to be still too high (McKinsey 2011b). Under such circumstances the drop in average sales prices for LEDs is expected to aggravate problems for vertically integrated companies:

"We believe Philips will find it difficult to pass price pressure up the supply chain as it has its own supply chain in this business [...]. We argue that, while owning an LED-component maker clearly brings some advantages, it also has the disadvantage that one of the levers available to management in an environment of price erosion, that of "supply chain management" (i.e. pushing the price pressure up the supply chain) is voluntarily given away. This leaves only the other lever: using R&D and marketing judiciously to generate a pricing premium" (HSBC 2011, 64–65).

The Philips lighting division thus may change its business profile to one that is exclusively oriented towards the sale of luminaires and lighting systems, while it still has the opportunity to participate in revenues achieved in the upstream industry through royalties on its intellectual property (JP Morgan 2010, 1, 6).

The trend towards EMS-like business models is expected to be accompanied by a geographical shift of the upstream industry towards Asia: "LED component manufacturing is set to be dominated by Asian manufacturers and—following trends seen in other industries—is likely to become a low-margin business over the medium term" (NSR 2010, 2). This leaves plenty of opportunities for emerging Chinese manufacturers to conquer market shares in the global industry. At the same time, the cost-driven quest for efficient and flexible manufacturing solutions provides a difficult envi-

---

71 The term "foundry" here refers to the regular semiconductor production models in the electronics industry where knowledge-intensive and highly profitable chip design functions have been separated from pure chip manufacturing in foundries. The latter is a low-margin OEM business based on manufacturing excellence (cf. Pawlicki 2010).

72 "EMS" (electronics manufacturing service) is a general term for supplier relations in which contract manufacturers produce electronics articles for brand companies (Lüthje et al 2013a, 45–51).

ronment for the development of more just patterns of work compared to those that are common in the "commodity business" of electronics contract manufacturing (Lüthje et al 2013a, Pun et al 2012) or at Chinese mass manufacturers of the conventional lighting industry.[73]

## 6.1.5  Conclusion

The application of LED technology in the field of general lighting leads to revolutionary changes in the industry's norms of technology that induce a structural shift on several levels:

1. The rise of a new generation of specialised LED light source manufacturers alongside established multinationals in the lighting industry.
2. A growing relative weight of luminaire production in the long term which in turn provides incentives for strategies of vertical integration sought by LED manufacturers.
3. Commoditisation and standardisation of LED production in the mid term fostering capital concentration and production models borrowed from the wider semiconductor and electronics industry.
4. A growing weight of Asian manufacturers, at least in the field of light source production

These tendencies create favourable conditions for industrial upgrading of the Chinese lighting industry. The global light source industry, which used to be highly monopolised by the three biggest international brands from Germany, the US, and the Netherlands, is in the process of being broken up which opens up growth perspectives for new entrants. This is supported by the growing importance of luminaire production, a regionally and structurally highly fragmented market segment in which specialised newcomers can gain a foothold comparatively easy.

Entry to the LED industry, especially in the lucrative field of upstream production, nevertheless comes at high costs since it requires sophisticated

---

73 Cf. Lüthje et al 2013b, 177–185 for the analysis of the regime of production at a leading Chinese manufacturer in the traditional lighting industry. Migrant workers in final assembly at this company suffer from excessive working hours of 12 hours per day, insufficient OSH protection and low wages with a base wage rate equal, if not below, the local minimum wage of RMB 770 at that time.

technological know-how and research capabilities. The prospects for success in the upstream segments of the industry therefore to a large degree depend on state support and the opportunities offered by local innovation networks. Most importantly, half a dozen of leading international companies control the core intellectual property that is needed to manufacture LED chips. For the time being, entry barriers therefore are much lower in the field of LED applications which has led to a crowding of the market by a large number of SMEs with often low technological capabilities.

Endemic pressures for cost reduction prospectively will drive a standardisation of production methods, and will presumably be accompanied by more mergers and acquisitions leading to bigger units. This in turn may raise entry barriers in the mid-term while a vast number of start-ups will encounter limits for further expansion in this very competitive environment. Trends towards overinvestment and the general volatility of the market add to the rather difficult business outlook for newcomers. The urge to reduce costs, to introduce more standardised methods of production, and to ramp up capacities in order to gain from economies of scale will shape the production models of the industry as it grows more mature. Yet, the lack of industry standards and a time lag between the innovation of technologies and implementation of standards for the time being constitute barriers for the establishment of mass production on an equally standardised level as is the case, for instance, in the consumer electronics industry.

## 6.2 The Chinese LED industry: Meteoric rise with obstacles

China's lighting industry can benefit from the geographical shift of production networks forecasted by industry analysts. In the incandescent lighting industry, the world market has been dominated exclusively by enterprises from Europe and the US. Large shares of their production volume was outsourced to suppliers in China, but Chinese brands didn't play any significant role on international markets. This situation, however, has been changing rapidly due to the rise of new energy saving technologies. Boosted by strong government support, China has already established itself as the global centre of CFL light source manufacturing, supplying about 80 percent of volumes (HSBC 2011, 32). In the course of this process, Chinese brands also succeeded in increasing their market shares in relation to the large three light source makers Philips, GE and Osram (Ton and du Pont 2008, 331f.). This geographical shift towards Asia is reaching a new quality with the proliferation of LED lighting. The US and Europe in 2011 controlled only one fifth of production volumes in the upstream and midstream segment which is clearly dominated by Asian manufacturers. Chinese manufacturers, whose products are generally considered to be technologically inferior, are still dwarfed by their peers in Korea and Japan. But the recent boom in the Chinese upstream industry, facilitated by government plans to gain technological leadership in this segment, is accelerating the rise of the Chinese industry which is about to leapfrog its competitors through large-scale investments in the upstream segment.

As explicated in the previous section, industry experts expect a further shift towards Asia, at least in the field of LED light source production. Several factors contribute to this shift: (1) the size and rapid growth of Asian markets, (2) the relatedness of LED technology and production methods to those of the electronics industry the gravity centre of which has continuously shifted towards Asia during the last decades and (3) already existing large manufacturing bases in the traditional lighting industry which have served as an outsourcing location for Western companies. All of this is creating favourable conditions for the upgrading of the Chinese industry which is proactively supported by the Chinese government. The following section gives an overview of the development and structure of the Chinese general lighting and LED industry and discusses the factors determining its upgrading prospects.

### 6.2.1 Market size and growth prospects of the general lighting industry in China

The increasing weight of Asian manufacturers in the general lighting market (i.e. conventional lighting plus energy-saving alternatives) is intertwined with its growing share in global demand. Currently Asia is absorbing 35 percent of lighting products worldwide, but this share is expected to rise to more than 45 percent until 2020 (McKinsey 2012a, 29). The effects of the global economic crisis have supported this trend and leading international brands have reinforced their efforts to conquer market shares in Asia. For instance, public orders under the framework of the New Lighting Project in China, which particularly focused on the investment of street lights, were a particularly attractive target for international bidders (LEDinside, 10.08.2012).[74] Within the expanding Asian market, the Chinese share is rising remarkably fast. The Chinese lighting market will prospectively conquer a volume of EUR 19 billion, around 23 percent of the global market, by 2020 (cf. figure 6.6). This extraordinary growth potential is rooted in the general social transformation of China. High urbanisation rates foster a thriving construction industry which is an important driver of luminaire demand (McKinsey 2012a, 29).

*Figure 6.6: Regional shares in the global lighting market 2011–2020 (all lighting technologies, EUR billions)*

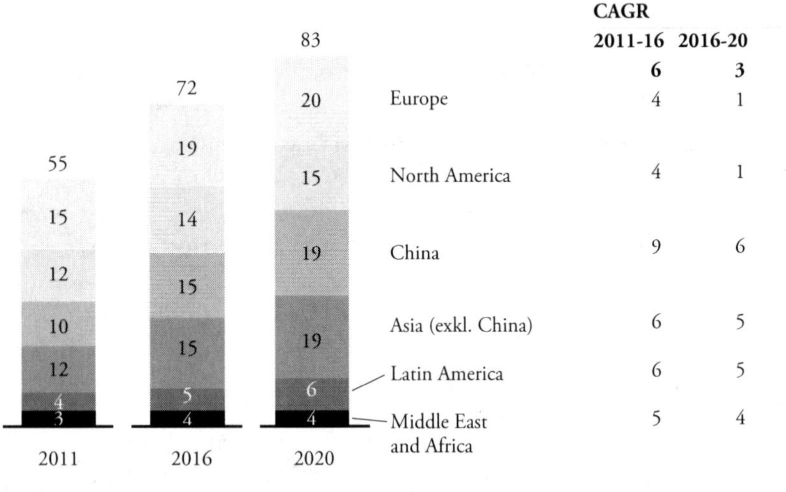
CAGR
2011-16 2016-20
6 3
55
15
12
10
12
4
3
72
19
14
15
15
5
4
83
20
15
19
19
6
4
Europe 4 1
North America 4 1
China 9 6
Asia (exkl. China) 6 5
Latin America 6 5
Middle East and Africa 5 4
2011
2016
2020

Source: McKinsey 2012a, 27.

This sets the stage for a skyrocketing development of the Chinese LED lighting market. It is expected to grow by 43 percent each year between 2011 and 2016 and prospectively will maintain high growth rates of 18 percent on average in the years 2016–20 (McKinsey 2012a, 27). This boom is the result of the combined effects of the replacement of conventional technologies in the

74 This is valid especially for prestigious projects in the field of architectural lighting. LED chips and installations for the Olympics in Beijing, for instance, were supplied by the American supplier Cree, and lighting fixtures on the 600 meter Guangzhou Tower built for the Asian Games in 2010 are equipped with chips by Philips Lumileds (LEDinside, 04.03.2011).

field of general lighting and the general above-average growth performance of the lighting market in China.

### 6.2.2 Structure of the Chinese general lighting industry

The general light source industry (all, technologies, excluding fixtures) in China has experienced rapid growth throughout the last 15 years at an annual rate of over 20 percent as a consequence of which China became the largest production base of lighting products, accounting for 70 percent of the global capacity (LEDinside 14.10.2011). Overall sales volumes of companies located in China grew almost sevenfold from USD 8 billion in 2000 to USD 55.6 billion in 2011. Exports rose even at a slightly faster average pace throughout the same period despite a drop of almost 12 percent in 2009. The export share of the industry amounted to 40 percent in 2000, then reached 48 percent in 2008 and dropped back to currently about 40 percent due to the repercussions of the global economic crisis. Yet, post-crisis recovery growth of exports has been strong—and faster than growth on the domestic market—with 31.2 percent in 2010 and 20.8 percent in 2011 (all figures from Chen 2012, cf. figure 6.7).

*Figure 6.7: Sales of general lighting companies in China (all technologies) and exports (USD billions)*

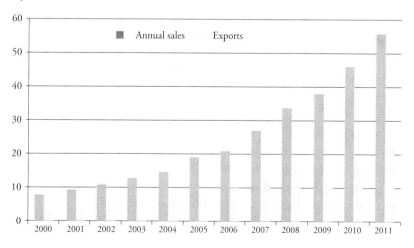

Source: Chen 2012.

These figures reflect the rise of China as a site for OEM production. All leading international lighting brands have established production sites or voluminous subcontracting agreements with Chinese producers. Regarding light sources, China truly has become the "workshop of the world" during the last decade. Fast growth of the energy-saving lighting market in China has been another growth driver. Sales volumes for CFL light sources produced by companies located in China outpaced those for conventional light bulbs in 2011 (Chen 2012). While the sales of the largest Chinese lighting companies still heavily depend on supplier relationships with foreign brands, they are also expanding their sales of OBM products. Some of these companies have also established production segments for LED lighting in recent years. Foshan Zhaoming, one of the largest domestic manufacturers, engages in cooperation with the US chip supplier Bridgelux since 2010, for instance (LEDinside 04.08.2010).

However, a full-scale conversion of production facilities from conventional lighting to LED is not an easy task because of vast technological differences between incandescent (or CFL) and LED light sources. Even in LED downstream production, where companies usually only integrate ready-made lighting modules into fixtures, different capabilities in the fields of heat reduction and optics are needed to arrange light sources in such a way that they create the desired lighting effects. What is more, current marketing strategies require different skills because of the great importance of state demand (realised via public tenders) in comparison to the classic marketing channels in the lighting industry directed at individual or corporate private consumers. Because of these difficulties, the majority of Chinese LED companies today does not originate from the traditional lighting industry. Even in Foshan, a long-established cluster of the lighting industry, only about half of all LED enterprises emerged from the established lighting industry, according to estimates (ID 10.12.2010).

### 6.2.3 Structure of the Chinese LED industry

As is the case for general lighting, production of LED lighting is also largely concentrated in the coastal provinces, especially in Guangdong, Zhejiang, Jiangsu and the Shanghai area. According to government data, the Chinese LED industry in 2011 counted around 3,000 enterprises. Around two thirds of these are active in the field of LED downstream production and often of a small scale. Additionally there are over 600 packaging companies and less than 100 companies that engage in the technologically sophisticated field of LED chip production (quoted in PS Quarterly Report I/2012, 51).[75]

This distribution reflects two characteristic features of the Chinese industry: its vertically disintegrated structure and the dominance of SMEs. Some well-established Chinese enterprises of a larger scale do exist, such as PACK-AGESTAR, a big encapsulation company with almost 2,000 employees in nine factories that is covered in this study. But, unlike the wider electronics industry, the LED industry so far is not organised based on giant contract manufacturers like those in the consumer electronics segment whose workforce often counts tens or hundreds of thousands (cf. Lüthje et al 2013a).

Until recently, the industry also remained quite strictly segmented vertically in companies that deal exclusively with upstream, midstream or downstream production. This contrasts with the production models of large international brands like Philips, Osram and their recently emerged Asian competitors LG and Samsung. Vertical disintegration reflects the history of the Chinese industry which, although some important players have emerged out of former SOEs, did not emerge from large scale investments by consumer electronics or lighting enterprises, but by small ventures that experimented with very specialised technological adaptations for certain products of the value chain. Usually such start-ups lack the resources and the know-how to develop capabilities across the segments of the industry and thus prefer to focus on a distinct technological field or sales model. In particular, technology start-ups, often spin-offs from or collaborators with universities and other state-funded research institutions, lack the market channels for a direct sale of applications to end consumers. In the field of applications, on the contrary, most companies usually are far from being able to build such comprehensive research activities and funds needed for LED midstream and upstream production.

Despite these obstacles, many LED companies are now making efforts towards a vertical expansion of their operations in concordance with global trends in this direction, as is illustrated by the case studies in section 6.3. From the perspective of downstream manufacturers, the motivation for moving upstream is driven by the recent profit squeeze in the very competitive application and encapsulation markets from which they seek to escape

---

75 The research institution Strategies Unlimited estimates the number of LED lighting companies in China to 4,000 (Bhandakar 2012).

through an advance to higher value-added production. Conversely, LED upstream and midstream companies, that suffer from severe price cutting competition in the field of light sources, are tempted to catch their share of the expanding market for luminaires, including state subsidies and tenders for general lighting products (ID 10.11.2011).

With view to the distribution of companies across the LED value chain, the small share of upstream enterprises is evident. This reflects the high dependence of the Chinese industry on foreign core technologies which are secured by intellectual property rights. This was considered to be a serious weakness by industry experts and government representatives alike (ID 05.11.2010; 10.11.2011; cf. section 6.2.4).

The asymmetry between China's attractiveness as a manufacturing site and its comparatively weak capacity for controlling the higher value-added segments of the industry sets the scene for the upgrading efforts of Chinese companies. According to a rough estimate, about 60 percent of global LED products in all application categories are manufactured in China (Bhandakar 2012). But up until recently most of these manufacturers inserted chips into their products that were supplied by foreign brands and mostly manufactured outside China. The quality of Chinese LED chips is generally considered to be lower and many midstream and downstream companies therefore prefer foreign products (ID 08.12.1010). A large share of profits is therefore siphoned off by foreign companies that control the upstream segment of the industry. The manufacturing process of applications often merely amounts for the assembly of components that are bought on the market (apart from chips, this also includes drivers and fixtures). Since downstream production, at least for the time being, is a low-tech and low-margin business, foreign providers of technologically more sophisticated light sources are the main beneficiaries from the Chinese LED boom. A higher level of self-sufficiency in chip production therefore belongs to the key targets of the government's 12th Five-Year Plan for the LED industry.

## 6.2.4 A strategic industry: Government support for the LED sector

Being the world's major production site for lighting products, the Chinese government has given strong support to energy-saving lighting technologies in general and the LED industry in particular during the last decade. In 2004, the Ministry of Science and Technology launched a national Solid

State Lighting (SSL)[76] Programme that included investments of RMB 140 million, primarily destined for funding research institutes and establishing cooperation with over 50 enterprises. This amount was expanded to RMB 350 million with the 11th Five Year Plan launched in 2006 (LEDs Magazine July 2006). In 2009, a large-scale subsidy programme for LED street lighting, labelled the "Ten Cities, Thousand Lights" was implemented which led to the installation of 350,000 street lights until 2010—74 percent of the total global amount. And this investment was only the overture for subsequent mass installations in the years that followed. The programme entailed the so-called energy management contract (EMC) mechanism through which 75 percent of investment costs were provided by cheap bank loans that are to be repaid by subsequent savings in operating costs obtained through energy saving. Guangdong Province, the national centre of LED luminaire manufacturing, spearheaded this programme with the installation of 100,000 LED street-lights in the capital Guangzhou alone (LEDs Magazine November 2011).

The 12th Five-Year Plan, launched in 2012, raises government support for the LED sector to new heights. Among the seven Strategic Emerging Industries listed in the 12th FYP are those categorised as "energy saving and environmental protection" and "new materials". The LED sector is promoted with reference to both categories (Digitimes 01.07.2011). The Five-Year Plan sets the following strategic goals for the Chinese LED industry until 2015:

- A 30 percent penetration rate of LED technologies in the general lighting market (from 7 percent in 2010)
- A sales volume of over RMB 500 billion (from RMB 31 billion in 2011)
- An LED chip self-sufficiency rate of 70 percent
- Establishment of 2–3 large scale LED chip companies
- Establishment of 3–5 leading SSL application companies (Chu 2010).

The main instrument to achieve these goals is an extension of subsidies. The New Lighting Project was expanded from 21 to 50 participating cities in 2012, and the government also financed rebates to consumers who switched from their old TV sets to "environmentally friendly" ones based on LED backlighting (China Daily 24.10.2012). On the local level, the implementation plans for public LED lighting are even more aggressive. In Guangdong,

---

76 Solid State Lighting is a general term for all kinds of semiconductor lighting. This mainly refers to LED lighting but also includes, among other, OLED lighting whose lighting capacity rests on an organic electroluminescent layer.

the provincial government plans to install LEDs in all public constructions until 2015, in the Pearl River Delta even until the end of 2013. These measures are expected to boost the market expansion of local manufacturers, such as the Shenzhen-based company Kingsun that currently delivers about half of the locally installed streetlights. The output target for the provincial industry proclaimed by the provincial government is set at RMB 500 billion and thus even matches the sales target established in the national Five-Year Plan (Digitimes 21.06.2012). Such investment programmes for LED applications are complemented by the roadmap for a phase-out of incandescent lighting that started in October 2012 for 100 watt bulbs and will be extended to all other incandescent products until October of 2016 (LEDinside 10.11.2011).

However, the strategically most important component of the government plans is a major initiative to develop the important segment of LED chip production by a subsidy of RMB 8–10 million for every newly installed MOCVD machine (Cooke 2010)—a measure that led to a surge of orders by Chinese chip manufacturers and created a hot market dynamic in this segment.

### 6.2.5 Overinvestment and consolidation in the Chinese LED industry

*"Currently the industry is a mess. There are strong and weak companies all mixed together. The current situation is as if the water washes the sand away so that gold remains at the end. This is a normal process. Foreign investors are observing this process and waiting".*

Sales manager of a small-scale packaging company (ID 15.11.2011)

Government subsidies in recent years have been vital for strengthening the domestic LED industry. They have contributed to the establishment of fairly sizeable Chinese LED manufacturers and have been relatively successful in reaching the goal of an increasingly competitive domestic upstream market segment. However, in the context of a volatile market development, government subsidies had a pro-cyclical effect that aggravated the tendencies of general market volatility. The LED industry seemed bound to grow fast at the end of the last decade, and even in early 2011 observers still expected "explosive growth" in the near future (LEDinside 04.01.2011). Chinese entrepreneurs accordingly took advantage of the opportunities offered by

the central and local governments which led to a veritable rush in investment. In the city of Foshan, for instance, 80 percent of traditional lighting
manufacturers ventured out for LED production between 2008 and 2012
which resulted in an increase in the number of LED companies to over 300
(Cens.com 23.05.2012). However, as explicated in section 6.1.2, the LED
market did only partially meet such high expectations. Unproductive investment and large overcapacities were the result, especially in those markets
that had particularly been supported by state subsidies—the street light and
LED chip industry. As a consequence, there was a wave of bankruptcies of
hundreds of small-scale LED makers in 2011 which continued in 2012 and
2013. LED chip makers, in general enterprises with high capital resources
and some advanced knowhow, were particularly hard hit. According to a
report by Reuters, about one fifth of Chinese LED producers were expected
to go out of business in 2013 (Reuters 07.02.2013). It is important to note
that these difficulties stemmed from massive overinvestment, not from a
general slump in demand. According to figures provided by a representative
of the Guangdong Solid State Lighting Association, the average growth rate
of LED revenues in China, which amounted to USD 551 billion in 2012,
was 31.2 percent between 2009 and 2012. Yet, growth slowed down from a
growth rate of 45.1 percent in 2010 to 30.0 percent in 2011 and 23.1 percent
in 2012 (cf. table 6.2).

*Table 6.2: Output and growth rates of the Chinese LED lighting industry 2006–2013*

|                          | 2006 | 2007 | 2008 | 2009 | 2010 | 2011 | 2012 | 2013  |
|--------------------------|------|------|------|------|------|------|------|-------|
| Output (billion CNY )    | 35.6 | 48.3 | 62.9 | 82.7 | 120  | 156  | 192  | 257.6 |
| Growth rates (percent)   |      | 35.7 | 30.2 | 31.5 | 45.1 | 30.0 | 23.1 | 34.2  |

Source: China-LED 2014.

The difficulties in the Chinese LED industry provoked criticism of the government's industrial policy. For instance, experts pointed out that the New
Lighting Project lacked sufficiently elaborated quality standards—an endemic problem given the fast development pace of technologies and the relative
time lag of the development of standards. As a representative of the Guangdong Solid State Lighting Association explains:

"There are more than 300,000 LED street lamps in China, but most of them are not mature technologically. Recently, many street light products from Chinese companies have been installed, but none of Osram and other leading multinationals because these companies did not participate in these public tenders. As a result, the available products are usually not the best ones; at least their quality varies to a great extent. As we expect that many of the smaller companies will go bankrupt as soon as bigger competitors enter the market, the government wasted a lot of money by providing artificial demand for companies that are technologically not mature and will die in the near future" (ID 10.11.2011).

As a consequence of this experience, a tender for public lighting was recalled and repeated in 2012 after it had become clear that the original tender would award contracts to companies that were not able to deliver adequate quality. The tender was then deliberately rewritten in a way that benefits bigger market participants and thus would foster further consolidation within the industry (LEDinside 18.06.2012, 24.07.2012).

In the field of LED applications in general, industry observers mock the low technological capabilities of many companies that were drawn into the business because of the shiny growth prospects. In Guangdong, industry experts during interviews frequently made reference to a former shoe manufacturer that entered the industry without sufficient technological capabilities in order to illustrate the problem (ID 10.12.2010; 15.11.2011). Faced with the oversaturation of markets after 2010, many of these companies went bankrupt. In October 2012 it was estimated that alone in the City of Shenzhen, the biggest LED cluster in Guangdong province, 80 LED companies were to close their gates. While mainly small companies were affected, the wave of bankruptcies also took its toll on bigger firms. For instance, the bankruptcy of a well-known local display manufacturer with annual revenues of more than RMB 100 million before the crisis received much attention in the industry (LEDinside 06.07.2012). In the process of the market adjustment the technologically more mature companies were expected to consolidate their leading position (Reuters 27.05.2012). One important question with regard to the current reshuffling of the industry is that about the role of large investors that have sufficient resources to boost the technological maturity and the sophistication of production methods of the industry. However, as one local industry expert explains:

"The big companies are hesitant with their investment. They wait until the market demand catches in. The traditional lighting companies have a lot of capital and human resources. They can keep on with the traditional lighting production and have time to wait until the technologies and markets are mature. New companies, on the contrary, have to move quickly [...]. We wish the big companies would do something to develop the industry, but most of them are just waiting. Companies like Osram and Phillips watch the small companies die and probably will buy the best that are remaining in the future" (ID 10.12.2010).

There have been signs of change in this respect. Cree, for instance, invested in a large scale chip factory in China and Osram opened an encapsulation factory in Wuxi, Jiangsu province, that will employ about 2,100 workers in 2017 (Osram 21.05.2014). Other companies are scanning the market in order to identify objects for possible acquisitions. NVC, the Chinese market leader in the field of general lighting, is plotting major plans for an expansion of its LED segment and aims at "[t]argeting branded suppliers with technological expertise for acquisition (mainly mid and downstream LED enterprises)" (NVC 2012). In 2012, NVC also announced a joint venture with Shenzhen Refond, one of the leading LED packaging companies in China in order to complement its production capacity in the field of LED applications with packaging facilities. Analysts expected that LED production will become a key growth driver for the company in the near future, whereas it currently only constitutes 2 percent of revenues (HSBC 2011).

The second high-profile state intervention for the development of the industry, namely, voluminous subsidies of RMB 10 million per piece for the acquisition of MOCVD reactors by LED chip companies, has had even more severe effects in terms of overinvestment. A well-known research institute projected a sweeping success of this strategy in late 2010 as it expected the Chinese industry to leapfrog Korea and Taiwan by the beginning of 2012 to become the world's largest production site (cf. optics.org 23.11.2010). Indeed, the subsidies provoked a run on the key production equipment. In 2010 and 2011, Chinese companies accounted for more than half of global orders of MOCVD reactors (SEMI 06.08.2013). This figure dropped to 33 percent in 2013 due to severe overcapacities, but Chinese companies are expected to order 44 percent of all reactors purchased worldwide in 2014 (Morrow 2013). Chinese companies operated 22.9 percent of reactors worldwide in May 2014, narrowly behind Taiwan (28.6 percent) and Japan (23.8 percent) (Digitimes 11.06.2014).

Frequently, the ambitions of emerging upstream companies have been confronted with an inadequate supply of human capital. MOCVD reactors need to be debugged in a complicated process that lasts four months before they can be operated. Since Chinese companies often lack suitably trained staff for this task, there have been frequent moves to attract experts from Taiwan by offering salaries of a multiple height of that of ordinary engineers (Digitimes 29.09.2011). The surge in investment for chip production equipment in 2011 coincided with the slowdown in demand on the general LED market (cf. section 6.1.1). Some orders for MOCVD reactors therefore were cancelled in 2012. It is estimated that about half of the 700 machines installed in 2009 and 2010 with the help of government money have remained idle until 2012 (Reuters 27.05.2012). The huge overinvestment in LED upstream production induced by MOCVD reactor subsidies thus aggravates the general tendency of crisis and consolidation, which are present all over the industry. But consolidation also drives leaps in productivity, as one analyst explains:

"With close to 100 companies involved in front-end LED manufacturing [i.e. epitaxial wafers production, F.B.] , the industry is still too fragmented to generate significant economy of scale, and the 2010–2011 investment cycle resulted in significant worldwide overcapacity at most levels of the value chain. However, a significant percentage of this excess capacity will be absorbed in the next 18 months via consolidations. This will have consequences on the equipment market, as many of the strongest LED companies will expand capacity through M&A rather than investing in brand-new equipment. Ultimately, consolidation will speed up process and tools standardization, allow vast economies of scale, and facilitate adoption of traditional semiconductor manufacturing best practices" (Virey 2012).

The current upheaval in the LED chip industry may therefore turn out to benefit larger manufacturers. It is expected that "the China LED chip industry will become increasingly concentrated in the hands of the big six manufacturers: San'an, Electech, Tsinghua Tongfang, Silan Azure, Epilight and Changelight. More and more smaller manufacturers in China are withdrawing from the LED chip sector altogether and selling off their MOCVD capacity to larger, more stable firm[s]" (Digitimes 24.11.2011). The Chinese government is pressing ahead with this process in order to create more competitive enterprises that can face up to their peers in the advanced industrial economies. In the words of one expert, "that's China's strategy. They want their biggest companies to survive" (quoted in Reuters 27.05.2012). While overinvestment is putting Chinese firms across the value chain under severe pressure and claims many casualties, it also fosters the consolidation of stronger and more competitive Chinese players in the vital segment of LED chip production.

## 6.3 LED case studies

Perspectives for fast growth—but devastating overinvestment, huge development potentials—but high competitive pressures: these are the characteristics of industry development in China's LED sector. How do companies respond to these challenges and what are the models of production that are chosen? The aim of the empirical study about the LED sector in Guangdong was to identify company strategies for industrial upgrading by which they could adjust to the competitive environment in the sector, and to discuss how these affect the respective patterns of work. In a broader perspective, the study addresses the relation between technological change, skill distribution, wages and working conditions. It aims to identify whether the rise of a new sector based on advanced technologies implies more just patterns of work than those that have dominated regimes of production in the labour-intensive segments of the region.

### 6.3.1 Overview of the LED industry in the Pearl River Delta

The case studies focus on companies in the Pearl River Delta, China's main production site for lighting products in general and LED lighting in particular. The industry in Guangdong maintained high growth in revenues from USD 151.5 billion in 2011 to USD 210 billion in 2012. It thereby contributed almost 40 percent of China's LED output of USD 550.7 billion in 2012 (ID 22.02.2013).

The industry structure in the PRD shows the characteristic prevalence of downstream production with so far relatively weak capacities in core technological development (GD LED Association 2011). In fact, this disproportion is particularly pronounced in this region, which has been the Chinese centre of low-end labour-intensive manufacturing during the past three decades. Many LED enterprises had also been active in the conventional lighting industry before, a business dominated by labour intensive production models in large scale units. They mostly continue to focus on the applications segment.[77]

---

77 Cf. Lüthje et al (2013b, 177–185) for a detailed analysis of the regime of production at a leading Chinese manufacturer in the traditional lighting industry. The production process at a leading European manufacturer in the same area in the PRD is similar in so far as

The provincial government, hand in glove with local industry associations, is strongly promoting industry development across the LED value chain with a particular focus on strengthening technology-intensive segments. LED lighting was selected as one of the three strategic industries to be strongly promoted alongside the new electronic information industry and electric vehicle production (CIES 04.11.2011). The PRD is also serving as a pilot area for the installation of LED public lighting with more aggressive plans for subsidisation and street lamp installation than those formulated by the central government. Moreover, the provincial government has set the ambitious target of an LED penetration rate of 30 percent for interior lighting until 2015 (Guangzhou Ribao 21.09.2011). Particular attention is devoted to LED upstream development. In September 2011, a cooperative innovation centre for the LED industry was inaugurated in the City of Foshan with the aim of promoting research in LED wafer production to help overcoming the key weakness of the local industrial structure (APT 19.09.2011). The government further aims to achieve breakthroughs in the development of industry standards, the lack of which is currently a handicap for market development and the establishment of economies of scale. The Guangdong Ministry of Science and Technology intends to set a benchmark for the industry that may create a common ground for national LED product quality standards in the future (APT 20.04.2012).

The efforts for fostering upstream development have shown some results in the recent past with large investments of foreign LED upstream producers (Cree, SemiLEDs, Epistar) and by some Chinese producers (Neo-Neon, Orient, APT) in the region. However, most large Chinese LED chip manufacturers (especially San'an and Silan Azure) are located outside of the province. LED upstream production currently remains mainly concentrated in Xiamen, Fujian Province, and in the wider Yangtze River Delta (especially the Cities of Hangzhou and Wuxi).[78]

The industry has formed several clusters within the PRD. Unlike in the garment industry, these are no "specialised towns" in which industry development and industrial policy are mainly shaped by one specific sector (cf.

---

labour-intensity in volume production of light bulbs was very high, as well, as the author was able to observe at a field visit (ID 20.10.2010). However, working conditions were better and skill requirements for manufacturing workers higher than in the case described by Lüthje et al.

78 Cf. for instance the list of prominent Chinese LED chip manufacturers published by LEDinside (24.06.2010).

chapter 7). Clustering rather takes place by agglomeration of several large enterprises in cities with a heterogeneous industrial landscape. Still, city governments in these clusters place heavy emphasis on the LED industry and compete against each other for investments by flagship companies. Some also support an industry agglomeration in special LED or lighting districts, such as in Foshan, where the government aims to streamline the supply chain and improve cooperation between companies by creating dense industry clusters (People's Daily 29.03.2010). In some cases (Shenzhen, Foshan) government policies are supported by local industry associations that support R&D activities and help to enact government measures to coordinate industry development (ID 16.11.2010, 22.11.2011a). The City of Shenzhen is by far the largest LED cluster in the region. Representatives of the local industry association claim a number of over 1,000 LED companies and a sales volume of around 40 percent of the Chinese total (ID 16.11.2010).[79] Other prominent clusters are the City of Foshan, a large production base of the traditional lighting industry in which the government fosters the conversion towards LED lighting, the provincial capital Guangzhou, and Huizhou, the site of recent investments by Cree and LG electronics and home to China's biggest lighting manufacturer, NVC.

## 6.3.2 Results of the case studies

Due to the marked diversity of the sample, each company and its respective upgrading strategy is introduced individually in the following paragraphs. The results concerning the effects of industrial upgrading are then presented in form of a summary discussion based on a systematisation of results of the single case studies.

### 6.3.2.1 *General information—introduction to the research sample*

The research sample consists of five companies in different vertical segments of the industry. The following paragraphs give a short introduction to the history, the ownership structure, and the main operations of the surveyed companies.

---

[79] However, these figures are probably inflated since even Guangdong's share in revenues of the Chinese LED industry is no higher than 40 percent, according to the figures quoted above.

*Table 6.3: Overview of research sample, LED industry*

| | CHIPSTAR | PACK-AGESTAR | SMART-PACKAGE | MULTI-APP | ARCHI-APP |
|---|---|---|---|---|---|
| Date of field study | Nov. 2010, Nov. and Dec. 2011 | Nov. 2011 | Nov. 2010, Nov. and Dec. 2011 | Nov. 2010, Nov. 2011 | Dec. 2011 |
| Location | Guangzhou | Foshan | Shenzhen | Shenzhen | Guangzhou |
| Ownership | Chinese PIE, founded 2003 in HK | Chinese PIE (listed), founded 1969 as SOE, privatised 2001-07 | Chinese PIE, founded 2002 | Chinese PIE, founded 2002 | Chinese PIE, founded in early 90s as SOE, privatised 2001 |
| Industry segment | Upstream, midstream | Midstream (mainly) | Midstream, downstream | Downstream | Downstream |
| Main products | High power chips (10%), wafer-level packages (40%), Packaged LEDs (50%) | Packaged LEDs (78%), LED applications (11%), other | Packaged LEDs (>75%), LED applications (<25%) | LED apps 100% Backlight modules, Lighting applications | LED apps 100% Entertainment and architectural lighting |
| Sales (RMB, 2011) | 132 mio | 1,071 mio | 100 mio | 103 mio | (50-70 mio)[i] |
| Markets/prod. model | PRC: 90% / OEM | PRC: 76.6% / OEM | PRC: 80% / OEM, OBM | Export: 60% / OBM, OEM | Export: 75% / OEM, OBM |
| No. of Employees (2011) | 350 | 1,789 | 350-400 | 5-600 | 600 |

i    Unverified estimation of the author. A company representative said that the average annual growth rate was 30-40% in 2009-2011 and that the company aimed to achieve revenues of RMB 100 million before the end of 2014.

Source: Interview data.

*CHIPSTAR: Pioneering integration of chip production and encapsulation
(up-/midstream segment)*
The company, founded in 2003 as a university spin-off by private investors
from Hong Kong and China, is among China's ten leading upstream producers according to a 2011 ranking (LEDinside, 24.06.2010). Its sales volume
considerably lags behind that of China's biggest chip producers, but CHIP-
STAR has been rapidly expanding in recent years at a rate of 39.9 percent per
annum in 2010–12.[80] The bulk of its products—over 90 percent in 2011—
was sold on the domestic market, mainly to large applications producers in
the field of general lighting, as OEM products. CHIPSTAR stands out from
the crowd of upstream manufacturers by offering a unique product based
on distinct product properties and production technologies. The company
proudly advertised in 2011 that it is the only high-power high-brightness
chip manufacturer in China with only a small technological lag compared
to leading Taiwanese vendors. Hence its main competitors on the Chinese
market are large scale foreign suppliers like OSRAM, Cree and Philips, rather than Chinese producers. The company's production model cuts across the
established distinction between upstream and midstream manufacturing, as
part of its products are LED packages that are encapsulated on wafer level.
The share of packaging (i.e. midstream production) in its total sales was
around 90 percent in 2011, 40 percent of which were wafer-level packages.[81]
A successful sales development enabled CHIPSTAR to more than double its
production capacity after opening a new factory near its former premises in
Guangzhou in early 2012.

---

80 According to the quarterly report of PACKAGESTAR, the largest Chinese LED chip
company achieved revenues of RMB 1.8 billion in 2011, i.e. about 18 times the amount of
CHIPSTAR's revenues in the same year (PS Quarterly Report I/2012).

81 The categorisation of CHIPSTAR as upstream company is therefore not without problems
since the company mainly engages in midstream production. The company also does not
engage in epitaxy, the core process of LED wafer production. CHIPSTAR is nevertheless
categorised as upstream company here since the company unlike other midstream companies engages in wafer level technologies and also supplies chips to external encapsulation
(midstream) companies. Chipstar is also listed as LED chip producer (i.e. upstream company) in the already mentioned ranking by LEDinside (24.06.2010).

*PACKAGESTAR: China's industry leader in LED packaging*
*(midstream segment)*
In the midstream segment, PACKAGESTAR is a mass producer of LEDs
with the largest LED encapsulation capacity in China, according to its company catalogue for the year 2012. It was also ranked at the 20th position of
LED companies worldwide in terms of sales volumes in 2010 (Research in
China 2011). A former SOE, founded in Foshan in 1969, the company entered LED manufacturing as early as 1976 in form of an export-processing
contract with a major Japanese electronics multinational. After privatisation
in 2001, PACKAGESTAR intensified its pace of technological development in order to gain from rising LED demand, and received heavy support
through measures of the central and provincial governments' development
plans for the high-tech industry. The company focuses on packaged LEDs
for backlight and general lighting applications, but since 2010 also offers
LED applications in the field of general lighting. On top of this, PACK-
AGESTAR is entering the upstream segment of the industry. It recently
placed an investment of over RMB 400 million in a joint venture with a
US LED chip manufacturer for a new factory in Foshan which entered test
production in 2011 and is expected to produce chips on a mass scale from late
2013 or early 2014 on. The company went public in 2010 and is listed at the
Shenzhen stock market. With an annual sales volume of over RMB 1 billion
in 2011 (PS Quarterly Report I/2012), the company outperforms the other
companies of the sample by far (cf. table 6.3). More than three quarters of
PACKAGESTAR's total sales were realised on the domestic market in 2011.
Its customers for OEM sales are large domestic and international consumer electronics companies like Panasonic, Sony, Sharp, Konka, Huawei and
TCL. It also supplies components to contract manufacturers, for instance to
the large Taiwanese company Foxconn. PACKAGESTAR's LED application
products are sold as own brand products to wholesalers, local governments
or private end consumers.

*SMARTPACKAGE: Expanding packaging company with ambitions for OBM*
*production (midstream segment)*
The second encapsulation company of this sample is a much smaller investment by Chinese businessmen (the CEO personally owns 60% of the company) founded in Shenzhen in 2002. The company developed its core encapsulation business to supply Chinese application manufacturers. Accordingly,
80 percent of the sales volume in 2011 was sold on the domestic market,

often, however, to Chinese applications companies that engage in export production. According to its own estimation, the company sells packages of an upper to middle quality in relation to other Chinese manufacturers. According to a sales manager, the products rather offer good value for money than peculiar characteristics (ID 14.12.2012). SMARTPACKAGE put a new factory with enhanced production capacities into operation in Shenzhen in early 2012. As many other producers within this field, the company broadened its product assortment by offering a selection of LED applications including street lights and indoor lighting products sold under its own brand name. Yet, packaged LEDs continued to constitute its core business in 2011, with over three quarters of total sales.

### MULTIAPP: Victim of the consolidation process in the field of LED applications (downstream segment)

MULTIAPP was an LED applications manufacturer founded in Shenzhen by private Chinese investors in 2003. The company became a mass producer of backlight modules, mostly of smaller dimensions like those used in mobile phones or netbook displays. In this function, it mainly acted as an OEM supplier to contract manufacturers like AUO or Wintek that produce LCD panels for large-scale consumer electronics manufacturers. In 2008, MULTI-APP added several own brand products to its assortment, mostly street lights and various types of indoor lighting. With 60 percent of the total in 2011, general lighting products constituted a growing share of MULTIAPP's sales. The company particularly focused on export markets to sell its LED lighting applications and opened a sales dependency in Belgium to this end. However, the company strategy did not turn out to be successful. MULTIAPP went bankrupt in May 2012 and ceased all its operations. It represents one of the many casualties of the recent phase of consolidation and may be seen as a typical case of early LED manufacturers that grew on basis of a high demand for backlight assembly, but could not cope with the enhanced requirements for product development and capital investment in a maturing industry.

### ARCHIAPP: Specialist for entertainment and architectural lighting (downstream segment)

With its focus on entertainment lighting and architectural lighting, this company is much more specialised on a particular market segment than MULTIAPP. It is a former SOE in Guangzhou that has been active in the general lighting industry since the 1990s. After privatisation at the turn of the century, the company entered LED production and specialised in developing and assembling entertainment lighting such as large spotlights that feature colour conditioning and functions of automatic motion. Three quarters of ARCHIAPP's sales were realised on foreign markets in 2011. The company pursues a split production model in which foreign clients, usually large lighting fixture brands, are supplied with ODM products. On the Chinese market, however, the company aims at a leading position with its own brand and competes against the very companies with which it is cooperating on the international level. In both functions, as ODM supplier and as Chinese OBM, the company has been able to implement high-profile projects such as the lighting system illuminating the Eiffel tower in Paris at its 120th anniversary, the installation of fixtures on the Great Wall, and some contracts for the 2008 Olympics in Beijing.

### 6.3.2.2 Industrial upgrading strategies

All company representatives stated in interviews that their enterprises have faced a difficult economic situation from late 2010 on. Problems resulted mainly from industry consolidation through overinvestment as described in sections 6.1.2 and 6.2.5. Companies have suffered under such conditions in terms of declining sales and a rapid drop in prices. Chronically weak foreign demand has further aggravated the situation even for primarily domestically oriented suppliers since many of their customers are large-scale consumer electronics companies with a high export share. This is especially the case in the field of backlighting modules where sales have suffered from a market development that remained beneath expectations. The performance of LED companies has to be measured against very high expectations for further expansion that were prevalent in the years 2009 and 2010 when much investment was placed. The surveyed companies all experienced growth in 2010 and 2011, but the performance did not meet the original expectations. Under the condition of falling end product prices, this led to a squeeze in profits. The most obvious victim of the current crisis is MULTIAPP which went out of business in 2012.[82]

---

82 In the light of the recent bankruptcy of MULTIAPP the projected growth rate 21.2 percent for the year 2011 provided by a company representative in November 2011 seems dubious. If it should correspond to the truth, an explanation for the subsequent insolvency also could lie in generally low profitability (despite a relatively good sales volume) and

These economic turbulences raised the pressures for enterprises to develop and upgrade their operations—and pressures already had been high in this very competitive and fast moving industry in which the lowering of production costs is an absolute condition for survival. Since products and processes for the time being remain little standardised and mass consumer markets in the field of general lighting are only in the process of being formed, a plethora of approaches exists on the micro level.

*CHIPSTAR: Entering volume production, focussing on wafer-level packaging*
The company's strategy is directed at a leading position for the mass production of high-power, high-brightness LED chips in China. As a spin-off from the Hong Kong University for Science and Technology (HKUST) it launched its operation on the basis of a specific product design (flip-chip technology), a relatively uncommon technology which is gaining ground internationally against other chip layouts (cf. Yole 2011).[83] In order to participate in the gains from this heterodox technological approach, one major international LED chip manufacturer from Taiwan holds shares of CHIPSTAR and supplies the company with high-quality epitaxial wafers which is one of the key reasons for CHIPSTAR's ability to produce chips with a fairly high lighting efficiency.

Based on its distinct chip designs, the company also has developed a technique for wafer-level packaging which company representatives described as the key to more efficient manufacturing. Through this technique, chips are packaged while still fixated on LED wafers and then cut, as opposed to the conventional procedure by which LED wafers are first cut into chips and then packaged (often by distinct LED packaging companies). Wafer-level packaging offers several advantages. First, the distinct steps of chip production and packaging are merged into one (also referred to as "vertical integration of the conventional packaging stream", ID 24.11.2011) which cuts out intermediaries between upstream and downstream production. Second, this practice offers new possibilities for automation because of the uniformity of processes that are performed while the wafer is still uncut. Third, and

---

the repercussion of the slowdown of foreign demand in 2012. The precise reason for the collapse of MULTIAPP could not be identified.

83 The main advantage of this packaging technique is that no bonding through a gold wire is needed. Thin gold wires by which electrical poles are connected are currently one of the main sources of defect of LEDs.

for the same reason, it is easier to guarantee equal lighting properties of the products.

*Table 6.4: Upgrading strategies of the surveyed LED companies*[i]

|  | CHIPS-TAR | PACKAGE-STAR | SMART-PACKAGE | MULTIAPP | ARCHIAPP |
|---|---|---|---|---|---|
| Sales 2011 | +15.3[ii] | +22.5% | n.s. | +21.2% | (+30-40% p.a.)[iii] |
| Product upgrading | STRONG | STRONG | MEDIUM | WEAK | STRONG |
| *Tech capability* | STRONG | STRONG | WEAK | WEAK | MEDIUM |
| *R&D* | 6 uni coop (3 HK, 1 TW), 30% R&D staff | 11 uni coop (PRC), > 10% R&D staff[iv] | 2 uni coop (local), 5-7% R&D staff | 2 uni coop (PRC), 4-6% R&D staff | 3 uni coop (local), 10% R&D staff |
| *IP*[v] | >50 patents (10 int.) | 141 patents (17 int.) | 3 patents (1 int.) | 90 patents (utility model) | n.s. |
| Process upgrading | STRONG | WEAK | STRONG | WEAK | WEAK |
| *New equipment* | New factory, large scale automation | Already largely automatic | New factory, large scale automation | No major changes in production process | No automation of manual labour |
| Funct. upgrading | MEDIUM | STRONG | STRONG | STRONG[vi] | MEDIUM |
| *Value added* | MEDIUM/HIGH | LOW | LOW | LOW | MEDIUM |
| *Vertical integr.* | MEDIUM[vii] | STRONG | MEDIUM | WEAK | WEAK |
| *Marketing* | More ODM, no OBM | More OBM | More OBM | More OBM | Unchanged |

|  | CHIPS-TAR | PACKAGE-STAR | SMART-PACKAGE | MULTIAPP | ARCHIAPP |
|---|---|---|---|---|---|
| Government support | MEDIUM | STRONG | MEDIUM | MEDIUM | MEDIUM |
| Relocation | No. New factory in same area | No | No. New factory in same area | Planned, but cancelled in 2011. | No |

i The evaluation of "product upgrading", "technological capabilities, "process upgrading", "functional upgrading", "value-added", "vertical integration" and "government support" are assessments by the author based on qualitative and quantitative data obtained through field studies and desk research.

ii CHIPSTAR experienced markedly slower growth in 2011 in comparison to 2010 (45 percent) and 2012 (31.4 percent).

iii No detailed data was provided because the data was considered to be sensitive. A representative stated in a follow up conversation in late November 2012 that the average annual growth rate was 30-40 percent "during the past three years".

iv There is no clear indication about the size of PACKAGESTAR's R&D staff. According to a company representative, there is a post-doc research station with 200 employees, but it was not clear whether this included all of the company's R&D staff. The quarterly report of the first quarter of 2012 gives a number of 601 employees in R&D and technical functions, but does not differentiate how many of these actually refer to R&D (PS Quarterly Report I/2012).

v The number and type of patents was used as an indicator for the possession of intellectual property (IP). There are different types of patents that can serve as an indicator for the innovative capacities of Chinese companies, cf. footnote 87.

vi MULTIAPP has pursued functional upgrading towards OBM production of general lighting products, but no vertical upgrading towards LED packaging or chip production.

Source: Interview data.

CHIPSTAR is putting all these advantages into practice in its new factory that took up production in spring of 2012. CHIPSTAR invested RMB 500 million in the new premises and expects to expand the factory in successive stages resulting in a total investment volume of RMB 1.5 billion. According to plans presented in December of 2012, the company's maximum production capacity will more than double after the launch of the already completed factory with substantial leeway for further expansion in the future. Nevertheless, the number of operators, around 150 in 2011, only rose slightly because of widespread automation of production. The labour intensity of production in relation to the company's output therefore was drastically reduced. In case of a further increase of production volumes in the future, the number of operators could rise to around 350, however. CHIPSTAR does not show any interest in entering consumer markets with OBM lighting products. On the contrary, it aims at a further vertical specialisation as a "foundry" of the LED industry (ID 14.12.2011).[84] This implies the possibility to offer custom-made LED packages to application producers. Requirements for such flexibility are supposed to be gained through the control of the complete upstream and midstream production chain. Prospectively, CHIPSTAR also wants to enter the production of LED wafers which has not been part of the company portfolio so far, unlike in virtually all other LED upstream companies (because wafers so far are delivered by CHIPSTAR's Taiwanese shareholder). While a broadening of functions takes place on this level, CHIPSTAR aims to abandon conventional packaging—perceived as an outdated procedure. For the time being this is only performed as a supplementary process.

CHIPSTAR received some government support by applying for certain projects. It also gained from efforts of the local government to foster a high-tech development zone in the area where both CHIPSTAR's old and new factories are located. The company has been granted several awards and is listed as innovative enterprise in Guangdong. However, it claims to not have received any direct subsidies. A company representative also complained that government support was not sufficient. Unlike virtually all other LED chip producers, CHIPSTAR did not take advantage of the huge subsidies for MOCVD equipment in 2011 because up to then it did not engage in wafer production. The large government subsidies for Chinese chip producers therefore have an adverse effect on CHIPSTAR's competitiveness. This may change, however, in case the company's plans to enter wafer production in the future by acquiring MOCVD reactors come true.[85]

---

84 This expression refers to foundries in the computer chip industry which are modularised suppliers of chips who do not deal with the production of applications (cf. Pawlicki 2010, 2).

85 CHIPSTAR did not implement its plans to order MOCVD reactors voiced in December 2011 as of December 2012 (ID 11.12.2012).

*PACKAGESTAR: Building innovative capabilities and pursuing functional diversification*

The upgrading strategy of PACKAGESTAR is pursued on two levels: ongoing improvements in products and processes on the one hand, and functional diversification on the other. With regard to the first strategy, the company is able to build on its control of advanced encapsulation techniques as well as on its intense efforts for product development during the last decade. Although foreign monopolies of intellectual property are conceived as a major problem, PACKAGESTAR is steadily improving its technological base in the field of packaging. The company owned 141 patents in 2011, among them 17 international ones. PACKAGESTAR entertains its own post-doc research station with around 200 researchers. The research institution has been recognised as "innovation centre" on the provincial, and recently also on the national level.[86] PACKAGESTAR is on the forefront of the national and provincial governments' efforts to gain in technological strength and to challenge foreign monopolies in high-tech IPs. The company received project funding under the framework of the 863 high-tech plan, the national torch plan and the 12th Five-Year Plan. It received RMB 18.6 million of direct subsidies alone in 2011, plus around RMB 60 million of subsidies for its LED chip joint venture with a Taiwanese chip producer (PS Quarterly Report I/2012, 43). The prominence of the company in China's high-tech development plans was underlined by a visit of former Prime Minister Wen Jiabao in 2008 and by visits of several national and provincial leading politicians subsequently. Independent innovation of products and processes remains a precondition for the company's development since further expansion in PACKAGESTAR's core business of encapsulation depends on the ability to increase yields and drive down production costs. The expansion of operations towards upstream and downstream production—segments in which the company owns virtually no IPs and' has virtually no experience—presents tough challenges in this respect. Hence, the cooperation with an established Taiwanese LED chip producer that can contribute technological and manufacturing know-how.

---

86 Industrial policy in Guangdong places heavy emphasis on creating innovation centres that support the technological capabilities of companies. While these often are organised in form of certain kinds of public private partnerships, the government also awards the title of a provincial (or even national) innovation centre to R&D departments of private companies.

This aim of a vertical expansion of operations beyond its current core business of encapsulation is the second main upgrading strategy pursued. In 2010, an investment of around RMB 80 million was placed in LED lighting production facilities. The company now produces a broad assortment of general lighting products under its own brand name, among them street lights and other outdoor applications through which it can benefit from investment programmes in the field of outdoor lighting. Complementarily, the already mentioned joint venture with the Taiwanese partner for LED chip production seems to play an even more prominent strategic role. It can be understood as a reaction to decreasing margins in an overcrowded and rapidly maturing encapsulation market which is also at risk of losing in relevance in the long term due to competing technologies such as CHIPSTAR's wafer-level packaging. By diversifying its investment, PACKAGESTAR can balance such risks and benefit from higher value-added production. Still, the company expects further growth in the encapsulation division and strives to further improve technologies in this field. For the time being, virtually all of its large R&D capacities are concentrated in this segment. Entering the stock market in 2010 can be seen as part of the company's strategy for vertical expansion, since it serves as a means to generate funds for the required investments, especially in the capital-intensive field of chip production.

*SMARTPACKAGE: Process upgrading and supplementary OBM production*
This company does not intend to enter the LED upstream business, but it pursues a strategy of vertical integration with regard to the downstream segment by adding LED lighting applications sold as own brand products to its portfolio. Although applications production was said to achieve almost a quarter of total company sales in 2011, it remained somewhat unclear whether the production of applications represents a fundamentally important long-term strategy of diversification or just served as a supplement to gain some extra income in a rapidly growing market (especially through street light subsidies). What is more, product development in this field was described to be difficult because know-how in prototyping, moulding and optics was necessary, which does not belong to the company's core competences. Currently, encapsulation clearly represents SMARTPACKAGE's core business. Still, its OBM applications are promoted with great fervour.

SMARTPACKAGE made a leap towards production of higher quality products and greater volumes in 2011 by opening new premises, an investment of RMB 50 million, including a newly built factory and office building. Like the old production site, then accommodated in a rented building, the new factory is also located in the City of Shenzhen, yet in a different district. Relocation from the Pearl River Delta to other places is not an option for SMARTPACKAGE because of the advantages of dense supplier relations, innovation networks and marketing channels in Shenzhen. In the new factory, the main process of encapsulation was transformed from manual and semi-manual production to fully automatic assembly. The company thereby approaches those manufacturing standards that are performed by large companies like PACKAGESTAR. The key equipment for this effort includes over 20 automatic die bonders from Taiwanese and American providers. Additionally, some older equipment was transferred from the old factory. There also remain some manual production steps, above all in LED applications production, but also in the assembly of a patented multi-chip module.

SMARTPACKAGE engages in some cooperation with two local universities and also has an R&D team that has so far acquired one international and three domestic patents. It is also ranked as a Shenzhen and China high-tech company and speaks of "very big government support" when attending fairs, applying for project funding and arranging credits (ID 19.11.2010a). The company benefited from the government's New Lighting Project subsidies as vendor of street lights. Yet, despite the overall emphasis on technological progress, the company's upgrading strategy currently clearly focuses on improving production yields and expanding in volume while simultaneously gaining additional income from its standard products for the rapidly growing lighting application market. As such, it resembles many mid-size LED companies in the area. SMARTPACKAGE has so far weathered out the storm of the crisis of overinvestment, which found some victims in companies of comparable strength, fairly well, but it may suffer from the ongoing process of consolidation which was described by a company representative as a process in which "the water washes the sand away so that gold remains at the end" (ID 15.11.2011). Yet, stable relations with some important customers, and not least the possession of own land using rights in a rapidly developing area of Shenzhen, act as a buffer against the worst effects of the crisis.

*MULTIAPP: A failed attempt to launch OBM production in general lighting*
The move towards general lighting products which could be observed at PACKAGESTAR and SMARTPACKAGE was most pronounced at the downstream producer MULTIAPP. The company did not engage in encap-

sulation, but has historically focussed on OEM assembly of lighting components in backlight modules. From 2008 on, it pursued a major shift in its business orientation by launching its own brand assortment of lighting products which in 2011 accounted for the majority of its sales. This was connected to a strategy of shifting from the domestic to overseas markets. OBM production of lighting products, although technologically not very sophisticated, potentially entails higher value added than backlight production. The latter consisted of few production steps at MULTIAPP, while most of the value was contained in packaged LEDs which were purchased on the market. MULTIAPP possessed its own moulding division, which guaranteed high flexibility in new lamp designs. Still, a great share of value (20–30 percent in street lights and up to 70 percent in desk lamps) was captured by chip and packaging providers. This dependence on key components created a profit squeeze in the context of overproduction. MULTIAPP expressed vague ideas of moving upstream towards packaging, at least in form of some technological cooperation agreements with packaging companies, but in late 2011 did not show any concrete plans to do so.

The company could benefit from government support in terms of project applications and, especially, through the New Lighting Project. It was listed as one of the 100 key enterprises of Shenzhen's Bao'an district and as a Shenzhen High-Tech enterprise. The company owned almost 90 domestic patents. Yet these were mainly utility model patents, an inferior type of intellectual property that is awarded for modifications of certain products and processes, as opposed to actual innovations.[87] The most important of these achievements of MULTIAPP are related to backlight production, not to the field of general lighting. The company claims to have a 30 percent share of university graduates in its staff, and 30 employees in R&D. However,

---

87 Chinese companies hold several types of patents which are considered to express innovative capabilities of varying strength. International patents (registered e.g. in the US, Europe or Japan) are considered to express the highest standards. Among national patents there are innovation patents, utility model patents and industrial design patents. Only the first are granted for inventions that imply new technical solutions. Utility model patents, very common among Chinese manufacturers, "protect any new technical solution relating to the shape, the structure, or their combination, of a product which is fit for practical use. They provide 10-year protection from date of filing and are not subject to substantive examination" (Stembridge 2010, 9). They indicate innovative capacities of lower complexity, directed at practical manufacturing solutions. While some commentators interpreted such patents as "junk", others hold that they play an important role for incremental innovation and catch-up growth (cf. Ernst 2011b, 5–7).

especially the latter seems to be based on a very loose definition of R&D. More concrete data counts five employees with a PhD and eight with an MA degree in the R&D department (ID 25.11.2011). There is some cooperation with two universities in form of joint labs. Despite inflated public statements about its R&D assets, the company seems to have a realistic assessment about its innovative strength. One representative admitted that its technologies were of "average" quality (ID 18.11.2010). Correspondingly, the improvement of products was seen as one major task for the company. The primary objective in this respect was not own product development, but better supply chain management, since much of the end product's quality depends on the standards of its supply products.

Process upgrading does not play a major role at MULTIAPP. Except for very large orders, backlight modules are assembled manually. The same is true for the division of general lighting in concordance with production standards for this segment in the region. In none of the departments are there any plans for raising the degree of automation. By and large, MULTIAPP's strategy of functional upgrading did not yield the expected results while earnings from the slackening backlight market were deteriorating. Yet, alternative orientations seem to have been out of reach. The company's innovative weakness did not allow for breakthroughs through product upgrading which could have distinguished the company's assortment either by superior quality or smart specialisation. Equally, there was little basis for moving upstream towards more complex and higher value added fields. Finally, there was little space for increasing production yields through process upgrading since the potential of automation is limited in the field of general lighting applications (and hypothetically would require high capital investment). This deadlock in the company's development outlook may explain its subsequent bankruptcy in 2012.

*ARCHIAPP: Deepening specialisation on highly lucrative application segments*
Conversely to most other cases, ARCHIAPP's upgrading strategy is rather directed at deepening its level of specialisation than at broadening its product portfolio. The company is trying to "stay ahead of the curve" in the market segments of entertainment and architectural lighting by making progress in product development. It thereby consciously refrained from producing low-tech products which was seen as a problematic effect of the LED boom (ID 30.11.2012). This is complemented by efforts to raise the share of higher value-added architectural lighting in its overall sales, and to also raise the

share of its own designs in OEM products. All of these steps decisively depend on its R&D capacities. ARCHIAPP employs 60 engineers (roughly 10 percent of the workforce) with at least an MA degree. These employees develop the main product architectures, designs for PCBs and even some smaller software elements. Yet, many high-tech components—apart from packaged LEDs: integrated circuits, power supplies and fans—are bought from suppliers. The company engages in cooperation with two universities and the Central Academy of Drama. It has attained over 20 patents (mostly practical ones), while many more were still pending in 2011. The company won an innovation award in the framework of the national semiconductor project and other awards. It has also benefited from public investment programmes, especially by selling fixtures for high-profile projects such as the Beijing Olympics or the Shenzhen Universiade sports event. However, a spokesperson emphasised that ARCHIAPP rather relies on its own product development than on government support, by which he also implied criticism of the general rush on subsidies in the sector.

The production process at ARCHIAPP is highly labour-intensive, since all products are assembled manually. The manufacturing of a diverse product assortment with low volumes of each product type demands high flexibility in assembly, which up until now can best be reached by manual assembly. There is some application of machinery in the mounting of PCBs and metal working, but no large-scale automation is envisaged. There has been an intensification of work however, since the number of the workforce is not rising as fast as revenues. According to a representative, "a worker that used to manufacture a USD 250 product in three hours is now able to manufacture a USD 450 product in two hours" (ID 30.11.2012). Yet, there does not seem to be a lot of pressure to increase yields through process upgrading because ARCHIAPP's production costs still are considerably lower than those of companies from advanced industrial countries that are its main competitors on the domestic market. For this reason the management also does not entertain any plans of relocating to regions with cheaper wages. In sum, the company's main development strategy clearly rests on improvements in product design instead, which is conceived to be a permanent challenge because of many imitators in this rapidly expanding segment.

### 6.3.2.3 Production process and work

Despite big differences in market positions and upgrading strategies, there are some regularities with regard to the surveyed companies' production processes. First, and most obviously, labour intensity is lowest in upstream production and increases further downstream, with the highest intensity in the assembly of general lighting applications. Labour intensity therefore stands in a converse relationship to the R&D intensity of production, which is highest in upstream and lowest in downstream production. However, high labour intensity does not automatically go along with low R&D capacities, as it could be observed in the case of ARCHIAPP, a company that allocates rather extensive resources to product development, but shows a very low degree of automation.

Second, there is a divide between automatic and manual production which runs through some of the companies of this sample. This has to do with varying production standards with respect to different products. Tasks of wafer processing in the upstream segment[88], like etching and photolithography[89], cannot be performed without relatively expensive high-end equipment. Encapsulation, a process that mostly implies the delicate placement of tiny gold wire connections, is mostly done with automatic equipment of equally high cost and dimension. However, manual wire bonders with amplification devices were still in use at SMARTPACKAGE in 2010, before these processes where automated in 2011.

In the field of LED applications, all surveyed companies (except CHIP-STAR which does not' produce applications) almost exclusively operated on the basis of manual assembly, and, according to a spokesperson at MULTIAPP, this is also the general manufacturing standard in China more generally (ID 17.11.2011b). LED backlighting production, as performed by PACKAGESTAR and MULTIAPP, occupies an intermediate position with view to the degree of automation. Large producers seem to organise this process by applying full-automatic machines, but manual assembly is also a widespread practice, as exemplified by MULTIAPP, where

---

88 As stated before, this analysis does not provide insights about the process of wafer production through epitaxy since none of the companies of the research sample performs this operation. An overview over the processes involved in LED chip production and packaging can be found in Yole 2011.

89 In photolithography, fine patterns from a photomask are transferred to a physical substrate.

virtually all backlight assembly was done manually, the small size of the components notwithstanding.[90] Because of the differentiated practices of automated and manual production, those encapsulation companies that supplement their core business with OBM production of general lighting products have a workforce that is split between machine operators and manual workers (cf. table 6.5).

*Table 6.5: Production process and working conditions at the surveyed LED companies[i]*

|  | CHIPSTAR | PACKAGE-STAR | SMARTPA-CKAGE | MULTI-APP | ARCHIAPP |
|---|---|---|---|---|---|
| Production process | Automated assembly | Automat./manual assembly | Automat./manual assembly | Manual assembly | Manual assembly |
| Labour intensity | LOW | MEDIUM | MEDIUM | HIGH | HIGH |
| Number of Employees | 350 | 1,789 | 350–400 | 5–600 | 600 |
| *Sales and management* | 40–50 | 160 | (52)[ii] | 75 | n.s. |
| *R&D* | 100 | 200 | 50 (12)[ii] | 30 | 60 |
| *Technicians* | n.s. | n.s. | (22)[ii] | n.s. | 120 |
| *Line workers* | 150 | 1,200 | 280–320 (110)[ii] | 350–400 | 450 |

---

90 The company does own an automatic machine for this process, but it was only used for very large orders. During two factory visits, it was never in use. The assembly of backlight modules at this company, which involved about 10 production steps, was organised in small assembly lines, while workers in other sections glued packaged LED chips on PCBs individually.

|  | CHIPSTAR | PACKAGE-STAR | SMARTPA-CKAGE | MULTI-APP | ARCHIAPP |
|---|---|---|---|---|---|
| **Social composition** | | | | | |
| *Migrant workers* | 150 | 1,200 | 280–320 | 350–400 | 450 |
| *Age and Gender div (line workers)* | 80% 20–30y, majority female | 76.6% 20 – 30y (entire workforce) | Most 18–23y, 55% female | n.s., 70% female | n.s. |
| Turnover/ recruitment | 5% p.a./ some problems | Quite stable/ no problems | 10% p.a./ problems | High (sales staff), less f. line workers | High (line workers) |
| **Human resources** | | | | | |
| *Skills(line workers)* | LOW | LOW | LOW-MEDIUM | LOW | LOW-MEDIUM |
| *Training (line workers)* | 2d-1w on the job | 1w on the job | Mixed: 1w, 1m, 1/2 y | 1m, new workers 3m | n.s. |
| Wages | 2–3,000 | 2,000 | 2,000–2,500 | 2,000–3,000 | (2,000–4,000) |
| *Base wage* | 1,300 | n.s. | 500–1,000 | 1,300 | (2,000)[iii] |
| *Flexible share* | 1,000–1,500 | n.s. | 1,000–2,000 | 700–1,700 | n.s., high |
| Working hours | 8h reg., 11h max, acc. to labour law | n.s. | 8h reg., 11h max | 8-9 reg., >12h max | 8h reg., 11h max |
| General conditions | GOOD | n.s. | BAD – AVERAGE | BAD – AVERAGE | AVERAGE-GOOD |

i  The evaluation of "labour intensity", "skills (line workers)" and "general conditions" are assessments by the author based on qualitative and quantitative data obtained through field studies and desk research.

ii  The figures in brackets were provided in 2013, yet these figures for line workers and R&D staff are much lower than the respective figures provided in 2010 (200-300, 50). Apparently, a significant reduction of the workforce had been taken place since then (ID 19.11.2010a; 06.04.2013)

Source: Interview data.

*Skill requirements and training for line workers*
Machine application in LED manufacturing generally does not require so-phisticated skills from line workers. There is a clear tendency to separate the sometimes difficult tasks of programming and setting up of the equipment from overseeing the machines' regular operation.[91] From wafer-level process-es to encapsulation and PCB mounting, the tasks of operators mostly consist of loading the machines, troubleshooting, and controlling some functions, the latter of which involves occasional adjustments of some settings.[92]

Nearly all company representatives emphasised the low skill requirements for operators in these functions. An engineer at CHIPSTAR justified the very short training periods for operators in his company by saying that workers "need to know how to make it, not why they make it" (ID 24.11.2011). In most statements there was a tendency to equate automated production directly with low-skilled functions. The generally short train-ing periods for machine operators vindicate such assertions. Training peri-ods between one week and one month on the job are typical even for new workers who have no prior experience in the industry (cf. table 6.6). The lowest data in this respect was provided by the technologically most so-phisticated company. At CHIPSTAR, management representatives spoke of a training of "only a few days" (ID 24.11.2011). Production in CHIP-STAR's new factory is not thought to be more demanding, since the level of automation is even higher.

Yet, despite the overall picture of low skill requirements, there seem to exist some differences with regard to the specific equipment used. At SMARTPACKAGE, a representative claimed that there was a training pe-riod for at least half a year for operators of automatic encapsulation ma-chines (ID 20.07.2012). These workers would need to master the digital controls of the machines and how to adjust settings, which apparently re-quires a lot of experience. However, there is considerable ambiguity about this issue. According to a representative of one of the machine producers

---

91 This does not necessarily have to be the case. As a representative of an American high-end equipment manufacturer explained, skill requirements for operators of automatic die and wire bonders can be relatively high. Such skilled workers would require comprehensive training of at least a year. But these machines are rarely used for high volume production in Chinese factories and much more expensive (ID 03.12.2012a).

92 As mentioned before this description does not cover the process of epitaxy which is not covered in this study.

of the wire bonding equipment used at SMARTPACKAGE, new workers needed no more than three days of training to master an automatic encapsulation machine. He emphasised that the machines were designed to have interfaces that are extremely easy to use and that these functions are usually performed by workers "off the street" in China, implying that no formal training whatsoever was needed (ID 03.12.2012b). The actual practice at SMARTPACKAGE seems to lie somewhere in between. During a shop floor visit, a production manager explained that the training periods for workers operating the two main types of packaging machines were one week and one month, respectively. A more comprehensive training of three months was only provided for technicians who set up the machines (ID 03.12.2012b).[93]

*Illustration 6.1: Automated LED packaging production line at PACKAGESTAR*

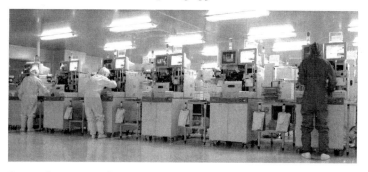

Source: Company catalogue.

---

93 The issue could not be definitely resolved in subsequent conversations with company representatives. In his last reply on the issue (after he was confronted with some evidence contradicting his earlier statements) a company manager replied: "I meant that skilled workers who are able to operate the auto die bonding machine skilfully need working experience of at least three to six months according to our experience. But if you refer to front line workers who simply watch the die bonding machine, insert materials and remove finished products, one month can do. Still I think that this is a little short for a worker in order to form a good habit and knowledge of his or her work [...]. For the more complex tasks, skilled workers are to be trained between three to twelve months. Technicians should be trained at least one year and gain three years of practical experience" (ID 14.12.2012). Apparently, the contradictions inherent in the data also have to do with different operating functions and different kinds of equipment used.

Manual production does not require much operating knowledge either since it generally consists of gluing packaged LEDs on PCBs or lighting cases. However, it does require some manual skilfulness given the small size of the packaged dies. A company representative at MULTIAPP said that the typical training period for new workers was 10–15 days plus a one month on the job training in both application and backlight production (ID 18.11.2010). Yet, a spokesman from ARCHIAPP claimed that skill requirements in manual production were high because of a need for calibrating components in products that performed dynamic functions (such as rotating spotlights) (ID 30.11.2012). However, "only a little experience in assembly processes, not necessarily in the field of LED" was required from new workers (ID 07.12.2011).

Taken as a whole, the available information suggest that the skill requirements for technologically highly complicated processes performed by use of sophisticated machinery are not higher than those in manual production. Automatic LED assembly in this respect echoes the common practices in electronics manufacturing, through which high-tech manufacturing processes are combined with very low-skilled and low-paid labour. The slightly contrary results of more demanding functions for machine operation at SMARTPACKAGE exemplify that some specific tasks in LED production may also foster the development of a new set of skills of operators. But given the contradictory evidence concerning this issue, such tendencies should not be overrated. Besides, indications of more demanding skills are absent in the other cases, most notably at PACKAGESTAR, the company possessing China's largest encapsulation capacity. A manager of this company stated that training periods for line workers generally amounted to one week (ID 22.11.2011b). In LED upstream and midstream manufacturing, the overall tendency of employment patterns and machine designs help to keep skill requirements for the workforce low. Processes of de-skilling may be part and parcel of this tendency. At CHIPSTAR the functions of workers in photolithography, which were considered to be among the most demanding tasks in terms of workers' skills, were eliminated through automation with the launch of the new factory (ID 24.11.2011).

*Illustration 6.2: Manual LED backlight module assembly lines at MULTIAPP*

Source: Author's photograhs.

It is an important result of this study that the assembly of LED lighting applications, for the time being, seems to be resilient vis-à-vis automation. Manufacturing in this field remains highly labour-intensive and based on manual skilfulness. But such skills, primarily fast gluing of chips to the devices and other simple assembly, do not seem to require a lot of experience, unlike it is the case with some garment functions in which very experienced workers can earn above average wages because of their proficiency. In a way, the typical functions in LED companies, especially the tasks in manual assembly, are not much different from those in many other labour-intensive industries in the region where workers take on extremely repetitive tasks of manual assembly of prefabricated components. It is ironic that such practices, deemed to be a hallmark of dated labour-intensive production in low-end industries, are widespread in the "strategic emerging industry" of LED lighting. It remains to be seen whether the expected expansion of the industry segment of general lighting applications and the simultaneous consolidation processes will lead to new forms of automation with different patterns of work. However, the high mix of products with the most diverse of shapes that need to be produced at relatively low unit costs currently constitutes a barrier for automation in the general lighting segment. Besides, automated production by no means is more demanding in terms of skills and does not imply wage gains for workers, as the results of these case studies and other studies about automated manufacturing in the electronics industry indicate (cf. Lüthje et al 2013a; Bernhardt and Milberg 2011[94]).

*Systems of employment*
The overall low skill requirements in manufacturing are clearly reflected in the observed employment patterns which are characterised by a strong polarisation between highly skilled and low-skilled employees. Without exception, low-skilled migrant workers are hired as line workers in manufacturing. As a representative of SMARTPACKAGE emphasised, these are not *nomingong*, i.e. peasant workers with little formal knowledge and skills, like those who took jobs in low-wage industries in earlier phases of the region's industrialisation (or still do so in some very low-end functions). Today's workers in LED manufacturing rather have a high school degree and many are socialised in urban regions which makes them better suited to acquire the necessary skills quickly (ID 08.12.2011). Despite their higher level of "cultivation", they have similar work biographies like their predecessors and equally build their existence on temporary migration to the manufacturing belts of the country, where they still are denied a full residential status. LED companies also do not seem to be very picky about their line workers: working experience, let alone formalised education, e.g. at technical schools, usually is no precondition for taking up a manufacturing job in an LED factory.

On the other end of the job hierarchy, there are professionals who excel in the development and application of LED technology. These experts are indispensable for assuring reasonable product quality and for keeping up to date on the latest technological trends. Several companies complained about the difficulty of finding sufficiently skilled employees and keeping them in their company. Bright career options result in a high turnover of experts who sometimes even dare to exit the labour market altogether by starting their

---

94 Bernhardt and Milberg discuss the social impacts of mobile telecommunication manufacturing. They do interpret the case of China as one where economic upgrading in the mobile telecom sector is combined with social upgrading (because of wage and employment growth). But all in all their conclusion of a cross-country analysis is that [t]he mobile telecom sector has experienced "widespread economic upgrading, but very little social upgrading" (2011, 57).

own businesses. What is more, educational institutions have difficulties of keeping up with the latest technological developments and as yet rarely offer courses that match the requirements of LED companies. Experience therefore is valued more than anything else, which means that the tussle for talent between companies is all the more intense. Professionals in the LED business can therefore earn very high salaries. At MULTIAPP, the monthly income of project managers, i.e. managers with technical proficiency, can amount to RMB 30,000 (ID 18.11.2010).

Technicians and sales people represent a middle ground in most companies. Usually these are young university graduates or staff from technical schools. They often accept a salary which is only little higher than that of line workers in order to have their share in the booming industry (ID 17.11.2011b). Often it is the prospect of advancing to a higher position that makes these employees accept low wages and long working hours.

This prospect barely exists for migrant workers in manufacturing because higher-paid functions usually require formalised education. Arguably, possibilities for upward mobility are therefore even more limited in the high-tech industry than it was the case in some low-end industries during the past two decades, when numerous migrant workers of the first generation even ended up starting their own businesses once they had learned the basics about their industry's operation. There also was no indication of a "practical specialisation" of workers as it sometimes occurs in the garment industry, where workers can improve their status because of their working experience in one particular function. There is some leeway for advancing one's position within manufacturing functions, however. Sometimes line workers can eventually advance to the position of foremen. At least two companies, CHIPSTAR and SMARTPACKAGE, also offer seniority bonuses to their workers, although they currently rarely have to actually make these payments, because most workers are newly hired. ARCHIAPP also expressed vague ideas about a "human resource development road-map" to be implemented in the future, by which workers should be able to advance to higher-skilled positions (ID 30.11.2012). Such measures must be seen in the context of the general labour shortage in the region, which aggravates the problem of an already relatively high turnover of the workforce, since workers engage in "individual bargaining" by changing to better-paid positions in other companies of the region. There is some chance that the increased market power of workers in the context of a widespread labour shortage may force companies to introduce incentives for long-term employment of migrant workers.

But on the other hand, skill requirements for line workers are deliberately kept low, which ensures the possibility of quickly replacing vacant positions by low-skilled workers. The growing technological sophistication that goes along with industrial upgrading furthermore creates relatively rigid barriers between different functions of which each requires its own specific profile in terms of professional education and training.

With regard to the social composition of the migrant workforce, LED companies show the typical characteristics known from electronics manufacturing and other industries in the region. The bulk of the workforce is aged below 30 years, e.g. 80 percent at CHIPSTAR (of manufacturing workers) and 76.6 percent at PACKAGESTAR (of the entire workforce) (ID 08.12.2010; PS Quarterly Report I/2012). According to an estimate by a spokesperson, the manufacturing workforce at SMARTPACKAGE is particularly young with most being only 18–23 years of age (ID 14.12.2012). As capacities in some enterprises have only recently been expanded, many workers are newly hired. Where manual mounting of PCBs is practised, companies tend to prefer young women, because they "can hold tiny things and process them more carefully", as a representative of CHIPSTAR explained. At MULTIAPP, the company with the highest proportion of manual labour, female workers constituted a majority of 70 percent of the manufacturing workforce (ID 25.11.2011). The preferred hiring of women in low-paid assembly functions echoes the experience in other segments of electronics manufacturing in the region where employment systems build on gender discrimination and companies thus preferably assign badly paid repetitive tasks to women (cf. Pun 2005, 145–150).

*Wages and wage systems*

Also the wages levels and wage systems show similarities to the standards in electronics manufacturing in the region. In the surveyed companies, workers usually receive the local minimum wage as a base wage (around RMB 1,300 in Guangzhou and Shenzhen in 2011). At SMARTPACKAGE, base wages for workers even amounted to RMB 500, 800 or 1,000 only, i.e. below the local minimum wage, depending on their function (ID 15.11.2011). A representative of ARCHIAPP claimed that base wages for different functions in the factory amounted to RMB 2,000–4,000, but stressed that he did not really know about the wage levels of workers (ID 30.11.2012). In general, performance bonuses and overtime payments constitute between 30 and 50 percent of the total wage (PACKAGESTAR and ARCHIAPP did not provide information on this). The total wage for line workers at the observed companies ranged between RMB 2,000 and RMB 3,000 (cf. table 6.6).[95] Most companies paid below RMB 2,500 on average. A representative of PACKAGESTAR thought that their total wage of RMB 2,000 for line workers was typical for the area where their factory is located (Foshan) (ID 22.11.2011b). Wage differentials between manufacturing workers usually are small. SMARTPACKAGE revealed that wages differed by no more than 10–15 percent between workers of comparable functions (ID 15.11.2011). At least in automatic production lines, performance bonuses are usually distributed across whole departments or production lines, not awarded individually. Similarly, overtime hours usually affect all workers of a shift and thus are distributed evenly.

Interestingly, there seem to be little efforts by companies to keep skilled manufacturing workers through offering wage incentives. At SMARTPACKAGE, the management complained about a drainage of skilled workers due to a relatively high turnover rate in the workforce. But the company does not offer higher wages for manufacturing workers, e.g. to those machine operators in encapsulation who allegedly need a more comprehensive training. A representative of the company argued that their "final salary is not far from the one of other [less-skilled, F.B.] workers, since their importance in the production lines is the same" (ID 20.07.2012). Benefits to these workers are limited to improved dormitory conditions (hot water, clean quarters) and other comforts.

In general, the production flows in the surveyed companies are quite stable, although the effects of oversupply on the market reduced production volumes somewhat in 2011. Still, there were less pronounced seasonal peaks in comparison to the seasonal changes in the garment industry. Overtime hours beyond the legal maximum are a common phenomenon. Regular working hours in most surveyed companies are 8 hours, and the maximum working time per day 11 hours, usually on 6 days per week (cf. table 6.6). At CHIPSTAR on the contrary, the management claims com-

---

95 From the available data, it cannot be excluded that wages for line workers at ARCHIAPP in 2011 could have been higher since base wages were said to amount to RMB 2,000, while flexible wage shares apparently constitute a high proportion of workers' incomes (ID 30.11.2012). This would also correspond to their claims of extensive occupation with workers' well-being (cf. below). ARCHIAPP also expressed little fear of losing their cost advantages vis-à-vis their international competitors (ibid). However, there do not exist any concrete figures or other reliable information to confirm such speculations.

pliance with the labour law with a regular working time of 8 hours per day on 5 days a week and not more than 32 overtime hours per month. At MULTIAPP, a company with a particularly high share of manual production, working hours can amount to 12 hours per day (ID 17.11.2011b). Yet all in all, working hours seem to be more regular and less extensive than in many low-end industries in which managers sacrifice their workers in order to meet short-term orders of large quantities. Most significantly, unlike in these industries, workers in LED manufacturing usually have one or even two days off per week. At least in automated production, an optimisation of productivity is rather achieved through appropriate equipment and its smart utilisation than by prolonging the working day beyond a sustainable maximum.

*General working conditions*
Similar conclusions can be drawn with regard to the general working conditions at LED factories. They do show some typical attributes of other labour-intensive industries where migrant workers are hired. Workers are accommodated in company-owned dormitories, catered for in factory canteens, and rarely leave the factory area. But dormitories are less crowded (usually rather 4–6 workers per room, instead of 8–12) and sometimes newly built. Some companies provide services like free wifi and reading rooms and consciously try to adjust to the young workers' expectations in order to prevent them from leaving (ARCHIAPP). Others (SMART-PACKAGE, CHIPSTAR) try to establish recreational activities to forge a sense of belonging. Representatives of MULTIAPP claimed that control of workers is less strict and military-like than in the much debated case of Foxconn. However, there was little way of confirming such claims in the course of this study. Except at PACKAGESTAR, a company with a long tradition as SOE, there are no branches of the ACFTU in the surveyed companies.[96]

Work environments, in some cases in newly built factories, are usually clean and professional—a precondition for some production steps where dust-free antistatic departments are needed (backlight assembly at MULTIAPP, chip production at CHIPSTAR). Requirements and practices are lower in this respect in most manual production steps of lighting

---

96 The interview data does not provide any insights about the activities of the ACFTU branch at PACKAGESTAR.

applications. Clean working environments do not necessarily imply good conditions, however. Virtually all machine operators in LED production stand upright during the entire work day. Some need to switch between machines, as it is the case at PACKAGESTAR, where one operator controls several encapsulation machines at the same time. In manual assembly, most tasks appear to be very tiring because of the tiny size of components. In manual encapsulation, workers use microscopes, whereas in LED application assembly the attachment of packages of about half a square centimetre size is usually done without any optical support. Workers need to remain highly concentrated and focus their vision permanently throughout the whole day. They also tend to lean, or rather bend, forward for better vision which surely creates orthopaedic problems in the mid-term (cf. illustration 6.2, p. 211). Another potential health problem concerns the chemical substances used. Workers mix and apply glue and phosphor powder without any respiratory protection.

By and large, wages and working conditions show some deviations from the standards in typical low-wage enterprises. But working conditions in most cases remain unsustainable because of the character of the tasks, the work and living environments, as well as low wages, which do not suffice to support an independent life outside of accommodation facilities provided by employers in the cities of the PRD. Like intended in the case of ARCHIAPP, companies may choose to create incentives for a more long-term employment of manufacturing workers by offering bonuses, but so far there is little substantial progress in this regard. Dormitory accommodation and low wages continue to constitute the standard of employment schemes which means that workers will barely stay in such factories once they want to start a family and look for long-term living perspectives. Occupation in the LED industry therefore continues to rely on a very young, low-skilled and badly paid temporary migrant workforce, and there are no signs of any major change in this respect.

## 6.4 Summary and outlook

The case studies from a sample of five companies in the Pearl River Delta reveal an ambivalent picture regarding the relationship between industrial and social upgrading. Confronted with the recent economic turbulences and the involved risks, most of the surveyed companies have striven to increase their technological strength by continuously improving products and processes. Most companies also have undertaken significant steps to broaden their functions by strategies of vertical diversification and the launch of own brand products sold at mass consumer markets or to public buyers. The difficult macro-economic environment makes continuous improvement through industrial upgrading a precondition for success. Technological strength is the single most important currency in this respect. Companies that lag behind or cannot provide enough sources to upgrade their products probably will not survive among high competitive pressures as the examples of MULTIAPP and many other LED companies of the region demonstrate.

Although innovative capabilities, which in the last instance rest on the cognitive abilities of the workforce, are of vital importance for the success of LED companies, the social upgrading effects of recent industry development is limited. A characteristic of employment systems in the industry is their strong polarisation between highly skilled professionals and low-skilled line workers. Professionals in R&D are a *sine qua non* in the LED industry and the fact that formalised education lags behind the pace of innovation in the sector makes the quest for talent all the more daunting. In this respect, the LED sector is markedly different from companies of the "low wage classic" regime of production. Arguably, it also differs from many other electronics companies of the "flexible mass production" type in which products and processes mostly are more standardised than in the still immature LED sector. In LED production, any company entering the field needs quite large capacities for product development, which is reflected in rates of up to 30 percent of R&D staff as a share of the total workforce. Requirements are much lower in downstream production in this respect, but still demanding because of the low degree of standardisation and the specific knowledge about heat reduction and optics that is needed. Because of this need for high R&D input, the LED industry currently drives the demand for professionals, which is also reflected in skyrocketing salaries for top personnel. Due to the fragmented structure of the industry, the divide between highly skilled and low-skilled work runs through every company, even if it may only have a few hundred employees in total. This high demand for upscale professionals may be regarded as one dimension of social upgrading. Even if there is a failure to elevate the general conditions for all employees, there is a strong segment in the workforce that is gaining ground.

With regard to the character of manufacturing work, the LED industry across the value chain does not transcend the typical characteristics of work as known from other RoP in the production of consumer electronics in the area. In particular, there is a failure to distribute tasks in a way that gives manufacturers incentives for long-term employment and better remuneration of manufacturing workers. Some LED companies try to reduce the turnover rates of the workforce by offering some benefits for line workers, but in the companies of this sample such measures—implemented as a reaction to labour shortages—did not lead to qualitative changes in wages and occupational statuses. Most importantly, companies do not have a necessity to extensively train a manufacturing workforce with comprehensive skills. The case studies delivered ample evidence for the fact that LED companies, be it in manual or automated functions, can operate on a basis of unskilled or semi-skilled workers who receive a short introduction to their respective functions and who can be quickly replaced in case they drop out of their positions. As cost-driven competition is ubiquitous in the LED industry, this option is the preferred choice for the surveyed manufacturers.

Especially in the upstream and midstream segment of the industry, there is a strong similarity of employment patterns, wages and working conditions with those that are common in electronics manufacturing, where skills and wages are equally polarised. This is also true for some downstream companies that use sophisticated equipment. In this segment, however, the low degree of automation is striking. Companies such as MULTIAPP and ARCHIAPP (and also the downstream sections of PACKAGESTAR and SMARTPACKAGE) hire large numbers of migrant workers to stick together their products manually, often without the use of any machinery or sophisticated tools in their assembly divisions. Behind the façade of its high-tech image, LED production continues to be a highly labour-intensive business and at the surveyed companies there were no efforts for a change towards a technology-driven intensification of LED downstream production in the general lighting segment. In fact, the weight of labour-intensive companies in the downstream segment will prospectively further increase in the future, since the market for applications in the field of general lighting will increase relative to upstream and midstream production or other fields of applications (cf. section 3.1.4.3).

Contrary to the expectation of an exodus of labour-intensive manufacturing from Guangdong that is dominant in mainstream discourse, labour-intensive functions in LED manufacturing are set to stay. Some downstream companies struggle with low margins due to a difficult market situation, but relocation to regions that offer more favourable terms for land and labour is not an option for the companies of this survey.[97] Relocation would cut these companies off from the dense networks of innovation and talent supply in the PRD. Most notably, companies would also lose the indispensable government support for innovation which is most abundant in Guangdong.

In the light of the general development trends of the industry outlined in section 6.1 and 6.2, the results of the empirical case studies allow for some considerations about general development trends of industrial and social upgrading in China. They leave the solid ground of research results and enter the uncertain realm of discussing future possibilities. But since the LED sector is a particular dynamic industry, it seems adequate to put the obtained picture from the empirical investigation "in motion" and to discuss them in a more general context.

First of all, China's LED industry represents a very successful case of industrial upgrading due to a favourable industry environment and heavy government support. The assumption that LED chip production and encapsulation, like so many other segments of the electronics industry, is moving towards Asia is definitely taking shape, and China is in a very good position to take advantage of this development. Key success factors are quickly expanding consumer markets, heavy government support and the likely emergence of manufacturing standards that resemble those of electronics manufacturing of mass consumer products, in which Asia has gained a competitive advantage over the last two decades. Government subsidies triggered a bonfire of investment which created serious overinvestment in the course of which a large number of companies was brought to their knees. However, the overall outcome of this process, at least partially intended by the government, most likely will be a more mature industry with fewer, but bigger and more competitive Chinese players. Foreign monopolies for intellectual property continue to constitute a problem

---

97 The cancelled plans for relocation of MULTIAPP to Shaoguan, a city in northern Guangdong, are the exception of the rule. Yet, the relocation plans of this company were motivated by very lucrative conditions that would have been offered at the new location, partly because of personal connections of the factory owner who grew up there. This site would also have been sufficiently close to the PRD to maintain important R&D, supplier and sales relations. Besides, the plans for relocation may be seen as an early indicator of the dead end in the company's development (which therefore paid greater attention to the question of labour costs than their peers).

for the Chinese industry, especially in the field of upstream production where Chinese producers currently lag behind the leading international suppliers. But because of the attractiveness of the huge and consistently expanding Chinese market, foreign companies have started to flock in. This is likely to create technology spillover effects, especially when foreign chip producers merge with local producers, such as in the joint venture between a Taiwanese upstream producer and PACKAGESTAR in Foshan. Cross-strait alliances between Taiwanese and mainland Chinese companies, like in the case of CHIPSTAR and its Taiwanese shareholder and LED chip provider, seem particularly promising in this respect and are encouraged by the government. The prospected entry of large Chinese consumer electronics companies to the LED business will also increase capital supply for large scale investments and back up the Chinese industry's capacity to engage in cross-licensing agreements and the like to gain in technological strength. The examples of LED latecomers like Samsung and LG demonstrate the possibilities for catching up and even overtaking long-standing LED brands in this respect. Of course, even large consumer electronics companies in China do not match the strength of these electronics giants so far, but still there are observers who predict that there will be one Chinese company among the world's ten largest LED producers until 2017 (LEDinside December 2012). Despite many casualties on the way and a large amount of unproductive investment as a result of broadly placed government subsidies, the Chinese industry therefore will most likely see a further rise in the future.

Considering the macro analyses of the LED industry discussed in the first section of this chapter, there is a certain irony behind China's quest for world leadership in the LED industry, however. The government strategy focuses primarily on the upstream segment. The production of LED applications, however, is rather looked down upon, except for some quality segments.[98] This mind-set reflects the status quo of the industry where

---

98 This tendency is not only documented in the strong focus on the upstream segment in the government's Five-Year Plan, but was also evident in most of the author's conversations with Chinese industry experts. It reflects the general focus of the industry in recent years: "Level 0 LED device development [LED wafer production, F.B.] has received a preponderance of research interest as the "sexy" technology that drives SSL device efficiency and performance [...]. Until recently, Level 3—System Level Assembly [applications like luminaires, F.B.], has not attracted the same level of interest as that of the three earlier assembly steps." (Chason 2012, 4).

the bulk of value added is achieved in LED upstream and midstream production. This view is also supported by the high potentials for LED chip
manufacturers to achieve above average profits as first movers, as long as
lighting efficiency of LEDs has not reached its maximum potential. But
while the Chinese industry embarks on the race for lighting efficiency in
LED chip development, analysts project a proportional shift of value in
the opposite direction. As outlined in section 6.1.4, chip manufacturing
prospectively will become highly commoditised "low margin business"
(NSR 2010, 2), as products and processes become more standardised. It
also seems likely that the pace of innovation will decelerate as LEDs approach their maximum lighting efficiency.[99] The LED upstream industry
will more and more become an issue of efficient and cost-effective high
volume manufacturing, which in this case primarily equals further automation.

On the contrary, the projected expansion of the LED applications market driven by the penetration of mass consumer markets means that this
industry may become a bonanza in the future offering chances for high revenues and increased value added. Currently, the Chinese LED application
industry remains highly fragmented. When this research was conducted,
there existed hundreds of SMEs in the downstream segment in the PRD
which, with the exception of specialised companies like ARCHIAPP, focused on a remarkably similar assortment of products which included street
lights (because of the investment programmes), tube lights, spot lights and
few other types of interior or exterior lighting. They mostly also produced
surrogates for conventional lighting products like retrofit light bulbs that
match conventional lighting fixtures. Product designs were very similar,
and quality differences mainly concerned the components used, first and
foremost the quality of LED chips bought from suppliers. Hence, value
added for the time being remained low and profits were under pressure
because of an overcrowding of the market. But market expansion creates

---

99 Primarily because miniaturisation, which is the main dimension of product innovation
   in the general IC industry, is barely an issue in the LED upstream industry. The quest
   for higher lighting efficiency in the LED sector is finite, since production standards are
   expected to reduce the gap to the theoretical maximum of LED lighting substantially
   within few years. Further increases then only result in negligible benefits regarding the
   lighting properties of products. However, the integration of lighting controls and other
   components on a wafer level may be one direction of future product improvements (cf.
   Virey 2012).

a positive environment for innovative product designs, including the sale of whole lighting solutions composed out of control elements and various types of luminaires. Such products would not only allow for a capture of higher value added by application producers, but for new "architectural innovations" (cf. Ernst 2009) that go beyond standard lighting solutions that were developed using the less versatile incandescent technology. One dimension of this general trend is a growing sophistication of specialised market segments such as automotive or architectural lighting, as the case study of ARCHIAPP exemplifies.

If the projection of a growing weight of the luminaire market, which is currently upheld by all relevant industry analysts, comes true, the question whether there can emerge strong Chinese application producers on national and international markets seems to be not less important than the question of technological leadership in the upstream and midstream segment. Although Chinese companies produce a very large share of products in this segment, there currently are no large Chinese OBM application producers that could face up to foreign giants like Philips, Osram, Samsung, or LG. The downstream segment of the Chinese industry, for the time being, continues to be highly fragmented and comparatively weak. Still, Chinese companies are in a good position to acquire technological excellence and leading market positions in the mid-term because of China's advantages as a production site for large volume manufacturing and its attractiveness as a consumer market. Technological capabilities of downstream companies need to be strongly enhanced, however, which will become easier if the industry moves beyond its current structure that is shaped by a myriad of small producers with little capital and innovative resources.

It is hardly possible to predict whether an emergence of large Chinese manufacturers in the field of LED applications would contribute to improving the conditions for manufacturing workers, in case there would be a concentration of production capacities towards larger units. The experience of low-skilled and labour-intensive work at large-scale electronics contract manufacturers rather supports a certain scepticism in this respect.[100] If a

---

100 Up until now electronics contract manufacturers that are active in the field of consumer electronics do not play any significant role in LED manufacturing. The Taiwanese company Foxconn, however, is experimenting with low volume production of LEDs through a subsidiary in the Pearl River Delta (ID 16.11.2011). In 2012, it was also announced that the company had invested USD 146 million in LED related ventures (LEDinside 20.07.2012).

trend towards automation would eventually emerge, as some analyses assume (cf. DOE 2012c, 17), there is also little hope that this would imply significant skill upgrading for manufacturing workers. The results of this empirical investigation prove that skill levels, wages and working conditions in automated manufacturing are not necessarily superior to those in manual production lines. The monitoring of working conditions in the rapidly evolving LED industry and the discussion of the conditions for social upgrading therefore constitutes an important field for future research. All in all, qualitative improvements for workers in this industry seem to depend less on the merits of advanced technologies by themselves than on the implementation of generally binding labour standards and the capacity of workers to enforce higher wages and better conditions.

# 7 China's textile and garment industry: Export leadership, booming domestic market and upgrading opportunities

The history of the Chinese textile and garment industry during the last two decades is one of rapid industrial upgrading as a result of which China emerged as the undisputed leader in terms of production volumes worldwide. The garment sector, which was the motor of China's rapid industrialisation in the late 1980s and early 1990s, flourished since China was an attractive low-cost sourcing site for foreign companies at that time. This especially pertained to lead firms or trading companies from Hong Kong, then one of the important centres of world garment production. During the last decade, the Chinese industry has developed more sophisticated functions of supply chain management and design which have set the industry apart from other South-East Asian competitors that have gained ground as alternative low-cost production sites. This tale of successful upgrading currently is being carried forward by a mushrooming growth of Chinese brands that are able to establish themselves taking advantage of a booming domestic market.

This chapter contains an overview of the dynamics in the global production networks that have provided the background for the rise of the Chinese textile and garment industry (7.1). Second, the structure of the Chinese industry and its recent transformation are analysed (7.2). In the final section the results of case studies of the knitwear, fashion and textile industry are presented (7.3).

## 7.1 The new landscape of global textile and garment production

The global textile and garment industry has recently been subject to a double shock that is affecting both its competitive dynamics and the global division of labour (Frederick and Gereffi 2011, 68–9). The first was the phase-out of the Multi Fibre Agreement (MFA) that began in 2005 and eventually was completed in 2009. Since 1974, the MFA had set maximum export figures for garment producing economies. It had been introduced in order to prevent a flooding of markets in advanced industrial countries by cheap garment products from developing countries. As will be analysed in more detail below, the phase-out not only enabled China to increase its export share, but also resulted in large overcapacities and a fiercer competitive landscape. The second shock was the global economic crisis which resulted in a slump in demand from the US and the EU in 2008/09 and ongoing weak sales in these markets. The crisis was a blow to economies that relied to a large extent on garment production for foreign markets. The combined effects of the MFA phase-out and the global economic crisis have transformed the competitive and geographical landscape of the industry. Yet, they should not be seen as incidences that transform the rules of the game by chance, but rather as catalysts that reinforce tendencies that are part and parcel of the maturing global production networks of the sector.

### 7.1.1  The garment supply chain

The garment supply chain is rather complex and heavily internationalised. With a total trade volume of USD 708 billion in 2012 for textile and garment articles, the industry is one of the main export sectors worldwide (WTO 2013, 125, 131). The garment supply chain is subdivided into four main production stages (cf. figure 7.1).

*Figure 7.1: The garment supply chain*

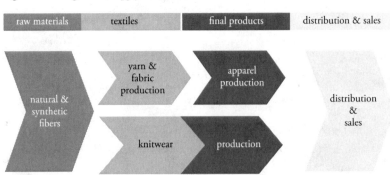

Source: Frederick and Staritz 2012, adapted by author.

The first step is the production of yarns from natural fibres, such as cotton or wool, or synthetic fibres which constitute a growing proportion of the total. In the second step, yarns are either woven by textile enterprises or knitted. In the third stage, garment companies produce a great variety of clothing products. This can involve complex subcontracting networks. In the fourth stage, there are various arrangements of distribution and sales. Again, there exists a great variety of models depending on the respective products and end markets, among other. It should be noted that this garment-centric supply chain model does not display the complete range of functions performed in the industry since not all textile production is destined towards the garment sector. For example, industrial textiles can be used in medical, automotive, and a broad range of other applications.

*Within* the garment supply chain, one important distinction concerns the difference between weaving and knitting. In the supply chain of woven garments, for which cotton is the paradigmatic raw material, the main production steps of fabric manufacturing and sewing are separated and mostly performed in different enterprises. The opposite is true for knitting, mostly based on wool or wool compounds. In this segment, garment companies generally combine the production steps of knitting and linking within the same factories which then produce a finished piece of garment (Frederick and Staritz 2012, 46–7). The case studies in section 7.3 cover the main production steps of garment production, that is to say, (1) weaving of fabric, (2) sewing of woven fabric and (3) knitting and linking of knitwear products.

In international trade, the garment industry is estimated to reach a much larger volume of USD 389 billion than the textile industry with a total volume of USD 74 billion in 2011 (Technopak 2012). One reason for the much lower export value of textiles is that a great volume of textiles now is produced domestically in major garment producing countries such as China. Backward integration to textile production is one major avenue of vertical upgrading in economies that used to be specialised on simple garment manufacturing functions (Frederick and Gereffi 2011, 73). A higher level of domestic trade of fabrics due to backward integration depresses the trade figures for fabric although gross production volumes may not have diminished. Within the segment of garment products, knitted and woven garments each constitute about half of the global trade volume. During the last years, the trade of knitted garments has grown faster than that of woven products.

The garment sector is a truly globalised industry. It was the first manufacturing sector in which the main assembly steps in manufacturing were outsourced to low-wage countries. It is therefore the paradigmatic case of global value chain (GVC) research that deals with the global dispersion of production (cf. Gereffi 1994; Gereffi and Memedovic 2003).

The global division of labour is characterised by the dominance of global brands and retailers, mostly located in advanced economies, which focus on design and sales functions. Mostly, they source the majority or all of their products from suppliers in low-wage countries, either from regional suppliers at the fringes of their home markets or, increasingly, from Asian firms. The current geography of garment consumption and production is characterised by the geographical disjunction of production and consumption with the notable exception of the Asian region which accommodates the world's largest production capacities and a large regional market of growing global importance.

The garment supply chain has been described as a "buyer driven commodity chain" in research (cf. section 4.2). Global brands control design and marketing functions in production networks which are the activities with the highest value added:

"In the context of heightened global competition at the supplier level, rents derive less from relatively standardized and commodified production-related activities that are globally available, and more from activities that differentiate the product in the eyes of the consumer. These activities are protected by higher entry barriers and are the core competencies of lead firms, typically large global retailers, and brand owners" (Frederick and Staritz 2012, 47–8).

From this relatively strong position, buyers can drive down sourcing prices for manufacturing steps in the value chain, which mostly are labour-intensive and often limited to basic manufacturing functions such as in the case of "cut, make and trim" (CMT) production models that are limited to pure assembly. In these, buyers do not only provide all specifications for the production process, but also deliver all supply products and manage logistics. Such models were the hallmark of the early globalisation of the sector and continue to constitute the entry stage for many developing countries. The actual manufacturing process thereby represents a highly commoditised, low-returns business.[101]

---

101 This interpretation should not be taken for granted for all types of end products including high-end garments which may be produced by *manufacturers* that capture a quite high share of value added. Yet, it represents a useful visualisation of relations in the bulk of garment manufacturing in globally dispersed production networks.

From this perspective, industrial upgrading primarily concerns an addition of more functions to the basic assembly process. Functional upgrading towards "full-package manufacturing" has therefore been identified as an upgrading dimension of high importance in literature. Frederick and Staritz even argue that all other upgrading measures can ultimately be seen as steps to achieve the end of functional upgrading (2012, 50). Such an enrichment of functions has been identified as the main criteria for success of development strategies in low-wage countries after the phase-out of the MFA:

"[C]ost competitiveness (particularly labor costs) and preferential market access have remained major competitiveness factors, but they are not the whole story. Upgrading—particularly to increase functional capabilities, establish backward linkages to important input sectors such as textiles, produce more sophisticated products, and diversify end markets—is crucial in understanding how different suppliers have fared post-MFA. Most countries' apparel sectors that increased market shares post-MFA have upgraded their industries to meet buyers' increasing requirements" (ibid, 80–81).

The addition of functions at garment manufacturers can result in a progression of production models. These are categorised as CMT models, Original Equipment Manufacturing (OEM, including functions of supply chain management and distribution), Original Design Manufacturing (ODM, in which suppliers co-design products) and finally Own Brand Manufacturing (OBM, in which enterprises also manage retail sales and marketing).

While a progression from CMT to OBM models is one way of achieving industrial upgrading, the theoretical literature often overlooks that this is not necessarily the only one. As the case studies in section 7.3 demonstrate, many Chinese brands did not enter the industry as producers, but as wholesalers or sales agents. They excelled in the field of distribution and therefore acquired the expertise to identify marketing options that then helped to launch their own manufacturing business through backward integration.

OBM enterprises can opt to exit manufacturing altogether, thereby launching a new cycle of outsourcing of manufacturing to lower-wage regions. This was common among Western brands and retailers during the last two decades. Also the recent history of the Asian garment industry is characterised by a dynamic of industrial upgrading and outsourcing of manufacturing. There has been a sequence of functional upgrading in which first Japan, then Hong Kong, South Korea, and Taiwan, and, finally, China, India, and some South-East Asian economies entered the industry as pure manufacturers and then upgraded their operations to more comprehensive functions. The relocation of CMT production towards Bangladesh, Cambodia, and Vietnam, starting in the mid-1990s, marks the most recent steps of this development to so-called fourth-tier suppliers (cf. figure 7.2).

*Figure 7.2: Industrial upgrading and outsourcing in Asia's regional production network*

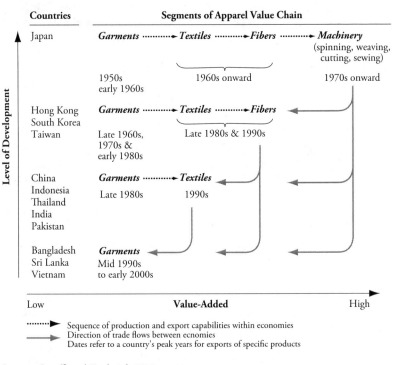

Source: Gereffi and Frederick 2010.

The result of these processes is a regional production network with dense interactions between the various segments of production. This characteristic division of labour in Asia that facilitates functional upgrading of producers in the whole region has been identified as the decisive advantage of China and other Asian suppliers in comparison to Central American production sites like Mexico, whose garment sector rapidly lost ground during the last decade:

"China has experienced regionally integrated development with East Asian neighbours, whereas Mexico and CAFTA [Central American Free Trade Agreement, F.B.] have largely emerged as competitors rather than as unified apparel producing network [...]. The East Asian division of labour is a much stronger integrated manufacturing model. The China model allows it to take much fuller advantage of strategies for moving up the value chain, and ultimately upgrading through tapping its own domestic and nearby regional markets using ODM and OBM" (Frederick and Gereffi 2011, 86).

In the case of China, the relocation of manufacturing functions from Taiwan and Hong Kong constituted the decisive jump start for the recent development of the national industry and later facilitated industrial upgrading of the involved firms.

Interpreted in a broader regional context, industrial upgrading is not only dependent on decisions on the company level, but also depends on the economic and political environment to a large degree. The existence of a domestic or regional textile industry is a precondition for an upgrading of garment companies towards OEM and ODM production that involve independent sourcing functions (Fernandez-Stark et al 2011, 52). The rationalisation of supply chains through industrial policies also plays an important role, since it may help to avoid unproductive competition between companies with similar profiles and foster interactions between companies that specialise in different functions. This is particular true with regard to functional upgrading that involves design, as the example of the Turkish industry illustrates:

"Upgrading into design and branding (ODM and OBM) requires a strong commitment to industry growth by both the public and private sectors. Turkey [has] major inroads in ODM and OBM, and it has done so with collaboration between strong industry associations and government organizations to strengthen Turkey's competitiveness in fashion and design. In addition, the full-package capabilities of Turkey's large integrated firms facilitate close relationships with global retailers, who are willing to facilitate Turkey's upgrading into design and brand services" (ibid, 50).

The Chinese central government and, even more importantly, governments on provincial and city level have been particularly committed to strengthen domestic industries by building industrial clusters and promoting functional interactions (cf. section 7.2).

## 7.1.2  Recent transformations in the garment supply chain: Structural

The phase-out of the MFA abolished maximum quotas for garment exporters. The effect has been enhanced competition in recent years. There exist no more barriers for leading exporters, in particular for China, to raise their world market share based on their industries' competitive advantages. At the same time, new competitors, especially in South and South-East Asia, are expanding their operations, while others struggle to maintain world market shares once acquired during the MFA quota era. The result are overcapacities which threaten the position of garment exporting companies and even whole regions. In this context, industrial upgrading is seen as a precondition for success, because it becomes increasingly difficult to survive solely based on the advantages of low-cost and abundant labour—after all, these assets are provided by a great number of competitors nowadays (Frederick and Staritz 2012, 56, 80–81).

The global economic crisis obviously has aggravated the situation, since garment exporting countries suffered from the slump in demand in Europe and the US. It is estimated that during the recession up to 10 percent of the garment workforce in Indonesia and Mexico (100,000 and 80,000, respectively) were laid off (Forstater 2010, 15). The crisis drove many suppliers in developing countries, especially those of lower technological capabilities, out of business. In general, it underlined the necessity for industrial upgrading in many of the exporting economies, including China, where the State Council launched a programme for restructuring of the sector in April 2009 (cf. section 7.2). The post-crisis recovery is characterised by faster growth in demand from emerging markets and developing countries which offers opportunities for firms in these regions to increase their market share, but also enhances price competition because of the demand structure in emerging markets where mid-range and lower price categories are predominant (Cattaneo et al 2010).

The combined effects of the MFA phase-out and the economic crisis have resulted in various structural changes that each influence the conditions for industrial upgrading for national economies and individual firms. Not all of these changes are an immediate product of this "dual shock". Yet, the economic ruptures of the last decade radicalised some general trends in the industry.

*(1) Changing roles of lead firms*
There has been a shrinking weight of brand marketers with large shares of own manufacturing facilities since the 1970s and 1980s. With the notable exception of Inditex, the group that launched the successful label Zara and commands a high share of own manufacturing facilities, garment production

has largely been outsourced to suppliers. This process has been accelerated in recent years through the growing weight of mass or specialty retailers. These companies, for example Walmart and C&A in the field of mass retailers and H&M and Benetton in the field of speciality retailers that exclusively focus on garment (cf. table 7.1), focus on their strengths in marketing and have limited capacities in terms of manufacturing (Frederick and Staritz 2012, 48). One particularly fast growing marketing strategy of such companies has been the launch of branded retail stores that replace or complement the traditional sales channels.

*Table 7.1: Garment lead firm and brand types with regional examples*

| Lead firm type | Type of brand | Description | Examples | |
|---|---|---|---|---|
| | | | United States | EU-27 |
| Retailers: mass merchants | Private Label: ownership or licencing of brand by retailer, but no own manufacturing | Department/discount stores that carry private label, exclusive, or licensed brands | Walmart, Target, Sears, Macy's, JC Penney | Asda (Walmart), Tesco, C&A |
| Retailers: specialty apparel | | Retailer develops proprietary label brands that commonly include the stores' name | The Gap, American Eagle, Abercromie & Fitch | H&M, Benetton, Mango, NEXT |
| Brand marketer | National brand: The manufacturer is also brand owner | Firm owns the brand name, but not manufacturing. Sales through a variety of retail outlets | Nike, Levi Strauss, Polo, Liz Claiborne | Ben Sherman, Hugo Boss, Diesel, Gucci |
| Brand manufacturer | | Firms own brand name and manufacturing: coordination of supplier networks | VF, Hanesbrands, Fruit of the Loom | Inditex (Zara) |

Source: Fernandez-Stark et al 2011.

## (2) A growing role of sourcing intermediaries

Due to the growing separation between the marketing functions of retailers and manufacturing by suppliers, there is an increased demand for intermediaries that are specialised in sourcing on behalf of lead firms. These companies take over important parts of the sourcing functions that used to be performed by lead firms in the brand marketing/manufacturing model. They also act as transmission belts of price pressures and supply chain consolidation, characteristic trends in the garment supply chain in recent years (Frederick and Staritz 2012, 47–52; Appelbaum 2009).

*Figure 7.3: Sales and production models in the garment supply chain*

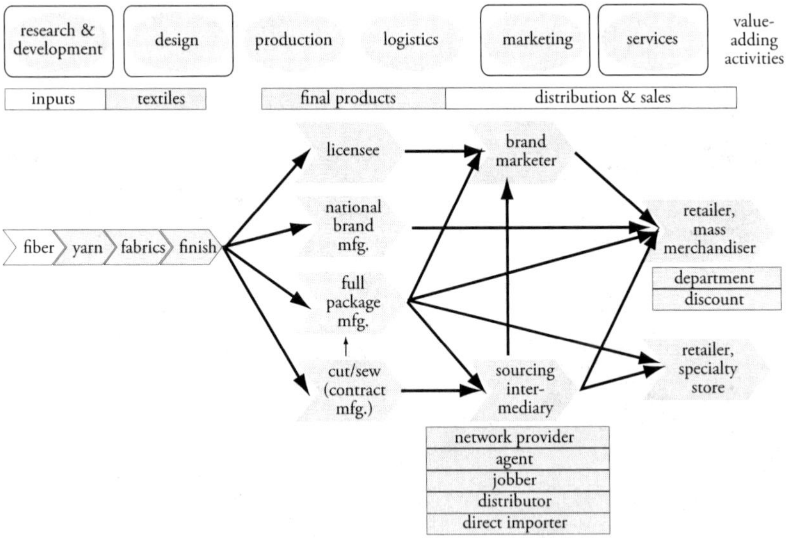

Source: Frederick and Staritz 2012.

## (3) A growing reliance on "full-package suppliers"

The growing weight of retail models, in which buyers do not directly interfere with the specifications of manufacturing, also results in a more pronounced role of leading suppliers with comprehensive functions. As Frederick and Staritz point out:

"Buyers have [...] increased the functions they demand from suppliers. Besides manufacturing capabilities, buyers desire nonmanufacturing capabilities such as input sourcing and financing on the supplier's account, product development and design, inventory management and stock holding, and logistics and financing [...] capabilities. The objective of buyers to concentrate on their core competencies and reduce the complexity of their supply chains has spurred the shift from CMT to full-package suppliers" (2012, 58).

Preferred suppliers to lead firms can even become intermediaries themselves as they manage a growing share of sourcing activities on behalf of their buyers (cf. Appelbaum 2009). This development implies that the competitive dynamics in the garment sector are not merely characterised by a cyclical shift of production to the next cheaper production site—the so-called "race to the bottom". Such processes of pure cost-related relocation of labour-intensive and low-tech CMT function do exist, but at the same time there is a historic evolution of manufacturing towards more sophisticated functions. It is therefore more appropriate to think of a bifurcation of production between strategic full-package suppliers and basic CMT suppliers that operate mainly on the basis of cost-advantages. Lead firms sometimes source from both types of suppliers for their respective product lines that include more sophisticated products and basic articles that can be delivered by suppliers with lower capabilities (Gereffi and Frederick 2010, 181). There are reasons to assume that both types of production models—full-package suppliers on the one hand, and basic CMT or OEM suppliers on the other—have sufficient space to expand. After all, a sustained demand for CMT functions is provided by the growth of the world market share of emerging markets where a large number of products of a lower price range is absorbed (cf. Cattaneo et al 2010). On these markets, entry barriers are comparatively low. However, in the context of overcapacities and heightened cost pressures, companies need to acquire considerable strength even to survive in the lower segments of the industry. The idea of a functional bifurcation of the supply chain is vital to understanding the competitive situation of the Chinese industry which will be discussed in section 7.2.

## (4) A consolidation of supply chains

The trend towards higher functional requirements for suppliers to global brands goes along with a growing reliance on key suppliers with whom lead firms may enter strategic relationships. Lead firms tend to establish permanent relationships with suppliers that have proven to be reliable in terms of quality, cost and lead times. After the MFA phase-out, there has been a tendency of consolidation due to which lead firms seek to reduce the complexity of their supply arrangements and look for larger and more capable partners. Correspondingly, there is a consolidation in the industry towards a limited number of (mostly Asian) supply regions and towards larger firms within each country (Frederick and Staritz 2012, 56–57). Yet, full-package suppliers frequently outsource a large share of manufacturing functions to subcontractors. The fragmentation of the industry is therefore continuously reproduced on the level of subcontractor networks (cf. Hale and Wills 2005; Lüthje et al 2013b, 260–264 for the case of China).

*(5) Fast fashion and lean production systems*
The fast fashion model pioneered by brands like Zara and Benetton revolutionised the sales models in the garment industry. These strategies are directed at faster product cycles through lean production methods resulting in a very quick linkage between design, manufacturing and sales:

"Retailers are exerting more efforts to curtail excess manufacturing expenses […]. Retailers such as Zara and H&M have successfully developed supply chains that facilitate quicker responses for fashion merchandise. Almost all retailers will continue to look at lower order quantities per style and reducing lead times as much as possible. Thus the typical sourcing time of 90 days could shrink to 75 days and, from 60 days, could drop to 45 days or even less in future" (Technopak 2012).

Especially, Zara became famous for its ability to produce a large number of styles in a very short amount of time which gives consumers a wide array to select from (Gallaugher 2008). Fast fashion is often interpreted as a response to rapidly changing consumer tastes, but the involved companies contribute to speeding up consumer habits as much as they react on these. In this sense, fast fashion can also be interpreted as a reaction to stagnant demand in the core markets in Europe and the US (Frederick and Staritz 2012, 58). Fast fashion exerts a countervailing influence on retail business models that imply a separation of sales and manufacturing processes because they rely on a closer communication between design and manufacturing. However, such requirements do not result in a broad-based reorientation of retailers towards integrated manufacturing, but rather contribute to expanding the roles of full-package suppliers and intermediaries who offer advanced sourcing strategies to fulfil these requirements. Another source of enhanced requirements for suppliers stems from the need for compliance with basic environmental and labour standards—a result of campaigns by activist groups that exposed frequent violations of basic environmental conditions and human rights in the garment supply chain (ibid, 58). However, critical analyses point out that increased pressures for cost competitiveness and flexibility related to the very lean production schemes that speed up product cycles and manufacturing lead times may undermine voluntary CSR initiatives by lead firms. Lead firms and intermediaries tend to rely on extensive subcontracting arrangements to achieve the required flexibility, which undermines workforce stability and creates precarious employment situations for workers. The complicated ramifications of subcontracting networks often also make it very difficult to monitor working conditions throughout the whole supply chain (WWW 2003, 10–26; Wick 2009, 4).

Taken as a whole, the combined effects of the MFA phase-out and the economic crisis have increased the pressures for cost competitiveness of suppliers, and at the same time have raised the requirements for quality, speed, and the ability to deliver advanced functions like co-design, supply chain management, and logistics. Lead firms in this way raise the bar for their suppliers by "requiring more for less" (Gereffi and Frederick 2010, 182), thus forcing suppliers to simultaneously improve their cost-competitiveness and upgrade their operations. As argued above, these contradictory requirements also result in a bifurcation of sourcing between more capable strategic suppliers and cost-effective manufacturers, especially those in thriving low-cost regions like Bangladesh and Cambodia.

These structural changes have contradictory effects in terms of the vertical power relations in the garment supply chain. On the one hand, the proliferation of the retail model has fostered a consolidation among lead firms that strengthens their position in relation to their suppliers, based on the sheer size of their buying power and their ability to quickly change supplier arrangements through advanced techniques of supply chain management (Gereffi and Frederick 2010, 186). On the other hand, key suppliers may strengthen their competitive situation and acquire additional bargaining power by performing a number of vital operations in the supply chain, including design and sourcing activities (Appelbaum 2009).

### 7.1.3 Recent transformations in the garment supply chain: Geographical

The structural changes described in the previous section have facilitated a stunning dominance of China, the "big winner" of the recent restructuring processes in the garment supply chain (Gereffi and Frederick 2010, 188).

Chinese companies not only export the highest share of finished garments worldwide, but also dominate all other stages of the supply chain such as fibre, yarn and fabric production (Technopak 2012).

The rise of China is the most radical expression of a regional consolidation of garment manufacturing. The top five garment exporting countries produced 71.8 percent of the total export volume in 2009—up from 59.5 percent in 1995 (Frederick and Gereffi 2011, 69). Behind this concentration lies a trend towards global sourcing. Regional suppliers like Mexico and other North American or Caribbean states as well as garment exporters from Central and Eastern Europe are the clear losers of this tendency: "The growth of regional suppliers for finished apparel to the European Union and the United States has decreased markedly since 2005, largely resulting from the expansion of China's exports to these markets" (Gereffi and Frederick 2010, 169). As outlined above, the functional division of labour in Asia's regional production networks with its cascade of differently specialised regions is a major source for the superior competitiveness of the whole area. It facilitates functional upgrading of all involved regions and enables companies to exploit the respective comparative advantages—from advanced and functionally diversified manufacturing to basic manufacturing tasks in countries with particularly low labour costs. The tendency of lead firms to demand more from their suppliers additionally heighten the chances for successful industrial upgrading in core manufacturing regions like China. Yet, higher requirements from buyers also threaten to marginalise other regions that cannot benefit in the same way from dense regional interconnections, proactive government intervention, or capital investments to raise productivity (Frederick and Staritz 2012, 73–80). Against this background, the garment industry in the future may partially lose its role as "pillar of export-oriented industrialisation" that it had taken in the 1970s and 80s (cf. Frederick and Gereffi 2011, 68).

However, as already described on a structural level in the previous section, there is still space for exporting countries to grow on CMT production models particularly in the lower-end product segments. A case in point is the Cambodian industry, the garment exports of which increased by 50 percent between 2005 and 2008 (cf. Frederick and Staritz 2012, 60). Again, the rise of fourth tier Asian exporters such as Cambodia has to be seen in the context of the wider regional production network. There is no other comparable case of the rise of low-cost manufacturers outside the Asian region. The era of a pure "race to the bottom" of functionally limited garment suppliers seems to be over.

The rise of Asian manufacturers does not only reflect their competitive advantages in the realm of production, but also a structural shift of global demand towards the global South and East. In the context of stagnating consumer markets in advanced industrialised countries, high growth in emerging markets has fuelled a regional shift of the industry. This was especially true during the height of the economic crisis and after:

"In 2009, the global apparel retail industry reached $1,032 billion, with the Asia-Pacific region increasing global market share to 25.5% from 21.9% in 2008 […]. The apparel retail industry in the Asia-Pacific region had a compound annual growth rate (CAGR) of 4.0% over the 2005–2009 time span, with strong growth from India (9.9%), China (7.9%), and South Korea (3.9%) offsetting declines in the Japanese market (–0.8%)" (Frederick and Gereffi 2011, 76).

Expanding consumer markets at home enhance the opportunities for brand building of Chinese wholesalers and manufacturers because they can take advantage of their advanced knowledge of local markets and offer fashion goods of cheaper price categories to the vast number of consumers with limited financial resources in these countries:

"Some of the larger, more advanced apparel suppliers such as China, India and Turkey are also reorienting production from export markets to large domestic and nearby regional markets […]. These largely untapped local markets often permit more opportunities for functional upgrading into ODM and OBM business models and may also provide easier entry for smaller exporters and can be used as a learning laboratory for more advanced activities" (ibid, 75).

From the perspective of many garment-exporting countries, the effects of the economic crisis have raised the importance of domestic or regional markets that compensated for some or all of the losses generated by the slump in demand from Europe, Japan and the US. Some garment exporters like Bangladesh, Turkey and Morocco whose exports had strongly depended on Europe and the US managed to diversify their exports during the last decade (ibid, 76).

China is the exception of the rule in this respect, since China's exports to Europe and the US have skyrocketed during the last decade, which means that they have grown faster than alternative end markets, where Chinese products are equally on the rise. Still, Chinese brands like CASUALYOUTH (cf. case study in section 7.3.2) especially expand on markets in South and South-East Asia, Eastern Europe and the Middle East—markets that have consumer profiles that often resemble those found in China (Li&Fung 2010, 11–12).

## 7.2 Growth and transformation of China's textile and garment industry

Like in many other developing countries, the garment industry had been an engine of China's early export-led industrialisation. But unlike in most other regions, the industry was in the position to look back on a history of mass production when the recent wave of growth kicked in after the beginning of the reform period. Back then, the sector was still dominated by SOEs and collectively owned enterprises (COEs) that often had a long history of textile and garment production and could draw on traditions stemming from China's first phase of industrialisation in the 1920s and 1930s, or even on ancient knowledge dating back centuries. What is more, the need to vest a large population meant that the Chinese industry in its recent history always had a strong domestic orientation, even in its recent history after the onset of the economic reforms in the 1980s.[102]

After the founding of the People's Republic of China in 1949, the Chinese government had strongly promoted the growth of the industry and facilitated the establishment of spinning, dyeing and textile factories. In the 1960s and 1970s it also promoted research in and production of synthetic fibres. As a consequence, the industry, which had already employed 745,000 workers in 1949, grew rapidly even before the onset of the reform era:

"By 1978 […] [p]roduction of cotton yarn reached 2.4 million tons, cotton fabric 11 billion meters, wool fabric 89 million meters and wool knitting yarn 378,000 tons. These products were respectively 7.3 times, 6 times, 16 times and 21 times more than their 1949 levels" (Qiu 2005, 3).

But the textile and garment industry made another leap towards high growth and, eventually, global dominance after 1978. The sector was pioneering the new possibilities brought by market opening and was once again strongly supported by the government. Close links with overseas Chinese entrepreneurs and especially Hong Kong investors played a decisive role for the integration of Chinese producers into global production networks that eventually resulted in a high growth in exports:

---

102 However, for much of the reform period the industry had been bifurcated between SOEs or COEs oriented at the domestic market and FIEs that operated on basis of assembly licences and were not allowed to sell their products on the domestic market.

"Hong Kong's textile and apparel industry boomed with the opening on China's economy in 1978. First, production was subcontracted to state-owned factories, but eventually an elaborate network of outward-processing arrangements were [sic!] established that relied on an assortment of manufacturing, financial, and commercial joint ventures. In 1995, Hong Kong entrepreneurs operated more than 20,000 factories employing an estimated 4.5–5 million workers in China's Pearl River Delta alone" (Frederick 2010, 178).

The main reasons for this move by Hong Kong investors were rising prices and shortages of space and labour within the small home territory. Both resources were available in abundance in mainland China at the time. Besides, outsourcing of production or the creation of own production facilities on the mainland helped to circumvent export quotas of the MFA which began to present a difficulty for Hong Kong exporters (Gereffi 1999, 57–59).

### 7.2.1 Development and structure of the industry

Since the beginning of the reform period, the Chinese textile and garment industry has constantly enjoyed high growth rates. Garment export almost doubled every year between 1980 and 1995 from an initial volume of USD 1.65 billion to USD 24.05 billion in 1995. In this year, China already had conquered the position as the largest garment exporter worldwide (Qiu 2005, 6). Fast export-led growth continued in the decade that followed and saw a particularly explosive development between 2005 and 2009, the period of the gradual MFA phase-out, when revenues in Chinese garment production doubled. Despite these high growth rates, the overall weight of textile and garment production in the total output of the Chinese economy has decreased. Garment production constituted a proportion of 7.8 percent of all merchandise exports in 2012, down from 9.7 percent in 2005 (WTO 2013, 123, 131).[103] Yet, this relative decline of the industry's weight only reflects an even faster growth of other industrial sectors, especially the electronics industry, during this period. The textile and garment industry continued to flourish throughout the entire reform period, including the last decade which was characterised by rapid industrial change.

---

103 The respective figures for the textile industry are 4.7 percent in 2012, down from 5.4 percent in 2005 (ibid).

The current development of the textile and garment industry remains one of fast and even accelerating growth, although projections for the coming decade are more modest, in line with global trends. What is more, China's textile and garment industry shows a huge trade surplus since imports barely play a significant role, despite the growing popularity of foreign brand products.[104] This reflects a high share of domestic content in the Chinese textile and garment industry. The bulk of value added in the sector, 66 percent in 2007, stems from companies in China, since the country accommodates a complete production chain from raw material production to final assembly (Koopmanns et al 2008, 20). This is a remarkable difference to many other industries, such as the electronics industry, where China's role has been centred on its role as assembly hub, implying that many valuable components are imported from foreign suppliers that siphon off much of the gains. Thus, the real economic weight of the sector is underestimated when only its relative proportion in total exports of finished products is taken as a measure.

The textile and garment industry, usually organised in a labour-intensive manner, is definitely the most important sector by employment, even though there is some ambiguity about the interpretation of the data. According to official statistics, 4.4 million workers were employed in the sector in 2009, a majority of 2.9 million of which were female (quoted in Lüthje et al 2013b, 253). However, some sources, such as the vice general secretary of China's main industry organisation, also claim a total employment figure of 20 million employees in textile and garment production (cf. Xu 2009). This somewhat speculative figure becomes more plausible, though not reliable, when one takes into account that the official figure for employment only covers employees in enterprises above "designated size", that is in those with an annual output higher than 5 million RMB. Since the Chinese industry infamously remains dominated by small-scale enterprises, most of which are far from reaching an annual output of this scale, it can be assumed that such small and micro units employ a large share of workers across the whole industry.

Today's ownership forms reflect the recent history of the industry as a pioneering sector for private investment that has marginalised former state

---

104 According to the Chinese customs statistics of February 2013, China imported textile and garment products of a value of USD 449.2 million while it exported textile and garment products of a value of USD 5.9 billion, i.e. imports constituted a proportion of 7.6 percent in this month (China Customs Statistics).

enterprises. The bulk of investment is from private sources with SOEs and COEs representing less than one percent of enterprises and only a slightly higher share in total revenues. Among private enterprises, the majority is now owned by mainland Chinese entrepreneurs.

The existence of a strong domestic fibre and textile base is an important advantage for garment enterprises which can cultivate backward linkages, a beneficial asset for a functional upgrading of garment suppliers towards OEM and ODM production models. This broad scope of the domestic industry is not a result of backward integration from CMT functions in garment manufacturing towards textile and yarn production. It is rather a result of China's rich natural resources (cotton, silk) and, in particular, of its long history of industrial development. In the Mao period, the CCP supported the foundation of large-scale textile mills as well as innovation in chemical fibres. This SOE heritage meant that at the beginning of the reform period, China's textile production constituted a larger share of output than the garment industry (Qiu 2005, 3).

The value of textile output to this day remains bigger than that of garments and accounted for more than double of the latter in 2009 (cf. figure 7.4). Both industry segments experienced high annual growth rates of 29.3 percent (textile) and 28.2 percent (garments), respectively, in the period between 2003 and 2009.

*Figure 7.4: Textile and garment revenues of Chinese enterprises above designated size 2003–09, billion RMB*

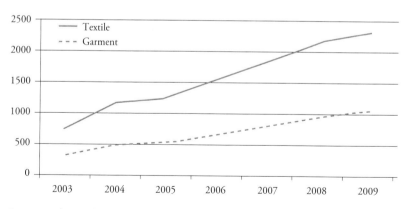

Source: Lüthje et al 2013b.

Yet, the quantitative relationship between garments and textile is opposite when only exports are considered (cf. figure 7.5). In 2011, garments constituted by far the largest industry segment with 52.9 percent of exports in 2011, whereas textiles only accounted for 32.7 percent of the total. The relatively lower share of textiles in total exports reflects that a very large share of the produced fabric is sold to domestic garment companies rather than exported[105] (China Customs Statistics 2011).

*Figure 7.5: Composition of textile and garment exports in 2011*

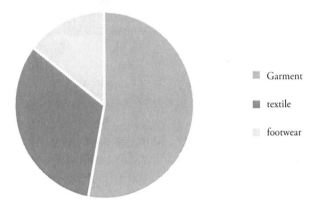

Garment

textile

footwear

Source: China Customs Statistics 2011.

Garment production is concentrated in the Southern and Eastern coastal provinces. According to the China National Garment Association, the combined output of five coastal provinces, Shandong, Jiangsu, Zhejiang, Fujian and Guangdong, in the first half of 2011 represented 77.5 percent of total textile and garment production volume in China (CTEI 08.08.2011). Guangdong Province is a major production base for both the textile and the

---

105 In fact, the discrepancy between garment and fabric exports is even underestimated by the quoted figures, since the Chinese customs statistics include various finished products such as carpets, hand bags, and suitcases, into the category "textile yarn, fabrics and made-up articles". If exclusively woven fabrics are considered, the respective export figure is USD 18.4 billion, only one fifth of the aggregate figure given for the broader category of "textile yarn, fabrics and made-up articles" (calculated from China Customs Statistics 2011). Regarding the composition of garment exports in 2011, 84 percent of garment exports consisted of textile garments (based on cloth), the remainder being products based on leather or fur and some woven products such as stockings or headgear (ibid).

garment industry (cf. table 7.2). Garment manufacturers therefore have the possibility to create close backward linkages to textile enterprises which is beneficial to their competitiveness.

*Table 7.2: Output of China's main textile and garment producing regions in 2012, billion RMB*

| Province | Textile output | Companies | Garment output | Companies |
|----------|----------------|-----------|----------------|-----------|
| Jiangsu | 608.5 | 5,227 | 451.3 | 2,233 |
| Guangdong | 232.6 | 1,810 | 290.1 | 2,856 |
| Zhejiang | 580.5 | 5,267 | 146.8 | 1,499 |
| Fujian (2011) | 166.8 | n.s. | 125.1 | n.s. |

Source: Statistical Yearbooks of Guangdong, Jiangsu, Zhejiang and Fujian.

While there is a strong concentration of manufacturing in the coastal regions, there is also an important traditional division of labour with provinces in the interior, such as Xinjiang Province or Inner Mongolia, acting as major suppliers of raw materials, such as cotton and cashmere wool. Additionally, in line with the general government strategy of a regional rebalancing of China's economy, the interior provinces are gaining some production capacities due to a relocation of industries from the overcrowded and more expensive coastal provinces. From January to May of 2011, garment output in the middle and western provinces increased rapidly by 42.1 percent and 38.6 percent respectively—much faster than in the Eastern provinces where output grew by 9.4 percent (ibid).

One characteristic feature of the textile and garment industry is its strong specialization and local conglomeration. Across China, there exist almost 150 officially approved industry clusters in the textile and garment sector. Such specialised towns mostly focus their industrial layout on one product category, such as in the case in the "capital of socks" Datang in Zhejiang Province, for instance, where more than 3.5 billion pairs of socks were produced in 2009 in a town of 70,000 resident inhabitants (People's Daily 21.12.2009).

Companies in specialised towns benefit from dense supplier interactions, as well as from proactive government support that often results in prestigious infrastructure investments to boost the sales of the local industry. Recently, the advantages of Chinese industrial clusters have served as blueprints for successful economic development in publications by the World Bank and the IMF (cf. Zeng 2010 and 2011).

## 7.2.2 Recent economic development

Although the domestic market absorbs the major share of China's textile and garment output, foreign trade has made an important contribution to its growth performance (cf. table 7.3). Due to this relatively strong export dependence, the contraction of demand from the United States and Europe in late 2008 and 2009 had a devastating effect on the garment industry, especially in the Pearl River Delta, where foreign investment and outward orientation of the industry are particularly pronounced.

In 2009, the effects of the global economic crisis lead to a contraction of textile and garment exports by 7.65 percent down from an annual growth rate of around 20 percent in the years 2003–2006 (cf. figure 7.6, p. 248). The global economic crisis thereby aggravated problems that low-end manufacturers already experienced in the course of the year 2007. National media reported a series of factory closures during that year due to rising wages and labour shortages (cf. Wong 2008,1–4). The crisis may therefore be seen as a catalyst for a structural change in which garment suppliers with limited technological capacities that relied solely on cost advantages went out of business.

*Table 7.3: Textile and garment production volumes and exports 2003–2009, billion RMB*

| | Revenues | | | Exports | Exports/ revenues[i] |
|---|---|---|---|---|---|
| | textile | garment | combined | combined | Combined |
| 2003 | 772.52 | 342.60 | 1,115.12 | 666.13 | 0.60 |
| 2004 | 1,165.51 | 466.85 | 1,632.36 | 805.97 | 0.49 |
| 2005 | 1,267.17 | 497.46 | 1,764.63 | 942.29 | 0.53 |
| 2006 | 1,531.55 | 615.94 | 2,147.49 | 1,147.70 | 0.53 |
| 2007 | 1,873.33 | 760.64 | 2,633.97 | 1,301.88 | 0.49 |
| 2008 | 2,139.31 | 943.58 | 3,082.89 | 1,285.95 | 0.42 |
| 2009 | 2,297.14 | 1,044.48 | 3,341.62 | 1,168.10 | 0.35 |

i   This figure for the proportion of exports as a share of revenues is not an accurate measure for the real export quota of China's textile and garment industry since data for "revenues" and for "exports" are calculated differently. Chinese official statistics for "revenues" do not provide data for the output of enterprises below "designated size", whereas customs statistics for "exports" capture any legally exported item. Since small-scale production below "designated size" constitutes a substantial share of output in this sector, the actual figure for "revenues" must be higher than the ones listed here. Therefore the real export quota should be even below the figures given in the last column of this table.

Source: Lüthje et al 2013a; China customs statistics; own calculations.

Yet, these aggregate figures about the slump in foreign demand in late 2008 and early 2009 insufficiently convey the extent of instant shock that the crisis gave companies and workers in export-oriented garment clusters. In the PRD, literally millions of workers left early for the New Year's break at the end of January of 2009, overcrowding the local train stations and bus terminals, often without having received their legitimate salary from their employers who in some cases had shut down operations and disappeared without a warning (Anti 2009; de Haan 2010, 72–76).

But what looked like a devastating collapse in early 2009 soon turned out to be a temporary shock. Foreign demand kicked in again in the second half of 2009 and China's textile and garment industry subsequently experienced two years of above-average growth which compensated for much of the losses during the crisis. Thereby the Chinese garment industry outperformed many of its competitors (though not low-cost locations like Vietnam or Cambodia): China's share in garment imports to the United States, for instance, rose from 32.0 percent in 2008 to 39.5 percent in October 2010 (Just Style 06.01.2011). The crisis proved to be a step towards a growing dominance of Chinese textile and garment manufacturers who were less hard hit than many of their international competitors. Rather than weakening the Chinese industry as a whole, the crisis eliminated some of the less competitive domestic companies and thus fostered a structural change towards more advanced production models resulting in a generally more competitive industry.

*Figure 7.6: Chinese textile and garment exports, billion USD 2003–11*

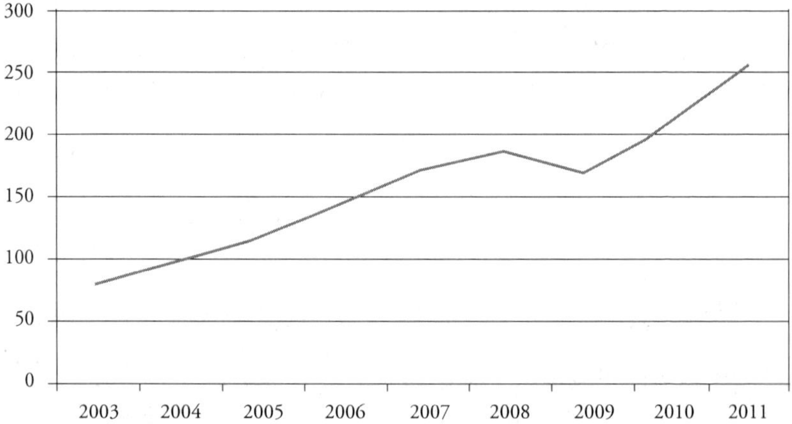

Source: Chen 2012.

Apart from government measures to support the weakly performing export industry, for instance through the reintroduction of export rebates, the strong performance of the domestic market helped many manufacturers to sustain the global economic crisis well. Due to unbroken growth in consumer demand, the textile and garment industry experienced growth rates of 17.0 percent in 2008 and 8.4 percent in 2009 during the crisis period (Lüthje et al 2013b, 253). The crisis thereby acted as a catalyst for structural change in yet another sense: it lastingly increased the share of domestic consumption in textile and especially garment output and thereby reduced the export dependency of the industry. In 2009, the volume of exports only corresponded to 35 percent of output of enterprises above designated size (down from a rate of 49 percent in 2007, cf. table 7.3). These figures provide a glimpse of the huge growth potential of the Chinese domestic market. While China increased its dominance among global garment exporters, domestic demand grew at an even faster pace, in the course of which the garment industry was transformed into a domestic-led industry.

Yet, the weak performance of its key export markets is continuing to put a strain on the Chinese textile and garment industry. According to the China Textile Association, it suffered a renewed setback in 2012, with a growth of only 1.04 percent in the first three quarters (China Daily 09.11.2012). The dire situation of the industry in 2012 is not specific to Chinese producers. The garment industry of Vietnam, for instance, is expecting similar difficulties and performing below targets set by the government, with exports to the EU expected to shrink by 15 percent in 2012 (CTEI 23.02.2012).

### 7.2.3 Restructuring and industrial upgrading

The Chinese central and provincial governments reacted to the crisis in the textile and garment industry with a mixture of immediate measures to curb its negative effects and initiatives for a structural reform aiming at an overall higher profitability and competitiveness. Both of these targets were presented in the "Plan for Adjustment and Revitalisation of the Textile Industry", published by the State Council on 24 April 2009.[106] The plan set targets for an annual growth of 10 percent and an export volume of USD 240 billion until 2011—both of which the industry eventually outperformed. It called for a rationalisation of the industry structure, and for the elimination of overcapacities along the production chain. It also promoted investment in China's interior provinces, more ecologically sound production techniques, and the elimination of outdated capacities which were supposed to be replaced by state-of-the-art production technologies that match international standards (USCBC 2009). The main instruments for achieving these goals were:

---

[106] In China, the expression "textile industry" (*fangzhe gongye*) refers to both the textile and the garment industry.

- A series of crisis-related interventions, e.g. the acquisition of cotton and silk factories; loan extensions; credit guarantees; reductions in social security obligations for companies that did not lay off workers; the raise of value added tax rebates for exporters.[107]
- Encouragement for mergers and acquisitions as a means to eliminate overcapacities in the sector.
- Measures to promote industrial upgrading, such as investment in and support of technological transformation in the fields of high-tech fibres, spinning, weaving, printing and dyeing; provision of public services and research to support innovative capabilities of SMEs; support for brand-building; a more proactive role of the government in guiding industrial development with national associations as a transmission belt between government planning and implementation.
- The promotion of domestic brands by enhancing product quality, encouraging brand building and creating a stronger marketing infrastructure. The plan set a target of 10 percent for brand products as a share of total exports and announced special support for the 100 companies with the strongest technological capabilities (ibid).

In order to reach its goals for the elimination of outdated production capacities, the authorities did not shrink back from rigorous actions. In August 2010, over 2,000 enterprises of all sectors, among them 200 textile and 25 synthetic fibre companies, were shut down on government orders because of violation of ecological minimum requirements (Gesamtverband textil+mode 2011, 26).

The implementation of the central government's Adjustment and Revitalisation Plan was mainly carried out by provincial, city or township governments. As the case studies illustrate, local governments of industrial clusters have been particularly eager to implement measures to strengthen the local industry through supporting local brands, subsidising the purchase of modern equipment, and constructing infrastructure. The Chinese system, in which the establishment and successful development of industry clusters is rewarded by the provincial and central authorities, has unleashed a strong competition between local governments. The by-product of this dynamic is a strong incentive for industrial modernisation among the local political cad-

---

107 The latter traditionally has been an instrument of industrial policy that had served to promote export processing during the reform period. The rebates were reduced from 2004 on, but raised above their previous level in 2008 (IBISWORLD 2011, 34).

re.[108] Within industrial clusters, governments devote much energy to foster smooth supply-chain interactions and a diversification of enterprises, instead of unproductive competition.

All of these measures have created an advantageous environment for industrial upgrading. In this sense, the long-established textile and garment industry is far from being mature. It is currently undergoing fundamental transformations that further improve the global (and national) competitiveness of enterprises and thoroughly affect the character of work (cf. Lüthje et al 2013b, 260–268). In fact, one study about the recent industrial transformation in China (certainly underestimating the dynamics of upgrading in high-tech industries) asserts that "[a]mong various industry sectors, garment enterprises are most outstanding in their pursuit of transformation and upgrade" (HKTDC 2011a). Most of the recent approaches entail some degree of functional upgrading towards "full-package production". This mostly implies incremental improvements on a trial-and-error base rather than a full-scale strategic shift towards a certain manufacturing model (cf. Lüthje et al. 2013b, 260–262). The following elements constitute prominent elements of upgrading initiatives in Chinese textile and garment enterprises:

*(1) Brand building*
Backed by a fast growing domestic market, brand building has become a major tendency among garment producers and wholesalers. The entry barriers are relatively low:

---

108 The benefits of a rationalisation of the industry structure through clustering became particularly evident during the author's field studies when visiting a garment company in Guangzhou's Baiyun district in 2010. This OEM supplier suffered severely under the crisis, showed little ambition to overhaul its production technologies and announced that it was going to go out of business within the following years (ID 27.10.2010). This stood in sharp contrast to the author's interviews with enterprise representatives in the thriving fashion industry of Humen, Dongguan, in 2010 and 2011. In the latter, the local government fostered the modernisation of local companies by supporting brand building, independent design capabilities and marketing. In Guangzhou's Baiyun district, the attitude of the government was the opposite since it was fostering the transformation of the area to a modern service hub where garment manufacturing did not fit in. The comparison illustrates that there is little chance for isolated garment companies without public support to cope with a changing business environment, whereas government policy has contributed to open new horizons for manufacturers in a town eager to establish itself as leading garment cluster.

"[I]t is easier for garment enterprises than those in other industries to develop and produce goods of their own designs and have them sold under their own brands in the mainland market while keeping their OEM production business for overseas buyers" (HKTDC 2011a).

However, brand building requires independent design capabilities and investment into advertisement and retail channels. Many brands organise sales through their own retail network:

"They will sell products of their own brands directly by running their own specialty stores [or] make active use of franchise and licensing operation [sic!] to recruit retail investors or participants across the country to become members of their chains" (ibid).

In their sales models, most Chinese brands tend to replicate the model of Western specialty retailers like H&M or Benetton. But unlike these, they mostly maintain their own production facilities. In a survey among 2,000 Chinese garment brands, 53.7 percent of respondents stated that they were not planning to outsource any manufacturing activities (HKTDC 2012b). The dominant production model in the industry therefore rather is one of brand manufacturing (like Zara or Fruit of the Loom) than that of fabless retailers.[109] One obvious reason is that some Chinese garment brands, yet not the market leaders, continue to engage in some OEM or ODM production, mainly for export customers. This has proven to be a successful transitional model in order to back up experiments in brand building by a solid source of income. Furthermore, Chinese brand manufacturers' know how with regard to the production process can turn out to be of a similar advantage as it was in the case of Zara, whose performance challenged the then dominant assumption by analysts that a retreat from manufacturing was the most successful model (cf. Gallaugher 2008).

## (2) Automation

As the costs of production factors like labour, land and cotton are rising fast, textile and garment manufacturers increase spending on advanced produc-

---

109 A counterexample is the Guangzhou Textile Group, a former SOE co-managed by the local branch of the ACFTU. The company now acts as a platform for design houses and fabless garment companies that outsource virtually all manufacturing to subcontractors. The large manufacturing capacity of earlier days was privatised or abandoned during the last two decades. The Group had 60,000 employees in 1990. This number shrunk to 30,000 in 2003 and 3,000 in 2009 (ID 26.10.2010 (b)).

tion equipment in order to raise productivity and maintain competitiveness. Process upgrading through the acquisition of new equipment also helps to improve product quality and enhance the versatility of manufacturers (e.g. through CNC weaving or knitting machines[110]). The result of the drive towards automation of the industry, which varies depending on the respective processes and products, sharply reduces labour intensity in manufacturing. At the same time, there is a higher capital intensity which raises the entry barriers for smaller companies with few resources.

China today by far constitutes the most important destination for textile machine vendors. China absorbed the lion's share in any of the most important machinery types in 2011 (cf. table 7.4), except in the category of long-staple spindles which are used for the spinning of wool (because raw wool is barely produced domestically). The surge in equipment sales in China bears witness to the rapid dynamic of process upgrading through automation which is supported by government subsidies.

*Table 7.4: Share of Chinese demand for main types of textile machines in 2011*

|  | Machine type | Growth of global shipments (percent) | Share sold in China (percent) |
|---|---|---|---|
| Knitting | Circular knitting | −16 | 73 |
|  | Flat knitting | 37 | 78 |
| Spinning | Short-staple spindles | 15 | 62 |
|  | Long-staple spindles | 35 | 21 |
|  | Open-end rotors | 27 | 68 |
| Texturing | Single heater draw | −86 | 84 |
|  | Double heater draw | 45 | 76 |
| Weaving | Shuttle-less looms | 44 | 83 |

Source: International Textile Manufacturers Federation.

---

110 Through Computer Numerical Controlled machines, manufacturers can enter (digital) designs directly into the machines which facilitates the production of complex stitches and patterns. Such equipment is usually sold together with matching design programmes, important tools to support independent design and a quick link between design and production (cf. case study on the Dalang knitwear industry in section 7.3.1).

The strong demand for equipment also nurtures a fast growing domestic textile machines industry. Chinese equipment producers have gained substantial market shares in recent years. Although Chinese machines are generally regarded to be of lower quality than those of top brands from Europe or the US like Stoll or Picanol, they present a reasonable alternative for customers since they are sold at a fraction of the price of imported models (ID 30.10.2010b; 21.11.2010a; 02.11.2011a). The development of a thriving equipment industry is an important dimension of industrial upgrading in textile and garment clusters, since it reduces the dependency of the Chinese textile and garment industry on foreign technology and in itself constitutes a field of relatively complex high value-added manufacturing.

*(3) Lean production*

In line with global trends, Chinese garment manufacturers increasingly adopt lean production schemes. These aim at a reduction of inventory, an improved coordination of time-cycles between retailers and their suppliers, as well as at quality improvements, e.g. through teamwork-based work organisation (Lüthje et al 2013b, 263–264). Lean production practices can streamline production and increase cost-effectiveness in such a way that it can counter the general tendencies of rising production costs. According to one consultant, there is a great potential for a professionalization in this respect, since many Chinese firms do not possess professional management systems and operate along traditional techniques similar to those that could be found in family-run businesses (ID 05.12.2010). Lean production schemes often interfere with the established wage systems. They mostly imply a change from piece rate systems towards hourly or de-facto hourly wages. While, theoretically, this could remove incentives for excessive overtime work that are inbuilt in the piece rate wage regimes, the change towards hourly wages often leads to wage losses for experienced workers and has been met with resistance in some cases (cf. Lüthje et al 2013b, 268–269).

Such measures for industrial transformation are far from representing the status quo in Chinese textile and garment enterprises. Despite lasting efforts to modernise production during the last decade, many companies still operate on basis of simple production technologies and a large share of companies is still limited to CMT or basic OEM operations. But the economic crisis has accelerated tendencies for a thorough structural change. Ongoing price increases for labour, land, and raw materials put further pressures on manufacturers to restructure their operations.

7.2.4 An exodus from Guangdong? Relocation dynamics after the crisis

Since the economic crisis there has been no shortage of reports that forecast a loss of competitiveness of Chinese companies against competitors in countries with lower production costs. This is argued in a recent report by McKinsey on the garment industry, for instance: "A growing number of chief purchasing officers (CPOs) are scrutinizing their sourcing strategies [...]. While China is starting to lose its attractiveness in this realm, the sourcing caravan is moving on to the next hot spot" which, according to this analysis, now is Bangladesh (McKinsey 2011c, 3).

A recent survey among 28 European and US Central Procurement Officers of garment brands and retailers representing a combined purchasing power of USD 46 billion found that 86 percent of buyers were planning to decrease levels of sourcing in China until 2016 "because of declining profit margins and capacity constraints" (McKinsey 2012c, 2). The assumption of a major shift in sourcing is also vindicated by announcements of well-known Chinese companies to relocate parts of their manufacturing to other countries, as it was the case with the large online apparel retailer Vancl that plans to start operations at new production facilities in Bangladesh. The company explained this step with rising wages and labour shortages in China (FT 08.08.2012). Without a doubt, there is a reorientation in global sourcing in which buyers strive to reduce their dependency on China. Outsourcing is even becoming an option for Chinese brands that equally look for ways to reduce costs in their supply chain.

But reports about a loss of production capacities, a relative decline in manufacturing, or even an end of cheap labour clearly overstate such tendencies and simply do not match trade statistics. In the period between 2005 and 2008, China's export value of textile and garment products has grown by USD 40,565 million, or 45.2 percent, whereas the combined exports of Vietnam, Bangladesh, India and Cambodia, i.e. those countries frequently named as sourcing alternatives to China, grew by USD 14,331, or 57.5 percent, at an only slightly faster pace.[111] The so-called fourth-tier suppliers and China all grew somewhat faster than the total volume of exports worldwide which means that they grew at the cost of other competitors whose production volumes declined during this period (cf. Frederick and Gereffi 2011, 70). The assumption of a relative loss of China's garment industry against its

---

111 Only the output of Vietnam grew at a substantially faster pace of more than 100 percent in this period.

Asian competitors also seems insupportable with view to the industry's immediate post-crisis development. The Chinese share in US garment imports increased by 5.1 percentage points from 32 percent in 2008 to 37.1 percent in February 2014, while those of Vietnam grew by 3.1 percentage points to 10.4 percent and that of Bangladesh by 1.4 percentage points to 6.2 percent during the same period (just-style 2011, FiveThirtyEight 23.04.2014). However, growth rates of Vietnamese and Cambodian garment exports have been much higher than those of China where there has been a stagnation of export volumes since about 2010.[112]

But even if the recent weak performance of China's garment exports seems to confirm the tale of a decline of China as a core destination for global sourcing, the scale of this process is often overestimated and mostly poorly understood. What is happening is not an all-encompassing geographical shift away from China, but an ongoing dominance of world trade by China with a partial diversification of sourcing strategies. In most cases, sourcing from fourth-tier suppliers is a supplementary strategy of global buyers, not an alternative. As described in section 7.1, there is a growing bifurcation of global sourcing between manufacturing of cheap labour-intensive goods and more sophisticated products, usually bought from full-package suppliers. Although also fourth-tier suppliers like Bangladesh and Vietnam experience rapid industrial upgrading, their manufacturing capabilities are centred on CMT and OEM production (Staritz and Frederick 2012: 213–272). This leaves China, while losing some of its more basic assembly activities, in a unique position to supply more complex products that entail design functions by full-package suppliers. One recent analysis puts this more bluntly:

"[E]veryone else competes to make the easy stuff, leaving China to mop up the profits elsewhere [...]. Ironically, China's competitors compete with one another. They do not compete with China [...]. Unlike the other countries, China's garment industry is diversified. Exports of the big four products [cotton T-shirts, cotton trousers, woven shirts and underwear, F.B.], while important, do not dominate China's garment exports" (Just Style 06.01.2011).

A recent statement from a representative from Vancl who stated that the production cycle for products sourced in Bangladesh could be as long as six

---

112 The share of Chinese garment imports to the US peaked at 39.7 percent in 2010 and never reached this value ever since (HKTDC 2011d).

months, as opposed to that of domestic Chinese suppliers who are required to deliver in 30 to 45 days implicitly confirms this assessment (quoted in FT 08.08.2012). Obviously, Vancl is looking for a supplementary production site for a basic production line while leaving its more complex "fast fashion" manufacturing in China.

Still, China's relative loss of competitiveness in cost-sensible CMT and OEM production may hurt domestic manufacturers, if competing export locations like Vietnam are able to maintain their cost advantages in the future. However, this can by no means be taken for granted. Vietnam has experienced a series of strikes and wage hikes similar to Guangdong in recent years (A.Chan 2011). A recent survey projects that average wages in Vietnam will grow at a similar pace like in China, and at a significantly higher pace in Bangladesh in the period 2013 - 2018. If average productivity growth, which is highest in China compared to most low-wage countries, is considered, China is even becoming cheaper as a production site relative to its competitors (The Economist, 23.05.2014).

A survey among Hong Kong manufacturers of all sectors from the first quarter in 2010 supports the view that China in general, and the PRD in particular, remains attractive as a production site (cf. table 7.5). Their responses are not representative of the investment and sourcing strategies of global companies, since Hong Kong entrepreneurs maintain strong cultural and economic ties to the PRD region and therefore may show less inclination to leave the region than other investors. However, Hong Kong investors historically do constitute an important share of investment in labour-intensive low value-added industries and their judgement therefore reflects the ongoing attractiveness of the PRD. Certainly it corrects the widespread impression of an exodus of low-end manufacturing, including basic garment manufacturing, from Guangdong.

*Table 7.5: Hong Kong manufacturers' assessment of the PRD's competitiveness as a production site.*[i]

| Region | Rating of competitiveness[ii] | Location to set up new factories (%)[iii] | Location to set up new outsourcing arrangements (%)[iii] |
|---|---|---|---|
| PRD | 3.59 | 46.2 | 46.8 |
| YRD | 3.59 | 12.7 | 20.8 |
| Other Guang-dong | 3.44 | 16.5 | 26.6 |
| Near inland | 3.11 | 13.5 | 19.0 |
| Bohai region | 3.08 | 3.8 | 7.1 |
| India | 2.95 | 1.5 | 3.4 |
| Vietnam | 2.92 | 6.2 | 6.9 |
| Rest of mainland | 2.79 | 10.8 | 12.9 |
| Indonesia | 2.73 | 3.1 | 2.8 |
| Cambodia | 2.57 | 3.8 | 2.0 |
| Bangladesh | 2.53 | 2.3 | 2.0 |

i   The survey was conducted in the first quarter of 2010 with more than 4,500 replies, of which more than 2,400 were manufacturers.
ii  On a scale of 1-5.
iii Multiplies replies possible.

Source: HKTDC 2010b.

## 7.3 Case studies from the textile and garment industry

The case studies cover ten enterprises in three relevant subsectors of the textile and garment industry: The knitting industry of Dalang, Dongguan (7.3.1), the fashion industry of Humen, Dongguan (7.3.2), and the textile industry of Xiqiao, Foshan (7.3.3). As each of the surveyed industries is clustered around townships in which they dominate the industrial structure, a broader focus was chosen in which the transformation on enterprise basis is discussed in the context of the respective upgrading policies pursued by local governments.

7.3.1 Automation, skill upgrading, and de-skilling in Dalang's knitwear industry

Dalang, a township within the city district of Dongguan with 69,000 permanent residents and a floating population of more than 400,000 migrant workers, has experienced a rapid transformation of its industrial structure during the last five years. Due to rapid upgrading of the town's knitwear industry, which has represented the town's core industrial sector since the beginning of the market reforms, Dalang has achieved the status of a model for the transformation of traditional labour-intensive and low value-added industries. Wang Yang, until recently CP party secretary of Guangdong, was a frequent visitor of the town and ensured that articles about Dalang's experience would be published in local media and government research reports (ID 13.12.10a). Dalang was one of the first out of 15 districts in Guangdong that were chosen for demonstrative cluster upgrading projects. It is also home to one of the three pilot projects in Guangdong's garment industry for the launch of international brands (Dalang Investment Promotion Office 2010).

After the beginning of the reform policies in the late 1970s, Dalang soon experienced a strong influx of foreign investment. Located on the Southern edge of Dongguan, the town benefitted from its proximity to Hong Kong, where most investment during the 1980s came from. The woollen knitwear industry was the first sector to flourish. Until recently, the industry was largely confined to assembly-type manufacturing.

*7.3.1.1 Economic structure of the town*

Due to the size of its local industry, Dalang earned the official title "Famous Town of Woollen Garments".[113] The significance of the knitwear industry for the local economy is clearly reflected in the town's layout. There is a specialised street of woollen knitwear products extending 6.5 km, as well as a 6 square kilometre woollen knitwear trade area and a giant newly-built wool-

---

113 Such titles are not self-chosen, but part of the central and provincial government's strategy to support clustering in certain industries. Township governments can apply for being officially recognised as industrial cluster which may entitle them to special attention regarding central industrial policies. This kind of governance has a parallel in awards provided to enterprises for brand names or particular products. Such awards are granted by government authorities and the respective industry associations.

len knitwear market building. The latter is also the site of the annual Dalang Woollen Knitwear Fair, a huge trade event that completely dominates the town's appearance during the fair and its preparations. The town's economy is shaped by a sheer infinite number of mostly small-scale knitwear companies. According to the Bureau of Statistics of Dongguan (2010), there existed almost 3,500 knitwear enterprises in town, 86 percent of them owned by mainland Chinese entrepreneurs. Yet, this is only the tip of the iceberg since the economic cluster stretches beyond the official town boundaries to involve roughly 10,000 knitwear enterprises in the wider area. Above 90 percent of enterprises within town limits are smaller companies with revenues of less than RMB 5 million per year. Yet, the bulk of output is produced by large companies. In 2009, the revenues of the town's 120 largest companies above designated size was RMB 5.5 billion which constituted about 80% of total output of the industry. Another 15 percent was produced by 1,200 medium-sized companies whereas small companies only contributed about five percent of revenues (ID 19.11.2010b).

Despite impressive dimensions of the knitwear industry, its relative economic weight has declined from a share of 50–60 percent of industrial output in 2003/04 to roughly one third, about the same level as the local IT industry and the machinery and industrial equipment industry.[114] Reflecting this trend, the Dalang authorities pursue an industrial policy that simultaneously supports each of these industrial sectors while especially promoting the service sector. It does not seek a replacement of the knitwear sector as the leading industry in town, but rather a "neck on neck" development of industries (ID 19.11.2010b). Despite the relative decline of the knitwear industry's output, it still dominates employment in Dalang. Government sources estimate the total number of employees in design, production and marketing at 100,000 persons, a higher number than in other sectors (ID 19.11.2010b).

---

114 There are 1,400 IT companies in Dalang that churned out two million display screens, 35 million integrated circuits, 500,000 hard disks, 500,000 solar panels and many other similar products in 2010. Apart from OEM production, which is dominated by Taiwanese investors, there are also high profile high-tech projects, above all the planned construction of a spallation neutron source, a device that enables the deciphering of molecular structures by the emission of neutron beams. A third pillar of Dalang's industry is the production of machinery and industrial equipment, a sector that consists of about 1,300 enterprises. The leading companies of this branch focus on the production of digital machines like precision moulding facilities, injection machines and industrial cranes (Dalang Government Website, ID 13.12.2010).

The total annual sales volume on Dalang's knitwear market is 1.2 billion sweaters, of which 800 Million are produced in Dalang. The US and Europe absorb 60 percent of Dalang's exports. The rest is mainly shipped to Russia, the Middle East and North Africa (ID 19.11.2010b). The town's authorities proudly claim that probably one in every five persons in the world owns a sweater that was produced in Dalang (Nanfang Ribao, 26.08.2010a).

During the economic crisis of 2008/09 Dalang at first experienced a similar fate like many export-oriented towns in Dongguan. Government sources claim that around 100 small companies shut down in 2009. Apparently, tens of thousands of migrant workers left town after the crisis hit (ID 19.11.2010b). However, Dalang, and in particular the knitwear sector, soon experienced high growth rates. About 150 small companies were newly founded in 2009, thus leading to a positive balance in the number of companies at the end of that year. More robust companies of larger size could expand at the expense of smaller competitors. Backed by the government, they heavily invested in modern production equipment. The crisis therefore triggered substantial process upgrading resulting in more efficient and less labour-intensive operations by large scale enterprises. According to government figures, the knitwear industry experienced a surge in growth between 2008 and 2012 with a total growth rate of 113 percent, well above the overall GDP growth rate of 10 percent in this period (ID 06.02.2013).

### 7.3.1.2 Industrial upgrading in the woollen knitwear sector

The splendid performance of the knitwear industry since the economic crisis is a stark contrast to the situation only a few years ago. According to an article in a regional newspaper,

"[i]n 2007, the Dalang wool industry was plagued by rising labour costs, rising raw material prices, an unfavourable adjustment of the currency exchange rate, reduced demand from the international market and many other factors. Profits were diluted [...]. Thus, a large part of labour-intensive industries of Dalang was relocated at this time. A greater emphasis was placed on corporate restructuring and upgrading" (Nanfang Ribao, 26.8.2010b).

Up until now, the transformation in Dalang has been fairly successful in reversing the negative trends in terms of growth and the former innovation deadlock. The provincial government is referring to Dalang as a vindication that industrial upgrading is possible even in traditional, labour-intensive sectors. A well-known statement by Wang Yang, according to which there existed no sunset industries, only sunset technologies, actually was coined with reference to the experience in Dalang (quoted in Nanfang Ribao, 26.8.2010b).

The Dalang government frames its upgrading policy as a "double transformation "from product marketing to brand marketing and from a production base to a modern commercial region. More specifically, the upgrading strategy in the knitwear sector is summarised as a programme of "six strokes" (*liu zhao*), according to a programme implemented by the local government since 2010. The agenda includes improvements in terms of innovation capabilities, the organisation of production, the development of marketing and the construction of infrastructure, in particular the so-called "six strokes" (*liu zhao*) aimed to (1) seize the opportunity for innovation and transformation, (2) digitalise production, (3) invest in the service platform, (4) develop an extended industry chain, (5) promote collaboration among enterprises and (6) create of a strong service environment (Guangdong EIC 22.10.2010). The main implications of these measures and their effects on enterprises is summarised subsequently.

*(1) Process upgrading: The introduction of the CNC knitwear machine*
Industrial transformation in the knitwear industry is closely connected to the introduction of the computer numerical control (CNC) knitting machine, as the following lofty passage from a local newspaper illustrates:

"Just like the industrial revolution in the mid-18th century in England, that originated from a small spinning jenny, which then changed the entire European continent and world's history, the technological revolution through the CNC machine is being carried out quietly in the town and will expand to other parts of the Pearl River Delta. It will gradually replace the manual knitting machine, with the effect to spur product design and development and to upgrade production" (Nanfang Ribao, 26.08.2010b).

CNC machines operate in a full-automatic manner, unlike their predecessors, semi-automatic or manual knitting machines. They tend to be operated 24 hours a day in two shifts whereas the older generation of equipment used to be operated during (at times excessively long) day shifts. Most notably, far fewer workers are needed to operate an automated knitting department. One operator can control eight to twelve machines on average whereas each worker operated only one manual or at most two semi-automatic machines in the previous system (ID 30.10.2010a; 30.10.2010b). Yet, even this comparison still underestimates the potential savings in labour power. Because of a productivity level that is 2.5 times higher on average, companies need to rely on less machines to produce the same output. Hence, companies that introduce new equipment can produce the same volumes with less than 10 percent of the former knitting workforce. One newspaper article even estimates that the productivity of the CNC knitting machine is equivalent to that of up to 20 skilled workers operating the older generation of machines, although this number is probably inflated (Nanfang Ribao, 26.8.2010a).[115] According to government information, automation is the main reason for the drastic layoff of 40–50,000 knitting workers between 2007 and 2009. In this period, 6,200 CNC knitting machines were installed and their number rose to around 10,000 in late 2010 (Bureau of Statistics of Dongguan; ID 19.11.2010b). Corresponding to this saving in man power, labour cost in the knitting sections of a company can be reduced by one eighth to one sixth (Yangcheng Wanbao 27.08.2010).

*Illustration 7.1: Manual and automatic knitting machines*

Source: Company website; author's photographs.

---

115 It is calculated as follows: Output of one 1 CNC operator = output of 8 manual machine operators x productivity increase of 250% = output of 20 manual machine operators. The article discusses automation at POWERKNIT, the largest company in town which is covered by the case studies below. However, this calculation ignores that companies with CNC machines tend to employ additional personnel for working the night shifts as was pointed out in my conversation with representatives at this very company. A representative of the machine manufacturer Stoll stated that one CNC machine can replace up to 15 manual workers based on the assumption that one worker can operate 12 machines simultaneously (ID 31.10.2010b).

Yet cost reduction is not the only advantage of CNC knitting machines. They also offer a new versatility in terms of styles and patterns.[116] Above all, designers can upload their digital designs to the machines via USB slots. Therefore, the modernisation of the knitwear industry in Dalang is labelled as a "digitalisation" of design, production and marketing. The direct link between digital design and the computerised machines has the effect that the knitting workers do barely interfere with this process. They also do not need to programme the machines or steer the production process, but merely oversee the faultless operation of the machines. The operability of the machines is furthermore kept simple by means of visual elements due to which "the machines can almost be operated by an illiterate worker", according to a salesperson of an equipment manufacturer (ID 10.04.2013). CNC machines furthermore offer advantages in terms of product quality which is as steady as their mode of operation. Progress in terms of the quality and versatility of styles allows suppliers to produce fabric that meets the requirements of high-end buyers once sufficiently sophisticated models of knitting machines are acquired.

The government of Dalang provides subsidies for the installation of CNC knitting machines. For each machine that costs more than RMB 50,000 it contributes the amount of RMB 2,000 and cheaper machines are subsidised at RMB 1,000 per piece. The government also cooperates with banks to facilitate credit financing, a service which was of great importance during the economic crisis and which for most companies is a prerequisite for buying the expensive knitting equipment (ID 19.11.2010b).

Automation of knitting is of such paramount importance to the development of the industry, that a sub-cluster of machine producers emerged in Dalang. In late 2010, eleven equipment companies had invested in manufacturing operations in Dalang and all in all there were sales dependencies of 59 knitting machine vendors (ID 19.11.2010b). In 2009, 28,900 machines were sold via vendors in Dalang, of which 4,000 were bought by companies in Dalang and the adjacent town Changping (Yangcheng Wanbao 27.08.2010).

---

116 According to a representative of one foreign equipment company, "the products fall out of the machines in an almost finished state. It is possible to create every possible form of textile with it, even for medical or other technical applications, so-called seamless textile parts" (ID 30.10.2010b).

## (2) Functional upgrading towards brand manufacturing

Brand building constitutes a second important element in the government's upgrading strategy. This is implemented in a double effort of establishing a regional brand and encouraging enterprises to create own brand products. Brand building is supposed to grant companies a "right to speak", i.e. a stronger market position, which is perceived to be denied as long as manufacturers stick to a supply function without any control of product development and marketing (Nanfang Ribao 27.08.2010).

The regional branding strategy focuses on the establishment of a local Dalang label that serves as a quality seal and is supposed to facilitate trade for local manufacturers. It was registered in 80 countries in late 2010. According to its own testimony, the government thereby emulates marketing successes of regional products such as those of Swiss watches or Italian shoes (ID 13.12.2010a).

Besides the marketing effects of a regional logo, the establishment of the Dalang brand is also intended to help restructure and rationalise the local industry. According to a local newspaper article, Dalang companies used to pursue a self-sufficient, combative developing course leading to a situation where Dalang knitwear companies were "fighting each other". The establishment of the Dalang brand, along with urban planning measures, was meant to rationalise the industrial structure. This way, a "fist should be formed out of the individual fingers" of the industry, as a frequently cited metaphor puts it (Nanfang Ribao 16.08.2010). These policies for fostering cooperation and diversification within the knitwear sector are based on a strategy to "develop an extended industry chain" by introducing machine production on the one hand and service functions from R&D to marketing on the other (Guangdong EIC 22.10.2010).

At the enterprise level, the government devotes special attention to the launch of private brands by knitwear companies. This is in line with an orientation of the Dongguan city government which published a catalogue of measures to transform the city's large number of processing enterprises, which accounted for almost 90 percent of imports and exports in 2010, towards more sophisticated forms of enterprises (DG Government 2010). The Dalang government intends to assume a coordinating and directing function for enterprise development by means of a new agency, especially founded for this task (Nanfang Ribao 27.08.2010). The 20 strongest knitwear brands are singled out and receive aid for advertising as well as for the participation at international and national exhibitions. The successful establishment of brands that are acknowledged on a national level is awarded by the town government by a sum of up to one million RMB while registering a brand on provincial level is supported by a reward of half a million RMB (Guangdong EIC 22.10.2010). The direct subsidies and support measures for brand building are closely linked to the government's general initiatives for R&D support. Moreover, a "Creative Dalang" special fund was established. It provides an annual budget of RMB 20 million for the support of enterprises in enhancing their capacity for independent innovation (Nanfang Ribao 27.08.2010).

The government further supports functional upgrading towards ODM and OBM production by special training courses for designers, technicians and marketing personnel. Dalang's well-equipped technical school is offering courses that include fashion design and the transmission of designs to CNC knitting machines. Each year 40–60 designers and 80–100 technicians graduate from the school. These designers later mostly work as design assistants in local companies. Design students can usually sign their work contracts while still at school because companies are desperately searching for suitable employees to equip their design departments (ID 31.10.2011b).

But despite all these efforts during the last 3 to 4 years to foster private knitwear brands, success was still very limited in late 2010. Dalang mayor Xie Jinbo is quoted in an article from August 2010 lamenting that up until then there were only nine provincial brands in Dalang and that the town was far from establishing a world-class brand (Dongguan Ribao 17.08.2010). This current weakness is illustrated by the fact that OBM production at POWERKNIT, the biggest knitwear company in Dalang in 2010, only contributed 2–3 percent of the company's total revenues which mainly remain based on OEM and some ODM production for foreign clients (ID 13.12.2010a). An update of information in early 2013 confirms that the government's brand building initiative so far showed only limited success. A representative of POWERKNIT admitted that their share of OBM sales was "too small to figure it out" and "not developing very good" and a government representative said that the brand building strategy was about to be re-launched as it had not borne many fruits in the recent past (ID 04.02.2013; 21.02.2013). Still, the public support for design functions seems to have strengthened innovative capabilities of some companies that venture on ODM production models in which they suggest own styles to (mostly foreign) buyers.

## (3) Relocation of industries

Automation is considerably reducing the labour intensity of knitwear manufacturing. Still, there are notable tendencies towards a relocation of industries motivated by a quest for cheaper labour. This does not only pertain to small enterprises that cannot afford investments in process upgrading, but also to some large companies that transfer distinct labour-intensive production steps to China's interior provinces and transport the half-finished products to Dalang for finishing and marketing. R&D, logistics and marketing usually remain in Dalang and relocation only affects operations based on manual, not automated, work (ID 19.11.2010b; 13.12.2010a). Rather than preventing relocation from taking place, the government's aim is an "orderly transfer" by taking advantage of the cross-regional deployment of resources (Guangdong EIC 22.10.2010). If a company intends to leave, the government makes an assessment of its strategic relevance (judged in relation to the criteria of the central government policies), the amount of its tax contributions and its energy consumption. Only if a company is regarded to be strategically important, the authorities make efforts to keep it in town. There is a strong interest to keep computerised production and to attract service industries to Dalang, in line with the strategies of the Guangdong government (ID 13.12.2010a).

According to government information, the proximity to Hong Kong, the advantages of dense industry links within the knitwear cluster and the presence of a strong IT and finance sector provide sufficient incentives for strategically important companies to stay (ID 19.11.2010b). However, this positive assessment needs to be qualified to a certain degree, as even the biggest knitwear company in town is shifting large production volumes to the rural district of Guiping in neighbouring Guangxi province. In March 2013 a new regional headquarter of POWERKNIT in Guangxi was about to be opened. (ID 31.10.2011a; 21.02.2013).

### 7.3.1.3 Impact of industrial transformation on the workforce

While the acquisition of CNC machines is leading to a reduction of knitting workers on a grand scale, the proportion of higher skilled employees in the knitwear industry has been rising recently (cf. table 7.6). In 2009, 125 knitwear enterprises above designated size, representing about 80 percent of the industry's revenues, entertained an R&D department. Consequently, the number of designers in the industry rose from 750 to 1,300 between

2007 and 2009 (Guangdong EIC 22.10.2010). According to government information, knitwear companies in Dalang also employed around 10,000 technicians in late 2010 (ID 13.12.2010b).

*Table 7.6: Proportion of higher skilled employees in the Dalang knitwear industry*

|  | College | Secondary school | Other |
|---|---|---|---|
| 2007 | 2.8 | 16.3 | 80.9 |
| 2009 | 5.7 | 27.1 | 67.2 |

Source: Dongguan Bureau of Statistics 2010.

These figures demonstrate a positive correlation between industrial upgrading and the demand for higher-skilled employees on a cluster level. Yet, it must be acknowledged that the proportional increase of higher-skilled work partially is the result of a large-scale reduction of the (lower-skilled) manufacturing workforce.

What is more, the situation is reversed when it comes to skill requirements for manufacturing workers. As the case studies demonstrate in detail, the introduction of CNC knitting machines leads to a de-skilling of knitting work. Correspondingly, process upgrading did not lead to higher wages for operators who earn roughly the same as operators of semi-automatic knitting machines and significantly less than workers in the linking departments who operate very basic mechanic machines.

### 7.3.1.4 Case studies: Process upgrading and de-skilling in Dalang's knitwear enterprises

The case studies cover two knitwear companies that have engaged heavily in the modernisation of their production systems in recent years. POWERKNIT, the largest garment enterprise in town, was visited twice in late 2010 and once in November 2011, and KNITCHUAN, a considerably smaller enterprise, was visited once in November 2010. Although they vary considerably in size, the production systems of POWERKNIT and KNITCHUAN exhibit remarkable similarities.

## A. General information—introduction to the research sample

Both companies were founded as investments by private businessmen, first registered in Hong Kong, and up until today remain mainly the property of one person. Yet, especially KNITCHUAN has strong links to the mainland and invests heavily in the city of Linshui in Sichuan province, the hometown of the owner. Both companies engaged in substantial upgrading of their operations, which was accelerated with the onset of the economic crisis. This included a complete replacement of equipment in the knitting departments by CNC machines and functional upgrading towards ODM production which now comprises a substantial share of income. Both companies also were about to launch their own brands for the domestic market at the time of this survey, although sales of OBM products up until then constituted only a marginal share of their income.

*Table 7.7: Overview of the research sample, Dalang*

| | Capital (mil. RMB) | Revenues (mil RMB, 2011) | Output (pcs) | Factory size (Dalang, m²) | No. of CNC mach. (2010) | No. of workers | Production model (main) | Main markets |
|---|---|---|---|---|---|---|---|---|
| POWER-KNIT | 500 | 1,500 | 800,000 | 85,000 | 1,040 | 3,000 | ODM: 70% OEM: 29% OBM: 1% | Export: 97-8% (EU: 60%, US 40%) |
| KNIT-CHUAN | 17.4 | 105 | 300,000 | 12,000 | 118 | 600 | OEM: 70%, ODM: 30% | Export: 80% |

Source: Interview data, material provided by the Dalang government.

Both companies produce knitwear products of a similar variety like sweaters, cardigans and knitted dresses. They execute a broad range of processes from wool spinning to knitting, linking of flat knitwear pieces and various finishing steps (attaching accessories and labels, ironing and packaging). This is done either on the basis of OEM or ODM contracts. In the case of the latter, buyers either deliver a vague idea to contractors, typically by giving the example of a piece by high end brands like Prada, or the contractor suggests styles from their own design department from which the buyer may chose.

At POWERKNIT, the contractors then buy a production volume of this item including the IP rights of the suggested design.

At the time of the field visits, both companies received the lion's share of their income from contracts with foreign buyers, mainly from the US and Europe. POWERKNIT's customers include famous fashion labels of an intermediate price level like H&M, Levi's, Dockers and Top Shop. The company exclusively maintains direct relations with its customers, unlike at KNITCHUAN where about 40 percent of products are sold via intermediate agents, some of it to retailers like the French supermarket chain Carrefour. The sales model and the customer base suggest a superior product quality of POWERKNIT whose director claims that it is "almost the best supplier" to its customers (ID 13.12.2010b).

Despite their almost exclusive reliance on export production, both companies appear to have fared well during the crisis. POWERKNIT claims a roughly estimated growth rate of 10 percent in 2008 and 5 percent in 2009, with higher figures in subsequent years. The company attributes this satisfying performance to the acquisition of new machines which enabled POWERKNIT to acquire a new customer base for products of a higher quality. Hence, revenues have risen, despite only marginally higher growth rates in production volumes (ID 13.12.2010b). Representatives of KNITCHUAN admitted that there had been adverse effects of the crisis, but claimed that these had not hit them particularly hard. According to the general manager's claim, the crisis was rather an opportunity to renew equipment supported by advantageous government loans and subsidies (ID 29.10.2010). The company registered positive growth by 15.6 and 16.0 percent in 2010 and 2011, respectively, but experienced a slump in revenues by 13.2 percent in 2012 (ID 21.01.2013).

POWERKNIT and KNITCHUAN both entertain a quite complex regional division of labour in their operations. POWERKNIT's legal headquarter is located in Hong Kong. All manufacturing activities, however, are located on the mainland with a volume of 80 percent in Dalang and a smaller, but rising, share in neighbouring Guangxi Province where the company already constructed four factories in 2008/09. The company experiments with distributing the manufacturing process over different locations. For instance, some products were knitted in Dalang, then linked in Guangxi and again finished in Dalang in 2010. Such arrangements balance the advantages of higher productivity in Guangdong and lower labour cost in Guangxi (ID 13.12.2010b).[117] In the case of KNITCHUAN, around one third of the production volume was produced in Sichuan province in 2012 where the company operates a factory since the end of 2007 (ID 21.01.2013). This factory is less automated and up until now used for simpler products and big orders (ID 29.10.10).

Both companies are pursuing major steps towards a relocation of production from Dalang in favour of their supplementary production sites. Rising labour cost and labour shortages were named as the primary reasons for this. POWERKNIT was constructing a new factory of equal size to the giant Dalang headquarters (illustration 7.2) in Guangxi.

*Illustration 7.2: Headquarters and workforce of POWERKNIT, Dalang*

Source: Company website.

It is supposed to be used for most of the products for foreign clients, whereas the current main factory will be used for OBM production. However, a complete relocation to Guangxi is not an option because of the lack of infra-

---

117 Companies thereby accept lower productivity levels in other provinces. According to a representative of POWERKNIT, one worker in their Guangxi branch will manufacture 12 pieces of garment during the same time in which a worker in Dalang produces 20 (ID 31.10.2011a).

structure for export trade, like a major shipping port, there (ID 13.12.2010b). Similarly, KNITCHUAN made the decision to relocate all manufacturing to Sichuan and keep only R&D and marketing activities in Guangdong. This step was projected for 2013/14. According to the company, there is an improving infrastructure and an almost complete industry chain in Sichuan, including a trade fair similar to the high-profile event in Dalang (ID 29.10.2010).

*B. Industrial upgrading strategies*

POWERKNIT and KNITCHUAN both focus their upgrading strategy on a complete automation of the knitting process. Beginning in late 2007, they acquired 1,040 and 118 machines, respectively (ID 29.10.2010; 13.12.2010b). Government subsidies acted as an additional incentive for this step. As the director of POWERKNIT explained, the strategy of automation, which is equated with a move towards higher quality products, was virtually forced upon them as they found themselves unable to compete in the cheaper market segment, especially with companies from Cambodia, India and Bangladesh. At the same time, the new investment places a large burden on POWERKNIT as they experience difficulties in creating enough cash flow to refinance the investment. In both companies, the machine outfit is divided between high-end models from Germany or Japan and domestic Chinese models. POWERKNIT has a high share of imported equipment (800 out of 1,040 machines), whereas the proportion is reversed at KNITCHUAN (ID 29.10.2010; 31.10.2011a).

By selecting standard CNC knitting machines, the companies chose a middle path of automation. At POWERKNIT, the management had experimented with full-automatic models that include linking operations, but found it unsuitable for their purposes. For this reason, the function of linking is not affected by the companies' automation investments and continues to be performed by manual workers with the support of basic mechanical equipment (ID 31.10.2011a).[118]

While the machines offer superior product quality due to their automatic and regular operation, the companies still need to make additional efforts

---

118 According to a machine vendor, full-automatic machine models are not used in the Pearl River Delta because "there are still enough manual workers to link the single parts of knitted fabric by using mechanical machines. Thus companies do not use full automation although it would be possible technically". However, full-automatic machines that combine the knitting and linking process are common in regions with higher wages such as Italy (ID 30.10.2010b).

in order to meet the quality requirements of international buyers. This concerns management techniques, market research, quality control and compliance with CSR provisions of buyers and the Chinese labour law. POWERKNIT had to struggle with complaints by their biggest customer H&M in 2011 who considered product quality to be insufficient (ID 31.10.2011a). At the same time, the companies experiment with measures to improve efficiency. At POWERKNIT, for instance, divisions that operate with German and Japanese equipment compete against each other for the highest possible output (ID 30.10.2010b).

But the efforts towards an upgrading of processes are not only about efficiency and product quality. The machines also offer an easy entrance to creating own design products, thus facilitating functional upgrading. Machine producers deliver the equipment that features computer programmes by means of which employees can develop digital designs relatively easy. Furthermore, these platforms offer an easy link between digital design and manufacturing by enabling data transfer between designers' computers and the machines (ID 30.10.2010b; 31.10.2011c). Still, designers need to become familiarized with the machines and some transcription between physical samples and digital data remains necessary, but the CNC knitting process significantly lowers entry barriers to engaging in design. Based on such technological advantages, both companies successfully launched ODM production in recent years which has enabled them to engage with customers of a higher price level.

However, the ongoing weakness on overseas markets demands a further reorientation. POWERKNIT regards it as doubtful whether the company can survive solely based on export, not least because of strong competition from countries with cheaper labour cost. Therefore, the domestic market is regarded to be the key to the company's future (ID 13.12.2010b). This is connected to a strategic shift towards own brand production. In 2011, the fashion line of POWERKNIT for the Chinese market aimed at a higher price segment than their export goods. Their brand products are manufactured in low numbers, sometimes of not more than 25 pieces per style, and include fur coats and woven garments that can reach a price of up to RMB 8,000. As knitwear only constitutes a share of its OBM product line, POWERKNIT sources a great share of articles from suppliers in Zhejiang Province. Whereas OBM production was only in its infancy in late 2011, the company aimed at raising the number of stores of its fully owned retail chain from five to 20–30 in 2012 and then add another 100 in 2013 (ID 13.12.2010b). KNITCHUAN has a similar strategic outlook with its focus on the domestic market (ID 29.10.2010b). The company already launched a brand in 2010. Its current performance and the further strategic outlook were less clearly spelled out than at POWERKNIT, however. As mentioned before, brand building did not show the desired results, so far. POWERKNIT only entertains 13 retail stores, so far, and a representative of KNITCHUAN stated that their products were launched on the domestic market in August 2012, only (ID 18.01.2013; 21.02.2013).

### C. Production process and work

The Dalang-based factories serve as the main sites for manufacturing and as headquarters at both enterprises. Apart from manufacturing, both companies run voluminous marketing and administration divisions and have installed their own design departments. The latter consist of few employees, but have a high output. POWERKNIT employs six senior designers that each lead a team of 30 employees. Together this team churns out at least 300 stitches per season that are offered to customers. Additionally, there is an, as yet smaller, design team for OBM production. The design division of KNITCHUAN is considerably smaller with only 3–4 employees (ID 29.10.2011; 30.10.2010a).

The manufacturing process consists of spinning, knitting, linking and finishing. Production is organised as a continuous flow through each of these departments. This makes it necessary to balance the output volumes of these tasks against each other and to adjust to alternations in demand in different seasons. The majority of workers at POWERKNIT are now employed in the finishing section, whereas the knitting section only amounts to one tenth of the manufacturing workforce (cf. table 7.8).

*Table 7.8: Composition of workforce at POWERKNIT and KNITCHUAN, Dalang*

|  | Employ-ees | Sales & Manage-ment | Designers & techni-cians | Workers in manu-facturing | Knitting | Linking | Finishing |
|---|---|---|---|---|---|---|---|
| POWER-KNIT | 2–3,000 | 350 | 30 | 1,600–2,300 | 200 | 500–1,200 | 900 |
| KNIT-CHUAN | 3–400 | 60–80 | 6–8 | 2–300 | 40 | 60 | 86 |

Source: Interview data.

The small proportion of knitters is a result of a drastic reduction of the knitting workforce due to automation. At POWERKNIT the number of knitters shrunk by some 80 percent between 2007 and 2010 (ID 31.10.2011a). At KNITCHUAN the total number of workers at the factory had fallen from 1,500 to 300 during the same period (ID 29.10.2010). While factors like a general economic downturn in 2009—although this was denied by my interview partners—and the gradual relocation to interior provinces probably aggravated the loss of employment, the automation of the knitting process can be regarded to be the primary reason for it.

At both factories, knitters operate around eight machines on average. A female worker at POWERKNIT even managed to operate 14 machines simultaneously which delineates the maximum number for experienced workers (ID 31.10.2011a). Most operators stand upright during their whole working day and switch quickly between machines. Their tasks consist of replacing yarn spools, adjusting some settings and (easy) troubleshooting. Work does not appear to be physically straining but is very repetitive. The shop floor is also quite noisy and workers wear earplugs as a protection against this. Since the task of the workers consists of simultaneously handling as many machines as possible, work may become stressful in dense periods. The companies also need technicians for maintenance of the machines, although services of installing and maintenance are provided by the local machine vendors (ID 30.10.2010b). At POWERKNIT, a group of 20–30 employees has been set up for these tasks (ID 31.10.2011a).

In contrast to the almost deserted knitting division where large full-automatic machines are hammering along, the shop floor in the linking division is crowded, but relatively silent, with dozens of linking workers arranged in rows operating vintage mechanical equipment (cf. illustration 7.3). According to management information, this process cannot be automated, except by buying the expensive integrated equipment referred to above. The almost exclusively female workers sit on small stools and lean over the machines with the help of which they attach the respective knitwear pieces loop by loop. Workers need to remain highly focused during the whole working day. As a manager at POWERKNIT explained, workers needed to be of good eyesight and manual skilfulness which was why they preferred "young ladies" for this task (ID 31.10.2011a). Interview partners at both factories regarded work in the linking department as "tougher" and "more difficult" than knitting work (ID 29.10.2010; 30.10.2010a; 30.10.2010b). According to a spokesperson at POWERKNIT, "it is easy to find knitting machine operators on the market, but not experienced linkers" (ID 13.12.2010b).

*Illustration 7.3: Linking department at POWERKNIT, Dalang*

Source: author's photograph.

In the finishing division, workers attach accessories and labels or iron the finished products. Workers sit or stand around large workbenches, some of them equipped with standard sewing machines or ironing equipment.

There are remarkable differences with regard to training and skills of the workers in the different divisions. In finishing, the workforce consists of unskilled migrant workers whose work is limited to very easy tasks. But it takes up to half a year to train linking workers which is why all companies prefer hiring experienced workers who are scarcely available. In both factories, the manual work of linkers is the highest skilled function in manufacturing. The work of operators of the technologically sophisticated knitting machines is regarded to be easier in comparison. Usually, workers receive an introductory training of one week supplemented by an on-the-job training that lasts between one week and one month (ID 29.10.2010; 30.10.2010a;

13.12.2010b).[119] Significantly, automation has resulted in a de-skilling of the knitting workforce. Knitters used to be responsible for the size and the tightness of products when using semi-automatic or manual equipment. They also needed to change needles and yarns in accordance to the desired styles, which is why they needed to become acquainted to some degree with the specific designs of their products. Automatic knitting skills, however, are limited to the function of overseeing the machines and occasionally changing yarn spools, while the designs are uploaded directly to the machines and therefore do not need to be known or understood in detail by the workers. The most difficult task, according to a manager of POWERKNIT, is the control of the tension of yarn threads (ID 30.10.2011a). Automatic knitting rests on some new skills of the workers, especially skills of coordinating the operation of as many machines as possible at the same time. But all in all, their tasks have become easier and new workers can quickly be introduced to their jobs.

These varying skill requirements are also reflected in differences in the wage levels of knitters and linkers. According to managers at POWERKNIT and KNITCHUAN, knitters usually earn around RMB 2,300–2,500, at most RMB 3,000 per month. The wages of linkers are estimated to be around 10–30 percent higher on average. A very experienced linker at POWERKNIT can even earn up to RMB 5,000 a month (ID 13.12.2010b; cf. table 7.9).

---

119 Companies provided very different and contradictory data on this question which probably had to do with the fact that they prefer to hire experienced knitters instead of training new ones. According to a representative from the machine vendor Stoll, on the-job-training usually lasts less than one month (ID 30.10.2010b). "To operate our machines, an on-the-job training of four weeks is easily enough [...]. The operation is kept very simple through a kind of sign language. Our machines can almost be operated by illiterate workers" (ID 10.04.2013).

*Table 7.9: Comparison of knitting and linking wages and training periods, Dalang*

|  | knitters | | linkers | |
|---|---|---|---|---|
|  | POWER-KNIT | KNIT-CHUAN | POWER-KNIT | KNIT-CHUAN |
| Number | 200 | 40 | 800–1,200 | 60 |
| Wages (RMB) | 2,300–3,000 | 2,000–3,000 | 2,700–5,000 | 2,200–3,300 |
| Training | 1w+1w/ 1m otj[i] | 1w+1 w otj[i] | 3–6 m | n.s. |

i    otj = on-the-job training.

Source: Interview data.

Workers usually receive a base wage of RMB 1,500—1,600 plus a piece rate bonus which varies according to their specific task. Curiously, the operators of knitting machines are paid according to a piece rate system, although productivity, speed and quality fundamentally depend on the machines. Yet, the management keeps a piece rate share of about 30 percent (at POWERKNIT) as an incentive for workers to simultaneously operate as many machines as possible—which positively affects their piece rate share (ID 31.10.2011a). The wage system in this respect is not fixed, but under permanent review by the management. As a representative of POWERKNIT explained, the company already had introduced a payment scheme which entirely rested on workers' performance. But as workers were not satisfied with this scheme and tended to leave the factory, a base rate of 1,600 was introduced. However, the management consciously refuses to switch to a wage system based on hourly wages, because then "workers would go to sleep" for lack of incentive (ID 31.10.2011a). According to an employee of the machine vendor Stoll, a base wage of RMB 1,500 that corresponds to 70–80 percent of the total wage in 2010 represented the industry standard in Dalang (ID 30.10.2010b).[120] While workers in this way benefit from a base wage above the local minimum wage, they do not have much chance of raising their total wage signifi-

---

120 These figures are also considerably lower than those provided by a company representative suggesting that his claims are inflated.

cantly through a high piece rate income, unlike the linking workers in the same factories. According to the information at a CNC equipment vendor, this also constitutes a difference with regard to the incomes that manual knitters used to achieve under the old system. Their average total income tended to be lower than that of CNC machine operators, but very experienced knitters could make up to RMB 3,000 which is about RMB 700 more than the income of an experienced CNC operator, according to his calculation (ID 30.10.2010b).[121]

Due to characteristic seasonal fluctuations in the industry, the production flow at the surveyed knitwear companies is irregular. At POWERKNIT, a share of at least a third of manufacturing workers is hired seasonally (ID 13.12.2010b). Still, both companies claimed that they did not have big problems with recruiting, although POWERKNIT admitted some difficulties with hiring unskilled workers for the ironing and finishing departments in 2011 (ID 31.10.2011a). It should be kept in mind, however, that the labour shortage in Guangdong was quoted as one of the main reasons for relocating manufacturing to other provinces. KNITCHUAN also reported of higher aspirations of the workers with respect to their income (ID 29.10.2010). A manager of POWERKNIT complained about the mentality of the workers which made it very hard to achieve the aspired quality standards in the company and made it necessary to exert "a lot of pressure through supervisors" (ID 31.10.2011a). The unstable production flow at the company is also reflected in working schedules. At POWERKNIT, the normal working hours are 8 hours on 6 days per week with overtime not exceeding three hours a day. According to the management, this was required in order to meet the standards of the Chinese labour law and requirements of their customers' codes of conduct. However, the director of the company added that "most customers understand what happens" and are tolerant about abundant overtime hours in peak seasons (ID 13.12.2010b). A representative of a large foreign machine vendor spoke of a two shift system in which CNC knitting machines are operated around the clock in twelve hour shifts (ID 30.10.2010b).

Regardless of these indications for excessive working hours, POWERKNIT cultivates an image of an employer with superior standards. The company is fully air-conditioned and provides sites for recreational activities

---

121 A representative of POWERKNIT stated that the average wages of CNC machine operators would be "roughly the same, maybe 10 percent more" than that of manual knitters.

like basketball and badminton courts and a table tennis room. The company also is proud to be a major taxpayer in Dalang and devotes money to charity projects. At POWERKNIT there is also a trade union which was installed from above because some of their buyers demanded this. It participates in negotiating certain general working conditions and was dealing with subsidies for canteen food at the time of the field visit.

### 7.3.1.4 Conclusion

The case of Dalang's knitwear industry illustrates an enhanced demand for higher-skilled work in design and administration due to the progression towards ODM and, eventually, OBM production. Yet, the approaches of the surveyed enterprises amount to a failure of social upgrading with regard to manufacturing workers. Comprehensive measures for process upgrading did not improve the situation of manufacturing workers in terms of wages and skills. Automation rather lead to a substantial reduction of the workforce and a de-skilling of knitting work which helps companies to keep wages and training times low and to quickly replace workers. Whereas this blend of upgrading does not entail improvements for manufacturing workers, it greatly reduces the labour intensity of production. One indirect effect of automation is that the proportion of skilled and highly skilled employees who do not work in the knitting departments affected by automation rose.

Yet, there are limits to further automation since the linking process can hardly be automated and knitwear companies continue to rely on a great number of unskilled workers for finishing tasks. In combination with the large amount of seasonal hiring this may be the main reason for both companies' decisions to relocate manufacturing to regions with lower costs and better supply of labour. Despite proactive initiatives by the Dalang government to upgrade the local knitting industry, the outlook of the companies of this sample seems to vindicate analyses that project an end of labour-intensive manufacturing in the Pearl River Delta. While manufacturing is expected to be relocated in the immediate future, both companies confirm that Dalang will continue to play a vital role as R&D and marketing centre for their operations.

7.3.2 Building brands without upgrading the workforce:
The Humen fashion industry

Humen is a town under the jurisdiction of the City of Dongguan with 124,000 permanent inhabitants and a "floating population" of migrant workers of at least 450,000 (Humen Government Website). The town was the setting for a fateful incident of Chinese history when some 20,000 chests of opium were destroyed by order of the government in 1839, thus provoking the First Opium War (1839–42). To this day, this act of patriotism, referred to as the "first page of modern Chinese history" (ibid), is officially seen with pride—Humen's central square shows a huge sculpture of two fists breaking an opium pipe.

After the onset of market reforms in 1978, Humen's economy quickly transformed from agriculture to industry. According to the vice-mayor of the town, there were three phases in Humen's industrial development corresponding to different product categories: first, mainly shoes and agricultural products were produced, second came household appliances and electronics, and finally garment, ICT and services like marketing and logistics (ID 09.12.2010a). However, the town already had been a trading hub for garment products throughout this period.[122]

Humen is located on the banks of the Pearl River in a corridor between Shenzhen and Guangzhou. Due to this favourable location in immediate vicinity to Hong Kong and with direct access to the sea, Humen proved to be an attractive target for investment. According to government information, Humen was the first site of garment production for overseas sales as well as the site of the first joint venture between foreign private and state investment (ID 09.12.2010a).

### 7.3.2.1 Economic structure of the town

The fashion industry dominates the appearance of Humen's townscape from the huge agglomeration of 22 wholesale markets and over 10,000 retail shops in the city centre to the myriad of factories and small workshop in the town's

---

122 The above chronology provided by the vice-mayor of the town therefore may be oversimplified. The history of Humen's industrialisation since the 1980s is narrowly connected to a special pattern of garment wholesale trade in which companies combined their trading functions with some own manufacturing functions (ID 03.11.2011a).

industrial zones. 250,000 people, or 40 percent of the total population, were employed in the town's fashion industry in late 2010, plus some 30,000 private enterprise owners and self-employed (South School Garment 2010, 15). Up to 2,500 garment processing enterprises churned out over 2.5 billion pieces of garment in 2009 and created demand for some 150 enterprises in supporting industries for zippers, buttons and accessories (ibid, 15). The prominence of the fashion industry earned the town the title "China's Famous Town of Lady's Fashion", awarded by the China National Textile and Apparel Council.

But as in Dalang, the IT industry matches the garment sector in terms of output. In 2011 it even contributed about 40 percent of industrial output whereas the share of the garment industry was somewhat lower with 30–40 percent (ID 03.11.2011a). Yet, numerous service functions, above all in marketing and trade, directly depend on garment manufacturing. Humen's economic life thus remains narrowly intertwined with the fashion industry, which becomes visible during the annual Fashion Fair that not only involves the town's garment manufacturers, but also features huge promotional efforts supported by the town's media, tourism and logistics industries. Humen's function as a trading hub may further deepen in the future as it is competing against Guangzhou for the designation as the main international trading centre for fashion production in Guangdong (ID 18.11.2011a).

While a successful bidding for this title probably would boost the town's international trade, Humen's enterprises are currently predominantly oriented towards the domestic market—in contrast to the knitwear industry in Dalang. According to government sources, 70–80 percent of garment products are sold on the Chinese mainland (ID, 09.12.2010a). This not only minimises the industry's economic dependency on foreign buyers, but also shapes its upgrading trajectory. Contrary to the experience in Dalang, most fashion brands in Humen emerged through a backward integration of wholesale traders to manufacturing, rather than through a supplier upgrading from OEM or ODM production (ID 03.11.2011a).

Due to its lower dependence on foreign trade, Humen's industry fared relatively well during the global economic crisis, better than other towns of the area, according to the vice-mayor. The town's GDP grew by 17.4 percent in 2008 and 13.5 percent in 2009. Industrial output rose by 7.7 percent in 2008 and by 6.3 percent in 2009 (ID 09.12.2010a). According to the government, the fast development of the service sector is another reason for the strong growth performance of Humen's economy in 2008–09. Finally the vice-mayor of Humen also attributes an advantageous role of industrial upgrading because companies had also begun to transform their operations which helped them to endure the difficulties of the economic crisis (ID 09.12.2010a).

### 7.3.2.2 Industrial upgrading strategies

Despite a satisfying growth performance in recent years, the government identifies several weaknesses in the town's overall economic development. First, the industry structure is conceived to be irrational due to the existence of an excessive proportion of low-end industries as well as an unhealthy internal competition between enterprises. Second, Humen's enterprises mostly have low innovative capacities with the high-tech sector only constituting 16.4 percent of all industries[123], a low figure for a town within the City of Dongguan. Third, the development of new sectors, such as a modern service industry, is conceived to be too slow (Humen Textile FYP 2009).

To overcome these shortcomings, Humen's general upgrading strategy primarily rests on the promotion of the service sector on the one hand and the modernisation of the garment sector, labelled as "Humen's most shining business card", on the other hand (Humen Working Programme 2009–2013). According to the town's development plan, the service sector is expected to contribute 55 percent to the town's GDP until 2013, up from about 50 percent in 2010. This includes the promotion of a "creative industry", closely related to the fashion industry, and the further expansion of Humen's role in garment trade. This strategy for structural change also includes a complete overhaul of the town centre with voluminous investments in road construction and other infrastructure. The development of transport, urban infrastructure and the town's industries are conceived to all contribute to the task of rebuilding Humen as a "commercial city by the beach" (ID 09.12.2010a).

The upgrading strategy for the garment industry primarily rests on functional upgrading towards OBM production. Like in Dalang, brand building involves initiatives on two levels: On the one hand the government pursues the creation of a regional brand to build the reputation of Humen as a fash-

---

123 Apparently, a large share of what is declared as "IT industry" in the before cited figure is not identified as "high-tech". The figure of 16.4 percent taken from the government development plans thus provides a more realistic picture.

ion cluster. On the other hand the government encourages the creation of enterprise brands which are seen as the main vehicle for moving towards higher value-added production and to develop domestic and overseas markets. As the vice-mayor explained, the experience of industrialisation in the Yangtse and Pearl River Delta shows that it is important to develop the big enterprises (that he calls "dragons") first in order to develop the whole industry. Selective government support for brand building is therefore also a means to rationalise the industry structure which is projected to be characterised by large brands that assume a pioneering role and by companies that remain limited to a supplier role (ID 09.12.2010a). The popular brand CASUALYOUTH that owns 14 factories in Humen and contributes about one fifth of its corporate tax revenues is the pride of the town in this respect (ID 9.12.10; cf. case studies below).

The branding strategy has been pursued with some success in the past years. In 2005, there had been no brand officially recognised as China Famous Brand and seven Guangdong Famous Brands. By 2011, the respective numbers had risen to three China Famous Brands and almost 30 Guangdong Famous Brands (ID 03.11.2011a). However, this is seen only as a beginning, as the government in its latest Five-Year Plan for the textile industry defined the goal of five to six national level and 50 provincial brands until 2015 (Humen Textile FYP). But progress in terms of the number of OBM enterprises cannot conceal the fact that currently the bulk of merchandise distributed at the town's voluminous wholesale markets consists of no-name products of a rather cheap product category. This becomes obvious at the annual fashion fair where one floor is reserved for the local brands while the remaining five floors of the town's central wholesale market are occupied by small scale vendors who trade products of a lower category.

Moving from a role as OEM producers or wholesalers to that of a brand company critically involves the acquisition of design and marketing capabilities. The local government heavily supports enterprises in acquiring these functions. In 2010 the "Humen Fashion Technology Innovation Centre" was inaugurated. Local companies can receive assistance and instructions in order to launch their brands and define their market segment, promote their products, find sales agents, improve management and find skilled employees in design and marketing. The centre engages in cooperation with many media stations and also trains designers and models (ID 03.11.2011b). The supply of talent is further supported by a local technical school at which 300 students graduate each year as technicians, assistant designers or models. The number of graduates has been expanding in recent years and will possibly rise to about 800 until 2016, according to the schools's vice-headmaster (ID 18.11.2011b)

Another important means to strengthen design and marketing capabilities of local enterprises is the annual "China (Humen) Fashion Fair". It is a major vehicle for achieving an increase in awareness for the town's products and to display distinctive styles developed by Humen's fashion brands. The fair regularly hosts various fashion shows and design contests as well as an ambitious cultural programme involving several celebrities and pop stars from Hong Kong. The fashion show also boosts the development of local media and the cultural infrastructure, like the planned fashion TV channel and the exhibition centre. All in all, the government plans to spend more than RMB 1.5 billion per year until 2015 for measures in relation to brand building (Humen Textile FYP).

With regard to the marketing structure of the town, the government strategy aims at increasing the number of wholesale markets to 26 until 2015 while at the same time rationalising their structure (ibid). Special attention is given to the development of e-commerce which is supposed to increase the range of Humen-based companies' sales and facilitate contacts between local companies.

In contrast to the upgrading strategy of Dalang, which particularly focused on the automation of manufacturing through the introduction of CNC knitting machines, process upgrading does not play a prominent role in Humen's garment industry. Some companies, first and foremost CASU-ALYOUTH, do engage in thorough rationalisation of the production process through the acquisition of machines and the introduction of lean production schemes. The government also inaugurated a wholesale market for garment machinery in order to provide access to the latest production technologies. Companies are encouraged to obtain machinery and in some cases can also receive subsidies for these acquisitions (ID 20.11.2010a; 09.12.2010b). But this seems not to be very common and all in all strategies for process upgrading do not rank highly in the government's development plans and are not implemented across-the-board by companies as the results of the case studies demonstrate. The main reason for this is the limited potential for automation of the sewing process which constitutes the core of garment manufacturing in Humen. Sewing work continues to depend on individual workers operating one sewing machine each. A local vendor of a major foreign sewing machines company claimed that the introduction of modern high-end machines can save half of the workforce, two thirds of electricity and one third of material in a jeans factory of 300 workers (ID 21.11.2010). But even in case companies make such an investment (which does not seem to be very common), it does not amount to automation on a large scale as is the case with Dalang's knitwear industry. Above all, investment in machines may turn out to be too expensive for garment enterprises that do not produce high-end products. Besides, the acquisition of more advanced sewing machines is not a precondition for producing higher-quality products, unlike it is the case with the CNC knitting machines that not only allow for faster knitting, but also enhance versatility and facilitate the link between design and production.[124]

### 7.3.2.3 Impacts of industrial transformation on the workforce

Economic upgrading towards the service industry and brand building in the fashion industry requires significant skill upgrading in the fields of design and marketing. In the words of the director of the government's Economy and Trade Office, "suppliers don't need an R&D department, but brands do" (ID 03.11.2011a). There is no precise data available about the numbers of skilled staff in these fields, but the director of the local technical school estimates that there are about 20,000 marketing specialists and between 10,000 and 20,000 designers active in Humen's fashion industry (ID 18.11.2011b). The development of the industry therefore results in pressures to meet the rising demand for skilled employees through more comprehensive training activities, formal technical education and the recruitment of professionals from universities and colleges.

According to a government official, industrial upgrading also results in higher skill requirements for manufacturing workers. They needed to be more experienced in order to react to quick changes in the production process and to meet higher quality standards. Supposedly, this is a difference to the repetitive tasks demanded at supplier companies. He holds that work-

---

124 The decision to invest in advanced sewing machines may be comparable to the option of introducing more advanced full-automatic machines in the knitting industry that even provide automatic linking. It involves high risks because of high capital investment. Given the availability of hundreds of thousands of low-waged migrant workers in the region, this option probably is not attractive. If there is a continuing tendency for labour shortages and rising wages, the balance might tilt towards more investment in machines, however.

ers today have a better school education and higher intellectual capabilities which makes them easier to train, but harder to discipline (ID 03.11.2011a). However, this claim conflicts with the explanation of a vendor of high-end sewing machines who said that the company's aim was "to enable unskilled workers as soon as possible to be on the same level as skilled workers" when designing the newest generation of machines. Accordingly, he estimated that the training for unskilled workers usually lasted one or two days (ID 21.11.2010b). This was confirmed by the director of Humen's technical school who asserted that it has become less difficult to operate sewing machines and that the programming of a modern sewing machine is "as easy as using a cell phone" (ID 18.11.2011b). The results of the company case studies presented below provide further evidence on this issue.

Aggregate data about wages provided by government sources is sketchy. A high-ranking government official estimated average wages for line-workers at RMB 3,000 in late 2011 and reported that wages had risen by about 20 percent annually in recent years due to labour shortages and government support for higher wages. He reported that many companies had problems with recruiting workers which set them under pressure to offer improved conditions. Workers responded to this situation by asking for higher standards in terms of working conditions, regular working hours and vacation (ID 03.11.2011a).

### 7.3.2.4 Case studies: Humen's enterprises between traditional management systems and lean production

The case studies cover three prominent brand name companies. The data stems from in-depth interviews with managers and shop floor visits in the autumn of 2010 (CASUALYOUTH) and late 2011 (GENTSSUIT, LADY-FIT). The results were complemented by additional interviews with sales personnel at the Humen fashion fairs in 2010 and 2011 and a review of printed and online sources.

### A. General information—introduction to the research sample

The companies pursue quite similar strategies of brand building and retail marketing, but differ enormously with regard to their size, products and organisation of production (cf. table 7.10). CASUALYOUTH dwarfs its peers in terms of revenues and production capacities. The company employed at least 25,000 workers in its 28 factories in 2011 and commanded thousands of sales people and management staff (ID 20.11.2010a).[125] There is a huge gap in size between CASUALYOUTH and all other garment enterprises in Humen, including GENTSSUIT, a company that also belongs to the most prominent Humen-based brands.

All companies represent investments by mainland-Chinese entrepreneurs. Most spectacular—and duly advertised—is the story of the founder of CASUALYOUTH, a former fruit vendor from Northern Guangdong, who launched the enterprise from virtually nothing as a 25 year-old (Beijing review 18.11.10). With a fortune of RMB 2.2 billion he ranked 22nd on the list of the richest Chinese with less than 40 years of age in 2011 (China. org.cn, 13.06.2012). Probably no other individual came that far in Humen, but many other companies were also founded by self-made men (and some women) who started to design, manufacture and sell clothes in Humen's thriving garment cluster. At the beginning of any of the surveyed brands stood a typical business model that combined comprehensive wholesale activities with some own production. None of the companies used to be a supplier to foreign brands and only GENTSSUIT engaged in voluminous manufacturing before creating its own brand.

---

125 In 2011, a salesperson of CASUALYOUTH at the Humen Fashion Fair even gave a number of 35,000 employees in total (ID 19.11.2011a).

Table 7.10: Overview of the research sample, Humen

|  | CASUALYO-UTH | GENTSSUIT | LADYFIT |
|---|---|---|---|
| Foundation | 1996, (1999)[i] | 1986, (2003)[i] | (2007)[i] |
| Revenues (RMB) | 8 billion (2009) | 400 million (2011) | 50 million (2011) |
| Employees | 30,000–35,000 | 600 | 160 |
| Products | mostly casual wear (age group 18-30) | Menswear, formal-casual | Lady's fashion |
| Price category (RMB) | 50–300, winter: up to 700 | 800–2,500, jackets: up to 4,000 | 500–700, winter: 1,200–1,600 |
| Production model | OBM | OBM | OBM |
| Main markets | Guangdong, 2nd tier cities in China[ii], exports to Asia, Middle East | Chinese mainland, 20% Guangdong | South/East/Northern China. 30% Guangdong |

i  The year in brackets indicates the year in which the brand was founded. All companies look back at a longer history as wholesalers and/or OEM producers.

ii  The term "second tier cities" refers to the large number of cities with millions of inhabitants that are not as rich and well-known as the political centres and trading hubs of Beijing, Shanghai, Guangzhou, Shenzhen and other comparable megacities.

Source: Interview data; company catalogues; Beijing review.

All companies have by now abandoned their wholesale activities and focus their attention on design, manufacturing and sales of their own brand products. They address different consumer groups and market segments. CASUALYOUTH emulates fast fashion business models of H&M or ZARA mainly directed at young customers, but at a slightly cheaper price category. Products of the summer collection rarely cost more than RMB 300 (Song 2012, 9). LADYFIT's styles are sold in lower quantities at double or triple the price. The company advertises a classy brand image to attract its female customers. With a focus on formal, but fashionable, menswear promoted under the slogan "creative business men", GENTSSUIT's products are considerably more expensive. Trousers and sweaters can cost up to RMB 2,000 and jackets are sold for up to RMB 4,000. The company therefore serves an intermediate price category in this market segment above casual retail chains, but well below foreign brands for formal menswear such as Hugo Boss, Armani or Pierre Cardin (ID 18.11.2011c; 19.11.2011b).

All surveyed companies almost exclusively pursue a strategy of brand manufacturing—as opposed to the fables retailer models described in section 7.1. None of them operates on a split production model in which brand manufacturing is supplemented by OEM or ODM production lines, as it is common in Dalang's knitwear industry. All companies maintain substantial in-house production capacities, although a significant share of production volumes is outsourced in each case (cf. table 7.11). Company representatives gave different reasons for this. Part of the motivation stems from limitations in their capacities which cannot keep track with the rapidly expanding demand.[126] At GENTSSUIT, a company representative also pointed to the regional labour shortage as one reason why it is preferred to look for suitable suppliers instead of ramping up production. Finally, the productive capacities of GENTSSUIT and LADYFIT are focused on woven garment products and are little diversified which forces these companies to source knitted products and accessories from suitable suppliers. CASUALYOUTH, on the contrary, is able to source a highly diversified assortment of goods from its network of specialised factories. The downsides of this business model are the challenges of supply chain management and quality control, as pointed out by the owner of LADYFIT. This company rather tends to outsource the production of basic articles while keeping manufacturing of more complicated products in-house (ID 09.12.2010b; 03.11.2011c; 18.11.2011c).

---

126 As one account analyses with view on CASUALYOUTH: "It is hoped that through self-production, its product quality and production plan can be effectively controlled to meet the needs of the retail network. However, as its sales are growing rapidly with an extensive array of styles and product mix, the group has outsourced nearly half of its products to mainland and Hong Kong manufacturers" (HKTDC 2011a).

*Table 7.11: Production networks of Humen-based fashion brands*

|  | CASUALYOUTH | GENTSSUIT | LADYFIT |
|---|---|---|---|
| Number of factories | 28 | 1 | 1 |
| Outsourcing (percent of volume) | 50% (2011) | 60–70% | 20% |

Source: Interview data; HKTDC 2011.

With regard to their distribution networks, all companies rely on a franchising model. Only GENTSSUIT sells a share of 60 percent of its products via sales agents (ID 03.11.2011c). CASUALYOUTH and LADYFIT are also developing their e-commerce platforms although they are of minor quantitative relevance so far. Franchising partners order brand products at the headquarters of the respective brand at a preferential price. At CASUALYOUTH their orders are directly fed back into production management and determine the production volumes of certain styles (ID 09.12.2010b). The growth strategy of the surveyed enterprises focuses on opening stores in strategically selected places. CASUALYOUTH, for instance, aggressively pursued a strategy of conquering so-called second-tier cities in China where they faced less competition from larger Chinese competitors (HKTDC 2011a). The company also opened pompous flagship stores in the commercial centres of large Chinese cities in order to spread the brand image. While all companies aim to be present all over China, they still have a higher density of stores in Guangdong.

*Table 7.12: Number of franchise stores of the surveyed companies, Humen*

|  | CASUALYOUTH | GENTSSUIT | LADYFIT |
|---|---|---|---|
| Revenue growth | 20% (2011) | 15% (2010) | 50% (2011) |
| 2009 | 1,000 | 160 | n.s. |
| 2010 | 3,000 | 210 | 50 |
| 2011 | 5,500 | 320 | 150 |

Source: Interview data.

Additionally, CASUALYOUTH caused some stir among industry observers with an ambitious expansion to overseas markets in Asia and the Middle East, most notably by entering a joint venture for the distribution of their products in India (Beijing review 18.11.2010). The company also aims at the European and US markets in the mid-term. Though fairly successful, exports still constitute a minor share in the company's total revenues.

As the mushrooming number of brand outlets suggests, all surveyed companies have experienced a high growth in revenues in recent years (cf. table 7.12). Yet, these figures probably do not reveal more than tendencies, because replies on this issue were characterised by a vagueness which is typical when questions touch issues that are considered to be sensitive. Still, the given figures are within a realistic range given the dynamic performance of garment retail sales in China which grew by 24.8 percent in 2010 and by 24.2 percent in 2011 (HKTDC 2012b).

## B. Industrial upgrading strategies

All of the surveyed companies launched their brands before the onset of the economic crisis of 2008/09. During the research period, none of them introduced sudden changes in their production model. However, in the period between 2008 and 2011 the brands succeeded to enter mass retail markets and gained increased market shares. The companies deepened their engagement in brand building and marketing and also introduced piecemeal changes, some of which affect their production systems.

*Table 7.13: Design capacities of Humen-based fashion brands*

|  | CASUALYOUTH | GENTSSUIT | LADYFIT |
|---|---|---|---|
| International input | Designers from Europe, Japan, Korea, HK | Consulting from Italy | Design centres in Korea and HK |
| No of designers | 500 | 30 | 10 |
| Styles per season | 3-4,000 | n.s. | 350-400 |

Source: HKTDC 2011; interview data.

## (1) Multiple challenges of brand building

Functional upgrading towards an OBM model primarily requires investments in design and marketing capabilities. Regarding the former, all companies rely on support from abroad to develop their styles. CASUAL-YOUTH employs designers in Europe, Japan, Korea, Malaysia and Hong Kong and LADYFIT runs design centres in Korea and Hong Kong on a part-time basis (HKTDC 2011a; ID 18.11.2011c). GENTSSUIT collaborates with an Italian consulting firm for which it spends RMB 1 million each year. This connection is proudly advertised in its 2011 catalogue under the motto "when business meets Italy" (ID 03.11.2011c). Input from abroad in each case is supplemented by more comprehensive design departments in Humen that adapt foreign styles to their perception of Chinese consumer tastes. This task also involves more or less elaborate functions of market research.

When launching a brand, the companies not only need to come up with independent design functions, but also meet enhanced quality standards. CASUALYOUTH's practice is most sophisticated in this respect with a RMB 20 million testing lab that controls flammability, content of chemicals, PH values and physical functionality of products, e.g. the quality of zippers and buttons (CY Website). The company also pursues the process-oriented technique of Total Quality Management (TQM) in its pilot factory in Humen (ID 09.12.2010b). Apart from quality control measures, quality also depends on the ability to coordinate the production flow in a way that balances the capacity utilisation of the factory and the seasonal demand for their products, as the general manager of LADYFIT explained (ID 18.11.2011c).

The coordination of marketing requires enhanced skills on the part of the management. This can be seen as one major challenge of industrial upgrading in this area where garment enterprises often are run by self-made men without any formal education in economics (ID 09.12.2010a). A representative of GENTSSUIT stated accordingly that the improvement of management skills and sales performance was their greatest challenge. Because of their fast growth, there was a lack of professional managers, especially in the field of retail sales. The company needed to develop their capacities to train sales managers and to summarise and generalise good experiences from franchising stores. GENTSSUIT received consulting from Chinese experts to support these tasks (ID 03.11.2011c). The experience of JEANSCHOKE, a fourth Humen based company whose general manager could be interviewed during the Humen fashion fair in 2010, very well illustrates the challenges involved in building a retail network. This producer of women's trousers engaged in an OBM model despite offering production of questionable quality

(ID 20.11.2010b). The enterprise apparently could not reach their goal of establishing a franchise network. In 2011, their website reported tensions between franchise partners and the management which suggest that the company could neither deliver products of sufficient quality nor possessed suitable management skills to master this task. The company was no longer present at the Humen fashion fair of 2011, and its website went offline in the meantime.

Establishing a popular fashion brand furthermore is a capital-intensive task. The surveyed companies attend fashion fairs for which they receive some financial support by the local government. CASUALYOUTH hosts own fashion shows displaying the latest collections and produces television and other advertising. CASUALYOUTH and LADYFIT also devote resources to developing sophisticated websites and e-commerce platforms. The expenses of GENTSSUIT give an adequate impression of the capital required to enter the league of mass retailers. The company spent more than RMB 10 million for a three-year advertising contract with a Hong Kong celebrity, RMB 15 million for a contract with the television channel CCTV and another RMB 10 million on fees for sales agents (ID 03.11.2011b).

*(2) Divergent results in terms of process upgrading*

While the case studies generally provide a quite unanimous picture with regard to the requirements for product and functional upgrading involved in the project of brand building, the results are less clear concerning process upgrading. The case of CASUALYOUTH reveals substantial changes with respect to the organisation of production that affect workers' skills and wages. At GENTSSUIT and LADYFIT, however, there is little evidence for process upgrading. By and large, the production systems of those companies are little different from CMT or OEM suppliers in the region that operate in a very labour intensive way with little demand for skill upgrading.

The case study of CASUALYOUTH is limited to the production department at its newly-built Humen headquarters complex. It houses comprehensive management and sales offices, logistics operations and a factory. Added together, there are 4,000 employees in this complex, of which 1,095 were manufacturing workers in December 2010 (ID 09.12.2010b). The production facilities in the building, inaugurated in 2010, assume a pilot function for CASUALYOUTH branch factories. The management is eager to introduce new production techniques with the intention of generalising them across CASUALYOUTH's dependencies. The factory is run according to a lean production system with the aim of reducing lead times and making the production process more efficient. This is linked to a fast fashion philosophy that allows for an easy and quick link between design and production in order to supply a large number of different styles. This production system is driven by a close communication with stores that select their orders according to their sales performance and own market assessment (ID 09.12.2010b).

Lean production at CASUALYOUTH implies improvements in the production flow that avoid unproductive jamming which is common in conventional garment companies and becomes apparent in the notorious piles of half-finished garment pieces on the shop floor (cf. the example of GENTSSUIT in illustration 7.4). CASUALYOUTH to this end introduced a General Systems Theory (GST) management system which helps to distribute tasks across the factory in an advantageous way and the before mentioned TQM system of process-oriented quality management. Production is organised in working teams steered by a digital performance control system (ID 09.12.2010b). This form of work organisation is not to be understood as a more participatory collaboration of workers, however, but merely as a form of less personalised performance control. Workers continue to receive very detailed specifications for their tasks and do not have a say in how to perform them. Likewise, there is no switching of tasks between different categories of workers.

In order to guarantee maximum flexibility, CASUALYOUTH applies a specific system of templates that guarantee easy and faultless sewing of different styles. The templates are provided by the designers and serve as a master plate attached to the fabric. The workers sew the fabrics along the templates and in this way do not need to be introduced in a detailed way in how to sew specific styles. According to a company presentation, and also confirmed by a government employee who closely followed the introduction of modern production techniques at the company's pilot factory, the template system allows CASUALYOUTH to employ workers with no prior sewing experience. This of course puts the company in an advanced position in terms of recruitment given the widespread shortage of experienced sewers in the region (ID 09.12.2010b; 18.11.2011a).

The template system is complemented by advanced production equipment. The company uses digitally controlled multifunctional sewing machines of high-end Japanese brands and has introduced automatic cutting machines that speed up the process and reduce the number of workers. There is also an automatic machine for attaching shirt pockets which apparently enables the simultaneous processing of several shirts. The combined effect of all of these measures is a steep increase in productivity which is permanently monitored by the management that continuously seeks to improve existing techniques and introduce new ones. Between September and December 2010, productivity rose by 21 percent and a further increase of 30 percent was projected for 2011. The average time for sewing shirt collars could be reduced from 1:37 to 1:07 minutes through the application of templates and the time for attaching shirt pockets from 2:12 to 0:45 minutes through mechanisation (ID 09.12.2010b).

*Illustration 7.4: Advertising vs. sewing departments of LADYFIT (left) and GENTS-SUIT (right), Humen*

Source: Company website; company catalogues; author's photographs.

None of these elaborate measures for an upgrading of the production process were introduced at GENTSSUIT and LADYFIT. Cutting and finishing was exclusively done manually, with workers crouching over the fabric on top of the cutting table at GENTSSUIT. Both factories use rather basic sewing machines without sophisticated functions or digital controls. According to the management, GENTSSUIT introduced some modern machines for supplementary tasks like the attachment of buttons (ID 03.11.2011c), but these were not demonstrated during the author's factory visit. In both factories, there were piles of half-finished garment pieces lying around, although this was organised in a slightly more orderly manner at LADYFIT where a hanger system was introduced to improve performance control and oversight. The organisation of production at GENTSSUIT and LADYFIT stands in stark contrast to their carefully created images of fashionable, upscale brands (cf. illustration 7.4).

*C. Production process and work*

The production process in each of the factories consists of cutting, sewing and finishing. The production process is very labour-intensive since finishing, and at GENTSSUIT and LADYFIT also cutting, is performed manually and sewing workers operate only one machine at a time. Despite its ambitious measures for process upgrading, CASUALYOUTH is no exception to this. At LADYFIT, there was a remarkable intensification of work without resorting to mechanisation: of the 300 workers in 2009, only 160 remained at the factory in 2011 due to a high workforce turnover and difficulties in recruiting. Yet, the output of the factory is said to have been significantly higher in 2011 than in 2009 (ID 18.11.2011c). In all of the factories, sewers are the largest group of workers, followed by workers in finishing and cutting (cf. table 7.14).

Apart from the manufacturing workforce, all companies employ a significant number of white collar workers. The share of employees in design and sales functions amounts to at least 13 percent of the total workforce at GENTSSUIT and 25 percent at LADYFIT. Data on the precise composition of the workforce at CASUALYOUTH was not available on request. The proportion between white collar and manufacturing work at the Humen factory complex (roughly 2.000 employees each) is not a valid indicator since the employees at the headquarter mainly perform functions that concern the whole enterprise group, not only the Humen factory.

*Table 7.14: Composition of the workforce at Humen-based fashion brands*

|  | CASUALYOUTH | GENTSSUIT | LADYFIT |
|---|---|---|---|
| Total workforce | 1,095 | 600 | 160 |
| Design | n.s. | 30 | 10 |
| Sample making | n.s. | 5-60 | n.s. |
| Cutting | n.s. | >20 | 9 |
| Sewing | 780 | >300 | 70 |
| Finishing | n.s. | >40 | 22 |
| Sales | n.s. | 50 | 30 |
| Proportion of designers | (1.4–1.7)[i] | 5 | 6,2 |

i    The figure for the proportion of designers at CASUALYOUTH is calculated by the aggregate number of designers and employees provided in secondary sources.

Source: Interview data; HKTDC 2011.

An approximation of the quantitative relationship can be achieved through the calculation of the aggregate numbers of 30–35,000 employees and the total number of 500 designers quoted in one secondary source (HKTDC 2011a). If the latter figure is valid, the proportion of designers in CASUALYOUTH's is rather low with a share between 1.4 and 1.7 percent. In sum, the data displayed in table 7.14 suggests a negative correlation between the overall company size and the proportion of higher-skilled design work. Obviously, the share of designers can be kept quite low even in a fast fashion type of production system once production reaches high volumes and sophisticated systems for a quick and easy link between design and manufacturing are introduced.

The gender proportion of the manufacturing workforce is more or less even, with a slightly higher share of women in sewing functions. At CASU-ALYOUTH there is a clearer majority of women, who constitute 60 percent of the workforce. At this company, the workforce is also the youngest, aged 25 on average according to the management, an estimation that still seemed rather high with view to the author's impressions during the shop floor visit (ID 09.12.2010b). But the relatively young average age at this factory is little surprising given the fact that most of the workforce was newly recruited with the opening of the factory, and that work at CASUALYOUTH allegedly requires no prior working experience due to its specific production system. At LADYFIT and GENTSSUIT, workers appeared to be significantly older, yet the management provided no data on this. At GENTSSUIT, the comparatively old age of workers reflects a management philosophy aiming at stable employment. The company recruits workers mostly from a city in Hunan province, the hometown of the owner. Through their common place of origin, the management aims to create bonds between the workers to overcome the "psychological difficulties of belonging to a lower class in a rich province" (ID 19.11.2011b). This solution, described as a typically Chinese approach, apparently succeeded in minimising a turnover in the workforce. According to the management, half of the workforce had joined the company more than ten years before, and 60 to 70 percent had worked there for more than 5 years (ID 3.11.2011c). LADYFIT has been less successful in holding on to its manufacturing workforce. According to the general manager, one or two workers leave per month which would correspond to a turnover rate of at least 7 to 15 percent per year. He referred to the widespread labour shortage as the reason for a reduction of the number of employees from 300 to 160 between 2009 and 2011. Recruitment represents a chronic problem for the company which is surprising because it offers comparably high wages (cf. table 7.15). The difficulties regarding recruitment are aggravated by the fact that the company exclusively hires experienced sewers due to its high quality standards and the requirements under its unsophisticated production system (ID 18.11.2011c).

The latter consists of a direct introduction of workers to product styles via foremen. Workers need to study each of the highly diverse items carefully and are individually responsible for the completion of each entire piece. One sample product is exhibited on the factory floor for workers to consult in case of doubts. As the quantity of products is quite low (ranging from 100 to a maximum of 1,000 pieces) styles often change. Small groups of workers instructed by three foremen each work on different styles (ID 18.11.2011c). The production process at GENTSSUIT is similarly based on a direct introduction of sewers by foremen, only that there is a larger sample-making department. Given the peculiarities of menswear, the styles are also less diverse and change less often. According to the management, production rhythms at GENTSSUIT are more even and relatively unhurried as opposed to the standards during their history as OEM supplier when the company had to reply to quickly changing orders from brand customers and wholesalers (ID 03.11.2011c). As explicated above, the link between design and sewing is greatly simplified at CASUALYOUTH through the introduction of the template system which saves time in the introduction of workers and reduces requirements for their skills.

The training times only partially reflect the different standards in this respect. At CASUALYOUTH and GENTSSUIT, training lasts one week, including the introduction to general rules and regulations at the companies (ID 09.12.2010b; 03.11.2011c). LADYFIT does not' provide any training at all, since the company only recruits experienced workers who need to work for one week on a trial basis before they are definitively hired (ID 18.11.2011c). Because the hiring policy at GENTSSUIT and, more pronounced, at LADY-FIT, aims at experienced workers, one week of training in these cases is not equivalent to the work introduction at CASUALYOUTH where the company management prides itself that new recruits do not need prior working experience. All in all, process innovations at CASUALYOUTH have resulted in a considerable de-skilling of the workforce, which is expressed by their social composition, their lack of experience, and their lower wages.

The wage system at all factories is based on a piece wage system, albeit with different modes of calculation. At CASUALYOUTH, the piece rate share only constitutes one third of the total wage of sewers, whereas it is about two thirds at GENTSSUIT and allegedly 100 percent at LADYFIT (ID 09.12.2010b; 03.11.2011c; 18.11.2011c). The latter company has a peculiar system of a unified piece rate independent of the style of the respective product. Differences in the complexity of the products are supposed to be balanced by the foremen who try to distribute the jobs in a fair manner. The different systems result in quite strong variations of total wages at the surveyed factories, which are lowest at CASUALYOUTH with an amount of RMB 2,000, and highest at LADYFIT where the average total wage for sewers is about RMB 3,400. Yet, according to a factory manager this would be a rather low wage for very experienced workers, who can up to RMB 6,000 through their ability to work faster and on condition of longer working days in peak production periods (ID 18.11.2011c).

At LADYFIT, wage levels differ substantially due to variations in capacity utilisation. In low season workers usually earn only RMB 1,700 to 2,500 which sometimes leads to discontent and may be the primary reason for the high turnover of the workforce (ID 18.11.2011c). There is no data available from GENTSSUIT on this issue, but there is a large disparity between simple manual tasks that sometimes can earn as little as RMB 1,000, and the average wage of sewers of RMB 3,000 (ID 03.11.2011c). At CASUALYOUTH, major variations in the wage levels seem to be absent because of the lower piece wage share of workers and the elaborate management techniques of optimising capacity utilisation. This provides workers with a reliable source of income, but the wage ceiling has rather tight limits and the total wage is much lower than at those enterprises that operate under a more old-fashioned production system (ID 09.12.2010b).

With respect to working conditions, better standards at CASUALYOUTH may compensate the disadvantage of lower wages to some degree. The company offers a modern and clean factory and dormitories with air-conditioning and hot water. The maximum amount of overtime is two hours per day and the maximum working time per week is 60 hours with one day off on Sundays (ID 09.12.2010b). At GENTSSUIT the maximum working time is slightly lower with 57 hours per week according to a company representative (ID 19.11.2011). Both factories demand working schedules beyond the legal maximum of 48 hours per week, but these are still much lower than the maximum working hours at LADYFIT. At this factory, workers toil up to 12 hours per day in peak production times with only one day off per month (ID 18.11.2011c) which amounts to a weekly maximum of 84 hours. GENTSSUIT grants workers a seniority bonus. It is claimed that dormitories are also air-conditioned and have hot water supply. The company also claims to have changed towards a more humanitarian style of workers control and devotes efforts to integrate workers by means of small anniversary gifts and the like (ID 03.11.2011c; 19.11.2011).

*Table 7.15: Wages and working hours at Humen-based fashion brands*

|  | CASUALYOUTH | GENTSSUIT | LADYFIT |
|---|---|---|---|
| Cutters | 2,200 | >1,000 | 2,300 |
| Finishers | n.s. | >1,000 | 2,200 |
| Sewers | 2,000–2,200 | 3,000 | 3,200–3,600 |
| Base wage | 1,600 | 2,000 | 0 |
| Flexible share | 400–600 | 1,000 | 3,200–3,600 |
| Spreading | n.s. | n.s. | 1,700–6,000 |
| Maximum working hours per week | 60 | 57 | 84 |

Source: Interview data; own calculations.

## 7.3.2.5 Conclusion

The upgrading strategy in Humen based on the creation of fashion brands for mass consumer markets rests on the ability of local companies to strengthen their capacities in product design and marketing. In these functions, local companies need an increased number of technically trained staff educated and trained in vocational schools and colleges. Although these workers have to meet high requirements with view to their output and receive substandard wages in comparison to international remuneration levels, the functional diversification of Humen-based garment enterprises towards independent design and marketing capabilities involves significant skill upgrading. The government follows suit by improving the availability of vocational training in technical or creative courses related to the fashion industry. Apart from that, brand building also raises the capital intensity of fashion enterprises considerably as they rely on expensive foreign input regarding product styles and high spending on advertising. Although the manufacturing process as such remains labour-intensive, companies rely less on the advantage of cheap labour alone for their success.

With regard to the organisation of production and the respective effects on line workers, the information from the surveyed companies differs. There is a certain common ground in an overall low degree of automation of the production process. This indicates that automation is difficult to realise in the core sewing function where workers continue to operate one machine each. At GENTSSUIT and LADYFIT this meant that brand building had no major effect on the production process at all, which continues to be organised on a low technological level and depends to a high degree on the working experience of sewers. Brand building may result in a higher frequency of styles and thus be more demanding as at LADYFIT, but this is not necessarily the case as the contrary example of GENTSSUIT demonstrates, where the production flow is more regular than during the company's past experience as OEM supplier. Contrary to both cases, brand building has induced a number of changes to the production process at CASUALYOUTH. In its pilot factory, the company introduced extensive measures for rationalisation through faster machinery and lean production schemes. These have had adverse effects with regard to skill upgrading. Sewers need to have little, or according to a government representative, even "no" working experience. Wages at CASUALFIT also were significantly lower than at the other surveyed factories, where working conditions were worse and working hours excessive, but where the skills of sewers constituted their very asset for gaining a higher wage.

All in all, the fashion industry in Humen is replicating the polarisation between creative and marketing functions on the one hand, and manufacturing functions on the other hand, that is the hallmark of the global garment industry. Unlike on the global scale, however, this polarisation mainly remains one *within* each factory. In each case, the growing sophistication of marketing and design does not require skill upgrading on the level of production. As the example of CASUALYOUTH demonstrates, a growing professionalization of the production process can even have adverse effects on skill requirements and wages of sewers.

### 7.3.3 A blueprint for cluster formation and industrial upgrading? The transformation of Xiqiao's historic textile industry

Textile production has a long history in Xiqiao, a town within the City of Foshan with about 140,000 inhabitants and a floating population of 70,000 migrant workers (GD Xiqiao TIB (no date), 4). Fabric production started in the Tang Dynasty (618–907 AD), then exclusively focusing on the production of silk. In the following centuries, Xiqiao became a prominent silk supply base profiting from the fame of the City of Guangzhou as source of superior quality silk. After the opium wars in the 19 century, global demand reached new heights, spurring the introduction of the first silk-reeling factory in 1872 which led silk production towards industrial mass production. By 1924, Xiqiao-based companies owned 12,000 sets of silk machines and produced one third of the total silk volume in the Pearl River Delta area. After the war with Japan had virtually destroyed the entire industrial base, the industry was first reconstructed on basis of a myriad of over 2,500 small producers that operated simple mechanic textile looms. In the 1970s, investment by the state in three silk factories and the simultaneous replacement of manual machines by automatic machines led to a renewed rise of the town's output until it produced goods that amounted to a GDP share of 12.98 percent of the city district of Nanhai (Wang and Yue 2010, 197–198).

The reform policies induced a major industrial transformation in the 1980s which involved a shift from silk to cotton products after the output of the state-owned silk factories had declined due to economic difficulties.[127] An increasing number of farmers subsequently began processing cotton on a small basis. These private enterprises often had no more than four weaving machines and some were run by cooperatives of farmers. The scarcity of fabric that existed in the late 1970s and early 1980s made the production of fabric a very lucrative business:

"With cloth still in very short supply, whatever the tiny new factories produced was snapped up by customers. Seeing the quick profits to be made and using the new little private factories as their model, people in Xiqiao who had no personal experience with electric looms began to open their own small enterprises. At that time they did not need to know much about doing business, for whatever they could manufacture got sold" (Unger 1999, 4).

Driven by this gold rush-like atmosphere, small scale production soon added up to a large industrial cluster with over 1,000 factories, 10,000 looms and an output of over 10 million meters of fabric per year. The industry supported 60–70 percent of the local population at this time. The introduction of the first cotton wholesale market in 1986 consolidated the agglomeration. During these years the local industry was able to take advantage of an increased national and international demand for industrially produced fabric (Wang and Yue 2010, 199–201).

Already in the mid-1990s the local industry suffered from overcapacities and enhanced competition that threatened its progress. Subsequently, it was restructured in two waves of government-led initiatives for industrial upgrading in the mid-1990s and the mid-2000s. In 2004, the Textile Industry Association of China (TIAC) chose Xiqiao as the first National Textile Industry Pilot Upgrading Area (Xiqiao FIB (no date)). By rationalising industrial development and creating a number of supporting institutions, the local government succeeded in raising the technological content of the Xiqiao industry and thereby has facilitated a successful economic development in the past years in spite of mounting economic pressures. Therefore, even more so than the other industrial clusters included in this study, the town of Xiqiao enjoys a model status in terms of industrial upgrading. The town's policies are a prominent object of academic research and even serve as

---

127 According to Unger, the main reasons for this decline were rising labour costs, a high level of pollution entailed in silk production and competition of cheaper substitute products such as nylon and rayon. Many industry participants also simply switched to cotton production given its outstanding attractiveness due to high domestic demand (1999, 4–5).

a showcase example in publications of the World Bank (cf. Arvantis and Qiu 2009; Wang and Yue 2010; Zeng 2011).

### 7.3.3.1 Economic structure of the town

Today, Xiqiao is no less focused on the production of textiles than it used to be in the past. The textile industry employed around 60,000 workers in 2011—almost one third of the total population. Its companies churned out 1 billion meters of fabric in 2011. It is the second biggest textile cluster in China and the largest production and distribution platform for fabrics in South China (Xiqiao Shan Tour Website). In 2008, its textile production volume constituted a market share of 30 percent in Guangdong, 11 percent in China and 6 percent internationally (Wang and Yue 2010, 195). Given these impressive figures, it is no wonder that the textile industry has remained the pillar on which the whole town's economy rests. In 2010, the revenues of the textile industry (excluding revenues of related services and trade) constituted RMB 8.5 billion, almost half of Xiqiao's GDP of RMB 17.6 billion (ID 08.11.2011a), a significantly higher amount than in Dalang and Humen, where the garment industry accounts for about one third of *industrial* output and is outperformed by the local IT companies in terms of output.

Besides textiles, there is some manufacturing of ceramics and hardware in Xiqiao. But only tourism, attracted by a huge historic temple complex on Xiqiao Mountain, is of noteworthy quantitative relevance. The government promotes Xiqiao as a tourist destination and finances extensive programmes for a modernisation and revaluation of the town (Xiqiao FIB (no date)). The IT, automotive or other industries that are considered to be strategically important by the central and provincial government are virtually absent in Xiqiao. Although the town government, on its own admission, does grant preferential policies for "new" and "high-tech" projects (e.g. tax breaks and favourable land transfer), there is no perspective for a gradual realignment of the town's economic structure towards reducing dependence on the textile industry. Asked about the government's vision for the future development, a leading CCP representative replied that the modernised textile industry should remain the pillar of the town's economy with a special focus on fabric production for denim, suits and leisure wear (ID 08.11.2011a).

There were around 800 textile enterprises in Xiqiao in 2010, about two thirds of which were small-scale operations. 100 bigger enterprises had a turnover of over RMB 5 million per year and nine large-scale enterprises an annual turnover of over RMB 100 million. 90 percent of enterprises are privately owned with only a small share of them being held by foreign investors. About half of the companies are owned by entrepreneurs from Xiqiao (ID 07.12.2010a; Wang and Yue 2010, 195, 212; Xiqiao FIB (no date)). According to government representatives, the industry is experiencing consolidation to some degree. About 20–30 companies are said to be dissolved every year, either because of bankruptcy or through mergers. Consolidation has been an ongoing tendency in the industry which had about the double number of enterprises in 1998. The government supports small enterprises by various measures, but does not try to stop the market-induced processes of consolidation which have been endemic during the industry's development over the last two decades (ID 08.11.2011a).

Facilitated by the upgrading strategy of the Xiqiao government, the diversification of the town's textile and garment industry has increased in recent years. Today, Xiqiao accommodates a "whole production chain" including some machinery producers, 37 dying and 36 garment companies. Still, the industry remains focused on the production of fabric with around 650 enterprises remaining specialised on this task (ID 07.12.2010a; Xiqiao FIB (no date)).

The industry is primarily oriented towards the domestic market. In 2008, exports constituted 0.11 billion meters of the total production quantity of then 1.2 billion meters, or 9.2 percent (Wang and Yue 2010, 195). However, the actual dependence of Xiqiao's fabric suppliers on overseas demand is higher than expressed in these figures because many of the textile companies' regional customers manufacture garments for export production.[128]

Accordingly, the slump in foreign demand during the crisis of 2008/09 did have some impact on Xiqiao's industry although the overall growth performance remained solid. There were a number of bankruptcies and mergers that accelerated the concentration process of the industry (ID 07.12.2010a). Yet, all in all, it remains unclear whether these difficulties are mainly the result of the global economic crisis or of a structural loss of profitability.[129]

---

128 For instance, a representative of a middle-scale textile company (the case of JUNGLE-JEANS, see below) estimated that one quarter of their revenues were obtained from Chinese companies producing for overseas markets (ID: 02.11.2011b).

129 Either way, difficulties of garment exporters in recent years do affect the industry of Xiqiao. According to Wang and Yue, "garment exporters' profits have been greatly reduced; as their fabric suppliers, Xiqiao producers are directly affected, although not as seriously as

Whatever the precise reason, many companies in Xiqiao took advantage of the situation to upgrade their operations. In 2008, the government of Foshan Nanhai launched the so-called Eagle Plan to support the upgrading of eight local industry clusters. 20 out of 70 enterprises that received this support were from Xiqiao (Wang and Yue 2010, 214). Due to past upgrading initiatives, the Xiqiao textile industry is already characterised by a relatively high degree of mechanisation. By 2008, there existed more than 20,000 spinning machines, about half of them of the more advanced shuttle less version—a higher proportion compared to national standards (ibid, 212).

Although the textile industry of Xiqiao remained relatively stable after the economic crisis, a government representative in late 2010 reported mounting structural challenges due to rising prices, mainly for cotton and labour. He explained the latter with the rising living costs in the region and the new aspirations of the so-called second generation of migrant workers, especially skilled ones. Another problem in the industry seems to be fraud, e.g. with regard to quality standards, which exposes local companies to enhanced price pressures (ID 07.12.2010a).

### 7.3.3.2 Industrial upgrading in Xiqiao—past initiatives and current strategies

Due to its pioneering role with regard to an upgrading of its textile industry, Xiqiao's present industrial policy carries forward past initiatives centred on rationalising the industry structure, enhancing innovative capabilities of local companies and supporting sales through a strong public infrastructure. This emphasis on qualitative improvements is linked to the general objective of raising production quantities substantially, "from one billion meters of fabric to two billion meters of fabric", as it was put by a government representative (ID 07.12.2010a).

Regarding the history of Xiqiao's industrial policy, Wang and Yue identify two major phases of government intervention to raise the technological level of the textile industry after China's market opening in 1978 (Wang and Yue 2009; cf. Wang and Yue 2010, 194–207). The first phase began in the mid-1990s and was a reaction to the uncoordinated growth of hundreds of small enterprises with very low technological capabilities. The government supported industry consolidation towards larger units and facilitated the

---

other regions. In addition, domestic and overseas competition is becoming increasingly stronger. This situation is especially difficult for small enterprises" (2010, 214).

expansion of Xiqiao Textile City, the town's wholesale market, in order to structure and develop the market. Additionally, it established a fabric sample manufacturing company in order to create a supply of innovative styles to local companies at subsidised prices. The latter initiative was expanded in the following years by the formation of the town's Technology Innovation Centre (TIC) in 2001, an investment project worth RMB 200 million which was realised with financial support from the provincial and city governments (Wang and Yue 2010, 206). The TIC is widely acknowledged for being of vital importance for Xiqiao's subsequent successful development. Wang and Yue sum up the changes after the foundation of the TIC as follows: "[T]he sales value of textiles rose from US$ 342.2 million in 1998 to US$ 788.8 million in 2003, although the number of enterprises fell from 1,590 to 1,380; the average R&D investment of enterprises increased from US$ 140 to US$ 4,280; and the total number of patents rose from zero to 188, while the number of employees increased by more than 10,000" (2010, 210). The detailed figures displayed in table 7.16 reveal a strong process of consolidation during this period with the number of employees at larger enterprises increasing six fold within five years.

*Table 7.16: Structure of Xiqiao's textile industry before and after TIC establishment, 1998 and 2003.*

| | 1998 | | | | | 2003 | | | | |
|---|---|---|---|---|---|---|---|---|---|---|
| Emplo-yees | Firms | Em-ployees | Out-put[i] | R&D[ii] | Pa-tents | firms | emplo-yees | Out-put[i] | R&D[ii] | Pa-tents |
| <10 | 795 | 7,055 | 44.6 | 0 | 0 | 465 | 3,715 | 31.9 | 0 | 0 |
| 11-50 | 583 | 26,235 | 130.1 | 0 | 0 | 634 | 25,299 | 94.5 | 0 | 0 |
| 51-100 | 205 | 19,475 | 106.1 | 0 | 0 | 359 | 33,387 | 323.2 | 2,257 | 22 |
| >100 | 7 | 1,094 | 61.5 | 230 | 0 | 22 | 6,445 | 339.2 | 3,648 | 166 |
| Total | 1,590 | 53,859 | 342.3 | 230 | 0 | 1,380 | 68,856 | 788.8 | 5.905 | 188 |
| Firm average | | 32.28 | 0.21 | 0.14 | 0 | | 49.86 | 0.58 | 4.28 | 0.14 |

i　USD, millions
ii　USD, thousands

Source: Wang and Yue 2010.

However, Xiqiao's textile industry in the mid-2000s was again plagued by economic difficulties due to "three cold fronts", that is, of a shortage of electricity, rising raw material prices, and intensified competition, especially on the low and medium quality product markets (Wang and Yue 2010, 201). These difficulties led to another round of upgrading initiatives, this time also supported by the Textile Industry Association of China, resulting in the official recognition of Xiqiao as the first "National Textile Industry Upgrading Pilot" area in 2004. The general line of the new upgrading policy was summarised as the "Five Ones", a set of measures for a comprehensive integration and coordination of the industry's economic structure with an emphasis on innovation (cf. figure 7.7).

The general orientations of this set of policies remain valid until today and were only slightly modified or intensified after the global economic crisis of 2008/09. However, some elements of the general strategy, such as the creation of a regional brand, have barely been implemented up until today,[130] while there is heavy emphasis on others. The following paragraphs summarise those initiatives that have enjoyed special attention in the recent past.

*Figure 7.7: The Five Ones—cornerstones of industrial upgrading policies in Xiqiao's textile industry*

- One System: integration of the entire supply chain
- One Platform: strengthen the TIC
- One Base: improve infrastructure of the production base
- One Market: develop Xiqiao Textile City as a communicative bridge between industry and buyers
- One Brand: establish a local Xiqiao fabrics brand

Source: GD Xiqiao TIB (no date).

### (1) The construction of the Xiqiao Industrial Park

The Xiqiao government advances the agglomeration of enterprises in special industrial zones mainly in order to facilitate efficient common access to infrastructure and to foster communication and cooperation between

---

130 This goal was mentioned in none of my interviews with Xiqiao government officials and company representatives, is absent from most printed material issued by the government and, to my cognition, was also not presented at the Xiqiao fabric fair in 2011 in any way.

enterprises throughout the production chain. The construction of two adjacent areas for different types of textile companies began in 1999. An investment of RMB 290 million in 2005 lead to the construction of the so-called "Three Unified" project that includes large scale facilities for water supply, power supply and sewage treatment (Xiqiao FIB (no date)). This offers important advantages for textile enterprises, especially for those engaged in ecologically sensitive dyeing processes. A Greenpeace report about heavy pollution by denim fabric producers in the nearby town of Xintang in the City of Guangzhou caused some stir about this issue (Greenpeace 2011). Due to stricter government regulations, a clean environmental balance has evolved as a competitive advantage for textile producing towns in recent years and all the more the Xiqiao government promotes its efforts as "the first ecotype textile and apparel industrial base in China", certified with the ISO 14001 label for environmental management (GD Xiqiao TIB (no date), 25). The availability of public infrastructure liberates private companies from the burden of setting up expensive facilities for power supply and water treatment. (GD Xiqiao TIB (no date), 18–27; ID 07.12.2010a). While these measures may help to attract technologically mature companies to Xiqiao, they also serve the purpose of rooting out backward industries. Companies need to qualify for placing investments in the industrial park and heavily polluting companies are asked to leave town (ID 08.11.2011a). As the case studies below demonstrate, the ecological merit of these policies is ambiguous. There is certainly a strong incentive for local companies in Xiqiao to improve their environmental balance, but two out of three companies of this sample execute their dyeing processes in nearby towns, thereby simply shifting the problem to regions beyond the town's borders.

*(2) Extension of the Technology Innovation Centre*
The TIC has been gradually expanded and diversified in terms of its functions. By now, it consists of five pillars that provide a range of professional services from product development to e-commerce and logistics (cf. figure 7.8).

*Figure 7.8: Structure and functions of the Technology Innovation Centre*

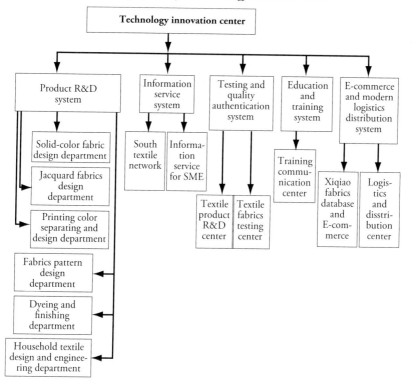

Source: Wang and Yue 2010.

The existing academic studies on Xiqiao's upgrading policy highlight the success of the TIC in improving independent design capacities of the local industry.[131] Wang and Yue claim that 20,000 products were developed by the TIC between its foundation in 1999 until 2007, 80 percent of which

---

131 This is vindicated by interview data from companies included in this case study which all take advantage of the TIC's services (see below). However, it is doubted to some extent by Arvantis and Qiu who state that "the innovation centre's development logic was rather different from the industrial logic. The industrial enterprises act as though [sic!] the innovation centre is of little interest. They develop their own design and development capabilities and have little interest in links with other enterprises or institutions. Nonetheless, the innovation centre has helped create better conditions for industry and attracted higher skilled labour to the city" (2009, 66).

were bought by local enterprises (2010, 212).[132] More than 20 of these were officially recognised as "China Popular Fabrics" and in sum more than 300 national patents were obtained for Xiqiao-made textile products. Significantly, the fostering of innovative capabilities also contributed to reducing the development cycle for new fabrics from 20–30 days to 1–5 days while the costs for developing new products were reduced by 50 percent. In the recent past the TIC has encouraged enterprises to apply computer-aided design and manufacturing functions to further modernise production (Wang and Yue 2010, 210–12). Within the last decade, there has also been a distinct shift towards more sophisticated products. The proportion of decorative cloth, considered to be technologically more demanding, in the total product mix rose from three percent in 1997 to 42 percent in 2009, while the proportion of fabric used in garment production dropped from 95 percent to 53 percent in the same period. At the same time, there was a slight increase in the share of industrially used fabric from two to five percent (Arvantis and Qiu 2009, 62).

Other functions of the TIC than those concerning product development are no less significant. A "Testing and Quality Authentication System" supports companies in maintaining high quality standards. Once a product obtains a certificate, its quality standard is recognized in more than 40 countries and regions such as Europe, the United States, South Korea and Japan. Furthermore, an "Education and Training System" is designed to enhance technological and management skills of the leading personnel in textile companies. Finally, the "Information Service System" and the "E-commerce and Modern Logistic Distribution System" support companies in obtaining market transparency and optimising their sales performance (GD Xiqiao TIB (no date), 44–7).

### (3) Upgrading of Xiqiao Textile City

Xiqiao's large production base has its major outlet in the Xiqiao Textile City, one of the three largest textile wholesale markets in China which accommodates more than 3,000 stores on 540,000 square meters. Products of a value of RMB 20 billion are sold annually, including apparel, cloth, chemical products and other raw materials (ID 07.12.2010a; Wang and Yue 2010, 195, Xiqiao FIB (no date)). The Textile City was expanded by functions with re-

---

132 They also give the figure of over 5,000 new products that are released by Xiqiao's enterprises each year with support of local government institutions (Wang and Yue 2010, 212).

spect to product display, business negotiations and e-commerce all of which are located in the newly constructed "Textile Business Building" that also provides additional office space. In 2011, the latter was the venue for Xiqiao's first textile fair, an attempt by the government to further boost the sales of local companies.[133]

*(4) Financial support*

The upgrading policies of the Xiqiao government from the beginning were complemented by financial assistance, mainly in form of cheap credits for enterprises. In late 2010, Xiqiao's financing platform controlled assets of RMB 100 million and granted credits of up to ten times that amount (ID 07.12.2010a). Additionally, the government decided in 2002 to offer extensive tax breaks to new investors, but also to companies that had stayed in Xiqiao for more than ten years.[134] Through its tax policy the government intends to attract investment from technologically progressed and export-oriented enterprises to the industrial parks (GD Xiqiao TIB (no date), 50). This has been fairly successful since the government managed to attract large investments by the huge denim manufacturer POWERDENIM, covered in the case studies, and the Humen-based garment manufacturer Yishion.

Another measure that directly affects the modernisation of industries is a payment of RMB 10,000 of subsidies for the acquisition of each modern machine. The government's total contribution to machine acquisition rose from RMB 6 million in 2009 to RMB 10 million in the following year leading to the installation of 800 imported machines (ID 07.12.2010a). Despite this high amount of subsidies, which is higher than that offered by the Dalang government for the acquisition of each CNC knitting machine, the case studies reveal that process innovation through automation of the weaving process has played a smaller role in Xiqiao than in Dalang during the research period. All surveyed companies already had upgraded their equipment in previous phases of modernisation. Still, there is a gradual renewal of equipment and a focus on sophisticated machinery for finishing tasks.

---

133 According to a representative of JUNGLEJEANS, a company included in the case studies, the fair was held on demand of local companies that faced a difficult market situation and wanted to take advantage of the fair to promote fabrics made from new materials (ID 02.11.11b).

134 In most of such agreements, enterprises were freed from tax burdens for two years and only needed to pay a reduced rate during the following three years.

### 7.3.3.3  Assessment of government policies and impact of industrial upgrading

In academic studies and political discourse, the development of Xiqiao's textile industry is treated as a blueprint for a successful government-led upgrading policy. Arvantis and Qiu identify it as "a typical success story in the Province of Guangdong" (2009, 59). The judgement of Wang and Yue in their study for the World Bank is equally positive. They emphasise the town's repeated success in overcoming economic difficulties by enhancing local enterprises' technological and innovative capabilities. Yet, they also report about ongoing challenges for the industry and state that "[f]rom the global perspective, the Xiqiao cluster, along with most clusters in China, is still counting on low costs for its competitive advantage rather than R&D, innovation, and branding" (Wang and Yue 2010, 214–215).

In terms of the composition of the workforce, the upgrading initiatives have created the need to hire designers and technicians. According to a government representative, large advanced companies may employ 20 or 30 highly skilled employees (ID 08.11.2011a). Arvantis and Qiu claim that 1,000 professional technicians in product development and process engineering were attracted to Xiqiao between 2006 and 2009 (2009, 62). However, apart from these estimations there is no reliable information available about the aggregate number of designers and technicians in Xiqiao. Taken at face value, the available data does reflect an enhanced demand for technical staff, but it also shows that this only affects a limited number of employees in a town with some 60,000 workers in the textile industry whose larger companies employ several hundred workers. Still, skill upgrading in Xiqiao seems to constitute a challenge for the hiring practices of local companies. Apparently, they have experienced some difficulties in attracting graduates from technical schools because these mostly shun employment in textile factories. The local government supports enterprises in attracting talent by establishing direct links to schools, including the nearest technical school that is located 10 km away from Xiqiao (ID 08.11.2011a).

According to government information, the wage standards in Xiqiao are surprisingly high. A spokesperson claimed a rise by 50 percent in 2011 from an average of RMB 3,000 to RMB 4,500 for manufacturing workers (ID 08.11.2011a). As the case studies show, these numbers are probably inflated since two of the surveyed companies paid wages below RMB 3,000 to weavers and only one company, the largest one in town, claimed to pay RMB 4,000 in 2011.

Apparently, a local wage standard exists in the town which sets a fixed minimum wage plus rates for overtime hours. In 2011, this determined that no line worker would receive a wage lower than RMB 1,500, a considerably higher amount than the local minimum wage which then amounted to RMB 1,100 (ID 08.11.2011a). If this information obtained from an interview with a government representative is correct, this industry-wide agreement can be seen as a significant step towards sector-wide wage agreements. It reflects the interest of the town government and entrepreneurs to collectively attract workers in the face of a severe shortage of workers which is creating problems for the local industry. Yet, the agreement, the detailed content and procedures of which were not further explicated, apparently only defines the absolute bottom line for wages and overtime payments and does not offer a detailed definition of hourly wages or piece rate payments. It is unknown whether the local branch of the ACFTU plays any role in negotiation the industry wage agreements.

According to a local government representative, the recent wage increases in Xiqiao were not the result of technological changes. In his view, the acquisition of modern production technology would not result in higher wages for workers in manufacturing functions. The driving factors for wage increases rather were the shortage of workers and the general increases in the cost of living (ID 07.12.2010a). Mechanisation also does not seem to result in higher skill requirements for line workers. According to the same source, the proportion of skilled workers remains unchanged in spite of a modernisation of production techniques. Training units at the local training centre are limited to especially skilled or management staff, whereas 80 percent of the workers typically receive an on-the-job training of ten days when they are hired (ID 07.12.2010a).

### 7.3.3.4 Case studies: Product upgrading and functional diversification in Xiqiao's textile enterprises

The case studies cover three enterprises of the Xiqiao textile industry cluster that produce fabrics as suppliers to garment enterprises. The contact to POWERDENIM, the largest enterprise of the town, was established via the foreign investment bureau of Xiqiao. The data on this company stems from field trips in December 2010 and November 2011 on which the author was able to visit the company's shop floor and conduct in-depth interviews with leading managers. Backup information on POWERDENIM was provided by the Xiqiao government and obtained via the company's website, company catalogues and two promotional films. The contacts to the remaining two enterprises covered in this study, DENIMSUIT and JUNGLEJEANS, were established at the Xiqiao textile fair in November 2011 where first interviews could be conducted with sales staff. These provided the basis for subsequent shop floor visits and interviews with management personnel one month later. The author also used material from DENIMSUIT's detailed website while no such information was available in the case of JUNGLEJEANS

### A. General information—introduction to the research sample

The sample consists of three private companies owned by mainland Chinese entrepreneurs. DENIMSUIT and JUNGLEJEANS are located in the Xiqiao industrial park whereas the premises of POWERDENIM are situated on an especially assigned area closer to the town centre. JUNGLEJEANS and DENIMSUIT are of local origin. JUNGLEJEANS entered business in 1989 as a garment manufacturer specialised on men's suits and jeans wear. However, the management decided to close the suits factory in 2002 and opened another factory for denim fabric the construction of which was completed in 2005. DENIMSUIT was founded in 1998 as a wholesaler. In 2006, the owners bought land and opened a factory which was equipped with 80 imported weaving machines in 2007. The third and largest company, POWERDENIM, also entered the industry as a wholesaler in 1995. The company first placed an investment for a small factory at its town of origin Xintang, a well-known cluster for denim garments in the City of Guangzhou. Subsequent investments lead to the opening of a larger factory in Xintang that had a production capacity of about two thirds of the one on the current premises (PD Company Catalogue 2009). However, the management decided to close down this factory and to entirely relocate to Xiqiao, mainly because of the town's advanced sewage conditions which help the company to meet official environmental standards (ID 07.12.2010b).[135] The new investment of around RMB 300 million in 2009 will be expanded by another RMB 300–350 million to a total amount of RMB 800 million until the end of 2013.[136] In the long term, this denim fabric specialist plans to open a

---

135 Moreover, this way the company apparently managed to keep out of the scandal regarding water pollution by Xintang-based factories revealed by the already mentioned report by Greenpeace on the issue.

136 The numbers given for investment in Xiqiao in 2009 (RMB 300 million) and for total

factory for jeans wear production on a huge area of 100 acres designated for investments by POWERDENIM. The existing enormous factory building currently only occupies about 6 percent of this area (ID 08.11.2011a). DENIMSUIT and JUNGLEJEANS equally announced plans to stock up investments. At JUNGLEJEANS these did not seem to be very concrete, whereas the owners of DENIMSUIT already possess ground next to its current factory earmarked to this end (ID 29.11.2011a). In 2012, the company built a new office building that extends beyond the factory area currently in use.

*Table 7.17: Overview of the research sample, Xiqiao*

|  | POWERDENIM | DENIMSUIT | JUNGLEJEANS |
|---|---|---|---|
| Founded (company, factory) | 1995, 2009 | 1998, 2006 | 1989, 2002 |
| Output 2011 (meters) | 32 million | 8 million | 10 million |
| Output 2011 (RMB) | 1.2 billion | 200 million | 150 million |
| Size of premises (sq m) | 174,000 (factory 150,000) | 31,000 (factory 13,000) | 12,000 |
| Number of weaving machines | 340 | 102 | 184 |

Source: Interview data; company websites; promotion material.

As table 7.17 illustrates, POWERDENIM by far is the largest company of the sample. Still, the company is "tiny" in relation to the global denim market, according to the vice-president of the company, who also estimated that POWERDENIM produced around 1.5 percent of global sales in 2011, a low figure in his view (ID 08.11.2011b).

All companies are specialised in the production of denim fabric. This product segment has seen a major diversification of materials and styles during the last decade. Enterprises nowadays offer a broad variety of prod-

investment in the current factory (RMB 460 million) differ. The most likely reason for this discrepancy is a reinstallation of expensive equipment that was already in use in Xintang in the new factory in Xiqiao. According to a company spokesperson, 40 percent of the equipment in use at the Xiqiao factory was brought there from Xintang.

ucts that differ in colour, appearance and physical properties. As will be elaborated in more detail below, these effects are achieved by sophisticated dyeing and finishing techniques that alter the products' morphology, look and feel on the one hand, and by special yarn blends that, for instance, alter the fabric's elasticity or the wearing comfort of the finished product on the other hand. The surveyed companies apply such techniques to create a distinctive product reputation. POWERDENIM builds its image on references to cowboy iconography as displayed generously in their promotional material (e.g.: "the oriental interpretation of cowboy culture", cf. PD Company Catalogue 2010, 51). The enterprise is also promoting its products as denim of a "new age" because of the company's advanced production techniques and the resulting novel product properties. Additionally, POWERDENIM cultivates an image of environmental sustainability and claims to adhere to higher standards in this respect (PD Company Catalogues 2010–12). Finally, the company boasts its great versatility and claims to be able to produce more than 1,000 different styles due to its broad range of high-end materials and its sophisticated finishing techniques. The management claims that the average sales price of products is highest among Chinese denim companies (ID 07.12.2010b; 18.11.2011b).[137] The product image of DENIMSUIT is defined more narrowly as a blend of formal menswear and denim styles, thereby paying tribute to its past as men's suit manufacturer. The company mostly produces T/R fabric, a blend of polyester and rayon that is popular in China due to its silk like feel. Apart from that, the company also produces pure cotton fabrics. The products are sold at a price range of RMB 28–35 per meter (ID 08.11.2011c; 29.11.2011a). JUNGLEJEANS has a similar product philosophy of a "combination of denim production with a suit experience". The company blends cotton and chemical fibres to manufacture "jungle products" somewhere in between casual and formal styles. Most products are sold for RMB 22–24 per meter, but the company seems to offer low-cost products of little more than RMB 10 per meter, as well (ID 02.11.11b; 29.11.11b).

Regarding production models, there is a predominance of OEM models whereas some contracts that require co-design functions are exercised by

---

137 Yet on request, a company representative quoted the amount of RMB 25 as average sales price which is lower than the number given by DENIMSUIT. This contradiction cannot be resolved (ID 12.04.2013). Based on the overall appearance of materials and production processes it can be guessed that the figure quoted by DENIMSUIT is inflated, however.

POWERDENIM and DENIMSUIT. JUNGLEJEANS operates exclusively on an OEM model. POWERDENIM's sales are mainly based on detailed customer specifications, too, although the company aims to raise its share of ODM products which currently constitute up to 20 percent of revenues (ID 08.11.2011b). DENIMSUIT, on the contrary, asserted that all of the company's sales were based on ODM contracts (ID 02.11.2011c). However, this claim is based on a rather loose understanding of the concept of ODM production. The company's website states: "[W]e can provide customized service and [a] professional design concept to our customers for their specific promotion demands. [P]lease [feel] free to contact us for customized [service] or design suggestion[s]. [O]ur design team will provide exactly what you want" (DS Website). As this statement exemplifies, the difference between OEM and ODM contracts seems to be less clear-cut in the textile industry than in the garment or IT business since supply contracts often imply notable elements of co-design. Where direct relations to buyers are maintained, textile contracts are often based on a dialogue between buyers and manufacturers that lead to the eventual specification of the final product which is produced according to the buyers specifications, but contains certain elements of design by suppliers.

*Table 7.18: Brand image, sales prices and production models at the surveyed textile companies, Xiqiao*

|  | POWERDENIM | DENIMSUIT | JUNGLEJEANS |
|---|---|---|---|
| Product image | "Cowboy culture", "new age" denim, versatility, eco-denim | Blend of formal menswear and denim styles | "Jungle wear" between casual and formal |
| Average sales price (RMB) | 25, "highest in China" | 28-35 | 22-24 |
| Production model | OEM, <20% ODM | (ODM) | OEM |

Source: Interview data.

All companies are focused on the domestic market. DENIMSUIT and JUNGLEJEANS do not sell their products outside China at all. Most of their merchandise is produced for Chinese garment companies that again are oriented towards the domestic market. However, JUNGLEJEANS estimates that about one quarter of sold fabric ends up in garments that are exported (ID 29.11.2011b). DENIMSUIT characterises its products as "high-end", but claims that the company's products are cheaper than those of a similar quality by competitors (ID 29.11.2011a). Among DENIMSUIT's customers are prominent Chinese garment brands like the menswear brands Youngor and Septwolves. JUNGLEJEANS also entertained a supplier relationship with Septwolves but apparently was not able to maintain it. This company does not have many fixed supply contracts and sells about 70–80 percent of its products via sales agents. The rest allegedly is directly sold to famous Chinese brands (ID 29.11.2011b). In contrast to its smaller peers, POWERDENIM places a heavy emphasis not only on the further penetration of national markets, but also on the expansion of its export production. Originally, the company's products had been exclusively sold in the jeans wear cluster of Xintang. In 2006, the company was represented at the Shanghai textile fair for the first time, thereby launching its offensive towards the national Chinese market. In 2009, POWERDENIM signed an agreement with a major Japanese sales agent that establishes contracts with large foreign brands. Today, the overseas market constitutes about 30 percent of POWERDENIM's sales. Among the company's major customers are the national brands Dancing with wolves and Yishion, as well as well-known international fashion companies like Levi's, Dickies, G-Star and VF (ID 08.11.2011b; PD Company Catalogue 2010).

In terms of its recent economic development, the large-scale enterprise POWERDENIM is a league of its own. According to management information, revenues grew by about 15 percent in 2011 (ID 08.11.2011b). The company advertises its large investment "against the odds", stating that "[i]n 2009, while the global financial crisis has blown most of the enterprises to pieces, [POWERDENIM received] all the attention from industry to announce the great opening of the [RMB] 0.3 billion investment in Xiqiao" (PD Promotion Video 2010). The company has remained on a solid growth path since the factory opened, not least because of its strategy of international expansion, despite a weak performance of overseas markets in recent years. The situation at DENIMSUIT and JUNGLEJEANS is not as promising. Interview partners at both companies admitted a zero growth rate in 2010 and stated that 2011 was a particularly difficult year. DENIMSUIT also explained that the great volatility of raw material prices in recent years has squeezed profits (ID 29.11.2011a). The fact that these domestically oriented companies experienced such problems despite overall growing demand for fabric during this period suggests that they are rather experiencing the effects of an oversupply of fabric on the Chinese market and generally heightened competitive pressures than some secondary effects of the global economic crisis.

### B. Industrial upgrading strategies

Industrial upgrading is not a new theme for the surveyed companies. In line with the policies of the Xiqiao government, their past investments already aimed at improvements in processes and products by acquiring advanced machinery, improving materials and enhancing innovative capabilities. As a consequence, the enterprises' upgrading strategies do not consist of a sudden technological leap comparable to the introduction of the CNC knitting machine in Dalang or the launch of fashion brands in Humen. Industrial upgrading in Xiqiao during the research period rather consisted of piecemeal improvements and is more diffuse, addressing a broad range of interconnected issues. These are of no less importance from the perspective of the respective companies, however. Particularly POWERDENIM attributes its success to its ability to "upgrade itself to a modernized textile enterprise" (PD Company Catalogue 2012). The replies given by representatives of the three companies when asked about their own understanding of industrial upgrading illustrate the diversity of approaches. The answers included the acquisition of high-end equipment (POWERDENIM, DENIMSUIT), the improvement of R&D capabilities (POWERDENIM, DENIMSUIT), the improvement of raw materials (DENIMSUIT), environmental sustainability (POWERDENIM, DENIMSUIT), improvement of market research (all), versatility of production (DENIMSUIT), highly skilled employees (POWERDENIM) and the ability to produce faster and at lower cost without compromising quality (JUNGLEJEANS) (ID 07.12.2010b; 02.11.2011; 08.11.2011 (b,c); 29.11.2011 (a,b); PD Company Catalogue 2012).

A more systematic analysis of the implemented upgrading measures at the surveyed companies reveals a general focus on product upgrading that encompasses all aspects of the companies' functions. Of predominant importance are the following aspects that will be explicated in more detail below: (1) the acquisition and blending of raw materials, including advanced chemical fibres, (2) the purchase of sophisticated machinery, first and foremost to guarantee a higher versatility of products through advanced finishing techniques[138], and (3) the enhancement of R&D capabilities to engage in co-design and guarantee the delivery of sophisticated materials in superior quality. These main initiatives are executed complementarily to the achievements of past upgrading efforts. In particular, the replacement of older loom models by electric power looms had already been completed before the research period. Some of the surveyed companies merely ramped up quantities, but none was operating on equipment of older generations in the recent past. For logical reasons, brand building did not play any role in the surveyed companies since their products are not sold on consumer markets but to garment companies. Yet, DENIMSUIT and POWERDENIM place heavy emphasis on a public image through marketing via expensive promotional materials and sophisticated websites. POWERDENIM also applies for IP licences for its products in order to undermine counterfeits, a widespread phenomenon in the industry.

### (1) Processing of advanced materials

Fabric prices decisively depend on the raw materials applied. According to a representative of JUNGLEJEANS, "the price of fabric has nothing to do with the production process, only with material and design" (ID 29.11.2011b). This statement may be viewed as exaggerated, and it is not accidental that it comes from a company with little efforts towards process and functional upgrading (cf. discussion below). Yet, similar views about the importance of raw material quality were also expressed in interviews at POWERDENIM and DENIMSUIT. Both companies entertain fixed supplier relations with cotton distributers. POWERDENIM only buys cotton from the best and DENIMSUIT from the second to best Chinese category, according to their own claim (ID 08.11.2011b).

But while denim fabrics famously were manufactured exclusively from cotton in the past, product quality nowadays depends on more than just the quality of cotton. Cotton yarn is usually interwoven with a variety of synthetic and natural fibres. DENIMSUIT and JUNGLEJEANS both use a blend of cotton and polyester or polyester and rayon for their products which gives them a lighter and softer feel. In contrast to JUNGLEJEANS, a company that purchases readymade fibre mixes on the market, DEN-

---

138 This mostly implies functional upgrading since versatility critically depends on adding manufacturing functions to the core function of weaving, like professional shrinking, dyeing or other surface treatments.

IMSUIT has acquired its own equipment for RMB 400,000 to blend different types of yarn (ID 08.11.2011c; 29.11.2011a). This machine gives the company higher autonomy to create own distinctive styles. POWERDEN-IM equally has the ability to create own mixes of yarn and the company applies this technique using high quality fibres. For instance, it adds the elastic fibre lycra to some of it products. Furthermore, it has signed a supply agreement with the Austrian chemical corporation Lenzing that delivers tencel, a refined natural fibre that enhances the durability of fabrics and reduces wrinkles of the cloth (PD Company Catalogue 2010, 2012).

The quality of chemicals used for dyeing and surface treatments is another criterion that defines the quality of end products. POWERDENIM places heavy emphasis on its supplier relations with international chemical corporations like Dow (US), Klein (SUI) and Clariant (ESP), which it classifies as technological cooperation agreements (PD Promotion Video 2010). Representatives from DENIMSUIT and JUNGLEJEANS did not mention anything about the origin of the applied chemicals.

*(2) Acquisition of advanced machinery*
The available information about the impact of the type of weaving machines on product quality is ambivalent. Certainly, there are major differences, first and foremost between domestic Chinese and imported machines. All companies mainly use imported equipment. POWERDENIM exclusively applies a comparably fast model of a well-known Belgian manufacturer. JUNGLEJEANS and DENIMSUIT both use a small share of Chinese machines, in the case of JUNGLEJEANS they constitute roughly one third of the weaving equipment (ID 29.11.2011b). DENIMSUIT uses various types of machines for different contracts which is explained by the need for enhanced versatility on the company website (DS Website). DENIMSUIT and JUNGLEJEANS both employ their equipment according to different quality requirements by their customers (ID 29.11.2011 (a,b)).

Despite these obvious differences in weaving speed and quality, the core potential in terms of process upgrading does not lie in the weaving process. As a manager of POWERDENIM explained, "the production steps [at POWERDENIM, F.B.] in comparison to a lower-end textile mill are more or less similar", thus underlining the uniformity of the automated weaving processes in modern textile enterprises (ID 08.11.2011b). This judgement was confirmed by a representative of a foreign weaving machine manufacturer who, referring to the Xiqiao industry, explained:

"Usually companies buy yarn on a mortgage from yarn producers and then receive a fee for weaving from their customers. So weaving is a rather low value-added industry. Quality and difference of the products are all about the yarn and the finishing of the fabric" (ID 02.11.2011a).

From this perspective, automatic weaving equipment is the entry ticket to the league of advanced fabric producers, but the decisive differentiating factor is what happens before and after the weaving process, especially in terms of the quality and blends of raw materials and further processing of woven fabrics.

With regard to the latter, there are fundamental differences between the surveyed companies. JUNGLEJEANS, the smallest company of the sample with the lowest average product sales price, performs merely the basic functions of denim production, which include dyeing, warp preparation, weaving and simple functions of finishing like washing and shrinking of the fabric. Just as is the case at DENIMSUIT, the dyeing process is not performed in Xiqiao because both factories did not meet the local ecological requirements. The functions at DENIMSUIT are similarly basic as at JUNGLEJEANS, with the exception of the already mentioned equipment for creating own yarn mixes, which places the company ahead of JUNGLEJEANS in terms of product versatility and originality.

Unlike these companies, POWERDENIM has obtained a variety of advanced and expensive finishing machines which give their fabrics distinctive properties. The most important installations are:

- two large scale computer-controlled dyeing machines that operate faster and deliver more precise results than conventional equipment.
- A machine for liquid ammonia mercerisation, a surface treatment that makes the fabric more shiny and stable. The machine was bought for the price of about RMB 24 million.
- A colour printing machine by which distinctive patterns and designs can be printed on the woven fabric (RMB 480 million).
- two giant imported machines for pre-shrinking the fabric that provide more reliable results than conventional equipment.
- A machine for glue finishing, another process of surface treatment that enhances the fabric's durability (RMB 3.6 million) (ID 08.11.2011b; PD Company Catalogue 2012).

This expensive machinery equips POWERDENIM with the necessary means to supply fabric to high-end denim brands. It also enables the company to develop its own innovative fabrics as an ODM supplier. The company accordingly advertises its versatility and originality, especially with reference to its colour denim product line that consists of a broad variety of denim fabric in unconventional colours with unique prints (PD Company Catalogue 2010).

*Table 7.19: Functional diversification of the surveyed textile companies, Xiqiao*

|  | POWERDENIM | DENIMSUIT | JUNGLEJEANS |
|---|---|---|---|
| R&D | 80 employees | 23 employees | 4 employees |
| Yarn mixes | X | X | – |
| Warp preparation | X | X | X |
| Dyeing | 2 large CNC machines | Facilities in nearby town | Facilities in nearby town |
| Weaving | 340 (all imported) | 102 (66 imported) | 184 (120 imported) |
| Washing | X | X | X |
| Shrinking | 2 huge imported facilities | Basic equipment | Basic equipment |
| Mercerisation | High-end equipment | – | – |
| Colour printing | Special equipment | – | – |
| Glue finishing | High-end equipment | – | – |

Source: Interview data; company websites; PD Company Catalogue 2012.

## (c) Strengthening R&D capabilities

All surveyed companies entertain R&D departments, yet they are of different dimension and function. At POWERDENIM, there is a large R&D department with 80 employees including some designers from Hong Kong. The department consists of a chemical lab and a centre that combines a showroom with market research and design functions. R&D is closely related to marketing at POWERDENIM. The company has created a one-stop service point where potential customers can select products, but also discuss their desires with technical personnel. To support this function, POWERDENIM even runs a small factory for garment samples with 20 employees. In 2011, most of the marketing and R&D functions were still located in Xintang, the site of the former factory, but about to be relocated to Xiqiao where they were supposed to be accommodated in a spacious building within the factory complex (ID 08.11.2011b).

DENIMSUIT also places high emphasis on its capabilities for product development. The company has been running an R&D centre for ten years, which in 2011 employed 23 people. DENIMSUIT advertises its ability to produce fabrics according to the customers' desires which involves substantial co-design activities. JUNGLEJEANS also claims to engage in some design cooperation with customers. However, its R&D department is relatively weak, with only four employees. Their workplaces are not located in the factory, but at the company's sales dependency in Xiqiao Textile City where the R&D staff closely cooperates with employees assigned to marketing (ID 29.11.2011b).

The surveyed companies all take advantage of the infrastructure provided by the Xiqiao government to back up their own R&D efforts, albeit to a different extent. DENIMSUIT emphasises the importance of public consulting institutes for developing their styles and improving processes. The company regularly purchases weaving patterns from the China Textile Information Centre in Beijing on which they have the exclusive rights of disposition for two years. Additionally, the company takes advantage of consulting services at the local Textile Innovation Centre (TIC). According to a manager at DENIMSUIT, employees at the TIC "tell them about market trends and how to organise production, e.g. environmentally friendly manufacturing" (ID 29.11.2011a). The company also runs quality tests at the TIC, which is considered to be important (ID 02.11.2011c). Likewise, JUNGLEJEANS uses the services of the TIC for product design and quality tests, although consulting in general seems to play a less important role for them (ID 29.11.2011b). In contrast to its smaller competitors, POWERDENIM exclusively relies on its own capacities for market research and the design of products. However, the company uses the services of the TIC in order to conduct physical tests of their products (ID 02.11.2011b). All in all, the public infrastructure has an important function of backing up private R&D capabilities, especially those of smaller companies. Apart from that, the product-testing functions provided at the TIC seem to be indispensable. After all, such tests identify whether certain products conform to product standards on international markets. As already mentioned, the quality standards employed at the TIC are recognised in 40 countries, which is of importance for direct exporters like POWERDEN-IM, but also for companies that sell their products on the domestic market to export-oriented garment companies.[139]

The Xiqiao government provides a number of other measures to support local companies, according to their statements. It reimburses some of the costs for attending domestic and international fairs and exhibitions. It also supports the acquisition of imported machinery on which neither VAT nor import tax need to be paid (ID 29.11.2011a). In the case of POW-ERDENIM in 2009, the Xiqiao government offered particularly tempting incentives to attract the company's huge investment. A company representative said that it was "better to skip the details" about this, thereby indirectly indicating the magnitude of this support (ID 07.12.2010b). As already mentioned above, the town's sewage system also helps companies to meet the tougher government requirements with regard to wastewater treatment (ID 08.11.2011b).

For all these reasons, there are no tendencies towards a relocation of the surveyed companies from Xiqiao. Companies only decide to allocate production steps to places outside of Xiqiao when these do not meet the local environmental criteria, as is the case with the dyeing processes of DENIM-SUIT and JUNGLEJEANS.

## C. Production process and work

The weaving process is the core operation in all of the surveyed companies. Weaving workers operate fully automatic machines. Their main responsibility consists of checking the appropriate supply of yarn in order to guarantee the correct operation of the machines. Unlike in the knitwear industry, they do not need to attach spindles of different coloured yarn, since the machines perpetually weave yarn of at most two or, rarely, three different colours. The product also does not consist of single pieces of gar-

---

139 As a salesperson at DENIMSUIT explained, there is a great variety of nationally specific standards for weaving patterns, materials, environmental criteria, and the like. Clients often order products according to nationally specific standards, which demands some effort on their part in order to understand such orders. To add to the confusion, the standards sometimes conflict with each other (ID 08.11.2011c). All the more, the physical product tests at the TIC seem to be of high importance for local companies.

ment, but of a steady output of fabric. Similar as in the knitting industry, weavers operate various machines at the same time. At POWERDENIM, their number ranges from four to ten machines, while at the other factories workers mostly operate a maximum of four machines (ID 08.11.2011b; 29.11.2011 (a,b)). At DENIMSUIT, the management set an explicit maximum of four machines per worker, in order to avoid quality defects (ID 29.11.2011a). All companies also employ workers for the preceding processes of warp preparation and dyeing. In each case this involves large-scale machinery with a comparably small number of workers controlling the processes of rewinding and dyeing of yarn. At DENIMSUIT and JUNGLEJEANS, this involves some minor manual tasks of winding yarns that are too complicated for automation, according to a manager at the former company (ID 29.11.2011b).

The remaining steps in the production process depend on the functional diversification of the respective company. POWERDENIM's huge digitally controlled equipment is operated by technicians who sometimes receive support from overseas experts to set up the machines and to train the operators. The technicians lead small teams of skilled migrant workers who are introduced gradually to their tasks (ID 07.12.2010b; 08.11.2011b).

Because of its higher functional diversification, the workforce at POWERDENIM has a larger proportion of technical staff than its peers. Since the weaving process at this company is also organised in a more efficient manner, its overall labour intensity, measured as the number of employees divided by total revenues, is slightly lower than at the other companies (cf. table 7.20).[140] At the same time, the high-end equipment at POWERDENIM has required substantial amounts of investment. The capital intensity of this enterprise is therefore particularly high.

---

140 As table 7.20 shows, the labour intensity at POWERDENIM is not lower when the relationship between the number of workers and the amount of produced meters is taken into account. This puts the assumption of a lower labour intensity at the most upgraded factory into perspective. However, it needs to be taken into account that the numbers for output at JUNGLEJEANS and JEANSSUIT are probably inflated.

*Table 7.20: Composition of workforce and labour intensity in the surveyed textile enterprises, Xiqiao*

| | | POWERDE-NIM | DENIM-SUIT | JUNGLE-JEANS |
|---|---|---|---|---|
| Composition of workforce | Number of employees | 850 | 220 | 200 |
| | Sales & management | 30 | 30 | n.s. |
| | R&D | 80 | 23 | 4 |
| | Technicians | 28 | 15 | n.s. |
| | Weavers | 240 | 100 | 50 |
| | Other workers | 368[i] | 40 | n.s. |
| Output | | | | |
| | Meters of fabric | 32 million | 8 million | 10 million |
| | Revenues 2011 (RMB) | 1.2 billion | 200 million | 150 million |
| Labour intensity | | | | |
| | Employees/ million meters | 26.56 | 27.5 | 20 |
| | Employees/ million RMB | 0.71 | 1.10 | 1.33 |

i   POWERDENIM provided the following detailed figures: warp preparation: 90; dyeing: 82; finishing: 95; inspection: 102 (ID 12.04.2013).

Source: Interview data.

With the exception of some technicians, the manufacturing workforce at all companies consists of migrant workers. The companies did not provide detailed data on the gender proportion of the workforce. Judging from observations during the company visits, the overall ratio is balanced with a manifest prevalence of female operators among weavers and a majority of male workers among technicians and operators of large scale machinery. This impression is vindicated by a salesperson at a foreign equipment manufacturer who indicated that weavers were generally female (ID 02.11.2011a).

With regard to the age structure, a JUNGLEJEANS manager said that most workers at her company were over 30 years old and had worked for the company for a very long time. Some had even settled permanently in Xiqiao, unlike most other migrant workers in the region (ID 29.11.2011b). The other companies did not provide details about the social composition of the workforce. All companies claimed, contrary to the statements of a government representative, that there were no grave problems in terms of hiring due to labour shortages. Only a representative at POWERDENIM said that they had experienced some difficulties, but that the government supported them in finding workers (ID 08.11.2011b). Given the complete relocation of this factory which implied that 80 percent of the manufacturing workforce were newly hired, some bottlenecks regarding labour supply are hardly surprising. The company plans to expand its workforce from currently 850 employees to about 1,500 and expects to recruit enough migrant workers to achieve this goal (ID 08.11.2011b).

With regard to training periods, weavers only receive a very basic introduction to their tasks. This is the case for newly trained workers and for experienced workers who are introduced to a new machine type. According to a representative of a vendor of advanced looms, the change to a new type of equipment was equivalent to that of "a car driver who switches from a BMW to a Mercedes". He added that today workers tend to have less work experience than five or ten years ago: "now the workers tend to be less skilled because companies need to hire any workers they find due to labour shortages". Only the workers who set up the machines, usually migrant workers with considerable work experience, needed a more substantial training of about two weeks which is provided by machine vendors (ID 02.11.2011a). This assessment about low skill requirements for weavers is vindicated by data from the surveyed companies, although training times for machine operators tend to be slightly longer than indicated in this statement. At POWERDENIM, new weavers are trained for two weeks and at JUNGLEJEANS for ten days. DENIMSUIT even claimed that new operators received a training that lasted between half a month and a month. At JUNGLEJEANS, where the workforce was of a comparatively old age, the management stressed that the company only recruited experienced workers. At this company, workers also receive a seniority bonus to keep them from leaving (ID 08.11.2011; 29.11.2011b). There are different estimates concerning the required skills of weavers. According to the equipment salesperson quoted above, the weavers only need to repair the yarn in case it breaks which was considered to be very easy (ID 02.11.2011b). A representative of DENIMSUIT, on the contrary, said that weaving tasks, especially checking the tension of the yarn and correcting its position, was the most critical and difficult step at his factory (ID 08.11.2011c). While this assessment may include a grain of truth in the case of this company, the relatively short training periods at all companies let weaving work rather appear as a largely de-skilled task with low complexity and a high degree of monotony.

At POWERDENIM, a number of other functions clearly demand higher skills. The training periods for dyeing and finishing workers, for instance, last about one or two months. Some of the corresponding tasks that involve the operation of complex high-end equipment afford a continuous refinement of skills. Work at complicated dyeing or finishing machines is less monotonous and requires more knowledge than standard assembly functions because each production run needs a precise adjustment of settings to guarantee the desired effects for a broad variety of styles (ID 08.11.2011b). A minority of migrant workers therefore evolves towards a form of more elaborate craftsmanship that in some cases may resemble tasks of junior technicians at the company.

Wages at the surveyed companies sometimes reach levels above the average payments for migrant workers in the region. However, they range considerably lower than the figure of RMB 4,500, which a local government representative quoted above gave as an estimate for wages of manufacturing workers. At POWERDENIM, actual wages are closest to this figure. A manager claimed that the average wage for weavers was RMB 4,000 per month. In other functions like dyeing and finishing, migrant workers earn about RMB 5,000 and RMB 4,000, respectively. Unskilled workers earn between RMB 1,500 and RMB 1,800. At JUNGLEJEANS and DENIMSUIT, however, workers seem to barely earn RMB 3,000, although the figures provided by different representatives were not unequivocal about this (ID 08.11.2011c; 29.11.2011 (a,b)).[141]

---

141 A representative of JUNGLEJEANS claimed that the weavers earned a total wage of RMB 4,000. However this person only held a sales position and was not very well informed about the details of the production process. The same is true for a representative

All companies pay their weaving staff according to a piece rate system, in order "to give workers an incentive to correct mistakes very quickly", as a representative of DENIMSUIT commented (ID 08.11.2011c). At POWERDENIM, piece rates constitute 50 percent of the total wage; at DENIMSUIT and JUNGLEJEANS the entire income of weavers is based on piece rate payments. In the case of DENIMSUIT, a base wage is only introduced when the business situation is not good enough to guarantee a sufficient income based on piece rate payments (ID 08.11.2011c; 29.11.2011a). Despite the predominance of performance-based wage payments, the available information suggests a rather low spreading of wages, although the data is not conclusive on this. Theoretically, there seems to be most potential for skilled workers to achieve an above average income at POWERDENIM. Wages decisively depend on the number of machines a worker controls simultaneously which at this company can amount to up to ten. At DENIMSUIT and JUNGLEJEANS workers regularly only control four machines each, and in the case of DENIMSUIT the management even forbids to operate a higher number. Workers in these factories thus have limited scope to improve their wages by better performance, although their wage fully depends on piece rates. Although more information on the issue would be needed for a definite judgement, it can be presumed that the wage levels at the surveyed textile companies are relatively even because of the steady rhythms of machines and the limited possibilities of workers to increase their incomes through above average performance. This is a significant difference to sewing workers at most companies in the Humen fashion industry, for instance, whose work experience can help them to achieve a much higher income, because their output decisively depends on their skilfulness in operating sewing machines.

The impression of more regular work rhythms due to an even mode of operation of the weaving equipment is supported by the available data on working hours. At JUNGLEJEANS, workers regularly work for eight hours in three shifts with one day off per week. Apparently, overtime work of up

---

of DENIMSUIT who claimed that weavers earned RMB 4,500, RMB 1,500 more than most other workers (ID 02.11.2011b; 08.11.2011c). The respective numbers given by factory managers were "almost RMB 3,000" at JUNGLEJEANS and RMB 2,700–2,800 at DENIMSUIT (ID 29.11.2011 (a,b)). This data seems to be more accurate due to the status of the interviewed staff and their greater proximity to the production process. However, the inflated numbers given by salespersons may also reflect some differences in wage levels of weavers who are paid according to piece rate wage systems.

to four hours a day in peak production times does occur, but this is rare according to a factory manager. The management of DENIMSUIT gave similar data of eight hours of work per day with two days off per month. A company representative added that workers could "choose to work more" if they wanted which, of course, is a euphemism for existing overtime hours (ID 02.11.2011c). Also at POWERDENIM, the regular working day for weavers usually amounts to 8 hours. Working hours in dyeing and finishing functions seem to be less regular and extensive. At POWERDENIM, a representative frankly admitted that regular shifts last for 12 hours (ID 12.04.2013).[142]

With regard to the general working and living conditions, there are considerable differences between the modern factory of POWERDENIM and the smaller factories of DENIMSUIT and JUNGLEJEANS. All workers, including all management staff, are accommodated in factory-owned dormitories at POWERDENIM. These resemble rather middle-class apartment buildings than the run-down and overcrowded dormitories that are typical for the region. A relatively low number of four migrant workers shares one room in these buildings, whereas white collar workers live in single, and management personnel in two room apartments. POWERDENIM provides free meals for all employees and is about to inaugurate a building with various offers for entertainment as well as recreation rooms for the staff. The newly-built and relatively clean factory buildings are fully air-conditioned. Comparable features are missing at the smaller, older and dustier factories of POWERDENIM's competitors, especially at JUNGLEDENIM, but also at DENIMSUIT.

Despite these differences in the work environments, weavers at all companies suffered from serious defects in health protection due to the ear-deafening noise produced by the hammering weaving machines. Most workers do wear respiratory protection against fibre dust, but lack any ear protection. Asked about this, a manager of JUNGLEJEANS replied that "workers get used to the noise and that there are no earplugs needed" (ID 29.11.2011b). Yet, there is little doubt that work in a textile factory without appropriate protection must permanently damage the weavers' sense of hearing. A representative of POWERDENIM claimed that their workers wore ear protec-

---

142 Since the interview partner had no problems with quoting the excessive working hours for dyers and workers in finishing functions, his statement about the regular working hours of 8 hours seems to be particularly credible.

tion, but this contradicted observations during the author's factory visit and pictures in the enterprises promotional material (ID 08.11.2011b).

### 7.3.3.5 Conclusion

The strategies of all surveyed companies in the Xiqiao textile industry are centred on product upgrading. Just as is the case with the general industrial policy of the local government, this involves a broad variety of measures that are implemented with varying scope and intensity at the companies of this sample. JUNGLEJEANS on all levels seems the least inclined to industrial upgrading which manifests itself in lower product prices, weak R&D capabilities and a low functional diversification, which means that the company remains limited to basic functions of weaving including basic preparatory and finishing functions. In comparison, DENIMSUIT invested more in R&D and equipment and thus supplemented the weaving functions with the capacity to blend yarn which gives the company a higher versatility. POWERDENIM clearly surpasses its competitors with regard to sophisti-cated machinery, a broad range of functions, and the corresponding advan-tages in versatility and product quality. The company has advanced towards the global leaders in the industry and has achieved above average growth by expanding its international sales.

The strategies for product upgrading chosen by the surveyed companies have not affected the work of weavers. The automation of weaving work through the introduction of electric power looms was completed before 2009 and thus its effects could not be studied during the research period. In 2010 and 2011, weaving work in all companies consisted of low-skilled and very repetitive tasks, similar to the work of CNC knitting workers in Dalang. Accordingly, training periods for weavers are very short and there is not necessarily a need to rely on staff with extensive work experience, even though one company of the sample nevertheless prefers to do so. Wages for line workers seem to have risen in the past and are higher than those of knit-ters in Dalang, but data from the surveyed companies suggests a much lower average wage level than the figure of RMB 4,500 provided by a government representative. Likewise, there is neither evidence of a sudden increase in wages in 2010 and 2011, nor of a critical labour shortage, both of which were claimed by the government. If there exists a common wage standard in the Xiqiao industry, up until now it has not helped to lift workers average in-comes significantly above the wage levels in Dalang and Humen. In the case of weaving workers, the production flow in automated weaving departments also seems to limit the ability to improve wages through obtaining bonuses for high performance based on work experience.

While industrial upgrading in the Xiqiao industry therefore only has a limited impact on weavers and most other groups of workers, there is some evidence for skill upgrading in other functions at POWERDENIM and, to a lesser extent, at DENIMSUIT. Both companies rely on R&D departments that constitute about 10 percent of the workforce. What is more, the operation of sophisticated dyeing and finishing equipment at POWERDENIM requires a relatively high proportion of skilled workers. The gradual training of dyers and other operators of large-scale machinery belong to the few examples of this whole investigation in which migrant workers are introduced to tasks that require a certain flexibility in terms of tasks and a deeper understanding of the involved processes. If such functions would be generalised in the industry, this could lead to a higher demand for skilled workers and possibly to a demand for more formalised vocational training which in turn could support more stable employment and higher remuneration. Workers at POWERDENIM, where there is a functionally diverse workforce, enjoyed relatively good working and living conditions—that is, except for the lack of appropriate ear protection. However, skill upgrading and higher wages at this company only affect a minority of at most 25 percent of migrant workers. Migrant workers in better-paid and relatively highly skilled dyeing function also suffer from excessive working hours of up to 12 hours per day.

### 7.3.4 Comparison of the case studies in the textile and garment industry

In comparative perspective, the upgrading strategies in the surveyed clusters are remarkably distinct. The chosen approaches depend on the respective product category, which is different in each case. Yet, they also depend on the respective histories of manufacturing and the companies' main customer base. The descriptions of upgrading trajectories in the previous sections displayed a variety of measures in each case and the author has tried carefully to avoid oversimplifications. Yet, in very general terms, the transformations in the surveyed clusters can be matched with specific upgrading types as discussed in section 4.5 (cf. table 7.21).

*Varying approaches to industrial upgrading*
The case of *Dalang* is a paradigmatic example for process upgrading with its heavy focus on automation through CNC knitting machines. This also results in product upgrading and some functional upgrading, both of which require special efforts by enterprises, but which are made much easier through the reliability of automated knitting as well as the low entry barriers to own design functions through CAD applications developed by machine producers. During the research period, functional upgrading towards OBM production, while emphasised in government programmes, did not bear fruit. The town government has recently stepped up its efforts to support local companies in this respect, but the barriers for success seem to be relatively high because OBM production models also imply a switch from export production to the domestic market where Dalang-based manufacturers are not very experienced.

The opposite is true for companies in the neighbouring town of *Humen*. The cluster traditionally is domestically oriented and most local companies started out as wholesalers, integrating their functions backwards towards manufacturing. Functional upgrading through brand building clearly is the dominant upgrading strategy of the town's largest manufacturers. They thereby continue on a path of growing sophistication of supply chain management and marketing which is interwoven with the function of the whole cluster as a major garment trading hub. But in order to succeed as fashion brands, companies also need to boost their design capabilities and develop independent sales networks. These are the functions of critical importance in the Humen industry and they are eagerly supported by government funding and infrastructure. Brand building does not necessarily involve comprehensive measures for process innovation, but the largest local company engages in a rationalisation of production which supports flexibility and efficiency. Such techniques, as promoted by international buyers, may become the production norm of Chinese garment brands in the future. Unlike their peers in advanced industrial countries, however, the production models of Humen-based brands for the time being generally rely on substantial in-house production.

The surveyed enterprises in the textile cluster of *Xiqiao* exclusively produce supply products for garment enterprises. Industrial upgrading in this cluster is equivalent to product upgrading, the only perspective of raising the share of value added in an industry in which automation of the weaving process is completed and profits are squeezed by rising costs for raw materials and labour as well as by fierce competition resulting from overcapacities. More so than in the garment clusters of this sample, the main strategy of product upgrading involves a variety of measures ranging from the choice and blending of high quality fibres to acquiring design functions, and, finally, a diversification of functions including superior dyeing and finishing tasks which in turn requires the acquisition of advanced machinery. Functional upgrading on the level of manufacturing and R&D seems to be the precondition for a step out of the cost-cutting game and it entails the potential to tap high quality segments on overseas markets, as the example of the biggest local company shows.

*Table 7.21: Upgrading strategies and government measures in the textile and garment industry*[i]

| | Dalang | Humen | Xiqiao |
|---|---|---|---|
| Inhabitants (migrants) | 470,000 (400,000) | 570,000 (450,000) | 210,000 (70,000) |
| GDP (RMB, 2010) | 13.5 billion | 27.28 billion | 17.7 billion (2012) |
| Revenues of textile/garment (RMB, 2010) | 6 billion | 16 billion | 9.3 billion |
| Primary upgrading strategy | Process upgrading | Functional upgrading | Product upgrading |
| Secondary measures | Product upgrading, functional upgrading | Product upgrading, (process upgrading) | Supply chain upgrading, functional upgrading, process upgrading |
| Main government measures | Trade fair, marketing infrastructure, financial support, technical school | Trade fair, marketing infrastructure, R&D support and counselling, technical school | R&D support, marketing infrastructure, financial support |

i    The hierarchisation of the upgrading strategies is based on the author's interpretation of the interview data.

Source: Interview data; secondary sources.

In all of the clusters, the municipal governments play a pivotal role in industrial transformation. They consciously assume this role by implementing elaborate upgrading programmes that involve a streamlining of local policies to this end. With diverging emphasis, the cluster policies imply the construction of a sales infrastructure including ambitious trade fairs, subsidies and tax breaks for evolving companies, R&D support and training facilities for skilled staff. The Technology Innovation Centre of Xiqiao is an instructive example for the collaborative efforts to raise the R&D capabilities of the local industry, an approach that recently has been adopted in Humen where the Humen Technology and Innovation Centre was inaugurated. While governments have frequently expressed aims for rationalising the industry structure and gathering companies from all steps of the supply chain in their clusters, a consolidation of the respective industries through hard-handed interventions is not intended. Beneath the progressive examples of modernising textile and garment enterprises like those covered by this sample, a huge number of small scale enterprises with low technological capabilities continues to exist. But the local governments of Dalang, Humen and Xiqiao seem to leave the decision about their fate to the market, instead of consciously cutting the number of enterprises. Still, the chosen upgrading strategies also support a further consolidation of industries because it is mostly large companies that benefit from government measures.

*Paths beyond labour-intensive manufacturing and their limitations*
Assessing the effects of industrial upgrading in very general terms, there is a transformation towards more capital-intensive and knowledge-intensive production models in any of the surveyed clusters. Yet, a closer look reveals important differences in this respect.

In *Dalang*, the intensity of labour was substantially reduced through the automation of the knitting process which at the same time raised the capital requirements for enterprises considerably. However, knitting enterprises continue to operate in a highly labour-intensive manner because of limits for automation in the linking and finishing functions. Knowledge-intensive design tasks are gaining in importance through the proliferation of ODM and prospectively also OBM production models, but the share of designers at the surveyed companies was smaller than at the surveyed companies in the fashion industry of Humen or at the more advanced companies in Xiqiao's textile industry.

In *Humen's* fashion industry, labour intensity is highest since industrial upgrading is not centred on a rationalisation of manufacturing. The largest local company of the town is an exception to this rule since it introduced lean production methods, but even so, potentials for automating and speeding up sewing and finishing work remain limited. Yet, production at the same time becomes more capital-intensive since the surveyed companies also ramp up their expenditures for advertisement and distribution. Finally, the success of their fashion brands depends on their ability to develop independent design capabilities with support of domestic and foreign experts thus making production more knowledge-intensive. The comprehensive design activities at Humen-based fashion brands certainly are a vivid example of skill upgrading. Whereas CMT or OEM suppliers usually received their orders from designers in advanced industrial countries in the past, such functions are now increasingly allocated in the Pearl River Delta and create a corresponding demand for highly skilled staff.

Labour intensity in *Xiqiao* is lowest due to past waves of automation of the weaving process and the prevalence of a product category that requires less manual finishing than garments. The town's larger textile factories are characterised by fully automatic production floors in the weaving departments and large-scale equipment for the surrounding tasks. The textile industry has therefore developed towards a very capital-intensive industry. Since the supply of a higher product quality also requires the ability to choose and combine advanced materials and to apply sophisticated finishing tasks, advanced textile companies need to hire a relatively high number of skilled employees for their R&D tasks.

It is fascinating to see how these varying requirements result in different attitudes towards the issue of relocation. These are strongest in *Dalang*, with definitive plans and measures for relocations at two large-scale companies of the town that both indicated labour shortage or labour costs as their primary motivations. Yet, they are absent at the surveyed companies in *Humen*, although their labour intensity is higher compared to that in the knitting industry. Obviously, the advantages of the local sales infrastructure for the time being are indispensable for those companies, and profits from rapidly expanding domestic sales seem to help withstand higher costs of labour and other production factors in the PRD. There is a certain amount of outsourcing which in part results from difficulties in keeping up with rising demand, but a full-scale relocation of manufacturing, like it is planned by the surveyed Dalang companies, is not on the agenda. Relocation plans are equally absent at the surveyed companies in *Xiqiao* where some of the surveyed companies have benefitted from strong government support for many years. The local government recently even raised the cluster's attractiveness as a production site by investing in comprehensive electricity, as well as water and sewage infrastructure which is of high importance for textile companies. In sum, these cases show that a relocation of labour-intensive industries does exist, but that the Pearl River Delta is not experiencing an exodus of labour-intensive traditional industries, at least where there are proactive efforts for industrial upgrading and strong government support. Furthermore, the disposition of companies to relocate does not only depend on the labour-intensity of their operations, but also on the possibility to establish "pure-play" manufacturers in distant regions without losing contact to dense supplier networks, government support and marketing opportunities in the PRD.

*A failure of comprehensive social upgrading: polarisation of the workforce in terms of skills and wages*
In terms of social upgrading, the results of the case studies reveal a strong polarisation of skills and wages in all garment clusters. On the one hand, industrial upgrading requires skilled staff in management, marketing and design functions. Local training institutions have difficulties in catching up with the demand for R&D and technical staff from local companies and experts in the respective fields can gain comparably high monthly wages of around RMB 6,000–10,000 and above. Due to this reliance on highly skilled work which breaks with the pattern of plain manufacturing functions as performed in CMT or some basic OEM production models, industrial transformation in the textile and garment industry of the PRD entails substantial skill upgrading with corresponding income effects for a minority of employees.

*Table 7.22: Labour intensity, relocation and skill requirements in Dalang, Humen and Xiqiao[i]*

|  | Dalang | Humen | Xiqiao |
|---|---|---|---|
| Labour intensity | High | Very high | Medium |
| Capital intensity | High | Medium | Very high |
| Knowledge intensity (R&D) | Medium | High | High |
| Relocation | Strong | Weak | Non existent |
| R&D departments | Weak | Medium | Medium |
| Skill requirements manuf. | Low (knitting), medium (linking) | Low (sewing), but work experience matters | Low (weaving), medium to high (finishing tasks) |
| Wages manuf. | 2,000–3,000 (knitters), 2,200–5,000 (linkers) | 2,000–3,600 (sewers), 1,700–2,300 (others) | 2,700–4,000 (weaving), 4–5,000 (dyeing, finishing) |

i   The judgements are based on the author's interpretation of the presented material.
Source: Interview data.

But, on the other hand, the story is very different for manufacturing workers. In most cases industrial upgrading in textile and garment companies does not require enhanced skills of knitters, sewers, weavers or other line workers. Quite to the contrary, the example of the Dalang knitwear industry as well as the case study of CASUALYOUTH, the most advanced fashion brand of Humen, demonstrate that process upgrading can even entail de-skilling of the workforce which is deliberately pursued in order to relieve the companies of the pressure to find skilled workers in the context of a widespread labour shortage. At CASUALYOUTH, the rationalisation of sewing work even seems to have negative effects with regard to workers incomes since average wages at this modern factory were the lowest of this sample. The same cannot be said about the other cases, but as a general rule, work with more advanced equipment did not affect workers' wages positively.

The surveyed variants of industrial upgrading therefore exhibit a failure in social upgrading for manufacturing workers. In different forms, there is a strong polarisation between (mostly) institutionally trained technical staff and low-skilled and low-paid migrant workers. Working conditions are slightly improving and in some instances there was a limitation of excessive working hours due to more regular production rhythms in modernised factories. But there are few incentives for companies to introduce more stable employment schemes, comprehensive vocational training and higher wages. The only example where the organisation of production resulted in higher skill requirements and potentially better terms for workers is the layer of migrant workers who are introduced to the operations of high-end equipment for dyeing and finishing at POWERDENIM in Xiqiao's textile industry.

# Part IV:
# Conclusion

# 8 Polarisation of skills and wages as obstacle for economic rebalancing

The presented case studies offer rich material for a comparison of industrial upgrading strategies in both investigated sectors and a discussion of their effects on employees. The following section reviews the results with regard to the main research question about the relationship between industrial upgrading and social upgrading in enterprises in the Pearl River Delta. The discussion is structured by the research hypotheses that were introduced in section 5.2 (cf. figure 8.1). Subsequently, the research results are related to the broader debate about the feasibility of a transformation of the Chinese growth model as presented in chapters 2 and 3.

*Figure 8.1: Hypotheses about the relationship between industrial upgrading and social upgrading*

1. There are overall favourable conditions for a vertical upgrading of Chinese industries in GPN
2. Functional upgrading supports skill upgrading of the workforce
3. The profoundness of social upgrading depends on the forms of segmentation of the workforce as well as on political factors, in particular:
3.1 The manner in which highly-skilled functions and basic manufacturing tasks are distributed between enterprises
3.2 The forms of task segmentation within enterprises
3.3 The regulation of labour relations and the agency of workers
4. Social upgrading is undermined by new segmentations into low-skilled and highly-skilled work

# Hypothesis 1: There are overall favourable conditions for a vertical upgrading of Chinese industries in GPN.

Industries in the Pearl River Delta are in a state of rapid and profound transformation—this is the most obvious result of the presented case studies. In both industrial sectors under consideration companies strive to acquire more sophisticated functions in higher value-added segments of the production chain, often with remarkable success as the proliferation of Chinese fashion brands, the fast growth of domestic LED producers, and other cases covered in this study prove. Significantly, such leaps are not limited to companies in "Strategic Emerging Industries". Enterprises in the garment sector, an industry widely thought to be mature technologically, are equally being transformed through a large variety of measures—be it the acquisition of design and marketing functions formerly executed by foreign lead firms, or the modification of manufacturing through automation, functional diversification, and lean production schemes. The companies of this investigation sample are not representative of all enterprises in the PRD since they were deliberately chosen in order to investigate the most progressive examples of industrial upgrading in the area. Yet, their story definitely reflects a broader tendency, as the mushrooming growth of sophisticated suppliers and fashion brands and the rapid transformation of the entire lighting industry in Guangdong towards advanced LED technology demonstrate (cf. HKTDC 2012b; section 6.2). Proactive government policies to push investment in SEI and to upgrade traditional industries are having a significant impact on the industrial structure of the Pearl River Delta. As argued in chapter 3, this does not automatically mean that the days of labour-intensive processing industries with comparably low margins are numbered. But it can be taken for granted that a functionally more diversified and sophisticated layer of industries is emerging in the region with great velocity.

The acquisition of technologically sophisticated functions by Chinese companies is taking place despite the persistence of hierarchies in GPN based on the control of advanced functions and intellectual property by companies in the advanced industrial countries. As discussed in chapter 4, these hierarchies are not static and allow for the entry of challengers from emerging economies. Not only are such hierarchies subject to permanent technological shifts which makes it possible for challengers—often with heavy support by local industrial policies—to acquire more powerful positions in newly emerging sectors. The increasing technological strength of Chinese companies can also be the result of the sourcing and manufacturing strategies of global lead firms themselves. The most important channels of such a technology transfer are sourcing strategies that require more comprehensive capabilities on the part of suppliers (as in the case of full-package suppliers in the garment industry), the allocation of high-tech capacities of foreign TNCs to China (as in the case of LED chip production) and the emergence of global innovation networks that imply investments by TNCs in R&D institutions in China (cf. Ernst 2011a). Business strategies of transnational companies in this respect should not be confused with the political interests of governments to maintain and expand technological leadership of national economies. While companies carefully watch their intellectual property, they are ready to tolerate technology transfer to Chinese companies if this serves their overall business interests. This is not only the legacy of joint ventures in the automotive industry, but also of recent investments by foreign LED companies which are keen to expand their operations in China and to establish joint operations with Chinese companies. Mergers and acquisitions and other forms of industrial cooperation do not mean that foreign investors share their intellectual property freely with Chinese partners, but they still constitute one avenue for technology transfer which puts Chinese companies in an advantageous position to emancipate themselves from a role of "pure-play" manufacturers.

The case studies also demonstrate that China's growing domestic market creates particularly favourable conditions for the acquisition of sophisticated functions in manufacturing as well as "intangible assets" in the realm of design and marketing. Chinese fashion brands are the most striking example of this, as especially the Humen fashion industry demonstrates. Functional upgrading towards OBM production is particularly thriving in this domestically-oriented garment cluster and potentially allows companies to acquire a higher share of profits than is the case for OEM suppliers that focus on volume production for foreign buyers. In the neighbouring, mainly export-oriented cluster of Dalang, on the contrary, brand building faces much higher barriers and companies are locked into supplier relationships that often only grant low margins.

Rising domestic demand for LED products is also projected to boost the Chinese LED industry. The high growth projections for LED markets in China provide ample space for the expansion of domestic companies and also attract investment from foreign companies that in the mid-term most probably will strengthen the Chinese industry as a whole. Government subsidies, most evident in the LED sector, constitute a particularly important form of domestic demand. Government authorities have supported industrial upgrading of local firms and indeed nourished a whole industry segment. As analysed in detail in chapter 6, the resulting rush in investment has supported the emergence of relatively strong Chinese LED brands, regardless of the huge problems that overinvestment in the sector creates for those companies that fall behind. Beyond government subsidies, rising private consumption of LED products is also projected to boost the Chinese LED industry. LED products are on the verge of becoming a competitive alternative on consumer markets and the proliferation of this technology is also supported by government regulations for the phase-out of conventional incandescent lighting in the coming years.

## Hypothesis 2: Functional/vertical upgrading supports skill upgrading.

Findings from the case studies confirmed that the functional diversification of enterprises in the Pearl River Delta creates an overall strong demand for highly skilled employees. This is particularly evident in the LED industry where the rapid technological development of the sector results in a shortage of adequately trained professionals who can often earn very high wages. Similarly, there is a broad demand for fashion designers in the garment industry and for technical staff that is needed to support product upgrading in the textile industry. In all of the surveyed sectors, companies complained about a shortage of professionals in their field. The local governments correspondingly invest in specialised technical schools and college programmes in order to meet the demand of local companies. In the surveyed garment clusters, these courses are mostly taken by local residents who are set to staff the more elevated functions in the respective industries. Yet, companies also aim to attract fashion designers and other professionals on the national and international level. A pragmatic choice to gain access to know-how about international fashion styles is often realised by employing designers from Hong Kong.

Based on a strong demand by companies, professionals in both sectors can gain comparatively high incomes. In the fashion industry, leading designers of mid-sized companies can earn around RMB 10,000 per month or more, while even a project manager at the relatively small and by now insolvent LED enterprise MULTIAPP earned more than RMB 30,000 per month (ID 18.11.2010). Employees in such highly skilled functions also possess an extraordinarily high bargaining power since they can easily switch to better-paid positions at competing enterprises in case they are dissatisfied with conditions offered by their employers. Beneath this segment of top personnel, wages for technical staff are substantially lower. In the fashion industry, the surveyed enterprises mostly employ teams of young assistant designers under the leadership of senior designers. Assistant designers, often graduates from local technical schools, do earn an above average income, which is about RMB 1,000 to RMB 3,000 higher than that of migrant workers in manufacturing, but they also shoulder a very high workload.

Sales staff in the LED industry hold positions that are roughly comparable to those of assistant designers in terms of salaries and workload. An employee of MULTIAPP who worked in this field reported about very long working hours and high pressures for employees. The turnover rate of sales personnel at this company was higher than among the manufacturing workforce (ID 17.11.2011). These examples only provide glimpses at the working conditions of employees of an intermediate skill level, a so far only scarcely investigated field.[143] Regardless of the often problematic working conditions of employees in these functions, industrial upgrading in local companies all in all provides ample opportunities for employment, income gains and favourable career options. Vertical upgrading of Chinese companies has the effect that many highly skilled functions in the industry, which used to be performed outside of China when Chinese companies remained limited to assembly or OEM functions, are now increasingly performed within China by local professionals. This is an important dimension of social upgrading which contributes to changing employment patterns and wage gains for a section of the workforce.

In the surroundings of the production sites of the surveyed enterprises in both sectors, there was also a layer of professionals working in diverse functions of the service sector such as media, logistics, event management and in publicly funded research institutions or government agencies. As the PRD moves on from its role as export-oriented production site for low-end processing industries towards a more diversified economic structure, there

---

143 But cf. M.Yu 2011 for an interesting case study on working conditions of professionals at the electronics company Huawei.

is also a need for a functional diversification of the involved economic clusters. Industrial upgrading thus indirectly enhances the demand for skilled employees across the entire respective region. Further research is necessary to assess the extent of such indirect effects of industrial upgrading at the regional level.

## Hypotheses 3.1: The profoundness of social upgrading depends on the manner in which highly skilled functions and basic manufacturing tasks are distributed *between* enterprises

This hypothesis assumes that a strong segmentation into highly skilled functions and basic manufacturing between enterprises has limited effects in terms of social upgrading because more advanced tasks tend to remain confined to lead firms, whereas suppliers only assume a subordinate role limited to basic manufacturing. This would limit opportunities for a skill upgrading of the workforce at suppliers.

Contrary to such a scenario though, the case studies reveal a relatively high integration of R&D functions and basic manufacturing tasks on the single enterprise level. In the LED industry, there is an overall segmentation between the more technology-intensive field of upstream production and the downstream field of application production which requires less innovative capabilities. But even SMEs in the latter case need to acquire significant R&D capabilities to survive in a very competitive and dynamic market. The low level of standardisation of the still immature LED industry means that there remains the necessity of relatively close interactions between manufacturers of LED chips, packages, and applications. Application producers therefore need to hire academically trained staff to adjust their products and screen future development possibilities. So far, the production models in the LED industry therefore are markedly different than in many more mature segments of the IT industry where there is a stronger segmentation between innovative functions in technology enterprises and assembly functions of contract manufacturers.[144] Since each LED enterprise requires a significant

---

144 Yet, this does not necessarily imply that contract manufacturers require less R&D input than LED enterprises. Especially ODM contract manufacturers are a vivid example of a "vertical integration from below" by which manufacturing specialists acquire design

share of engineers, the industry creates a quantitatively strong demand for professionals and hence promotes skill upgrading in any enterprise of the supply chain.

In the garment industry of Humen, Chinese fashion brands rely on a relatively high share of in-house production, contrary to the dominant global norms of production which brought about a widespread separation of design and marketing functions, performed by global lead firms, and manufacturing functions, performed by suppliers in low-wage countries. The Chinese garment companies covered in this case study rather build on advantages of combining own design capabilities with the merits of those efficient manufacturing techniques that have turned China into the largest supply base for garments worldwide. None of the surveyed companies pursued plans to drop manufacturing altogether, although CASUALYOUTH and GENTSSUIT have outsourced substantial shares of their production volume to suppliers. As in the case of the LED industry, it remains to be seen whether a vertical integration of R&D and manufacturing on a company level will be maintained. It is possible that Chinese companies start to mimicry production models of foreign fashion giants like H&M by abandoning manufacturing altogether as some industry analysts suggest (cf. HKTDC 2012b). Yet in 2012, only a small majority of 53.7 percent of a sample of 2,000 Chinese garment brands stated that they were outsourcing any manufacturing functions at all, which illustrates the strong proliferation of integrated production models in the industry (ibid).

The case studies of companies in Dalang's woollen knitwear industry and Xiqiao's textile industry also reflect a need for individual enterprises to assume highly skilled functions. However, other than with OBM in Humen, companies in these clusters remain highly dependent on supply contracts with international and national buyers. Their strategies to increase their share of value added rests on the creation of own R&D departments and sales offices in order to advance to ODM production models or increase their flexibility with regard to OEM orders. The surveyed companies pursued such strategies with different intensity. The extent to which highly skilled functions are performed on the single-company level therefore differs strongly. With

---

responsibilities that are being outsourced by lead firms. Yet, highly skilled functions in these mass manufacturers are confined to engineering staff, whereas the large majority of employees consists of low-skilled employees, i.e. low-paid migrant workers in the case of China (Lüthje et al 2013a, 183-199; 217–231).

the exception of the case of POWERDENIM, an enterprise that possesses relatively high R&D capacities, the companies of Dalang and Xiqiao have quantitatively smaller design departments and are rather strongly confined to commoditised manufacturing activities, i.e. standardised high-volume production with relatively low margins.[145]

The comparison of enterprise cases with regard to their integration of skill-intensive functions of R&D and marketing reveals that the chosen industrial upgrading strategies, to a variable extent, require high-skilled functions at the level of *each* enterprise. Such tendencies to a certain degree counteract a strong vertical polarisation of knowledge-intensive and labour-intensive tasks along the supply chain. So far, all surveyed companies maintain substantial levels of in-house production and show little efforts to completely outsource assembly-type manufacturing functions to specialised suppliers. Highly skilled functions are therefore spread out relatively evenly across the enterprises under investigation.

However, a more fundamental question with regard to a polarisation of skills between different production sites is whether vertically integrated enterprises reproduce an *internal* segmentation of design and manufacturing between different *fully-owned* branches. If so, "pure-play" manufacturers that are formally owned by the respective parent companies could assume functions that are similarly limited like those of independently-owned CMT or OEM suppliers, while formally belonging to the same enterprise group. This tendency could be observed in the garment industry.[146] Design functions at CASUALYOUTH are organised in a highly centralised manner, with most of the 28 factories operating according to quite detailed specifications provided by the headquarters.[147] If production models at the newly

---

145 This especially accounts for the cases of DENIMSUIT and JUNGLEDENIM both of which have relatively low technological capabilities. These companies hardly are able to leap beyond a production model of highly automated volume production with relatively low margins.

146 Possibly, it is no less relevant in the case of the LED industry. Unfortunately, the data on PACKAGESTAR, the only company that commands various production sites, does not provide much information on this. R&D seems to be largely centralised in the company's research centre. The factories are specialised in different product categories. Apparently each of them hires a large number of technical staff (ID 22.11.2011b).

147 The five seasonal collections are created by five chief designers who direct their own design teams. In terms of its production model, CASUALYOUTH pursues the aim of maximum flexibility. Production is organised according to orders from franchising store managers who order individual styles according to their sales figures. The supplier factories, most of

emerging Chinese fashion brands were to entail such hierarchical supplier relations *within* the legal form of a vertically integrated enterprise, highly skilled functions would again be concentrated at the top, whereas manufacturing at "supplier" factories would not necessarily depend on more sophisticated functions than provided by regular suppliers to global brands. The enterprise group could acquire a higher degree of market control through vertical integration, but the division of functions between enterprises would be no less hierarchic and polarised than in globally organised supplier relations—with correspondingly weak effects of a skill upgrading of workers in pure manufacturing factories that receive orders from the headquarters. The data from this investigation does not provide a conclusive picture with regard to this question. The skill distribution within production networks of Chinese enterprises would be an important issue for further research.

The question of task segmentation between regions constitutes a special dimension of this issue since it may have the effect of a regional polarisation between highly skilled and low-skilled tasks. The strongest tendency in this direction was evident in the knitwear industry of Dalang where both surveyed companies had begun to relocate the bulk of their manufacturing activities to production sites in provinces with cheaper labour costs while keeping their design and sales departments in the Pearl River Delta. Obviously, such arrangements imply a strong segmentation into highly skilled functions in the PRD and low-skilled manufacturing work in the interior. The skill upgrading effects of industrial transformation therefore prospectively would remain largely confined to employees in the companies' headquarters. The enterprises thereby are circumventing the pressures on labour-intensive manufacturing by setting their sails for cheaper regions. The surveyed companies obviously pursued such a strategy while at the same time implementing measures for large-scale automation in order to upgrade their products and reduce their workforce in the field of knitting. The contrary examples in the Humen fashion industry, the textile industry and the LED industry, where companies intend to stay in the PRD despite rising cost pressures, indicate that there is no overall tendency towards a regional division of labour between knowledge-intensive and assembly functions. Again, this result is only

---

which are specialised in one single product category, need to be able to flexibly adjust their production flow to these orders (ID 09.12.2010b; 19.11.2011a). They clearly are located at the bottom end of the hierarchy similar to OAM or OEM suppliers in international supplier arrangements.

valid for the companies of this sample which show very eager strategies for industrial upgrading. The picture therefore could be markedly different if less innovative enterprises were examined the production models of which all the more depend on the availability of cheap labour.

All in all, the case studies reveal that highly skilled functions and the corresponding effects in terms of social upgrading are distributed relatively widely across Chinese companies. However, the discussion also revealed that a more profound assessment of the division of labour between factories must look beneath the legal enterprise form in order to identify renewed segmentations and hierarchical supply chain arrangements *within* enterprises that divide their production volumes up between fully-owned factories with varying functional capabilities.

## Hypotheses 3.2: The profoundness of social upgrading depends on the forms of task segmentation *within* enterprises

Much more relevant in terms of the profoundness of social upgrading is the internal task segmentation within single factories. The results of the case studies suggest that the strong polarisation of employees' skills on a factory level currently constitutes a major obstacle for a broader distribution of the gains of social upgrading across the workforce.

On an abstract level, the results from the LED industry and the textile and garment industry are remarkably similar in this respect. In all companies, there persists a strong segmentation between academically or technically trained employees with urban *hukou* on the one side and low-skilled migrant workers on the other. The case studies provide a comprehensive set of data on the mechanisms of segmentation by which highly skilled functions—in the case of the LED industry even functions that involve high-tech matters—can be combined with low-skilled, repetitive manufacturing work. This segmentation rests on deliberate management decisions by which even technologically advanced companies can continue to take advantage of the cost advantages of China's segregated labour market. In fact, the combination of a pool of highly skilled professionals on the one hand and low-skilled and cheap migrant workers on the other hand can be seen as a strong competitive advantage of China in comparison to the emerging Asian low-cost regions in which wages for manufacturing workers may be lower, but where the business environment is not as favourable in terms of the availability of sufficiently trained staff, industry linkages, government support, and infrastructure.

While Chinese enterprises thus continue to harvest the advantages of a segregated labour market which are specific to the Chinese system, the strong segmentation between top-notch professionals and low-skilled workers is not mainly a Chinese-bred phenomenon. By implementing production models that rely on a strong polarisation of highly skilled and low-skilled functions, Chinese companies are also adopting certain global norms of technology and production in the field of commodity mass manufacturing that have emerged internationally during the past decades. These norms are often built into the layout of (foreign) manufacturing equipment which is designed in a way to guarantee easy operation by low-skilled workers. Particularly telling in this respect are the results from interviews with foreign machine vendors in all surveyed subsectors, who advertised the easy operability of their equipment as a particular product advantage (cf. table 8.1).

*Table 8.1: Examples for equipment vendors' recommendations for training periods of unskilled workers*

| Sector | Equipment | Training periods |
|---|---|---|
| Knitwear | High-end; imported CNC knitting machine | Four weeks on-the-job |
| Woven garments | High-end; imported, digitally-controlled sewing machine | One or two days |
| Textile | High-end; imported CNC rapier power loom | "very basic" (i.e. < one week) |
| LED encapsulation | Imported high-speed wire bonder | Three days |

Source: Interview data.

As explicated in the respective chapters, sophisticated finishing equipment in the textile industry and arguably also some types of encapsulation machines in the LED industry are an exception to this rule, since they require more comprehensive training periods for operators. But in general, the middle ground between high-skilled and low-skilled functions is thin, i.e. there is a drastic polarisation of the workforce. What is more, process upgrading can even imply further de-skilling as the case of the knitwear industry in Dalang and similar developments in the LED industry demonstrate. Particularly interesting in this context is the impact of CASUALYOUTH's lean production system on the workforce. Unlike textbook knowledge would have it (cf. Womack et al 2007), lean production in this case does not imply more diverse responsibilities of employees who needed to acquire more comprehensive skills to master their tasks. Through the implementation of CASUALYOUTH's lean production system, sewing rather becomes an even more de-skilled task. Workers are thus less able to reap financial benefits based on their working experience. They earn a more steady income because of the more even production flow at the company, but their wages are lower than at the other garment factories of this sample.

The polarisation in skill levels and wages within each single company undermines a comprehensive skill upgrading that affects all employees and which therefore could be the basis for a social upgrading of manufacturing work. As skill requirements in manufacturing can be kept low, companies mostly develop little interest in encouraging long-term employment of experienced manufacturing workers by improving their conditions and raising their wages substantially. High turnover rates and overall employment flexibility remain the hallmark of employment regimes of the surveyed industries in the PRD. Thereby companies continue to base their strategies on the availability of temporary migrant work.

The recent labour shortages in the PRD, however, constitute a countervailing trend to all-encompassing labour flexibility. Employers are under increasing pressure to offer better conditions than their peers if they are to attract workers and avoid a high turnover rate, which could negatively affect their productivity. Yet, the case studies demonstrate very clearly that the resulting improvements in wages are not to be seen as a result of industrial upgrading but of the general macroeconomic environment and the demographic structure of the Chinese population. Decades of fast growth in labour-intensive manufacturing industries have absorbed ever larger shares of China's seemingly indefinite supply of cheap labour. At the same time, migrant workers today are less prepared to tolerate appalling working conditions than the generations before them. The resulting tendency of rising wages affects high-end and low-end industries alike. Wages for line workers at companies that barely engage in a modernisation of the manufacturing process—such as at Humen's LADYFIT or Xiqiao's JUNGLEJEANS, for instance—may therefore be higher than at such enterprises that show a very dedicated activity in terms of process upgrading, such as at Humen's CA-SUALYOUTH or the LED chip producer CHIPSTAR. In general, wages at textile and garment companies even tended to be higher than at companies in the technologically sophisticated LED industry.[148]

The exogenous factor of labour shortages as well as the proliferation of labour conflicts in the area drive average wage increases that could support a social upgrading of workforces and alter the employment systems in manufacturing industries in the mid-term. Eventually, higher wage levels could make labour-intensive manufacturing unsustainable and force companies to invest in a more stable workforce of skilled employees. However, the case studies also show that the dominant *responses* of companies to these circumstances rather seek to relieve themselves from cost pressures while sustaining employment systems based on the exploitation of flexible and cheap migrant labour than to qualitatively improve working conditions and wages. The means to do so are accelerated automation and other modifications of production systems that raise the productivity of labour in the PRD. As the examples from Dalang's knitwear industry show, companies ultimately may rather chose to relocate their manufacturing operations to areas with cheaper labour costs than to offer substantially better conditions to their local manufacturing workforce. Furthermore, enterprises can counteract the pressures of rising legal minimum wages and stricter regulations through the labour law by modifying wage systems (e.g. by lowering performance-based, flexible wage shares relative to the base wage) and exploiting loopholes in government regulations. As there is a lack of collective regulations of basic employment and working conditions and government enforcement of the labour law is weak, social upgrading largely remains dependent on the willingness of the management to grant better conditions. In the context of high com-

---

148 In the surveyed LED companies, the wages for line workers typically constituted between RMB 2,000 and RMB 3,000. In the textile and garment companies, RMB 2,000 equally constituted the bottom line of salaries, but experienced linkers and sewers could earn substantially more (roughly between RMB 3,500 and RMB 5,000 in different cases). Experienced operators of automated knitting machines can also earn around RMB 3,000. The difference between wages in the two industries is all the more striking since the minimum wages in Shenzhen and Guangzhou where most surveyed LED factories are located are significantly higher (RMB 1,500 and RMB 1,300 in 2011, respectively) than in Foshan and Dongguan where the surveyed textile and garment factories are located (RMB 1,100 in 2011).

petitive pressures through cost increases and overinvestment, the disposition for voluntary generousness certainly is not very widespread.

But even if most companies refuse to grant substantial improvements for the workforce and rather resort to technology-central paths of upgrading, their reactions to a changing macroeconomic environment nevertheless are bound to change employment systems in the Pearl River Delta. The effects of automation in the Dalang knitwear industry, for instance, could indicate one scenario of the regional effects that enterprise strategies could have: widespread automation did not improve the situation of line workers, but it changed the quantitative relationship between higher-skilled tasks and plain manufacturing functions because hundreds of low-skilled knitters in both visited companies were laid-off. If all companies were to react in the same way, the share of skilled employees on a regional level would rise in relation to low-skilled migrant labour (and laid-off workers probably could find alternative employment options in the context of labour shortages). The indirect repercussions of company measures to counter the pressures of labour shortages and wage rises could therefore bear the paradoxical effect of raising the overall skill dependency of enterprises in the region in the mid-term since low-skilled manufacturing tasks are automated.

Such a vision of comprehensively automated manufacturing controlled by a small number of highly skilled staff is reminiscent of utopias of completely automated production systems which could free mankind of the burden of stultifying and monotonous work. The history of industrialisation saw the frequent resurgence of such visions which have been particularly widespread since the emergence of computer-integrated manufacturing techniques since the mid-1960s (cf. Waldner 1992). As the implementation of fully automated systems proved to be more difficult than the futuristic projections would have it and many labour-intensive functions were rather outsourced to cheap wage regions than automated, public attention to this discussion has rather faded in advanced industrial regions. But ironically, it is again resurging in debates about the future of Chinese manufacturing. The announcements of Foxconn in 2011 to introduce one million industrial robots in the group's factories within three years has received the most attention in this respect and raised fundamental questions about the future of manufacturing in China (Businessweek 29.11.2012).

Yet, fully automated manufacturing indeed seems very distant if one inspects factories in the Pearl River Delta today. While some tendencies towards automation certainly do play a strong role in company strategies, other examples from the case studies demonstrate that an actual end of labour-intensive production based on cheap labour is fairly remote.[149] Particularly striking is the example of LED application manufacturing, where the level of automation is very low while companies are set to stay in the Pearl River Delta. Since potential gains in some fields of LED manufacturing are high, companies may be able to handle rising wages for quite some time. LED application manufacturing constitutes one example of a new industry where labour-intensive assembly is on the rise—contrary to the frequently voiced expectation that it is about to die out. The examples from Humen's fashion industry, where the potential for automation is equally limited, is another. As discussed in chapter 3, the resilience of labour-intensive assembly operations is generally stronger then the tale of the end of cheap labour would make believe.

## Hypothesis 3.3: The profoundness of social upgrading depends on the regulation of labour relations and the agency of workers

The presented case studies prove that the doubts about an automatic link between industrial and social upgrading, as voiced in recent academic literature, are well-founded. The political consequence of this insight should be to discuss under what circumstances technological change can actually lead to improvements in working conditions. Curiously, the insight that social change is not an automatic product of technological change has a very long history which is rarely reflected in the recent upgrading literature.

For instance, the sociologist Friedrich Pollock from the Institute for Social Research in Frankfurt extensively discussed the question whether automation would result in an "upgrading" or "downgrading" of the workforce. In his fundamental work on the issue he critically remarked that optimistic assumptions about this question tended to "prematurely project single processes that only affect a minority to the workforce as a whole" (Pollock 1964, 252)—an insight which could also be taken as a pointed summary of the basic findings of this study. This scepticism towards exaggerated expectations about the merits of technological change as expressed in critical theory was

---

149 This is also true for companies of Dalang where relocation, not full automation, of labour-intensive manufacturing constitutes a major tendency.

completely lost in the theoretical upgrading literature which, as discussed in chapter 4, tended to equalise industrial upgrading with social benefits without asking more precisely about the winners and losers in these processes. In recent discussions on the issue though, the critical question about the social implications of industrial upgrading has received renewed scholarly interest. However, this debate still suffers from the one-sidedness of the technology-centred view on social change. The social upgrading conception in recent literature still represents a "top-down" approach in which social improvements in the last instance result from the agency of firms, states or international institutions, whereas the agency of workers is neglected (cf. critically: Selwyn 2013, 76).

Yet, the present study highlights that *companies* in the Pearl River Delta have little interest in voluntarily improving workers' employment conditions. The *central and the provincial governments*, on the contrary, do show a motivation to harmonise labour relations, but the close bonds between enterprises and state officials that developed on the local level in the course of China's reform era, as well as the ineffectiveness of mechanisms for an effective regulation of labour relations, mean that such efforts often end in talk. *International institutions* have placed their hopes mainly in voluntary initiatives for Corporate Social Responsibility (CSR), which may have contributed to curb some excessive instances of exploitation, but which suffer from a lack of accountability and enforcement mechanisms. They are often undermined by competitive pressures as well as downward pressures exerted by the very international brands that at the same time urge suppliers to improve their CSR practices.

A decisive question in relation to the issues of industrial upgrading and social upgrading therefore concerns the balance of forces between workers and management on a factory and an industry level. Due to the notorious absence of effective regulations and bargaining mechanisms in China, working conditions are mainly dependent on management decisions in which workers do not have a say. Consequently, industrial upgrading is implemented in a one-sided technology-centred way that responds to employers interests under the circumstances of high competitive pressures while depriving workers of potential benefits that the transformation of industries in the Pearl River Delta might entail.

In concrete terms, the critical issues concerning social upgrading in China include the question of democratic representation of workers and their right to organise, the implementation of effective collective bargaining systems, and the determination of basic standards concerning the conditions of employment and wage systems in collective contracts. A fundamental change furthermore concerns the abolition of discriminatory employment systems through the *hukou* system which still represents the main anchor for the extensive regimes of production that are common in the PRD. Faced with escalating inequality and mounting labour conflict, the government in Guangdong has reinforced its efforts to implement effective systems of collective bargaining that also rest on democratic elections of ACFTU branches on a factory basis. But as discussed in chapter 2, such approaches are still far from showing fundamental results and ridden with internal contradictions due to the resistance of industry groups and the unsteady commitment of the authorities. As the recent attempt at reform in 2010 was a direct reaction to the most dynamic wave of strikes in recent years, it seems likely that workers' agency needs to be the pacemaker for more comprehensive reform measures. The results of this investigation as well as various reports about the expectations of the so-called "second generation of migrant workers" suggest that there still exists a virulent contradiction between higher ambitions of migrant workers and those conditions that employers in the PRD are prepared to offer. It therefore seems likely that the coming years will see a further proliferation of labour conflict in this region which during the last decade has constituted the epicentre of labour unrest in China.

An interesting parallel to the period of Fordism, the reference point of the theoretical framework presented in chapter 1, comes to mind. Actually, the transformation of extensive regimes of accumulation after the implementation of Roosevelt's New Deal never was a product of "social upgrading" in the sense of passive modifications of the labour process as a consequence of technological change. Quite on the contrary, work organisation under Fordism relied on a Taylorist division of labour that implied a strong segmentation into knowledge-intensive work and relatively low-skilled manufacturing tasks (Aglietta 2000, 111–118). The decisive moment that lead to a transition of the mode of regulation towards an acceptance of trade unions, the implementation of collective bargaining, and the construction of the welfare state was a series of militant labour conflicts during the years of the Great Depression (ibid, 130–134). This in turn brought about a period in which workers' wellbeing (despite ongoing racial and gender discrimination) could be significantly improved. Though it was stated in the deliberations on this issue in chapter 2 that the historic experience of Fordism should not be taken as a blueprint for the case of China, the genesis of Fordism still seems to entail a valuable lesson for the future of social upgrading in China: in the last analysis, workers agency needs to play a prominent role in aligning economic development in a way that allows workers to reap its rewards.

## Social upgrading and macroeconomic rebalancing

A final consideration concerns the relationship of the empirical findings of this study to the wider issue of the future of China's growth model as discussed in chapter 3. In the theoretical discussion about the interconnectedness of China's mode of world market integration, the widespread proliferation of extensive regimes of accumulation, and the contradictions of the current growth model, the augmentation of wage incomes was identified as one essential aspect of economic rebalancing towards a domestically-led growth model. The discussion of the case studies in chapters 6 and 7 demonstrated severe obstacles to this goal because they show that the majority of workers do not benefit from industrial upgrading in the surveyed companies. While there is some quantitative progress in terms of rising incomes due to macroeconomic factors, a qualitative improvement of wages is undermined by ongoing wage polarisation which reflects the social segmentation of the workforce. Under these conditions, it cannot be taken for granted that the total wage sum will increase faster than GDP growth, which would be the precondition for a rise of wages as a share of GDP. Yet then again, industrial upgrading creates a strong demand for highly skilled employees who earn above average incomes. The breadth of this layer varies corresponding to the industry under consideration, but by and large, social upgrading for these segments of the workforce will boost the spending capacity of middle income groups.

The obstacles to social upgrading analysed above may just as well be interpreted as obstacles to economic rebalancing. There is no way to quantify this assertion based on the results of this study since the small sample of enterprises barely allows for an extrapolation of results to all industries in the area, let alone the rest of China. The presented empirical data also does not include precise data about the long-term development of wages since it merely constitutes a spotlight on the situation in the years 2010 and 2011. However, this study shows that the widespread failure of social upgrading for manufacturing workers *prolongs* the existence of predominantly extensive regimes of accumulation in the Pearl River Delta, and therefore acts as a burden on efforts for rebalancing. Significantly, this is not only true for the so-called "old birds" of Wang Yang's metaphor, but also for newly emerging industries, as the case studies from the LED industry reveal.

With a broader view on the effects of urbanisation, the construction of social security systems, and the strong growth of minimum wages in coastal provinces it seems likely that the efforts for a rebalancing of the economic growth model nevertheless will make some gradual progress in the future. However, in the face of ongoing economic difficulties due to sluggish foreign demand as experienced in 2012 and 2013, it is doubtful whether the pace of rebalancing will suffice to avoid major social confrontations and political instability. Despite the successful balance sheet of the Chinese leadership during the past decades in which it managed to uphold political stability backed by an exorbitant economic growth performance, the spectre of economic slowdown and political crisis remains present in the current struggle to rebalance growth. But possibly, political ruptures and social conflict are not an obstacle, but a precondition for turning the practice of stability-oriented piecemeal reform into qualitative changes towards a more sustainable pattern of economic development.

# Figure and illustration credits

# Table credits

# Bibliography

## Literature

Aglietta, Michel (2000). *A Theory of Capitalist Regulation. The US Experience*. London and New York: Verso.

Ahuja, Ashvin, Nigel Chalk, Malhar Nabar, Papa N'Diaye, and Nathan Porter (2012). *An End to China's Imbalances?* (= IMF Working Paper WP/12/100). Washington: International Monetary Fund.

Akamatsu, Kaname (1962). A historical pattern of economic growth in developing countries. In *Journal of Developing Economies*, 1 (1), 3–25.

Akyüz, Yilmaz (2011). Export Dependency and Sustainability of Growth in China. In *China & World Economy*, 19 (1), 1–23.

Amin, Samir (1976). *Unequal Development: An Essay on the Social Formations of Peripheral Capitalism*. New York: Monthly Review Press.

Amsden, Alice (2001). *The Rise of "The Rest": Challenges to the West From Late-Industrializing Economies*. Oxford: Oxford University Press.

Anderson, Jonathan (2007). *Is China Export-Led?* (= UBS Investment Research – Asian Focus). 22.03.2013 http://www.allroadsleadtochina.com/reports/prc_270907.pdf

Anti, Michael (2009). China's Millions of Jobless Migrants. In *World Policy Journal* (Spring), 27–32.

APCO Worldwide (2011). *China's National People's Congress (NPC): Fine-tuning the Economy With an Eye on Social Stability*. 12.12.2012 http://www.apcoworldwide.com/content/PDFs/npc_briefing_2011.pdf

Appelbaum, Richard (2009). Big Suppliers in Greater China: A Growing Counterweight to the Power of Giant Retailers. In Hung, Ho-Fung (ed.), *China and the Transformation of Global Capitalism*, 65–85. Baltimore: John Hopkins University Press.

Arrighi, Giovanni (2007). *Adam Smith in Beijing: Lineages of the Twenty-First Century*. London and New York: Verso.

Arvantis, Rigas, Pierre Miège, and Wei Zhao (2003). A Fresh Look at the Development of a Market Economy in China. In *China perspectives*, 48.

Arvanitis, Rigas, and Haixiong Qiu (2009). Research for policy development: Industrial clusters in South China. In Graham, Michael and Woo, Jean (eds.): *Fuelling*

*Economic Growth. The Role of Public-Private Research in Development*, 39–86. Bourton on Dunsmore: Practical Action Publishing.

Arvantis, Rigas, Wei Zhao, Haixiong Qiu, and Jian-nu Xu (2006). Technological Learning in Six Firms in Southern China: Success and Limits of an Industrialisation Model. In *International Journal for Technology Management*, 36, (1/2/3), 108–125.

Ashman, Sam (2009). Capitalism, Uneven and Combined Development and the Transhistoric. In *Cambridge Review of International Affairs*, 22 (1), 29–46.

Bair, Jennifer (2005). Global Capitalism and Commodity Chains: Looking Back, Going Forward. In *Competition and Change*, 9 (2), 153–180.

Bair, Jennifer (2009). Global Commodity Chains: Genealogy and Review. In Bair, Jennifer (ed.). *Frontiers of Commodity Chain Research*. Palo Alto: Stanford University Press.

Barbieri, Elisa, Marco R. Di Tommaso, and Stefano Bonnini (2012). Industrial Development Policies and Performances in Southern China: Beyond the Specialised Industrial Cluster Program. In *China Economic Review, 23 (3), 613–25.*

Barrientos, Stephanie, Gary Gereffi, and Arianna Rossi (2010). *Economic and Social Upgrading in Global Production Networks: Developing a Framework for Analysis* (= Capturing the Gains Working Paper 2010/03). Manchester: University of Manchester. 22.10.2013 www.capturingthegains.org/publications/workingpapers/index.htm

Becker, Joachim (2002). *Akkumulation, Regulation, Territorium. Zur kritischen Rekonstruktion der französischen Regulationstheorie.* Weimar bei Marburg: Metropolis Verlag.

Bernhardt, Thomas (2013). *Developing Countries in the Global Apparel Value Chain: A Tale of Upgrading and Downgrading Experiences* (= Capturing the Gains Working Paper 2013/22). Manchester: University of Manchester. 24.10.2013 http://www.capturingthegains.org/pdf/ctg-wp-2013-22.pdf

Bernhardt, Thomas and William Milberg (2011). *Economic and Social Upgrading in Global Value Chains: Analysis of Horticulture, Apparel, Tourism and Mobile Telephones* (= Capturing the Gains Working Paper 2011/06). Manchester: University of Manchester.

Bhandakar, Vrinda (2012). *LED Lighting. Global Manufacturing Trends.* Presentation 13.06.2012.

BMI = Business Monitor International (2009). *China Textile & Clothing Report Q4 2009.* London: Business Monitor International.

Brandt, Loren, and Eric Thun (2010). *The Fight for the Middle: Upgrading, Competition, and Industrial Development in China* (= University of Toronto Department of Economics Working Paper 395). Toronto: University of Toronto.

Brandt, Loren and Eric Thun (2011). Going Mobile in China: Shifting Value Chains and Upgrading in the Mobile Telecom Sector. In *Journal for Technological Learning, Innovation and Development*, 4 (1/2/3), 148–180.

Brenner, Robert, and Mark Glick (2001). The Regulation Approach: Theory and History. In *New Left Review* I/188, 45–119.

Breslin, Shaun (2011). China and the Crisis: Global Power, Domestic Caution and Local Initiative. In *Contemporary Politics*, 17 (2), 185–200.

Braun, Anne J. (2010). *Das Ende der billigen Arbeit in China. Arbeitsrechte, Sozialschutz und Unternehmensförderung für informell Beschäftigte.* Wiesbaden: VS Verlag.

Bureau of Statistics of Dongguan (2010). *dong guan dai lang chanye tiaozheng shengji shixian liu ge zhuanbian (Adjustment and Upgrading of the Industry in Dalang, Dongguan, through "Six Changes").* Dongguan: Dongguan Government.

Butollo, Florian, and Tobias ten Brink (2012). Challenging the Atomization of Discontent. Patterns of Migrant-Worker Protest in China during the Series of Strikes in 2010. In *Critical Asian Studies*, 44 (3), 419–440.

Cai, Fang (ed.). (2010). *Transforming the Chinese Economy.* Leiden: Brill.

Callinicos, Alex (1991). Periodizing Capitalism and Analyzing Imperialism: Classical Marxism and Capitalist Evolution. In Albritton, Robert, Makoto Itoh, Richard Westra, and Alan Zuege (eds.). *Phases of Capitalist Development. Booms, Crises, and Globalizations.* New York: Palgrave Macmillan.

Callinicos, Alex (2009). *Imperialism and Global Political Economy.* Cambridge, Oxford and Boston: Polity Press.

Cardoso, Fernando H., and Enzo Faletto (1979). *Dependency and Development in Latin América.* Berkeley: University of California Press.

Casey, Joseph, and Katherine Kolesky (2011). *Backgrounder: China's 12 Five-Year Plan*, U.S.-China Economic & Security Review Commission. 14.10.2012 http://origin.www.uscc.gov/sites/default/files/Research/12th-FiveYearPlan_062811.pdf

Cattaneo, Oliver, Gary Gereffi, and Cornelia Staritz (2010). Global Value Chains in a Postcrisis World: Resilience, Consolidation, and Shifting End Markets. In Cattaneo, Oliver, Gary Gereffi, and Cornelia Staritz (eds.). *Global Value Chains in a Postcrisis World. A Development Perspective.* Washington: The World Bank.

CCCWS = China Center for Contemporary World Studies and Rosa Luxemburg Foundation Germany (2009). *Post-Financial Crisis Era: Reform and Competition of Development Models.* Beijing: CCCWS/RLS.

Chan, Anita (2001). *China's Workers Under Assault: The Exploitation of Labor in a Globalizing Economy.* Armonk: M.E. Sharpe.

Chan, Anita (2011). Strikes in Vietnam and China in Taiwanese-owned Factories: Diverging Industrial Relations Patterns. In Chan, Anita (ed.). *Labour in Vietnam.* Singapore: Institute of Southeast Asian Studies.

Chan, Anita, and Kaxton Siu (2010). Analyzing Exploitation. The Mechanisms Underpinning Low Wages and Excessive Overtime in Chinese Export Factories. In *Critical Asian Studies*, 42 (2), 167–190.

Chan, Chris King Chi (2010). *The Challenge of Labour in China: Strikes and the Changing Labour Regime in Global Gactories. New York: Routledge.*

*Chan, Chris King Chi, and Elaine Hui (2012). The Dynamics and Dilemma of Workplace Trade Union Reform in China: The Case of the Honda Workers' Strike. In Journal of Industrial Relations, 54 (5), 653–668.*

Chan, Kam Wing (2010). The Global Financial Crisis and Migrant Workers in China: 'There is No Future as a Labourer; Returning to the Village has No Meaning'. In *International Journal of Urban and Regional Research, 34* (3), 659–677.

Chang, Kai, Boy Lüthje, and Siqi Luo (2008). *Die Transformation der Arbeitsbeziehungen in China und ihre Besonderheiten* (IfS Working Paper). Frankfurt am Main: Institut für Sozialforschung.

Chason, Marc (2012). SSL Products and Manufacturing – Winners and Losers. In *Global LEDs/OLEDs,* 2 (2), 2.

Chen, Feng (2010). Trade Unions and the Quadripartite Interactions in Strike Settlement in China. In *The China Quarterly,* 201, 104–124.

Chen, Xiangli (2012). Ten Years: Growth and Gains. In *China Textile,* November, 22–25.

Chen, Yansheng (2012). *Lighting Industry in China* (presentation at the Global Lighting Association Conference in New Delhi, 09.10.2012).

Chu, Roger (2010). *LED Industry Outlook 2011.* Presentation from 02.11.2010, 28.04.2012 http://issuu.com/trendforce/docs/led_industry_outlook_in_2011

CLB = China Labour Bulletin (2009). *Going it Alone. The Workers' Movement in China (2007–2008).* Hong Kong: China Labour Bulletin.

CLB = China Labour Bulletin (2011). *Unity is Strength. The Workers' Movement in China 2009–2010.* Hong Kong: China Labour Bulletin.

CLB = China Labour Bulletin (2012). *A Decade of Change. The Workers' Movement in China 2000–2010.* Hong Kong: China Labour Bulletin.

CLNT = China Labor News Translations (2008). *The Chinese Trade Union's Big Rush to Set Up Unions in Fortune 500 Companies. Background Information August 2008.* 22.01.2011 http://www.clntranslations.org/article/33/the-chinese-trade-unions-big-rush-to-set-up-unions-in-fortune-500-companies

Coase, Ronald, and Ning Wang (2012). *How China became capitalist.* London: Palgrave Macmillan.

Cooke, Mike (2010). Chinese Burn into LED Market Driving MOCVD. In *Semiconductor Today,* 5 (7), 94–98.

Credit Suisse (2012). *China in 2015.* Hong Kong: Credit Suisse. 12.01.2013 http://wpc.186f.edgecastcdn.net/00186F/mps/Equity_Research_Test_Account/9/865/China_in_2015.pdf

Dalang Investment Promotion Office (2010). *da lang zhen jing ji she hui fa zhan gai kuang (Overview over the economic and social development of Dalang town).* Unpublished text provided by the Dalang Investment Promotion Office in December 2010.

Das, Mitali, and Papa N'Daye (2013a). *The End of Cheap Labor.* In *Finance & Development,* 50 (2), 34–37.

Das, Mitali, and Papa N'Daye (2013b). *Chronicle of a Decline Foretold: Has China Reached the Lewis Turning Point?* (= IMF Working Paper WP/13/26). Washington: International Monetary Fund. 27.07.2013 http://www.imf.org/external/pubs/ft/wp/2013/wp1326.pdf

DB Research = Deutsche Bank Research (2010). *China's Provinces. Digging One Layer Deeper.* Frankfurt am Main: Deutsche Bank. 12.11.2013 http://www.dbresearch. com/PROD/DBR_INTERNET_EN-PROD/PROD0000000000247520.pdf

de Haan, Arjan (2010). The Financial Crisis and China's "Harmonious Society". In *Journal of Current Chinese Affairs,* 39 (2), 69–99. 11.06.2012 http://hup.sub. uni-hamburg.de/giga/jcca/article/view/255/255

DG = Dongguan Government (2010). *guanyu tuidong lai liao jiagong qiye zhuanbi-an xingtai, gongzuo jinzhan de qingkuang tongbao (Transformation of Processing Enterprises, Briefing on Progress).* Dongguan: Dongguan Municipal People's Government.

DOE (2012a). *Life-Cycle Energy Consumption: Incandescent, Compact Fluorescent, and LED Lamps.* Washington: US Department of Energy. 22.04.2013 http://apps1. eere.energy.gov/buildings/publications/pdfs/ssl/2012_LED_Lifecycle_Slipsheet. pdf

DOE (2012b). *Life-Cycle Impact Analysis: LED Manufacturing and Performance.* Washington: US Department of Energy. 22.04.2013 http://apps1.eere.energy. gov/buildings/publications/pdfs/ssl/2012_lca-pt2_slipsheet.pdf

DOE (2012c). *Solid-State Lighting Research and Development: Manufacturing Roadmap.* Washington: US Department of Energy.

Dorsheimer, Jed (2012). *Economics of LED manufacturing: Yesterday, Today and Tomorrow.* Presentation at the DOE SSL Market Introduction Workshop, 07.08.2012.

Dunn, Bill, and Hugo Radice (2006). *100 Years of Permanent Revolution. Results and Prospects.* London: Pluto.

Egger, Georg, Daniel Fuchs, Thomas Immervoll, and Lydia Steinmassl (eds.). (2013). *Arbeitskämpfe in China. Berichte von der Werkbank der Welt.* Wien: Promedia.

Ernst, Dieter (2007). Beyond the Global Factory Model: Innovative Capabilities for Upgrading China's IT Industry. In *International Journal of Technology and Globalization,* 3 (4), 437–460.

Ernst, Dieter (2008). *Innovation Offshoring and Asia's 'Upgrading through Innovation' Strategies* (= East-West Center Working Papers, Economics Series, no.95). Honolulu: East-West Center.

Ernst, Dieter (2011a). Global Production and Innovation Networks. In Juergensmeyer, Mark, and Anheier, Helmut (eds.). *The Encyclopedia of Global Studies.* Thousand Oaks: Sage Publications.

Ernst, Dieter (2011b). *China's Innovation Policy is a Wake-Up Call for America* (= AsiaPacific Issues. Analysis from the East-West Center, 100). Honolulu: East-West Center.

Ernst, Dieter, and Barry Naughton (2008). China's emerging industrial economy. Insights from the IT industry. In McNally, Christopher (ed.). *China's Emergent Political Economy. Capitalism in the Dragon's Lair,* 39–59. London: Routledge.

Esser, Josef, Boy Lüthje, and Ronald Noppe (1997). Europäische Telekommunikation im Zeitalter der Deregulierung - Fragestellung und theoretischer Bezugsrahmen. In Esser, Josef, Boy Lüthje, and Ronald Noppe (eds.). *Europäische*

*Telekommunikation im Zeitalter der Deregulierung. Infrastruktur im Umbruch.* Münster: Westfälisches Dampfboot.

Eurasia Group (2011). *Chinas Great Rebalancing Act.* New York: Eurasia Group. 20.10.2011 http://eurasiagroup.net/item-files/China%27s%20Great%20Rebalancing%20Act/China%20Rebalancing.pdf

EUSME Centre (2009). *Textile and Apparel Market in China.* Beijing: EUSME Centre.

Feenstra, Robert (1998). Integration of Trade and Disintegration of Production in the Global Economy. In *Journal of Economic Perspectives,* 12 (4), 31–50.

Ferguson, Niall, and Moritz Schularick (2009). *The End of Chimerica* (= Harvard Business School Working Paper 10-037). Harvard: Harvard Business School.

Fernandez-Stark, Stacey Frederick, and Gary Gereffi (2011). *The Apparel Global Value Chain. Economic Upgrading and Workforce Development.* Durham: Center for Globalization, Governance and Competitiveness at Duke University. 03.12.2012 http://www.cggc.duke.edu/pdfs/2011-11-11_CGGC_Apparel-Global-Value-Chain.pdf

Forstater, Maya (2010). *Sectoral Coverage of the Global Economic Crisis. Implications of the Global Financial and Economic Crisis on the Textile and Clothing Sector.* Geneva: International Labour Office.

Frank, Andre G. (1966). *The Development of Underdevelopment.* New York: Monthly Review Press.

Frederick, Stacey (2010). *Development and Application of a Value Chain Research Approach to Understand and Evaluate Internal and External Factors and Relationships Affecting Economic Competitiveness in the Textile Value Chain.* Dissertation submitted to the Graduate Faculty of North Carolina State University.

Frederick, Stacey, and Gary Gereffi (2011). Upgrading and Restructuring in the Global Apparel Value Chain: Why China and Asia are Outperforming Mexico and Central America. In *International Journal of Technological Learning, Innovation and Development,* 4 (1/2/3), 67–95.

Frederick, Stacey, and Cornelia Staritz (2012). Developments in the Global Apparel Industry after the MFA Phaseout. In Lopez-Acevedo, Gladys, and Raymond Robertson *(eds.). Sewing Success? Employment, Wages, and Poverty following the End of the Multi-fibre Arrangement,* 41–86. Washington: The World Bank. 03.12.2012 http://siteresources.worldbank.org/EXTPOVERTY/Resources/SewingSuccess_FullReport.pdf

Freedonia Group (2011). *Focus Report Lighting Fixtures China.* Cleveland: Freedonia Group.

Fröbel, Folker, Jürgen Heinrichs, and Otto Kreye (1980). *The New International Division of Labour. Structural Unemployment in Industrialised Countries and Industrialisation in Developing Countries.* Cambridge: Cambridge University Press.

FYP = *China's Twelfth Five-Year Plan 2011–2015.* Translation by Delegation of European Union in China, 25.06.2012 http://cbi.typepad.com/china_direct/2011/05/chinas-twelfth-five-new-plan-the-full-english-version.html

Gaulier, Guillaume, Françoise LeMoine, and Deniz Ünal-Kesenci (2007). *China's Integration in Asian Production Networks and its Implications* (= RIETI Discussion Paper Series 04-E-033). Tokyo: RIETI. 24.11.2011 http://www.rieti.go.jp/jp/publications/dp/04e033.pdf

Gallaugher, John M. (2008). Zara Case: Fast Fashion from Savvy Systems. Online publication. 04.09.2012 www.gallaugher.com/Zara%20Case.pdf

Gereffi, Gary (1994). The organization of buyer-driven global commodity chains: How U.S. retailers shape overseas production networks. In Gereffi, Gary, and Miguel Korzeniewicz (eds.). *Commodity Chains and Global Capitalism*, 95–123. Westport: Praeger.

Gereffi, Gary (1999). *International Trade and Industrial Upgrading in the Apparel Commodity Chain*. In *Journal of International Economics*, 48 (1), 37–70.

Gereffi, Gary (2005). The Global Economy: Organization, Governance, and Development. In Smelser, Neil J., and Richard Swedberg (eds.). *The Handbook of Economic Sociology*, 2nd ed., 160–182. Princeton: Princeton University Press and Russell Sage Foundation.

Gereffi, Gary (2009) Development Models and Industrial Upgrading in China and Mexico, In *European Sociological Review*, 25 (1), 37–51.

Gereffi, Gary (2014). Global value chains in a post-Washington Consensus world. In *Review of International Political Economy*, 21 (1), 9–37.

Gereffi, Gary, John Humphrey, Raphael Kaplinsky, and Timothy J. Sturgeon (2001). *Introduction: Globalisation, Value Chains and Development* (= IDS Bulletin 32.3). Brighton: Institute for Development Studies.

Gereffi, Gary, John Humphrey, and Timothy Sturgeon (2005). The Governance of Global Value Chains. In *Review of International Political Economy*, 12 (1), 78–104.

Gereffi, Gary, and Stacey Frederick (2010). The Global Apparel Value Chain, Trade, and the Crisis: Challenges and Opportunities for Developing Countries. In Cattaneo, Oliver, Gary Gereffi, and Cornelia Staritz (eds.). *Global Value Chains in a Postcrisis World*, 157–208. Washington: World Bank,

Gereffi, Gary, and Olga Memedovic (2003). *The Global Apparel Value Chain: What Prospects for Upgrading by Developing Countries?* Vienna: UNIDO.

Gereffi, Gary, Ghada Ahmed, and Marcy Lowe (2011). *Case Study: Cree, Inc. Local Markets and Global Competitiveness: A Value Chain Analysis*. Durham: Center for Globalization, Governance and Competitiveness at Duke University. 04.05.2012 http://www.cggc.duke.edu/pdfs/CGGC_Cree_CaseStudy_10-22-10.pdf

Gläser, Jochen, and Grit Laudel (2010). *Experteninterviews und qualitative Inhaltsanalyse: als Instrumente rekonstruierender Untersuchungen*. Wiesbaden: VS Verlag.

GM = Globalization Monitor (2010). *Investigation and Monitoring of the Post-MFA Impact in China*. Hong Kong: Globalization Monitor.

GPRDBC = The Greater Pearl River Delta Business Council (2010). *2008–2010 Term Report*. Hong Kong: GPRDBC.

Gore, Lance (2012). *Wang Yang's Reform Program in Guangdong* (= EAI Background

Brief no. 727). Singapore: East-Asian Institute.

Greenpeace (2011). *shishang wuran liang ge zhongguo fangzhi zhuanye zhen huan-jing diaocha (Fashion pollution. Environmental investigation of two Chinese textile clusters)*. Beijing: Greenpeace China.

Guangdong LED Association (2011). *guangdong sheng LED xinpian fazhan zhuyao tedian yu qushi fenxi (The main characteristics and development trends of the LED chip industry in Guangdong Province)*. Unpublished manuscript.

Guangdong Xiqiao TIB = Textile Industry Base (no date). [Printed information brochure distributed by the local government].

Guo, Kai, and Papa N'Diaye (2009). *Is China's Export-Oriented Growth Sustainable?* (= IMF Working Paper WP/09/172). Washington: International Monetary Fund.

Guo, Kai, and Papa N'Diaye (2010). *Determinants of China's Private Consumption: An International Perspective* (= IMF Working Paper WP/10/93). Washington: International Monetary Fund.

Hale, Angela, and Jane Wills (2005). *Threads of Labour: Garment Industry Supply Chains from the Workers' Perspective*. Oxford, UK: Blackwell.

Hall, Peter A., and Soskice, David (eds.). (2001). *Varieties of Capitalism. The Institutional Foundations of Comparative Advantage*. Oxford: Oxford University Press.

Hart-Landsberg, Martin, and Paul Burkett (2005). *China and Socialism. Market Reforms and Class Struggle*. New York: Monthly Review Press.

Hart-Landsberg, and Martin Burkett (2006). China and the Dynamics of Transnational Accumulation: Causes and Consequences of Global Restructuring. In *Historical Materialism*, 14 (3), 3–43.

Harvey, David (2005). *A Brief History of Neoliberalism*. Oxford: Oxford University Press.

He, Dong, and Wenlang Zhang (2010). How Dependent is the Chinese Economy on Exports and in What Sense Has its Growth Been Export-led? In *Journal of Asian Economics*, 21 (1), 87–104.

Heilmann, Sebastian (2004). *Das politische System der Volksrepublik China*. Wiesbaden: VS Verlag.

Herrigel, Gary, and Jonathan Zeitlin (2010). Inter-Firm Relations in Global Manufacturing: Disintegrated Production and Its Globalization. In Morgan, Glenn, John Campbell, Colin Crouch, Peer Kristensen, Ove Pedersen, and Richard Whitley (eds.). *The Oxford Handbook of Comparative Institutional Analysis*, 527–61. Oxford: Oxford University Press.

Herrigel, Gary, Volker Wittke, and Ulrich Voskamp (2013). The Process of Chinese Manufacturing Upgrading: Transitioning from Unilateral to Recursive Mutual Learning Relations. In *Global Strategy Journal*, 3 (1), 109–125.

Hess, Martin, and Henry W. Yeung (2006). Whither global production networks in economic geography? Past, present and future. In *Environment and Planning A*, 38 (7), 1193–1204.

HKTDC Research (2007). *Cost Escalation and Trends for Export Price Increase—A look at the rising production costs in the PRD.* Hong Kong: Hong Kong Trade Development Council. 12.09.2012 http://economists-pick-research.hktdc. com/business-news/article/Economic-Forum/Cost-Escalation-and-Trends-for-Export-Price-Increase-br-A-look-at-the-rising-production-costs-in-the-PRD/ef/ en/1/1X000000/1X006T8D.htm

HKTDC Research (2010a). *Dongguan and Suzhou: Pilot cities for processing trade transformation.* Hong Kong: HKTDC. 24.10.2012 http://economists-pick-research.hktdc.com/business-news/article/Business-Alert-China/Dongguan-and-Suzhou-Pilot-cities-for-processing-trade-transformation/bacn/en/1/1X-000000/1X0786I0.htm

HKTDC Research (2010b), *The competitive supply chain: China v arising Asia,* Hong Kong: HKTDC. 24.10.2012 http://economists-pick-research.hktdc.com/business-news/article/Economic-Forum/The-competitive-supply-chain-China-v-arising-Asia/ef/en/1/1X000000/1X06XO6U.htm

HKTDC Research (2011a). *China's Industry Upgrade and Opportunities for Hong Kong Expertise.* Hong Kong: HKTDC. 12.09.2012 http://economists-pick-research. hktdc.com/business-news/article/Economic-Forum/HKTDC-Research-China-s-industry-upgrade-and-opportunities-for-Hong-Kong-expertise/ef/en/1/1X-000000/1X07MUYK.htm

HKTDC Research (2011b). *Are "China Prices" Becoming Yesterday's Trade Story.* Hong Kong: HKTDC. 07.01.2013 http://economists-pick-research.hktdc. com/business-news/article/Economic-Forum/Are-%E2%80%9CChina-prices%E2%80%9D-becoming-yesterday%E2%80%99s-trade-story-/ef/en/1/1X-000000/1X07R3HA.htm

HKTDC Research (2011c). *The New Clusters: China's Regional Boost.* Hong Kong: HKTDC. 12.09.2012 http://china-trade-research.hktdc.com/business-news/ article/Industry-Development/The-new-clusters-China-s-regional-boost/tq/ en/1/1X3BDU8A/1X07HODN.htm

HKTDC Reseach (2011d). *Of Prices and Productivity.* Hong Kong: HKTDC. 07.01.2013 http://economists-pick-research.hktdc.com/business-news/article/ Trade-Quarterly/Of-prices-andproductivity/tq/en/1/1X000000/1X07QZJK. htm

HKTDC Research (2012a). *China Garment Market.* Hong Kong: HKTDC. 22.11.2012 http://china-trade-research.hktdc.com/business-news/article/China-Consumer-Market/China%E2%80%99s-garmentmarket/ccm/en/1/1X-000000/1X002L72.htm

HKTDC Research (2012b). *China's New Value Added.* Hong Kong: HKTDC. 07.01.2013 http://economists-pick-research.hktdc.com/business-news/article/ Research-Articles/Main/rp/en/1/1X000000/1X09QLWD.htm

HKTDC Research (2012c). *Aggressive Brand-Building by Mainland Garment Manufacturers,* Hong Kong: HKTDC. 22.11.2012 http://economists-pick-research. hktdc.com/business-news/article/Economic-Forum/HKTDC-Research-Aggressive-brand-building-by-mainland-garment-manufacturers/ef/en/1/1X-

000000/1X07X1GH.htm

HKTDC Research (2013a). *Foreign Trade and Investment*. Hong Kong: HKTDC. 14.02.2013 http://china-trade-research.hktdc.com/business-news/article/Fast-Facts/Foreign-Trade-and-Investment/ff/en/1/1X000000/1X09PHD8.htm

HKTDC Research (2013b). *PRD Economic Profile*. Hong Kong: HKTDC. 14.02.2013 http://china-trade-research.hktdc.com/business-news/article/Fast-Facts/PRD-Economic-Profile/ff/en/1/1X000000/1X06BW84.htm

HKTDC Research (2013c). *Latest Development Trend on Production Costs on the Chinese Mainland*. Hong Kong: HKTDC. 14.03.2013. http://economists-pick-research.hktdc.com/business-news/article/Research-Articles/Latest-development-trend-on-production-costs-on-the-Chinese-Mainland/rp/en/1/1X-000000/1X09SGK4.htm

HKTDC Research (2014). *Economic and Trade Information on China*. Hong Kong: HKTDC. 30.06.2014 http://china-trade-research.hktdc.com/business-news/article/Fast-Facts/Economic-and-Trade-Information-on-China/ff/en/1/1X-000000/1X09PHBA.htm

HSBC Global Research (2011). *LED lighting. A revolution, but few long-term winners*. Düsseldorf: HSBC Trinkaus and Burkhardt AG.

Hirsch, Joachim (2005). *Materialistische Staatstheorie. Transformationsprozesse des kapitalistischen Staatensystems*. Hamburg: VSA.

Hopkins, Terence, and Wallerstein, Immanuel (1977). Patterns of development of the modern world-system. In *Review*, 1 (2), 11–145.

Huang, Yasheng (2008). *Capitalism with Chinese characteristics: Entrepreneurship and the State*. Cambridge: Cambridge University Press.

Huang, Yasheng (2010). *Urbanization, Hukou System and Government Land Ownership: Effects on Rural Migrant Works and on Rural and Urban Hukou Residents* (= Background Paper, Global Development Outlook 2010). Paris: OECD Development Centre.

Huang, Yanjie, and Shaofeng Chen (2009). *Crisis of Industrialization in the Pearl River Delta* (= Background Brief no. 444). Singapore: East-Asian Institute.

Humen Town Working Programme for Industrial Upgrading 2009–2013 (2010). Dongguan: Humen Government.

Humen Textile FYP = Humen Government (2010). *humen zhen shier wu fang zhi chanye fazhan guihua* (*Second Five-Year Plan for the textile industry in Humen town*). Dongguan: Humen Government.

Humphrey, John, and Hubert Schmitz (2001). *Governance in Global Value Chains* (= IDS Bulletin 32.3). Brighton: Institute for Development Studies.

Humphrey, John, and Hubert Schmitz (2002). How Does Insertion in Global Value Chains Affect Upgrading in Industrial Clusters? In *Regional Studies* 36 (9), 1017–1027.

Hung, Ho-Fung (2009a). A Caveat: Is the Rise of China Sustainable? In Hung, Ho-Fung (ed.). *China and the Transformation of Global Capitalism*, 188–202. Baltimore: John Hopkins University Press.

Hung, Ho-Fung (2009b). America's Head Servant? The PRC's Dilemma in the Global Crisis. In *New Left Review*, 60, 5–25.

IBISWorld (2011). *Apparel Manufacturing in China*. (no place): IBIS World.

Itoh, Makoto (2003). Sozialistische Marktwirtschaft und der chinesische Weg. In *Sozialismus*, 7–8 (supplement).

Jessup, Bob, and Ngai-Ling Sum (2006). *Beyond the Regulation Approach. Putting Capitalist Economies in their Place*. Cheltenham: Edward Elgar.

Jiang, Xiao, and William Milberg (2012). *Vertical Specialization and Industrial Upgrading: a Preliminary Note* (= Capturing the Gains Working Paper 2012/10). Manchester: University of Manchester.

JPMorgan Cazenove (2010). *Electrical Engineering & Semiconductor Equipment. Winners and Losers in a Radically Changing Lighting Industry Driven by LED*. London: JPMorgan Cazenove.

Kaplinsky, Raphael (2000). Globalisation and Unequalisation: What Can Be Learned from Value Chain Analysis? In *The Journal of Development Studies*, 37 (2), 117–146.

Kogut, Bruce (1984). Normative Observations on the International Value-Added Chain and Strategic Groups. In *Journal of International Business Studies*, 15 (2), 151–167.

Koopmann, Robert, Zhi Wang, and Shang-Jin Wei (2008). *How Much of Chinese Exports is Really Made in China? Assessing Domestic Value-Added When Processing Trade is Pervasive* (= NBER Working Paper 14109). Cambridge: National Bureau of Economic Research.

KPMG (2011). *China's 12 Five-Year Plan: Overview*. (no place): KPMG China.

Lan, Tu, and John Pickles (2011). *China's New Labour Contract Law: State Regulation and Worker Rights in Global Production Networks* (= Capturing the Gains Working Paper 2011/05). Manchester: University of Manchester.

Lardy, Nicholas (2011). *Sustaining and Rebalancing Economic Growth in China*. Washington: Peterson Institute for International Economics.

Lardy, Nicholas, and Nicholas Borst (2013). *A Blueprint for Rebalancing the Chinese Economy* (= Peterson Institute for International Economy Policy Brief 13-02). Washington: Peterson Institute for International Economy.

Lee, Ching Kwan (2007). *Against the Law. Labor Protests in China's Rustbelt and Sunbelt*. Berkeley, Los Angeles and London: University of California Press.

Lee, Ching Kwan, and Eli Friedman (2010). Remaking the World of Chinese Labor: A Thirty Year Retrospective. In *British Journal of Industrial Relations*, 48 (3), 3–17.

Lee, Joonkoo, and Gary Gereffi (2013). *The Co-evolution of Concentration in Mobile Phone Global Value Chains and its Impact on Social Upgrading in Developing Countries* (= Capturing the Gains Working Paper 2013/25). Manchester: University of Manchester.

Li&Fung (2010). *China's Apparel Market 2010*. Hong Kong: Li&Fung.

Li&Fung (2011). *China's Apparel Market 2011*. Hong Kong: Li&Fung.

Li&Fung (2011). *Overview of China's Regional Development.* Hong Kong: Li&Fung. 22.02.2013 http://www.funggroup.com/eng/knowledge/research/china_dis_issue94.pdf

Li&Fung (2012). *China's Apparel Market 2012.* Hong Kong: Li&Fung.

Li, Gan, and Haixiong Qiu (2010). *Woguo LED chanye fazhan de zhiyue yinsu yu duice fenxi. Jiyu chanye jiqun wangluo fanshi de jiedu* (Study on the Influences of Cluster Construction on the Development of LED in China. An Analysis Based on the Network Paradigm). In *Economic Geography,* 30 (10), 1675–1680.

Li, Kunwang, and Ligang Song (2011). The technological content of Chinese exports and the need for upgrading. In Golley, Jane, and Ligang Song (eds.). *Rising China: Global Challenges and Opportunities.* Canberra: ANU E Press.

Li, Hongbin, Lei Li, Binzhen Wu and Yanyan Xiong (2012). The End of Cheap Chinese Labor. In *Journal of Economic Perspectives,* 26 (4), 57–74.

Lipietz, Alain (1987). *Mirages and Miracles. The Crisis of Global Fordism.* London: Verso.

Liu, Xielin, Boy Lüthje, and Peter Pawlicki (2007). China: Nationales Innovationssystem und marktwirtschaftliche Transformation. In Gerlach, Frank, and Astrid Ziegler (eds.). *Innovationspolitik: Was kann Deutschland von anderen Lernen?,* 222–249. Marburg: Schüren.

Liu, Weidong, Clifton Pannell, and Hongguang Liu (2009). The Global Economic Crisis and China's Foreign Trade. In *Eurasian Geography and Economics,* 50 (5), 497–512.

Lopez-Acevedo, Gladys, and Raymond Robertson (eds.). (2012). *Sewing Success? Employment, Wages and Poverty following the End of the Multi-Fibre Arrangement.* Washington: The World Bank.

Lüthje, Boy (2001). *Standort Silicon Valley: Ökonomie und Politik der vernetzten Massenproduktion.* Frankfurt am Main and New York: Campus.

Lüthje, Boy (2011). Which Side Are You On? Lessons from the Strikes at Auto Suppliers in South China. In *Asian Labour Update,* 78, 15–19.

Lüthje, Boy, Siqi Luo, and Hao Zhang (2013b). *Beyond the Iron Rice Bowl. Regimes of Production and Industrial Relations in China.* Frankfurt am Main and New York: Campus.

Lüthje, Boy (2014). *Why no Fordism in China? Regimes of Accumulation and Regimes of Production in Chinese Manufacturing Industries* (= IfS Working Paper #3). Frankfurt am Main: IfS.

Lu Zhen, and Xiang Deng (2011). *China's Western Development Strategy: Policies, Effects and Prospects* (= MPRA Paper 35,201). Munich: Munich Personal RePEc Archive.

McKinsey&Company (2011a). *Lighting the Way: Perspectives on the Global Lighting Market.* (no place): McKinsey&Company.

McKinsey&Company (2011b). *LED at the Crossroads: Scenic Route or Expressway?* (no place): McKinsey&Company. 04.04.2012 http://www.mckinsey.com/client_service/semiconductors/latest_thinking/led_at_the_crossroads

McKinsey&Company (2011c). *Bangladesh's Ready-Made Garment Landscape: The Challenge of Growth*. (no place): McKinsey&Company.

McKinsey&Company (2012a). *Lighting the Way: Perspectives on the Global Lighting Market*, 2nd edition. (no place): McKinsey&Company.

McKinsey&Company (2012b). *Healthcare in China: "Entering Unchartered Waters"*. (no place): McKinsey.

McKinsey&Company (2012c). *Bangladesh: The next hot spot in apparel sourcing?* (no place): McKinsey&Company. 14.12.2012 http://www.mckinsey.com/insights/consumer_and_retail/bangladesh_the_next_hot_spot_in_apparel_sourcing

McKinsey&Company (2012d). *McKinsey Consumer & Shopper Insights. Meet the 2020 Chinese Consumer*. (no place): McKinsey&Company.

McNally, Christopher (2006). *Insinuations on China's Emerging Capitalism* (= East-West Center Working Paper no.15). Honolulu: East-West Center.

McNally, Christopher (2012). Sino-Capitalism: China's Reemergence and the International Political Economy. In *World Politics*, 64 (4), 741–776.

McNally, Christopher A. (2013). *Refurbishing State Capitalism: A Policy Analysis of Efforts to Rebalance China's Political Economy*. In *Journal of Current Chinese Affairs*, 42 (4), 45–72.

McNally, Christopher, and Yin-Wah Chu (2006). Exploring Capitalist Development in Greater China: A Synthesis. In *Asian Perspectives*, 30 (2), 31–64.

Meyer, Marshall (2011). Is it Capitalism? In *Management and Organization Review*. 7 (1), 5–18.

Nahm Jonas, and Edward Steinfield (2013). Scale-Up Nation: China's Specialization in Innovative Manufacturing.In *World Development*, 54, 288–300.

Naughton, Barry (2007). *The Chinese Economy: Transition and Growth*. Boston: MIT Press.

Naughton, Barry (2009). The Scramble to Maintain Growth. In *China Leadership Monitor*, 27, 1–11.

NDRC = The National Development and Reform Commission of the People's Republic of China (2008). *The Outline of the Plan for the Reform and Development of the Pearl River Delta (2008–2020)*. Beijing: NDRC.

NSR = New Street Research (2010). *The Future of Lighting. Who Will Win?* London: New Street Research.

NVC (2012). *2011 Annual Results*. Presentation. 12.01.2013 http://m.todayir.com/todayirattachment_hk/nvclighting/attachment/2012040220344017_en.pdf

OECD (2010). *OECD Territorial Reviews: Guangdong, China*. Paris: OECD.

Pawlicki, Peter (2010). New Industries and Locations in Semiconductors—the Role of Industry, State and Markets. The Case of the Taiwanese Fabless Chipdesigner Mediatek. Paper presented at the international workshop "Understanding the emergence of new industries. Between path dependency and path plasticity" (University of Torino 7./8.10.2010). Unpublished manuscript.

PD = POWERDENIM (2010). *Denim New Age* (=Company Catalogue 2010). Foshan: POWERDENIM.

PD = POWERDENIM (2010). *Denim New Age* (=Promotion Video 2010). Foshan: POWERDENIM.

PD = POWERDENIM (2012). *Denim New Age* (=Company Catalogue 2011/2012). Foshan: POWERDENIM.

Pettis, Michael (2013). *The Great Rebalancing. Trade, Conflict, and the Perilous Road Ahead for the World Economy.* Princeton: Princeton University Press.

Pickles, John, and Jane Godfrey (2012). *Economic and Social Upgrading in Global Apparel Production Networks* (= Capturing the Gains Revised Summit Briefing No 06.2). Manchester: University of Manchester.

Pohlmann, Markus (2002). *Der Kapitalismus in Ostasien. Südkoreas und Taiwans Wege ins Zentrum der Weltwirtschaft.* Münster: Westfälisches Dampfboot.

Pollock, Friedrich (1964). *Automation. Materialien zur Beurteilung der ökonomischen und sozialen Folgen* (= Frankfurter Beiträge zur Soziologie Band 5). Frankfurt am Main: Europäische Verlagsanstalt.

Porter, Michael (1985). *Competitive Advantage.* New York: Free Press.

PS = PACKAGESTAR (2011). Company Catalogue. Foshan: PACKAGESTAR.

PS = PACKAGESTAR (2012). *Quarterly Report I/2012.* Foshan: PACKAGESTAR.

Pun, Ngai (2005). *Made in China. Women Factory Workers in a Global Workplace.* Durham and Hong Kong: Duke University Press and Hong Kong University Press.

Pun, Ngai, Huilin Lu, Yuhua Guo, and Yuan Shen (2012). *Wo Zai Fushikang*, Beijing: Zhishi Chanquan. German translation: Ruckus, Ralf (ed.) (2013). *iSlaves.* Vienna: Mandelbaum.

Pun, Ngai, and Jenny Chan (2012). Global Capital, the State, and Chinese Workers: The Foxconn Experience. In *Modern China*, 38 (4), 383–410.

Qiu, Larry (2005). *China's Textile and Garment Industry.* Manuscript. 14.12.2012 http://s3.amazonaws.com/zanran_storage/www.bm.ust.hk/ContentPages/18112599.pdf

Qiu, Haixiong et al (2012). guang dong gai ge fa zhan bao gao 2011–2012: Chan ye zhuan xing sheng ji guang dong xing ren min zheng fu zhuan xiang ke ti bao gao (Guangdong Industrial Development Report (2011–2012): Industrial Upgrading and Transformation). Guangzhou: Guangdong Provincial Government.

Research in China (2011). *Global and China LED Industry Report, 2010–2011.* (no place): Research in China. 22.04.2013 http://www.researchinchina.com/Htmls/Report/2011/6075.html

Roach, Stephen (2009). *The Next Asia. Opportunities and Challenges for a New Globalization.* Hoboken: John Wiley & Sons.

Roach, Stephen (2011). *China's 12 Five-Year Plan. Strategy vs. Tactics.* (no place): Morgan Stanley. 12.06.2012 http://www.law.yale.edu/documents/pdf/cbl/China_12th_Five_Year_Plan.pdf

Rostow, Walt W. (1960). *The Stages of Economic Growth: A Non-Communist Manifesto.* Cambridge: Cambridge University Press.

Sauer, Dieter, and Volker Döhl (1994). Arbeit an der Kette. Systemische Rationalisierung unternehmensübergreifender Produktion. In *Soziale Welt*, 45 (2), 197–215.

Schiller, Daniel (2013). *An Institutional Perspective on Production and Upgrading. The Electronics Industry in Hong Kong and the Pearl River Delta*, Stuttgart: Franz Steiner.

Schmalz, Stefan (2013). Neue Vögel im Käfig? Chinas steiniger Weg zu einem neuen Akkumulationsregime. In Atzmüller, Roland et al (eds.), *Fit für die Krise? Perspektiven der Regulationstheorie*, 329–352. Münster: Westfälisches Dampfboot.

Schucher, Günter (2009). China's Employment Crisis—A Stimulus for Policy Change? In *Journal of Current Chinese Affairs*, 38 (2), 121–144.

Schucher, Günter (2011). *"Unausgeglichen, unkoordiniert, nicht nachhaltig" – Chinas Entwicklung vor großen Problemen* (= GIGA Focus Asien no.3). Hamburg: Global Institute of Global and Area Studies.

Schüller, Margot (2008). *Technologietransfer nach China – Ein unkalkulierbares Risiko für die Länder der Triade USA, Europa und Japan?* Berlin: Friedrich-Ebert-Stiftung.

Schüller, Margot, and Yun Schüler-Zhou (2009). China's Economic Policy in the Time of the Global Financial Crisis: Which Way Out? In *Journal of Current Chinese Affairs*, 38 (3), 165–181.

Schüller, Margot, Yun Schüler-Zhou, and Lisa Peterskovsky (2010). *Chinas Telekommunikationsunternehmen drängen an die Weltspitze* (= GIGA *Focus* Asien, no. 12). Hamburg: Global Institute of Global and Area Studies.

Selwyn, Ben (2011). Beyond Firm-Centrism: Re-integrating Labour and Capitalism into Global Commodity Chain Analysis. In *Journal of Economic Geography*, 12 (1), 205–226.

Selwyn, Ben (2013). Social Upgrading and Labour in Global Production Networks: A Critique and an Alternative Conception. In *Competition and Change*, 17 (1), 75–90.

Shen, Jie (2007). *Labour Disputes and Their Resolution in China*. Oxford: Woodhead.

Silver, Beverly, and Lu Zhang (2009). China as an Emerging Epicenter of World Labor Unrest. In Hung, Ho-Fung (ed.). *China and the Transformation of Global Capitalism*, 174–187. Baltimore: John Hopkins University Press.

Smith, Ted, David Sonnenfeld, and David Naguib Pellow (eds.). (2006). *Challenging the Chip. Labor Rights and Environmental Justice in the Global Electronics Industry*. Philadelphia: Temple University Press.

Song, Haifeng (2012). *The Marketing Strategy Suggestions for Yishion in Jing County*. Thesis. Varkaus: Savonia University of Applied Sciences.

South School Garment (2010). Characteristic and versatile Humen fashion industry cluster. In *South School Garment* (Magazine of the Humen Garment and Fashion Association), 2, 15.

Staritz, Cornelia, Stacey Frederick (2012). Summaries of the Country Case Studies on Apparel Industry. Development, Structure, and Policies. In Lopez-Acevedo, Gladys, and Raymond Robertson (eds.). *Sewing Success? Employment, Wages, and Poverty following the End of the Multi-fibre Arrangement*, 211–297. Washington:

The World Bank.

Staritz, Cornelia, Gary Gereffi, and Oliver Cattaneo (2011). Editorial. In *Journal for Technological Learning, Innovation and Development*, 4 (1/2/3), 1–12.

Steinfeld, Edward (2004). China's Shallow Integration: Networked Production and the New Challenges for Late Industrialization. In *World Development*, 32 (11), 1971–1987.

Stembridge, Bob (2010). Chinese Utility Models—a Lesser-Known IP Strategy. In *International Asset Management*, 9.

Streeck, Wolfgang (2010). *E pluribus unum? Varieties and communalities of capitalism* (= MPIfGDiscussion Paper 10/12). Cologne: Max Planck Institut für Gesellschaftsforschung. 30.01.2013 http://www.mpifg.de/pu/mpifg_dp/dp10-12.pdf

Sturgeon, Timothy (2009). From Commodity Chains to Value Chains: Interdisciplinary Theory Building in an Age of Globalization. In Bair, Jennifer (ed.). *Frontiers of Commodity Chain Research*, 110–135. Stanford: Stanford University Press.

Sturgeon, Timothy, and Momoko Kawakami (2011). Global Value Chains in the Electronics Industry: Characteristics, Crisis, and Upgrading Opportunities for Firms from Developing Countries. In *Journal for Technological Learning, Innovation and Development*, 4 (1/2/3), 120–147.

Taylor, Bill, Kai Chang, and Qi Li (2003). *Industrial Relations in China*. Cheltenham: Edward Elgar.

Technopak (2012). *Textile and Apparel Compendium 2012*. Gurgaon: Technopak Advisors.

ten Brink, Tobias (2008). *Geopolitik. Geschichte und Gegenwart kapitalistischer Staatenkonkurrenz*. Münster: Westfälisches Dampfboot.

ten Brink, Tobias (2013). *Chinas Kapitalismus. Entstehung, Verlauf, Paradoxien*. Frankfurt und New York: Campus.

Gesamtverband textil+mode (2011). *Textil+Modewelt 2011+12*. Berlin: Gesamtverband textil+mode.

The Climate Group (2012). *Lighting the Clean Revolution. The Rise of LEDs and What it Means For Cities*. London: The Climate Group.

Ton, My, and Peter du Pont (2008). *An Inconvenient Truth: The Reality of "Shoddy" CFLs, in Developing Asia, and a Plan for Eliminating Them* (= Proceedings Paper, American Council for Energy-Efficiency Economy). 22.04.2013 http://www.aceee.org/files/proceedings/2008/data/papers/9_729.pdf

Tong, Sarah, and Yang Zhang (2009). *China's Responses to the Economic Crisis* (= EAI Background Brief no. 438). Singapore: East-Asian Institute.

Traub-Merz, Rudolf (2011). *All China Federation of Trade Unions: Structure, Functions and the Challenge of Collective Bargaining* (= Global Labour University Working Paper 13). Berlin: International Labour Office and Global Labour University.

UNCTAD (2013). *World Investment Report 2013: Global Value Chains: Investment and Trade for Development*. Geneva: UNCTAD.

Unger, Jonathan (1999). *The Rise of Private Business in a Rural Chinese District: The Emerging Characteristics of Entrepreneurship in the PRC* (= Asia Research Working

Paper nr. 90). Perth: Murdoch University.

USCBC = The US-China Business Council (2009). *USCBC Summary of the PRC Textile Industry Revitalization Plan*. (no place): USCBC. 15.11.2011 https://www.uschina.org/public/documents/2009/04/textile_revitalization_plan.pdf

Virey, Eric (2012). 2010's Blow-Out Cycle Marked LED Industry Investment Peak. In *iLED*, 5, 16–18.

Walder, Jean-Baptiste (1992). *Principles of Computer-Integrated Manufacturing*. Hoboken: John Wiley & Sons.

Walker, Richard A. (1995). Regulation and Flexible Specialization as Theories of Capitalist Development. Challengers to Marx and Schumpeter? In Ligget, Hellen, and David Perry (eds.). *Spatial Practices. Critical Explorations in Social/Spatial Theory*, 167–208. Thousand Oaks, London, New Dehli: Sage.

Wang, Jun, and Fangmin Yue (2009). *Cluster Development and Government Role: the Case of Xiqiao Textile Cluster in Guangdong Province, China*. Presentation.

Wang, Jun, and Fangmin Yue (2010). Cluster Development and the Role of Government: The Case of Xiqiao Textile Cluster in Guangdong. In Douglas Z. Zeng (ed.). *Building Engines for Growth and Competitiveness in China. Experiences with Special Economic Zones and Industrial Clusters*, 181–222. Washington D.C.: World Bank.

Watson, Andrew (2009). Social Security for China's Migrant Workers—Providing for Old Age. In *Journal of Current Chinese Affairs*, 38 (4), 85–115.

WEED (2008). *The Dark Side of Cyberspace. Inside the Sweatshops of China's Computer Hardware Production*. Berlin: WEED.

Wick, Ingeborg (2009). *Soziale Folgen des liberalisierten Weltmarkts für Textil und Bekleidung: Strategien von Gewerkschaften und Frauenorganisationen* (= OBS-Arbeitsheft 62). Frankfurt am Main: Otto-Brenner-Stiftung.

Womack, James, Daniel Jones, and Daniel Ross (2007). *The Machine That Changed the World: The Story of Lean Production—Toyota's Secret Weapon in the Global Car Wars That Is Now Revolutionizing World Industry*. New York: Free Press.

Wong, Staphany (2008). *Impacts of the Financial Crisis on Labour Conditions in China*. Heidelberg: Werkstatt Ökonomie.

Wong, John (2013). *China's Economy: Rebounded in 2012, Gearing up for Rebalancing in 2013 and Beyond* (= EAI Background Brief no. 782). Singapore: East-Asian Institute.

World Bank and State Environmental Protection Administration of the PRC (2007). *Costs of Pollution in China. Economic Estimates of Physical Damages* (Conference Edition). New York and Beijing: State Environmental Protection Administration, World Bank Rural Development, Natural Resources and Environment Management Unit (East Asia and Pacific Region) and World Bank Office Beijing. 01.07.2012 http://siteresources.worldbank.org/INTEAPREGTOPENVIRONMENT/Resources/China_Cost_of_Pollution.pdf

World Bank (2012). *China 2030: Building a Modern, Harmonious, and Creative Society*. Washington: The World Bank Group.

World Bank (2014). *China Economic Update. June 2014.* Washington: The World Bank Group. 30.06.2014 http://www.worldbank.org/en/country/china/publication/china-economic-update-june-2014

Wright, Maury (2013). Packaged LED Market Resumes Moderate Growth While the SSL Market Will Enjoy 12% CAGR through 2017. In *LEDs Magazine* (March), 35–40. 22.04.2013 http://ledsmagazine.com/features/10/3/4.

WWW = Women Working Worldwide action research in Asia and Europe (2003). *Garment Industry Subcontracting and Workers' Right.* Manchester: Women Working Worldwide.

Xiqiao FIB = Foreign Investment Bureao (no date*). xi qiáo zhèn zhāoshāng tuījiè xiàngmù shuucè* (Xiqiao investment promotion brochure). Material provided by the Xiqiao foreign investment bureau.

Xu Yingxin (2009). *Die Textilindustrie Chinas* (presentation at the Heimtextil Fair, Frankfurt am Main, 13.01.2009).

Yeung, Wai-Chung (2004). *Chinese Capitalism in a Global Era: Towards a Hybrid Capitalism.* London: Routledge

Yole Développement (2010). *Status of the LED Industry* (= Industry, Market & Technology Report November 2010). Lyon: Yole Développement.

Yole Développement (2011). *LED Packaging 2011. A Comprehensive Survey of the Main LED Packaging Technologies and Marketing Metrics.* 22.04.2013 http://www.marketresearch.com/product/sample-6490053.pdf

Yole Développement (2012). *Status of the LED Industry. Market Analysis, Industry Status, Players and Main Applications for LED.* 07.11.2012 http://www.i-micronews.com/reports/Status-LED-Industry/14/308/

Yu, Hong (2011). *Class Formation, and China's Informationized Policy of Economic Development.* Plymouth: Lexington.

Yu, Hong (2012). *China's Western Development Strategy 10 Years On* (= EAI Background Brief no. 715). Singapore: East-Asian Institute.

Yu, Miaojie (2011). *Moving up the Value Chain in Manufacturing for China* (= Peking University China Center for Economic Research (CCER) Working Paper). Beijing: China Center for Economic Research. 22.04.2013 http://dx.doi.org/10.2139/ssrn.1792582

Yu, Min (2011). *Working Conditions of White Collar Workers in the Chinese IT Industry* (presentation at the conference "Global production, economic development, and labor standards in the information technology industry", Guangzhou. 05.12.2011).

Yu, Yongding (2009). *China's Policy Responses to the Financial Crisis* (Richard Snape Lecture, Melbourne 25.11.2009). Melbourne: Productivity Commission of the Australian Government.

Yu, Yongding (2012). China's Rebalancing Act. 26.04.2013 http://www.project-syndicate.org/commentary/five-year-plan-imf-chinese-exports-by-yu-yongding

Yu, Hong, and Yang Zhang (2009). *New Initiatives for Industrial Upgrading in the Pearl River Delta* (= EAI Background Brief no. 464). Singapore: East-Asian Institute.

Zeng, Douglas Zhihua (ed.). (2010). *Building Engines for Growth and Competitiveness in China. Experience with Special Economic Zones and Industrial Clusters.* Washington: The World Bank.

Zeng, Douglas Zhihua (2011). *How Do Special Economic Zones and Industrial Clusters Drive China's Rapid Development?* (= World Bank Policy Research Working Paper 5583). Washington: The World Bank.

Zhao, Litao, and Yanjie Huang (2010). *China's Labor Shortage in the After-crisis Era* (= EAI Background Brief no. 538). Singapore: East-Asian Institute.

Zhu, Andong and David Kotz (2011). The Dependence of China's Economic Growth on Exports and Investment. In *Review of Radical Political Economics*, 43 (9), 9–32.

# Newspaper articles and online sources

APT Electronics Ltd (19.09.2011). *Guangdong LED Industry Joint Innovation Center Settled in Nanhai*, Foshan. 22.04.2013 http://www.apt-hk.com/en/html/?162. html.

APT Electronics Ltd (20.04.2012). *Guangdong Initiates Major Research Project of Standard Optical Elements for LED Luminance.* 22.04.2013 http://www.apt-hk. com/en/html/?186.html.

AustCham = The China-Australia Chamber of Commerce's (11.07.2011). *China's labour revolution continues: New social insurance law.* 18.04.2013 http://www.austcham.org/search/node/labour%20revolution.

BBC news (13.08.2012). *China's ghost towns and phantom malls.* 26.04.2013 http://www.bbc.co.uk/news/magazine-19049254.

Beijing review (18.11.10). *From Rags to Riches.* 13.12.2012 http://www.bjreview.com.cn/16th_Asian_Games/2010-11/18/content_313364.htm#

Bloomberg (17.12.2012). *China May Delay Plan to Reform Income Distribution, Caijing Says*, 08.01.2013 http://www.bloomberg.com/news/2012-12-17/china-may-delay-plan-to-reform-income-distribution-caijing-says.html

Businessweek (15.06.2009). *A Talk with Wang Yang*, 26.04.2013 http://www.businessweek.com/globalbiz/content/jun2009/gb2009065_691758.htm

Businessweek (19.11.2009). *China's Reverse Brain Drain*, 26.04.2013 http://www.businessweek.com/magazine/content/09_48/b4157058821350.htm

Businessweek (29.11.2012). *The March of Robots into Chinese Factories*, 26.04.2013 http://www.businessweek.com/articles/2012-11-29/the-march-of-robots-into-chinese-factories

Businessweek (26.01.2013). *Obama Speech to Embrace Manufacturing Rebirth as Job Creator.* 10.04.2013 http://www.businessweek.com/news/2012-01-26/obama-speech-to-embrace-manufacturing-rebirth-as-job-creator.html

Cens.com (23.05.2012). *Fury of IPOs Continues in 2012 for China's LED Lighting Sector.* 22.04.2013 http://www.cens.com/cens/html/en/news/news_inner_40264.html

China Briefing (23.03.2010). *Guangdong Province Adjusts Minimum Wage.* 26.04.2013 http://www.china-briefing.com/news/2010/03/23/notice-on-adjusting-the-minimum-wage-in-guangdong-province.html

China Briefing (10.06.2010). *Shenzhen Raises Minimum Wage.* 26.04.2013 http://www.china-briefing.com/news/2010/06/10/shenzhen-raises-minimum-wage.html

China Briefing (30.12.2012). *Foreign Investment Industrial Guidance Catalogue Promulgated,* 26.04.2013. http://www.china-briefing.com/news/2011/12/30/2011-foreign-investment-industrial-guidance-catalogue-promulgated.html#more-15148

China Daily (11.01.2010). *China overtakes US as world's largest auto market.* 26.04.2013 http://www.chinadaily.com.cn/china/09achievements/2010-01/11/content_9306920.htm

China Daily (10.07.2012). *Guangdong LED industry set for losses,* 08.11.2012 http://europe.chinadaily.com.cn/business/2012-07/10/content_15566312.htm

China Daily (28.07.2012). *No fear of a hard landing.* 26.04.2013 http://www.chinadaily.com.cn/cndy/2012-07/28/content_15625535.htm

China Daily (24.10.2012). *Pushing the reset button* 24.10.2012 http://usa.chinadaily.com.cn/business/2012-09/15/content_15760559.htm

China Daily (09.11.2012). *China's textile industry faces poor export growth.* 29.04.2013 http://www.chinadaily.com.cn/china/2012-11/09/content_15899931.htm

China Economic Watch (24.01.2013). *China Rebalancing Update Q4/2012.* 24.04.2013 http://www.piie.com/blogs/china/?p=2250

China LED (01.01.2014). *CSA chan yan: 2013 nian zhong guo ban dao ti zhao ming chan ye shu ju ji fa zhan gai kuang* (CSA market research: overview of the state and development of China's semiconductor lighting industry in 2013). 12.03.2014 http://www.china-led.org/article/20140101/3979.shtml

Chinaview (08.03.2013). *Dongguan Continues Industrial Upgrade.* 09.03.2013 http://www.icbc.com.cn/icbc/investment/financial%20news/Dongguan%20Continues%20Industrial%20Upgrade.htm

China.org.cn (13.06.2012). *Top 33 richest Chinese under 40.* 23.01.2013 http://www.china.org.cn/top10/2012-06/13/content_25635580_6.htm

CIES = China Illumination Engineering Society (04.11.2011). *Director of the Office of Guangdong Science and Technology Said That the Development of LED Industry is a Revolution.* 12.04.2011 http://en.lightingchina.com/news/news_info.asp?newsID=2481

CS = Compound Semiconductor (18.07.2012). *LED Industry Faces Tough Times, Reports Research in China.* 07.12.2012 http://www.compoundsemiconductor.net/csc/news-details.php?cat=news&id=19735260

CTEI = China National Textie and Apparel Council (08.08.2011). *2011 First Half China Garment Industry Report.* 26.04.2013 http://english.ctei.gov.cn/reports/

rts/201108/t20110808_307405.html

CTEI = China National Textie and Apparel Council (23.02.2012). China textile and garment exports USD 249.89billion. 26.04.2013 http://www.ccpittex.com/eng/statistics/49483.html

Digitimes (01.07.2011). *China's LED industry under the 12th Five Year Plan.* 05.07.2013 http://www.digitimes.com/Reports/Report.asp?datepublish=2011/7/1&pages=RS&seq=400

Digitmes (13.09.2012). *Trends in Asia's LED Chip Manufacturing Industry.* 22.04.2013 http://www.digitimes.com/Reports/Report.asp?datepublish=2012/9/13&pages=RS&seq=400&read=toc

Digitimes (29.09.2011). *China LED Industry Should Not Blindly Increase Capacity but Focus on Improving Technology, Management, and Quality.* 25.10.2011 http://www.digitimes.com/NewsShow/MailHome.asp?datePublish=2011/9/29&pages=PD&seq=216

Digitimes (24.11.2011). *Overview of Chinas LED Chip Industry.* 22.04.2013 http://www.digitimes.com/Reports/Report.asp?datepublish=2011/11/24&pages=RS&seq=400&read=toc

Digitimes (21.06.2012). Guangdong province announces plans to switch to LED lighting for all public areas in 3 years 22.10.2012 http://www.digitimes.com/news/a20120621PD202.html

Digitimes (18.03.2013). *Global High-Brightness LED Market Forecast.* 17.04.2013 http://www.digitimes.com/Reports/Report.asp?datepublish=2013/03/04&pages=RS&seq=400

Digitimes (11.06.2014). *Digitimes Research: Taiwan makers take up 28.6% of MOCVD in operation globally in May.* 30.06.2014 http://www.digitimes.com/news/a20140610PD209.html

Dongguan Ribao (Dongguan Daily) (17.08.2010). *zong zuan jiagong fei dao gan chang zi mou chuang yi dai lang mao zhi zhuan xing huo wangyang kending* (From earning processing fees to brand building – Dalang's transformation was confirmed by Wangyang).

FiveThirtyEight (23.04.2014). *Where the U.S. Gets Its Clothing, One Year After the Bangladesh Factory Collapse.* 30.06.2014 http://fivethirtyeight.com/datalab/where-the-u-s-gets-its-clothing-one-year-after-the-bangladesh-factory-collapse/

FT = Financial Times (02.07.2007). *750,000 a Year Killed by Chinese Pollution.* 24.03.2013 http://www.ft.com/cms/s/0/8f40e248-28c7-11dc-af78-000b5df10621.html#axzz2OeEz6600

FT = Financial Times (10.06.2009). *China's Plan to Empty the Bird Cage.* 26.04.2013 http://www.ft.com/intl/cms/s/0/4accc3bc-5556-11de-b5d4-00144feabdc0.html#axzz2Rb6RUzJm

FT = Financial Times (26.02.2012). *China to Tighten Shadow Banking Rules.* 26.04.2013 http://www.ft.com/intl/cms/s/0/223777b6-7fec-11e2-adbd-00144feabdc0.html

FT = Financial Times (08.08.2012). *China's Vancl Shifts Production Overseas.*

29.04.2013 http://www.ft.com/cms/s/0/ea439996-e13c-11e1-839a-00144fea-b49a.html#ixzz22y106loe

FT = Financial Times (19.08.2012). *Economists Weigh Chinese 'Hard Landing'.* 26.04.2013 http://www.ft.com/cms/s/0/cc05e828-e860-11e1-8ffc-00144fea-b49a.html#axzz2OeEz6600

GTAI = Germany Trade and Invest (31.03.2011). *Neues Sozialversicherungsgesetz erhöht Lohnnebenkosten*

Guangdong EIC = The Economic & Information Commission of Guangdong province (22.10.2010). *dong guan shi dai lang zhen zai liang jian tuichu liu zhao ju cuo tuijin mao zhi ye zhuan xing shengji* (Dalang Town, Dongguan, launched the "six strokes" initiative to promote industrial upgrading in the wool industry).

Guangzhou Ribao (21.09.2011). *LED deng mingnian ni mianfei huan* (LED lights are supposed to be free of charge in the next year). 22.04.2013 http://gzdaily.dayoo.com/html/2011-09/21/content_1481885.htm

International Textile Manufacturer's Association (26.05.2012). *Textile machinery shipments hit record levels.* 29.04.2013 http://www.knittingindustry.com/textile-machinery-shipments-hit-record-levels/

Just Style (06.11.2011). *COMMENT: Has China hijacked the global garment industry?* 04.01.2012 http://www.just-style.com/comment/has-china-hijacked-the-global-garment-industry_id109932.aspx

LEDinside (24.06.2010). *Ranking of LED Chip Manufacturers in China–Report on China's LED Epitaxy Industry.* 07.11.2012 http://www.ledinside.com/research/2010/6/led_china_epi_rank_2010_en

LEDinside (04.08.2010). *Foshan selects Bridgelux as LED supplier for SSL.* 22.04.2013 http://ledsmagazine.com/news/7/8/4

LEDinside, (04.01.2011), *Outlook of LED Industry Trend in 2011.* 14.04.2011 http://www.ledinside.com/ledoutlook_2011

LEDinside (04.03.2011). *Luxeon LEDs Shine Brightly on the Guangzhou TV tower.* 22.04.2013 http://ledsmagazine.com/press/30569

LEDinside (14.10.2011). *Chinese LED Lighting Market Report in 2011—2015(II): Supply Chain Analysis.* 22.04.2013 http://www.ledinside.com/research/2011/10/report_cnledlighting_b

LEDinside (10.11.2011). *China to Raise LED Market Demand with Incandescent Bulb Phase-Out Policy and LED Subsidies.* 08.11.2012 http://www.ledinside.com/research/2011/11/china_led_market_2012_in_fob

LEDinside (15.12.2011). *Samsung, LG to Release 60W LED Light Bulbs of US$10-12.* 22.04.2013 http://www.ledinside.com/news/2011/12/samsung_lg_20111215

LEDinside (18.06.2012). Large Manufacturers to Benefit Most from Chinese Subsidy Program for LED Lighting. 15.11.2012 http://www.ledinside.com/news/2012/6/large_manufacturers_benefit_subsidy_program_20120618

LEDinside (06.07.2012). *Shenzhen Sinolight Optoelectronics Closed down.* 22.04.2013 http://www.ledinside.com/news/2012/7/shenzhen_sinolight_optoelectronics_

closed_down_20120706

LEDinside (20.07.2012). *Foxconn Invested US$146 Million in LED-Related Ventures*. 22.04.2013 http://www.ledinside.com/news/2012/7/foxconn_led_ventures_20120720

LEDinside (24.07.2012). *Bidding for China LED Subsidies Restarted, Taiwan LED Firms in Advantageous Position*. 15.11.2012 http://www.ledinside.com/news/2012/7/taiwan_ledfirms_20120724

LEDinside (10.08.2012). *Global LED Lighting Market Focus Shifting to Asia under European Debt Crisis*. 22.04.2013 http://www.ledinside.com/intelligence/2012/8/led_eu_lighting_report

LEDinside (07.11.2012). *Interview with Louis Lam, President & CEO of OSRAM Opto Semiconductors Asia*. 29.04.2012 http://www.ledinside.com/interview/2012/11/osram_os_asia_ceo_inter_2012

LEDinside (15.11.2012). *Manufacturers Form Alliances within the Industry as LED Market Becomes Over-Competitive*. 21.11.2012 http://www.ledinside.com/research/2012/11/manufacturers_form_alliances_within_the_industry_as_led_market_becomes_over_competitive

LEDinside (09.01.2013). *Long-term Optimism about LED Lighting Despite Temporary Downturn*. 16.01.2013 http://www.ledinside.com/news/2013/1/long_term_optimism_led_lighting_20130109

LEDs Magazine (July 2006). *China Pours Millions into Solid-State Lighting Program*. 22.10.2012 http://ledsmagazine.com/features/3/7/6

LEDs Magazine (28.04.2011). *Luxeon LEDs Shine Brightly on the Guangzhou TV Tower*. 22.04.2013 http://www.ledsmagazine.com/press/30569

LEDs Magazine (March 2012). *LED lighting Market to Grow While LED Component Market Goes Flat*. 22.04.2013 http://ledsmagazine.com/features/9/3/2

LEDs Magazine (September 2012). *LED Lighting Market Holds Steady in 2012*. 20.11.2012 http://ledsmagazine.com/features/9/9/8

LEDs Magazine (November 2011). *LED Revolution Advances in China with Government Backing*. 08.11.2012 http://ledsmagazine.com/features/8/11/12

LEDs Magazine (27.11.12). *GE Lighting will Acquire Albeo Technologies, an LED Fixture Manufacturer, Allowing GE to Offer a Broader Range of SSL Products Across More Applications*. 27.11.2012 http://ledsmagazine.com/news/9/11/18

LEDs Magazine (December 2012). *China will Develop a Global Leader in the LED Manufacturing Space*. 22.04.2013 http://ledsmagazine.com/features/9/12/5

Nanfang Ribao (16.08.2010). *dong guan dai lang zhen mao zhi ye zouchu ni shi shang yang zhi lu chuangxin cu shengji zhitou bian quantou* (The Wool industry of Dalang Town, Dongguan, grows against the trend. Promote innovation to upgrade and form fingers to a fist).

Nanfang Ribao (26.08.2010a). *bian xi yang wei chao yang jie du dong guan dai lang zhen mao zhi ye zhuan xing shengji mima (shang pian)* (Change from "sunset" to "sunrise" industry: Interpreting the key to upgrading of the wool industry in Dalang, Dongguan).

Nanfang Ribao (26.08.2010b). *pinglun: gaizao tisheng chuantong chanye ye shi chanye zhuan xing shengji* (Comment: transform and upgrade industries by reforming and developing them).

Nanfang Ribao (27.08.2010). *bian xi yang wei chao yang jie du dong guan dai lang zhen mao zhi ye zhuan xing shengji mima (shang pian)* (Change from "sunset" to "sunrise" industry: Interpreting the key to upgrading of the wool industry in Dalang, Dongguan).

Nanfang Ribao (15.01.2012). *dong guan zhuan xing sheng ji cheng gong zhi ri guang dong ke xue fa zhan sheng li zhi shi* (If transformation and upgrading in Dongguan is successful in Dongguan, scientific development in Guangdong also succeeds). 26.04.2013 http://epaper.nfdaily.cn/html/2012-01/15/content_7049377.htm

Nanfang Ribao (07.04.2014). *sheng bu he zuo zhi chi LED zhao ming biao zhun guang zu jian ji hua* (Cooperation in the context of the provincial ministry's plan to develop standards for optical components of LED lighting products). 30.05.2014 http://epaper.southcn.com/nfdaily/html/2014-04/07/content_7290891.htm

Optics.org (23.11.2010). *China to Lead World's LED production by 2012.* 14.04.2011 http://optics.org/news/1/6/26

Optics.org (08.08.2012). *Osram Breaks Ground on Huge China LED Fab.* 22.04.2013 http://optics.org/news/3/8/10

Osram (21.05.2014) *Osram opens new LED assembly plant in China.* Press Release.

People's Daily (21.02.2009). *China's "sock capital" grows on clustering.* 29.04.2013 http://english.people.com.cn/90001/90778/90860/6848212.html

People's Daily (29.03.2010). *Foshan Special: Foshan massing strength in LED lighting.* 07.11.2011 http://english.peopledaily.com.cn/90001/90778/90860/6933046.html

Project Syndicate (29.08.2012). *China is Okay.* 26.04.2012 http://www.project-syndicate.org/commentary/china-is-okay-by-stephen-s--roach

Reuters (08.02.2012). *China sets target of average 13 percent annual minimum wage rise.* 26.04.2013 http://www.reuters.com/article/2012/02/08/us-china-economy-jobs-idUSTRE8170DY20120208

Reuters (27.05.2012). Analysis: *Falling Prices to Kill Off Half of Chinese LED Chipmakers.* 22.04.2013 http://www.reuters.com/article/2012/05/27/us-led-china-idUSBRE84Q0FJ20120527

Reuters (23.07.2012). *China eyes new strategic industries to spur economy.* 26.04.2013 http://www.reuters.com/article/2012/07/23/us-china-economy-strategic-idUSBRE86M03R20120723

Reuters (18.01.2013). *China lets Gini out of the bottle; wide wealth gap.* 26.04.2013 http://www.reuters.com/article/2013/01/18/us-china-economy-income-gap-idUSBRE90H06L20130118

Reuters (20.01.2013). *Analysis: China upturn underscores need to rebalance economy.* 26.04.2013 http://www.reuters.com/article/2013/01/20/us-china-economy-idUSBRE90J0I820130120

Reuters (07.02.2013). *Analysis: Failing Firms Cloud China's LED Lighting Vision.* 22.04.2013 http://www.reuters.com/article/2013/02/08/us-china-led-idUS-BRE91701H20130208

Reuters (09.03.2013). *China data show uneven economic recovery, policy dilemma.* 26.04.2013 http://www.reuters.com/article/2013/03/09/us-china-economy-idUSBRE92806M20130309

SEMI (05.11.2011). *LED Makers Shifting Focus from Efficacy to Manufacturing Efficiency for Mass-Market Leap.* 29.11.2012 http://www.semi.org/en/node/38171?id=s-gurow0711

SEMI (06.08.2013). *LED Equipment Spending on Track for a 2014 Rebound.* 22.04.2014 http://www.semi.org/en/node/46491

Siemens (15.03.2013). *Siemens to Drive Osram Spinoff* (Press Release). 17.04.2013 http://www.siemens.com/press/en/pressrelease/?press=/en/pressrelease/2013/corporate/axx20130326.htm

The Guardian (05.03.2013). *China's Wen Jiabao signs off with growth warning,* 26.04.2013 http://www.guardian.co.uk/world/2013/mar/05/china-wen-jia-bao-growth-warning

The Economist (03.04.2012). *Top of the heap.* 26.04.2013 _http://country.eiu.com/article.aspx?articleid=1080340292&Country=China&topic=Economy&sub-topic=Regional%20developments

The Economist (11.08.2012). *Social security with Chinese characteristics.* 20.03.2013 http://www.economist.com/node/21560259

The Economist (23.05.2014) China to maintain manufacturing supremacy 30.06.2014 http://gfs.eiu.com/Article.aspx?articleType=wif&articleId=2557

Washington Post (02.10.2012). *As China's economy slows, real estate bubble looms.* 26.04.2013 http://articles.washingtonpost.com/2012-10-02/business/35500560_1_home-prices-real-estate-chinese-home-buyers

WTO (2013). *International Trade Statistics.* Geneva: WTO 30.06.2014 http://www.wto.org/english/res_e/statis_e/its2013_e/its13_toc_e.htm

Yangcheng Wanbao (27.08.2010). *dong guan dai lang mao fangzhi ye bujin mei bei fangqi, faner shixian baozha xing fazhan—xi yang chanye heyi neng lirun fan fan* (The wool industry of Dalang (Dongguan) is not only resilient, but achieves explosive growth. How to double profits in a "sunset industry").

## Websites and databases

Capturing the Gains Project: http://www.capturingthegains.org/

China Customs Statistics are documented on the website of HKTDC Research: http://china-trade-research.hktdc.com/business-news/article/Fast-Facts/China-Customs-Statistics/ff/en/1/1X39VTVQ/1X09N9NM.htm

Dalang Government Website: http://en.dalang.gov.cn/index.aspx
Humen Government Website: http://www.humen.gov.cn/
ILO Decent Work Agenda http://www.ilo.org/global/about-the-ilo/decent-work-agenda/lang--en/index.htm
World Bank Statistical Database: http://databank.worldbank.org/data/home.aspx
Xiqiao Shan Tour Website: http://www.xiqiaoshantour.com/eng/travelguide_nid474.html
Zhaga Consortium: http://www.zhagastandard.org/

## List of interviews

2010

26.10.2010, Guangzhou Textile Group, trade union representative and management staff, interview on outsourcing of manufacturing capacities in Guangzhou and business strategies in the creative industry park, Guangzhou.

27.10.2010, interview and factory visit at a garment OEM company in Guangzhou, Guangzhou.

29.10.2010, KNITCHUAN, general manager, interview on sector development and company strategy, factory visit, Dalang.

30.10.2010a, POWERKNIT, employee at human resources department, factory visit, Dalang.

30.10.2010b, Stoll knitting equipment, area consultant technology, interview on CNC knitting technology, skill requirements for operators and local practices in terms of training arrangements and remuneration in Dongguan, Dalang.

05.11.2010, Guangdong LED Industry Association, chairman, interview on general developments in the sector, industrial upgrading and state policies, Guangzhou.

09.11.2010, Qiu Haixiong, director of the Research Institute for Social Development at Sun Yat-sen University, Guangzhou and Chairholder UNESCO Chai in Science and Technology Policies, interview about recent developments in the LED lighting industry, Guangzhou.

16.11.2010, Shenzhen LED Association, chairman, interview on general developments in the sector, industrial upgrading and state policies, Shenzhen.

18.11.2010, MULTIAPP, general manager of semiconductor department, interview on sector development and company strategy, factory visit, Shenzhen.

19.11.2010a, SMARTPACKAGE, sales manager, interview on sector development and company strategy, factory visit, Shenzhen.

19.11.2010b, Dalang government, employee at Foreign Trade & Economic Office and co-workers, interview on government strategies for industrial upgrading in

Dalang, perspectives for the local knitwear industry and progress in the implementation of upgrading strategies, Dalang.

20.11.2010a, CASUALYOUTH, sales staff, company introduction, Humen.

20.11.2010b, JEANSCHOKE, general manager, interview on company strategy, Humen.

20.11.2010c, LADYFIT, director, interview on company strategy, Humen.

21.11.2010a, Kingtex sewing equipment, sales staff, interview on sewing machine technology, skill requirements for operators, Humen.

21.11.2010b, Singer sewing equipment, sales staff, interview on sewing machine technology, skill requirements for operators, Humen.

23.11.2010, Chris King-Chi Chan, Department of Applied Social Studies, City University of Hong Kong, interview on industrial transformation and changing employment patterns in the PRD, Hong Kong.

24.11.2010, Pansy Yau, Hong Kong Trade and Development Centre Chief Economist, interview on business development after the economic crisis and industrial transformation in the PRD, Hong Kong.

25.11.2010, Apo Leung, Asia Monitor Resource Centre, interview about changing employment patterns of migrant workers in the PRD, Hong Kong.

26.11.2010a, Geoffrey Crothall, China Labour Bulleting, interview on industrial transformation and changing employment patterns in the PRD, Hong Kong.

26.11.2010b, Sze Wan Chan, Students and Scholars Against Corporate Misbehaviuos, interview about changing employment patterns of migrant workers in the PRD, Hong Kong.

26.11.2010b, Ngai Pun, Hong Kong Polytechnic University, interview about changing employment patterns of migrant workers in the PRD, Hong Kong.

29.11.2010, Shenzhen Semiconductor Association, secretary general, interview on development of the industry, Shenzhen.

30.11.2010, Huang Qiaoyan, School of Law, Sun-yat Sen University Guangzhou, interview about changes in migrant workers' social statuses, employment conditions and wages, Guangzhou.

03.12.2010, Foshan Lighting Association, chairman, interview on general developments in the sector, industrial upgrading and state policies, Foshan.

05.12.2010, Asia Management Consultants, managing director, interview on management systems in garment factories in the Pearl River Delta and process upgrading, Guangzhou.

07.12.2010a, Xiqiao government, CCP committee member, interview on government strategies for industrial upgrading in Xiqiao, perspectives for the local textile industry and progress in the implementation of upgrading strategies, Xiqiao.

07.12.2010b, POWERDENIM, factory manager, interview on sector development and company strategy, factory visit, Xiqiao.

08.12.2010, CHIPSTAR, sales manager, interview on sector development and company strategy, factory visit, Shenzhen.

09.12.2010a, Humen government, vice-mayor, interview on government strategies for industrial upgrading in Humen, perspectives for the local fashion industry and progress in the implementation of upgrading strategies, Humen.

09.12.2010b, CASUALYOUTH, interview on company strategy, factory visit, Humen.

10.12.2010, Guangdong Solid State Lighting Alliance, secretary-general, interview on general developments in the sector, industrial upgrading and state policies, Foshan.

13.12.2010a, Dalang government, vice-mayor and CCP chairman of Dalang, interview on government strategies for industrial upgrading in Dalang, perspectives for the local knitwear industry and progress in the implementation of upgrading strategies, Dalang.

13.12.2010b, POWERKNIT, director, interview on sector development and company strategy, Dalang.


2011


31.10.2011a, POWERKNIT, director, interview on sector development and company strategy, factory visit, Dalang.

31.10.2011b, Dalang vocational school, director, interview on education for junior designers in the local knitwear industry, Dalang.

31.10.2011c, Chemtax, knitting equipment vendor, sales staff, interview on CNC knitting technology, skill requirements for operators and local practices in terms of training arrangements and remuneration in Dongguan, Dalang.

02.11.2011a, Picanol weaving equipment, sales manager and product manager, interview on weaving equipment technology, skill requirements for operators and local practices in terms of training arrangements and remuneration in Xiqiao, Xiqiao.

02.11.2011b, JUNGLEJEANS, sales staff, interview on company strategy, Xiqiao.

02.11.2011c, DENIMSUIT, sales staff, interview on company strategy, Xiqiao.

03.11.2011a, Humen government, director of Economy and Trade Office, interview on government strategies for industrial upgrading in Humen, perspectives for the local fashion industry and progress in the implementation of upgrading strategies, Humen.

03.11.2011b, Humen Fashion Technology Innovation Centre, general manager, interview on functions of the Humen Fashion Technology Innovation Centre, Humen.

03.11.2011b, DENIMSUIT, general manager, interview on company strategy, factory visit, Humen.

08.11.2011a, Xiqiao government, CCP committee member, interview on government strategies for industrial upgrading in Xiqiao, perspectives for the local textile industry and progress in the implementation of upgrading strategies, Xiqiao.

08.11.2011b, POWERDENIM, vice president, interview on sector development and company strategy, factory visit, Xiqiao.

08.11.2011c, DENIMSUIT, export manager, interview on company strategy, Xiqiao.

10.11.2011, Guangdong Solid State Lighting Alliance, secretary-general, interview on general developments in the sector, industrial upgrading and state policies, Guangzhou.

14.11.2011, Guangdong LED Industry Association, chairman, interview on general developments in the sector, industrial upgrading and state policies, Guangzhou.

15.11.2011, SMARTPACKAGE, sales manager, interview on sector development and company strategy, Shenzhen.

17.11.2011a, Shenzhen Mobile Communications Association, chairman, interview on development of the industry, Shenzhen.

17.11.2011b, MULTIAPP, sales manager, interview on sector development and company strategy, factory visit, Shenzhen. Supplementary information provided by employees in the sales department of the company.

18.11.2011a, Humen government, director of Economy and Trade Office, interview on process innovation at CASUALYOUTH, Humen.

18.11.2011b, Weiyuan technical school, director, interview on education for junior designers in the local fashion industry, Humen.

18.11.2011b, LADYFIT, director, interview on company strategy, factory visit, Humen.

19.11.2011a, CASUALYOUTH, sales staff, company introduction, Humen.

19.11.2011b, DENIMSUIT, sales manager, interview on company strategy, Humen.

22.11.2011a, Foshan Lighting Association, Chairman, interview on general developments in the sector, industrial upgrading and state policies, Foshan.

22.11.2011b, PACKAGESTAR, senior engineer in R&D centre, interview on sector development and company strategy, Foshan.

24.11.2011, CHIPSTAR, product marketing manager, interview on sector development and company strategy, visit to the company's showroom, Guangzhou.

25.11.2011, MULTIAPP, sales staff, clarification of open questions, information provided per e-mail.

29.11.2011a, DENIMSUIT, director, interview on sector development and company strategy, factory visit, Xiqiao.

29.11.2011b, JUNGLEJEANS, production manager, in-depth interview on sector development and company strategy, factory visit, Xiqiao.

07.12.2011, ARCHIAPP, vice-president marketing, interview on sector development and company strategy, factory visit, Guangzhou.

08.12.2011, SMARTPACKAGE, sales manager, interview on sector development and company strategy, factory visit, Shenzhen.

14.12.2011, CHIPSTAR, product marketing manager, interview on sector development and company strategy, visit to the company's showroom, Guangzhou.

## 2012

20.07.2012, SMARTPACKAGE, sales manager, clarification of open questions, information provided per e-mail.

30.11.2012, ARCHIAPP, vice-president marketing, clarification of open questions, information provided per e-mail.

03.12.2012a, Polamar (LED production equipment manufacturer), managing director Europe, supplementary interview about skill requirements for operators of LED equipment, telephone conversation.

03.12.2012b, Kulicke & Soffa Orthodyne GmbH (LED production equipment manufacturer), European sales agent, interview about skill requirements for operators of LED equipment, telephone conversation.

11.12.2012, CHIPSTAR, product marketing manager, clarification of open questions, information provided per e-mail.

14.12.2012, SMARTPACKAGE, sales manager, clarification of open questions, information provided per e-mail.

16.12.2012, SMARTPACKAGE, sales manager, clarification of open questions, information provided per e-mail.

## 2013

21.01.2013, KNITCHUAN, sales staff, clarification of open questions, information provided per e-mail.

04.02.2013, Dalang government, employee at Foreign Trade & Economic Office, update on industrial upgrading in Dalang's knitwear industry, telephone conversation.

06.02.2013, Dalang government, employee at Foreign Trade & Economic Office, update on industrial upgrading in Dalang's knitwear industry, information provided per e-mail.

21.02.2013, POWERKNIT, director, clarification of open questions, information provided per e-mail.

22.02.2013, Guangdong Solid State Lighting Alliance, secretary-general, update on sector development, information provided per e-mail.

06.04.2012, SMARTPACKAGE, sales manager, clarification of open questions, information provided per e-mail.

09.04.2013, McKinsey, co-author of the McKinsey reports "Lighting the Way" (2011, 2012), backup on research report "Lighting the Way" (2012), telephone conversation.

10.04.2012, Stoll knitting equipment, area consultant technology, clarification of open questions, information provided per e-mail.

12.04.2013, POWERDENIM, sales staff, clarification of open questions, information provided per e-mail.

# Index

# Political Science

**campus**

Frankfurt. New York

# International Labour Studies – Internationale Arbeitsstudien

Dennis Eversberg
**Dividuell aktiviert**
Wie Arbeitsmarktpolitik Subjektivitäten produziert
2013. Ca. 700 Seiten. Band 7. ISBN 978-3-593-50059-1

Peter Bescherer
**Vom Lumpenproletariat zur Unterschicht**
Produktivistische Theorie und politische Praxis
2013. 267 Seiten. Band 6. ISBN 978-3-593-39973-7

Stefan Schmalz, Klaus Dörre (Hg.)
**Comeback der Gewerkschaften?**
Machtressourcen, innovative Praktiken,
internationale Perspektiven
2013. 454 Seiten. Band 5. ISBN 978-3-593-39891-4

Boy Lüthje, Siqi Luo, Hao Zhang
**Beyond the Iron Rice Bowl**
Regimes of Production and Industrial Relations in China
2013. 356 pages. Volume 4. ISBN 978-3-593-39890-7

Klaus Dörre, Karin Scherschel, Melanie Booth (Hg.)
**Bewährungsproben für die Unterschicht?**
Soziale Folgen aktivierender Arbeitsmarktpolitik
2013. 423 Seiten. Band 3. ISBN 978-3-593-39797-9

Karin Scherschel, Peter Streckeisen,
Manfred Krenn (Hg.)
**Neue Prekarität**
Die Folgen aktivierender Arbeitsmarktpolitik –
europäische Länder im Vergleich
2012. 316 Seiten. Band 2. ISBN 978-3-593-39656-9

Klaus Dörre, Dieter Sauer, Volker Wittke (Hg.)
**Kapitalismustheorie und Arbeit**
Neue Ansätze soziologischer Kritik
2012. 513 Seiten. Band 1. ISBN 978-3-593-39657-6

**campus**

Frankfurt. New York